A FAMILY
OF FAITH

A FAMILY OF FAITH

An Intimate View of Church History
through the Journals of Three Generations
of Apostles—Willard Richards, Franklin D.
Richards, and George F. Richards,
1837–1950

EDITED BY
KENT F. RICHARDS

DESERET
BOOK

Salt Lake City, Utah

Selections from the journals of Willard Richards, Franklin D. Richards, and George F. Richards are used by permission of Intellectual Reserve, Inc.

Except as noted otherwise beside individual photos, images are courtesy Church History Library, The Church of Jesus Christ of Latter-day Saints, Salt Lake City, Utah, and are used by permission.

Library of Congress Cataloging-in-Publication Data

A family of faith : an intimate view of church history through the journals of three gen-
erations of apostles—Willard Richards, Franklin D. Richards, and George F. Richards,
1837–1950 / Kent F. Richards, editor.
    pages cm
  Includes bibliographical references and index.
  ISBN 978-1-60907-394-7 (hardbound : alk. paper)
1. Richards family. 2. Richards, Willard, 1804–1854. 3. Richards, F. D. (Franklin
Dewey), 1821-1899. 4. Richards, George F. (George Franklin), 1861–1950. 5. The
Church of Jesus Christ of Latter-day Saints—History. I. Richards, Kent F., 1949– editor.
  BX8693.F36 2013
  289.3092'2—dc23   2013009074

Printed in the United States of America
Publishers Printing, Salt Lake City, UT

10 9 8 7 6 5 4 3 2 1

CONTENTS

PREFACE

"Believing blood" was the phrase President James E. Faust used when my wife, Marsha, and I sat in his office in the LDS Church Administration Building in Salt Lake City to be called as a mission president and companion. The Richards family, he said, was one of the stalwart families of the Restoration. He was quick to say that the same pioneering, believing legacy is being passed from generation to generation all over the world as individuals and families choose covenants and faithfulness. In my own family, there are six generations behind us of "believing," seven generations to which our children may look, and eight generations to bless our grandchildren.

All my life I have heard stories of faith and service of early Richards men and women in this dispensation. I knew that three of the men in my direct lineage had served in the Quorum of the Twelve Apostles and that one of them was a member of the First Presidency. In my boyhood days, we knew and loved "Uncle LeGrand," an Apostle, and we looked forward to seeing him and hearing from him at family reunions. In reality, however, coming to know these men was still a future adventure.

In the early 1980s, as a newly trained surgeon, young bishop, and father of six little boys, I had a quiet urging in my heart to study and find out more about these ancestors. I went to the LDS Church archives, navigated the approval process, and received the privilege of sitting in the archives of the library reading room to receive sequential cartons, each containing several handwritten volumes of Great-Grandfather George F. Richards's journals. In those days before laptop computers and digital records, I began taking notes by hand or speaking into a bulky tape recorder as I read aloud the entries. At home in the evenings, I transcribed the work of the day. I progressed through several years of his journals—until about 1907, shortly after his call to the Quorum of the Twelve. It was a fascinating view of the challenges his family faced in Utah's rural, pioneering beginnings; of his thoughts, feelings, and experiences; and of the workings of the leadership of the Church. As life became busier for me, I put aside the project.

After my service as a mission president concluded in 2001, I felt a great desire to return to my early work. I found my notes and returned to the archives, supposing that I could resume my work from where I had left off. I was disappointed to discover that the journals of George F. Richards had since been placed in a secure vault with no access to outside parties. Gratefully, as a descendant with the goal of providing information for family members, I was given authorization to once again read the journals, with the proviso that I would not publish anything without the approval of the Church History Department and the First Presidency.

Over the next few years, I read all of the George F. Richards's journals and transcribed portions of them. In many ways, this work anchored my soul to sound gospel principles, to the goodness of his heart, and to his sweet, pure, humble willingness to serve. For me, what had begun as a *project* became a commitment to serve, to grow, and to lead my own family, emulating his faith and faithfulness. I submitted the 450 pages of notes through channels to the presiding Brethren for their approval to allow publication of them for the descendants of George F. Richards. Then I had more to do.

I began to do the same work from digital images of available journals of Franklin D. Richards, who was George's father, and of Willard Richards, who was Franklin's uncle. Franklin and Willard each served in the Quorum of the Twelve Apostles, and each was a father to George.

Willard died as a relatively young man, leaving his first wife, Jane Snyder Richards, and several young plural wives as widows. Family lore suggests that Brigham Young instructed Franklin to raise up posterity to Willard. As a result, Franklin married Nanny Longstroth Richards, one of Willard's widows, and George was a child of that union. Franklin often referred to George and his siblings as "Willard's family." They were linked to Willard by sealing and to Franklin by blood. In a letter to George, Franklin sent copies of both his and Willard's patriarchal blessings, explaining that George was "blessed to have two fathers."

A question I have often been asked—"Are you related to Willard Richards?"—has always required explanation. He is my great-great-grandfather by priesthood sealing. My bloodline comes through Franklin and Nanny, but I am sealed to Willard. I am grateful to have two connected, righteous lines.

This volume is an abbreviated collection of experiences, many of them overlapping, from the journals of Willard, Franklin, and George. The selection of these excerpts is intended to give the reader an overview of a period of history lasting one hundred and thirteen years through the eyes of three generations of related, humble men, each writing his living, day-by-day witness of the Restoration. Excerpt by excerpt, year after passing year, their message becomes greater and more powerful.

When excerpts from the journals overlap in time, they are

identified with the initials of their respective writers to allow the reader to keep track of who is speaking. It was impossible to include everything here of value from the journals. If the complete journals were published, the pages would number in the thousands. Readers who desire a more extensive study will find an expanded eBook edition of this volume, *Family of Faith,* at DeseretBook.com. It includes a lengthier life sketch of each of the three men as well as many more quotations from their journals, with annotations only when necessary for understanding. Readers who wish to study the complete journals of Willard Richards and Franklin D. Richards will be pleased that the Church History Department of The Church of Jesus Christ of Latter-day Saints is considering plans to publish at a future date online images of the journal pages side-by-side with a corresponding transcript.

This story does not belong to the Richards family alone but to families everywhere who are striving to live after the manner of happiness, "believing," and passing the legacy of faith from generation to generation.

ACKNOWLEDGMENTS

For their invaluable assistance in bringing this volume to fruition, I gratefully acknowledge Elder Marlin K. Jensen, Richard E. Turley Jr., Reid Neilson, Matt Grow, and others from the Church History Department of The Church of Jesus Christ of Latter-day Saints; Cory Maxwell and Suzanne Brady from Deseret Book; and Rebecca Maxfield, who checked the transcriptions and helped with early editing from the original images.

I also express appreciation to the First Presidency of the Church and to the advisers to the Church History Department of the Church who have reviewed my manuscripts and authorized their being made available to the public in print and in digital formats.

INTRODUCTION

Three Generations of Apostles

From Willard Richards's baptism and mission to England in 1837 to his death in 1854, followed by the experiences of Franklin Richards from 1844 to his death in 1899, and capped by the writings of George F. Richards from 1882 to his last entry in 1950, we have a daily record of feelings, perspectives, and experiences as The Church of Jesus Christ of Latter-day Saints developed from its early days in Nauvoo to the modern era. These three great men served a combined one hundred and seven years in the Quorum of the Twelve Apostles. There were only seven years during this historic period—1899 to 1906—that one of them was not serving in the quorum.

Their journals offer us a daily view of life, service in the Church, marriage and family concerns, personal growth, and Church leadership. They also offer insights into many difficult circumstances and situations they had to deal with while establishing a new society and building up the kingdom of God on the earth.

Willard Richards

Willard Richards is one of the unsung heroes of the Restoration. Once converted, he dropped everything and devoted himself entirely to the Lord and to the newly restored gospel of Jesus Christ for the rest of his life. He immediately went into the service of the Lord as a missionary. Over time, Willard was called to be an Apostle, personal secretary to the Prophet Joseph Smith, scribe, historian, and counselor to Brigham Young in the presidency of the Church. After arriving in Utah, he served as editor of the *Deseret News,* postmaster, and territorial secretary. His personal journal and correspondence give us a wonderful view of the establishment of the Church, the workings of the leaders of the Church in the early days, and his own personal life and experiences.

Willard's life was not easy. As a missionary and full-time servant of the Prophet and the Church, he always depended upon others for his temporal well-being. He had poor health, yet he worked long and hard to fulfill his responsibilities with devotion and care.

I had heard stories about Willard—languishing in jail, crossing the plains, and participating in early activities in the Salt Lake Valley. But as I read his journals, I was pleasantly surprised to come to know him as a man of great intellectual ability, yet also as a humble, willing servant of the Lord. I believe he was raised up to perform a critical function as the Prophet's secretary and companion and as historian for the Church.

Willard accomplished much in the short forty-nine years of his life—seventeen years as a member of the Church. For me, the measure of the man came together as I was studying his journal, specifically the riveting hour-by-hour account of the events that unfolded in Carthage Jail. I saw in his own journal handwriting the dialog he had with his friend the Prophet just moments before the mob burst up the stairs and started firing. Joseph asked him if he would stay with him. In response, he offered to take the Prophet's place. Joseph responded that he could not. Willard wrote two simple words in his journal: "I will." That expression became the defining nature of his character and his commitment to all he was asked to do.

Willard's first journal begins as he recounts his baptism and immediately prepares to leave with Heber C. Kimball in 1837 to serve on the first foreign mission. Often the journals are cryptic, with few words. Later, when he was appointed Church historian in 1847, his journals became more full and informative, especially as he keeps the "Camp Journal" of the migration from Nauvoo to Winter Quarters in 1846. At times, when he was ill or too occupied, he would dictate to an assistant, who recorded some of the text of the journals. After his arrival in Utah, the journals were often kept by an assistant, becoming abbreviated again. Then his correspondence becomes even more important as a source of information about his life and duties.

Willard Richards was born June 24, 1804, in Hopkinson, Massachusetts, to Joseph and Rhoda Richards. He was the sixth son and the youngest of eleven children. Willard's father, Joseph, was born in Middlesex County, March 17, 1762. His mother, Rhoda, daughter of Phinehas and Susannah Howe, was born July 8, 1762. They were married December 20, 1781. Joseph served in the Army of the Republic in the Revolutionary War, fighting in Boston.

As a boy, Willard eagerly sought education and demonstrated both an affinity and an aptitude for leaning. Biographer Clair Noall suggests that Willard occasionally provoked the displeasure of his father by staying up late to read by candlelight and then being unable to arise the next morning in time for his chores on the family farm at Richmond.[1] In his quest for religious knowledge, Willard apparently became disillusioned with the brand of Calvinism being preached in the family's Congregational church and so remained aloof from organized religion.[2]

During his studies in many different fields, Willard taught school for a short time.[3] In his scientific pursuits, he became interested in electricity and subsequently presented lectures on the subject in some nearby towns. While on one of these lecture tours, he acquired a copy of Dr. Samuel Thomson's *Practice of Medicine* and was persuaded to become an herbal doctor. He launched a medical career by successfully prescribing herbs for his two ailing sisters, and after purchasing a patent for twenty dollars, he expanded his practice to the community.

Willard's life took a new direction when he happened upon a copy of the Book of Mormon. The book had been left by his cousin Brigham Young, who had already joined the Saints in northern Ohio. Willard read the book through twice in ten days and, having received a witness of its truthfulness, immediately began selling his medicines, "settling his accounts," and making preparations to travel seven hundred miles to the Church headquarters at Kirtland, Ohio.[4]

1. Clair Noall, *Intimate Disciple: A Portrait of Willard Richards, Apostle to Joseph Smith, Cousin of Brigham Young* (Salt Lake City: University of Utah Press, 1957), 40–41.

2. "History of Willard Richards," in "History of Brigham Young," *Millennial Star* 27, no. 7 (February 25, 1865): 118–20.

3. On April 6, 1823, the inspectors of common schools in Nassau, Rensselaer County, New York, gave him a certificate. He commenced a school there in April and continued until August, having an average attendance of about forty students (ibid.).

4. Howard C. Searle, "Willard Richards as Historian," *BYU Studies* 31, no. 2 (1991): 1.

Upon arriving in Kirtland, Willard sought out Brigham Young to request baptism. Willard was baptized in an icy river on the last day of 1836. His journal begins with an account of his baptism and his new life as a member of the restored Church. "I was baptized at Kirtland under the hand of Elder Brigham Young December 31st, 1836 after the sun had set in the West."[5]

Shortly after his ordination as an elder in the Church, he was assigned to serve a mission to the eastern states with Brigham. A couple of months later, he was suffering physically, which he described as being "much fatigued, stomach foul, head ache." He "felt a strong desire to start for Kirtland immediately" and received a spiritual prompting that he should follow his desire. Immediately after his arrival, Willard learned of the assignment of Heber C. Kimball and others to leave on the first foreign mission to England. Willard had received an earlier promise from Heber that if he was called to leave, Willard could accompany him. Heber told him, "I am now ready to fulfill my engagement with you. You recollect it don't you. I start for England tomorrow and you may go with me. Get ready &c." He was set apart for the mission the day after he arrived in Kirtland and made immediate plans to depart. He did not know then that he would be away for four years and that when he returned, he would bring a wife and son with him.

Willard and his companions arrived in England after a difficult passage across the ocean, sailing in the *Garrick*—the same vessel his nephew Franklin would take in 1856 while returning home from England. Willard and Elder John Goodson, a recent convert from Canada, were assigned to labor in Bedford.

---

5. Willard Richards Journal, Church History Library, The Church of Jesus Christ of Latter-day Saints, Salt Lake City, Utah; hereafter cited as Church History Library.

Willard later labored in the Preston area, where, in March 1838, he met a twenty-one-year-old convert who had recently been baptized by Elder Kimball. Elder Kimball told him, "Willard, I baptized your wife today." Heber recorded in his journal:

"On Wednesday, August 2nd, Miss Jen[n]etta Richards, a young lady, the daughter of a minister òf the Independent Order, who resided at Walkerfold, about fifteen miles from Preston, came to the house of Thomas Walmesley, with whom she was acquainted. Calling in to see them at the time she was there, I was introduced to her and we immediately entered into conversation on the subject of the Gospel. I found her very intelligent. She seemed very desirous to hear the things I had to teach and to understand the doctrines of the gospel. I informed her of my appointment to preach that evening, and invited her to attend. She did so; and likewise the evening following. After attending these two services she was fully convinced of the truth."[6]

Jennetta, baptized in the River Ribble, was the first convert to be confirmed a member of the Church in Great Britain. After their marriage, Willard and Jennetta had two sons born to them while in England. Both were named Heber John—Heber in honor of Heber C. Kimball, John to honor her father, the Reverend John Richards. The first son lived only six months before expiring from small pox. It was a brief illness of only ten days from the onset of two spots on his arm on December 1839 until his death on the 28th.

On July 18, 1838, the Prophet Joseph Smith received a revelation naming John Taylor, John E. Page, Wilford Woodruff, and "also my servant Willard Richards, [to] be appointed [as new

---

6. Orson F. Whitney, *Life of Heber C. Kimball* (Salt Lake City: Stevens & Wallace, 1945), 137, 143.

Apostles] to fill the places of those who have fallen, and be officially notified of their appointments" (D&C 118:6). Willard was still serving in England and could not be ordained until Brigham Young and the other members of the Twelve arrived in England by assignment in 1840. On April 14, 1840, Willard became the first and only Apostle ordained on foreign soil in this dispensation.

In December 1841, Willard was appointed private secretary to President Joseph Smith and called as general Church clerk. While building a house, he lived in the upper story of the Prophet's Red Brick Store. In December 1842, Willard was appointed Church historian and recorder. As historian, he was responsible for keeping the diary of Joseph Smith and for gathering and writing Church history. He became the pen for much of the correspondence that emanated from Church headquarters.

The month of June 1844 saw the frenzied activities of a mob culminate in the assassination of Joseph and Hyrum Smith in Carthage Jail. As an eyewitness, Willard recorded most of the events that transpired. After the Nauvoo City Council destroyed the *Nauvoo Expositor* press as a city nuisance, a mob served writs for Joseph's arrest and imprisonment. Legal activities and maneuvering ensued. At one point, Joseph, Hyrum, and Willard crossed the Mississippi River with the intention of fleeing west to escape persecution. They returned to face the charges, however, knowing that their lives would be in jeopardy.

All but Joseph, Hyrum, John Taylor, and Willard were ultimately excluded from the jail cell in Carthage. Willard kept a careful secretary's and historian's account of the events as they unfolded there. Gratefully, Willard recorded not only the events but also the conversation he had with the Prophet just moments before the mob stormed the cell. Willard kept a detailed account of the events up to a certain point in the attack. Then he left a blank page—probably intending to go back and complete the historical record. He never did. His was the only contemporary account. John Taylor, the other survivor, was asked to write his account twelve years later by then-Church Historian George A. Smith.

After the Martyrdom, Willard had to step into a leadership role to guide the Saints in Nauvoo and vicinity. John Taylor was recuperating from serious wounds, and Brigham Young and the other Apostles were in the East. Willard immediately penned an important note to Emma Smith and the citizens of Nauvoo:

Carthage jail, 8 o'clock 5 minutes P.M., June the 27th 1844

Joseph & Hyrum are dead. Taylor wounded not fatally very bad. I am well. Our guard was forced as we believe by a band of Missourians from 1 to 200 the job was done in an instant and the party fled towards Nauvoo instantly. This is as I believe it. The Citizens here are afraid of the Mormons attacking them. I promise them NO!

From December 1845 to February 1846, under the direction of Brigham Young, the Saints busily worked day and night to complete the Nauvoo Temple and receive their temple ordinances. Church leaders were packing and preparing to leave Nauvoo in mid-February 1846. Willard's diary gives some insight into the challenges they faced. In his capacity as Church historian, he kept a journal that became the "Camp Journal" of the pioneer migration. He wrote a detailed account of the challenges Brigham Young faced in leading a large group of ill-prepared people across a barren wilderness. There was no feed for the animals. Men had to be sent out to buy corn and oats from surrounding farmers. Any work the men could do for the local people was recompensed in food products. Wet weather was a great challenge. Streams had to be crossed, heavy wagons became stuck in mud, and there was no protection against the storms. Delays were inevitable.

Willard's journal record of the first pioneer company's journey to the valley of the Great Salt Lake in 1847 is brief and terse—he records the times of departure, lunch, arrival, and a few other facts. Some of his letters give wonderful historical insight into the final days of the trek as the pioneers approached the valley.

After a short stay in the valley, most members of the pioneer company reversed their journey and followed the same route back to Winter Quarters, where they had spent the previous winter. In December 1847, Brigham Young was sustained as prophet and president of the Church. He chose Willard to be his second counselor.

Once Willard arrived again in the valley to stay, he resumed his journal writing, but the most important information he recorded comes from his correspondence. Letters to various individuals detail an interesting view of the challenges of carving out a home, a society, and a government in a barren location far from any established society. In 1850 he wrote John M. Bernhisel, who had been assigned to travel to Washington, D.C., to seek a governmental solution to the Indian "problem," asking that the Indians be sent to a new location where they could hunt and fish without the need to steal the pioneers' cattle and corn.

In 1854, at age forty-nine, Willard passed away. He had suffered for some time from a condition known as dropsy, which we know today as congestive heart failure, with edema, or fluid retention, in the legs and body. Willard was sick much of his life. Perhaps he developed heart disease after contracting rheumatic fever, which may have made him more vulnerable to infectious diseases.

In retrospect, it is amazing that Willard accomplished all he did in his short life. One author estimated that he wrote more than 1,884 pages of Church history.[7] Other than a period of employment in his early years before joining the Church, he never really had a profession to sustain his family. He served with his full capacity and devotion as secretary, recorder, historian, editor, letter writer, and Apostle. He served as second counselor to President Brigham Young from 1847 until his death seven years later. Perhaps one of Willard's greatest admirers was his nephew Franklin, who wrote about him after his death:

"My uncle occupied the position of historian up to March, 1854. He was said to be a person of high character and a rather handsome person. He had a handsome classical face and head, and he had a very genial, pleasant disposition. He was always kind and pleasant and was always considered an able man. His literary abilities were very high. He did all the important writings of the Apostles, and if President Young had any important writing to do, he was just the man to do it."[8]

Franklin D. Richards

Franklin Dewey Richards was born in Richmond, Massachusetts, on April 2, 1821, to Phinehas and Wealthy Dewey Richards. Phinehas and his brothers, Willard and Levi, were cousins of Brigham Young. In the summer of 1836, Brigham, then

7. H. Dean Garrett, *Utah History Encyclopedia,* edited by Allan Kent Powell (Salt Lake City: University of Utah Press, 1994); available online at http://www.media.utah.edu/UHE/r/RICHARDS,WILLARD.html.

8. Franklin D. Richards's dictation while staying with H. H. Bancroft in San Francisco, 1880. Included in his personal journal, Church History Library.

one of the Twelve Apostles, and his brother Joseph brought the gospel to the Richards family in Massachusetts.

Franklin was not immediately converted, taking two years to study and reflect before joining the Church. On June 3, 1888, the fiftieth anniversary of his baptism, Franklin recorded, "Fifty years ago today about 4 or 5 o'clock P.M. my Father Phinehas baptized me in Mill Creek, sometimes called Markham's Creek in the town of Richmond, Berks Co, Mass, after having spent the day mostly with Edwin D. Peirson & myself explaining the scriptures & removing our seeming objections."

Once baptized, Franklin committed himself to his new church. He was serving his second mission in 1844 when he heard of the martyrdom of the Prophet Joseph Smith. He returned to Nauvoo and was soon busily engaged in building the temple. As the Saints prepared to leave for the West, Franklin and his brother Samuel were called to return to England to complete their mission, leaving their wives in the care of the pioneer group going west as they headed east to England. His heart was broken when he belatedly learned of the premature birth and death of his first son, soon followed by the death of his precious little daughter, Wealthy—his only two children at the time.

In February 1849, between missions to England, Franklin was called as to be an Apostle as a young man of twenty-eight. He had returned to the States to join the final 1848 migration to the Salt Lake Valley. He and his little family weathered their first winter living in their covered wagon while Franklin built a small cabin.

By 1868, as he returned from England from his final foreign assignment, he had fulfilled seven missions, all without purse or scrip. Three of his missions were in the United States, while the other four were in Europe. He presided over the British Mission or European Mission three times. By his calculation, he was "absent on distant missions 12 years less 14 days."

Franklin was a dedicated journal writer. Some of his journals are missing, but the ones we have are rich in perspective on his life, family, faith, and commitment to serve the Lord. His first journal begins in 1844, and with the exception of a span of nearly ten years, from 1856 to 1865, there is an almost daily account of his activity and experiences.

Franklin's missionary journeys meant that he was often absent during the early years of his married life. "Ten of the first fourteen years of married life was spent away from my loved ones in the mission field," he wrote of himself in his journal. He crossed the plains between the Missouri River and the Salt Lake Valley seven times before the railroad entered the Salt Lake Valley.

In 1868, Brigham Young asked him to move his family to Ogden, preside over Church affairs there, and become a probate judge in Weber County. He served faithfully as a judge for fourteen years, handling everything from divorce cases to capital murder cases. He was replaced only after the federal government declared him unfit for public service because he had practiced polygamy. In addition, Franklin served as a brigadier general in the Utah militia, a member of the Utah Legislature many times, and a regent of the University of Deseret (now the University of Utah). He was editor of the *Millennial Star* for a time and the founder and first editor of the *Ogden Junction*.

As early as August 1, 1845, Franklin began to work with Church historical records. His uncle Willard Richards, Church historian, employed him to assist in the historian's office. Franklin's work consisted of copying Church history and, during the brief time the Saints used the Nauvoo Temple, he personally recorded many of the ordinances performed there.

Franklin worked tirelessly in the temple from December 1845 until February 8, 1846, to help as many as possible to receive their temple ordinances. On February 8 he took part in the last ordinances performed in temple before the main body of the Saints departed Nauvoo for the West. Three months later the temple was publicly dedicated and then abandoned as the remainder of the Saints left Nauvoo.

Franklin ultimately became the historian of the Church. He developed a devout interest in family history research and gathered a large personal collection of resource books. Later, at the request of the First Presidency, he donated all of his books to the Church, forming the first genealogical library. He was then appointed as the first president of the Utah Genealogical Society while simultaneously serving as the president of the Utah State Historical Society.

Franklin married a total of eleven wives and fathered twenty-eight children. His first wife, Jane Snyder, was the love of his life. After accepting the doctrine of celestial marriage, Franklin took Elizabeth McFate as a plural wife. The Richards family left Nauvoo in May 1846, and almost immediately Franklin was called to go to England. Jane and Elizabeth continued their journey westward, but Elizabeth died and was buried along the way. Even though Franklin married additional wives, Jane was the only one he actually lived with. This became very important in the late 1880s when those Brethren who were living with more than one wife were subjected to increased persecution. Franklin, however, was left alone and was able to attend to Church matters and preside over conferences in the absence of the members of the First Presidency and more senior members of the Twelve. After the death of his uncle Willard, Franklin married four of his widows. One biographer explained: "It seems to have been an ancient custom in Israel for the brother of a deceased man to marry his brother's widow or widows, so President Young counseled Franklin to marry his uncle's widows. The size of his own family made this seem a heavy responsibility, but as always, he obeyed [counsel] and married four of uncle Willard's wives."[9]

Three of Franklin's wives had no children; two had one child each. After 1868, Franklin maintained his residence in Ogden, and only his first wife, Jane, and their children lived in the primary residence. He often referred to his wives who had been previously sealed to Willard as "Willard's family." Each wife was expected to manage her home and affairs without much financial support from Franklin. Occasionally, when one was sick or in need, he would give her five dollars a month to help out. His journals recount visits, blessings, and concern for their welfare. He took the train from Ogden to Salt Lake nearly every day to attend meetings and fulfill his calling as an Apostle. He often stopped in Farmington, between Ogden and Salt Lake, to visit his three wives there.

Franklin labored for the completion of the Nauvoo Temple, and as a senior member of the Twelve, he participated in the building and dedication of three Utah temples. President Wilford Woodruff asked him to write a draft for the dedicatory prayer of the Manti Temple. A few years later, the dedication of the Salt Lake Temple became the crowning temple experience for many of the pioneer Saints. They had worked on it for forty years and had made many great sacrifices to complete it. After the second dedicatory session, Franklin wrote on April 7, 1893:

"At Temple met with Saints. After music I spoke some 10 or 15 minutes & GQC. JFS delivered the prayer in 40 minutes.

---

9. From a talk given by a grandson, Franklin D. Richards, at the Mt. Olympus Sons of Utah Pioneers, Salt Lake City, Utah, April 1981.

Prest. WW stated his night vision. WW said Joseph Smith, Brigham Young, & J. Taylor had gathered together all the Church of the Firstborn in the Latter-days & the ancient Saints & with Christ in their midst. When we shout, they shout, & the work is more earnest with them than with us because they know more than we do. Prest. WW testified that Prest. B. Young has twice since his death delivered to him the Keys of this Temple & commanded him to dedicate it. He first saw the dedication of this Temple 50 years ago while in Boston. No one is more rejoiced over these things than the Prophet Joseph Smith."

Perhaps the political issue that dominated much of Franklin's Church leadership experience was the practice of polygamy and the federal government's efforts to use all of its political and legislative power to stop it. Because Franklin had decided to live with only his first wife, Jane, after the Edmunds-Tucker Act was passed in 1887, he was not as vulnerable to arrest and imprisonment as the other leading Brethren. While President John Taylor and his counselors and other leading Apostles were hiding from persecution by the federal government, Franklin became the tacit leader of the Church, presiding at several general conferences. He communicated with the president and other Brethren, and he had to work hard to protect the interests, assets, and even historical documents of the Church.

Franklin passed away in the fall of 1899. At the time of his death, he was serving as president of the Quorum of the Twelve Apostles. He fulfilled his great desire to serve the Lord with the fulness of his heart and soul. He has become a great example to me of humbly accepting life, graciously attempting to be happy, and leading his family in all good things. Evidencing great faith and humility, he recorded the following early in his life:

"I hope to overcome every obstacle and be not a whit behind

the chiefest of my brethren in the celestial kingdom of God, having kept my covenants and being sanctified thereby; and not myself only, but all those who belong to me."[10]

At the time of Franklin's death, Elder Orson F. Whitney, a member of the Quorum of the Twelve Apostles, wrote:

"Endurance is the crowning quality, and patience all the passion of great hearts. Perhaps no man in this community ever exemplified to a greater degree these sublime qualities than Franklin Dewey Richards. If there were nothing else in his character and career . . . to entitle him to the distinction of greatness and nobility among his fellows, these grand qualities would suffice, for he was preeminently a patient man, a meek man, one who endured much and was faithful to his principles and convictions.

"But he was also one who achieved much, and will long be remembered for the noble works that he performed, not only within the State, but in lands far distant from this, where he wrought with mighty zeal and marvelous success in the interests of the sacred cause to which he had consecrated his life. As an Apostle of the Church of Christ through a full half century; as a member of the Utah Legislature, a regent of the University, brigadier-general, probate judge, Church Historian, president of the State Genealogical and Historical Societies, and finally, as President of the Twelve Apostles, he labored in every capacity with intelligence, wisdom, and zeal and carved out a name and fame that will be as lasting as the archives and records of the Church and Commonwealth that he so faithfully served."[11]

10. Franklin L. West, *Life of Franklin D. Richards* (Salt Lake City: Deseret News Press, 1924), 71–72.

11. West, *Franklin D. Richards*, 255–56.

George F. Richards

George F. Richards, like his father, was a dedicated journal writer. His numerous journals, written in a daily format, occupy a total of 8,520 pages. He began writing at age twenty-two in 1883. For a long time his journals have been largely unavailable even to the family because of sacred materials recorded therein. Gratefully, we now have the opportunity to make approved excerpts available. George F. Richards will become better known through these excerpts from his journals. From time to time he mused about his journals and their possible future use. In July 1924 he wrote:

"Thoughts about my journal. When I think that some one may undertake to look through my journals after I shall have gone hence with a view to accumulating information for a book on my biography, I feel ashamed that I have written so much into my journal that is of so little worth and so lacking of interest. I have thought that notwithstanding I have been closely associated with others in the making of Church history, I would leave the making or writing of such history to [others]."

The life of George F. Richards, who was born in 1861, stretches from the pioneer era—he was born five years after the handcart migration began and eight years before the railroad arrived—to the age of airplanes and television. His mother was Nanny Longstroth Richards. She had been a plural wife of Willard Richards. After his death in 1854, she married his nephew Franklin D. Richards as one of his plural wives. Nanny was thus the wife of two Apostles (Willard and Franklin), the mother of one Apostle (George), and the grandmother of two Apostles (LeGrand Richards and Stephen L Richards).

George followed his father into the Quorum of the Twelve seven years after Franklin's death. Years later, after reading a biography of his father, he humbly wrote: "Wed. July 16 I finished reading the biography of my Father. . . . The life of my father as there portrayed is most interesting and inspirational. When I think of the accomplishments of my father, it makes me feel very small and inadequate for the responsibility which has come to me from the Church. I do feel that the Lord has helped me in every direction of my life actively. I have been measurably successful in raising my family. Notwithstanding I have but one wife, I have 15 children, 5 boys and 10 girls. As counselor in the Tooele Stake Presidency, as a Patriarch, as an Apostle, as President of the European Mission, and as President of the Salt Lake Temple I have been uniformly blessed of the Lord. Thankful for these blessings, I feel that I have done but very little for the cause as compared with what my father has done for it. How am I to correct my record, but by plodding along in faithfulness and devotion to my calling."

George was a humble man who had given his heart to the Lord. Shortly after the birth of his first son, he received an inquiry about his availability to serve a mission. He copied into his journal the letter he wrote in answer. The spirit of his response has become a guiding principle in my life.

"I am twenty-three years of age, was born and raised in Farmington, Davis Co. I have a wife and one child, have never been on a foreign mission. Financially, I am in poor circumstances at present, being in debt more than four-hundred dollars, and paying interest on a part of the same.

"I have no ready means and all the property I have is a set of harness, wagon (both been in use more than five years), six head of horses, a cow and two calves and not quite two acres of land worth from seventy-five and one-hundred dollars.

"While I feel that I am poor, I do not wish to let that stand between me and my duties as a latter-day Saint. That which I have is upon the altar and subject to the direction of those in authority, as is also my time and life if necessary."

Before his call to the Quorum of the Twelve Apostles in 1906, he had a dream in which he saw the Savior and was embraced by him. He would later refer to that dream, which "seems to have prepared me in a measure for this call":

"Thu. July 26 [1906] I related a dream or Vision I had wherein I saw and embraced the Savior on the 22nd of March last. The seeing of Him was something beautiful but that in itself would have been of little significance as compared with the results of my embracing him. My whole being seemed to be thrilled with the power of His love and I was indeed in Heaven."

This humble farmer from rural Tooele was a willing servant of the Lord. He never complained or criticized the Brethren in his journal. His attitude was to go and do and serve whenever the Lord called. The day his son LeGrand married Ina Ashton, George F. performed the sealing; then he went to his Thursday meeting in the Salt Lake Temple with the First Presidency and the Twelve. He was assigned to go to a stake conference assignment requiring him to leave that afternoon. He did so without any complaint or resistance, thus missing the reception at his home for LeGrand and Ina.

"Wed. Jan. 2, 1907 Among other things, I told the President my health is good, & my shoulders broad and if he had any work more difficult than any other that he could trust me, to lay it upon me; that my greatest hope & most earnest prayer is that the Lord will sustain me in my calling & the discharge of my duties."

When called to leave his wife and family for three years to preside over the European Mission during World War I, he wrote:

"I came home and made known to my family the above

information. It broke up my wife's feelings and the children cried with her. The Lord has said we should live together in love so that we should mourn for those who die. We should so love that we sorrow at separation. It is pleasing to the Lord that we love one another so it cannot be an offense that we sorrow at parting.

"My true feelings are that I would naturally shrink from such responsibility and having to leave home and loved ones for such a time as this mission will mean, but that having put my hand to the plow, there is for me no turning back. I appreciate the honor if I can succeed and I believe I shall have his help else he would not through his servant have called me. Perhaps I have said enough."

Shortly after his return from presiding in England, George was called to be the president of the Salt Lake Temple. He served in that role from 1921 to 1937 while still serving as an Apostle. After George had served for a year as temple president, the Brethren determined that the matron, who had served for many years, should be released. President Heber J. Grant asked George who he thought might be called as the new matron of the temple. In all humility, he suggested that it would be appropriate for his wife, Alice, to be called so that they could work together. He recorded how President Grant told him, "with tears in his eyes," that the Presidency had already come to that conclusion. The call of George's wife to be the matron was the first in a pattern that has been followed ever since in all temples. After their release from the Salt Lake Temple, they were called and set apart to preside over all the temples in the Church, which they did until George's death.

In his service as a member of the Quorum of the Twelve, George experienced almost every weekend for forty-five years every kind of travel available. He traveled by train (both passenger and freight), horse, buggy, wagon, stagecoach, auto stage, bus, automobile, ship, and finally airplane. The train was his mainstay—convenient for study and preparation if he had a sleeper car. To travel to Arizona, he was required to take the train to Los Angeles and then transfer to the train traveling East to Holbrook, Arizona. He experienced all kinds of delays and difficulties, such as washed-out roads, railroad accidents, changed schedules, severe weather, camping out beneath a wagon, and broken axles. Often at the end of a long train ride he still had fifty miles of rugged road yet to traverse. He slept in the homes of members when he could—often with another priesthood leader.

"Friday May 7, 1909 Pres Hart and I slept together in the attick and had a terrible time with the bugs."

"Returned to the Sierra Hotel at 12 o'clock midnight and rassled with the flees."

"Sund. Jun 9 Am well but feel that I need more sleep. My rest was greatly disturbed during the night by vermine."

In a letter responding to his younger brother who had asked for advice, he wrote:

"It is by the observance of these little things that men show whether theirs is an obedient and willful spirit. A man with a willing and obedient spirit can be used for positions of trust and honor though not otherwise very well qualified, but if qualified so much the better. Success will follow his ministry and be attended by the blessing of the Lord. But the man who has demonstrated an unwilling and disobedient spirit can scarcely be trusted with grave responsibility and high honor lest the same be trailed in the dust as it were and the man himself be in reproach before his brethren. One may say I am not seeking any such honors. Of course not, but that is no reason why we should not be prepared for what the Lord has for us and wants of us. God showed

Abraham certain intelligences and said: 'These are my noble ones whom I have chosen to be my rulers. Thou Abraham wast one of them.' You, my dear brother, may be one of them and you should not hedge up the way of your coming to this honor. A straw thrown up indicates the direction of the wind, even so the small things of our lives indicate largely our future destiny. . . . By doing the small duties we plant our feet in the narrow way and fix our faith permanently."

George F. Richards served for forty-four years as an Apostle and was president of the Quorum of the Twelve Apostles when he died. He had seen the maturing of the Church and its doctrine. He was faithful in his devotion and willing service as a humble servant of the Lord.

At the funeral of Elder Richards, Elder Harold B. Lee said: "With the passing of every great and beloved leader, there has always been an assembling of those who are close to them to reflect upon the admonitions and counsels and the teachings of that one who had passed. It was a similar feeling in the minds of President Richards' close associates the other morning, when we learned of his passing and as the Twelve assembled, the hour was spent conversing about the things that Brother Richards had so recently taught us. And the feeling seemed to be expressed and summed up in a quotation from the scriptures. Brother [Spencer W.] Kimball quoted to us these words: 'Brother Richards was like Moses. His eye was not dimmed nor his natural force abated, but God took him unto himself.'"

Chapter 1

WILLARD RICHARDS

DECEMBER 1836 TO FEBRUARY 1844

I was baptized at Kirtland under the hand of Elder Brigham Young December 31st, 1836 after the sun had set in the West.

From this time I enjoyed uninterrupted peace of mind and continued improvement of bodily health until the eve of the 6th of March, 1837, when I was ordained to the office of an Elder in the Church of "Later Day Saints" under the hand of President Beman and Counsel at his house.

January 8 1837 Partook of the sacrament of the Lord's Supper. I was confirmed in the Church by the laying on the hands of Elder Cahoon when I received such a measure of the Spirit.

Monday, March 13 Received the prayers of President Joseph Smith Jr. and Sidney Rigdon with the laying on of hands for the recovery of my health. I was set apart especially to accompany Elder Brigham Young on a brief mission to the East.

Tuesday, March 14 Left Kirtland with Elder Young and travelled by stage to Buffaloe, 200 mi.[1]

June 5 Much fatigued, stomach foul, head ache, in the evening received a letter from Elijah Fordham N.Y. on business. And on reading it felt a strong desire to start for Kirtland immediately, but wishing to know the mind of the Spirit I submitted the case

---

1. Willard's journal lists the locations they visited and records some success in their mission: "April 13 Bro. Young, baptized uncle, aunt, and Miss Miller."

to the Lord. Praying that my head might be <u>relieved from pain immediately</u> if it was the Lord's will I should start for K. at day break or 2 o'clock, which prayer was answered.

June 11 Sabbath. Arrived in Fairport after 24 hours sail and walked immediately to Kirtland. It was excessively hot and I came near melting. Evening went with Brother Brigham to President Joseph Smiths. Those were present Brothers Heber C. Kimball, O. Hyde, & Joseph Fielding. Also Presidents S. Rigdon H. Smith and others. Elders K. H. and F. had been ordained to a mission to England & President Smith was giving them counsel on the subject when I felt my heart burn within me strongly desiring that I might be one of the no., but I do not recollect that it once entered my mind that it would be possible for me to go, for I was deeply involved in the Temporal affairs of the Church with Bro Brigham and knew not how to extricate myself from the dilemma So I let my mind rest over night quite contended with the simple fact I could not go although months before I had entered into a covenant with Elder Kimball that I should be one of the [number] to constitute the first mission to a foreign land.

June 12 Made a few calls. Met with Elder K. in the St. when he said Elder Richards I am now ready to fulfil my engagement with you. You recollect it don't you. I start for England tomorrow and you may go with me. Get ready &c. But I saw no way to extricate myself or to procure means to cross the water.

Walked to Pres. Hyrum's and after doing my business enquired if it was my privilege. He replied it was if I wished it. Walked with him to P. Rigdon who said he had "no objection" & did not know why the Lord should have any. Accordingly with the approbation of Bro. Brigham, who agreed to the charge of all our business, & I was ordained Monday P.M. 6 o'clock to a mission to England under the hands of Presidents S. Rigdon and H. Smith.

June 13 Closed all my business—bade my Kirtland friends farewell & started for a foreign shore at 9 A.M. in Co. with Brother Heber C. Kimball, Orson Hyde & Joseph Fielding.

June 23 Engaged passage in ship Garrick, 2nd cabin.

June 24 This day 33 years old.

July 16 Sabbath. Elder Hyde preached on the aft Quarter Deck. Was on deck and heard the Sermon but was severely afflicted with pain in the head & different parts of the body so that it was difficult for me to stand. Brethren Kimball & Hyde laid their hands on me and prayed. Then E. K. took me by the hand & in the name of Jesus Christ told me to "arise" which I immediately did and found myself quite comfortable. Thanks be to the Lord for his special healing power which has been repeatedly manifested toward me.

July 20 Awoke this morning in the utmost horror. It appeared to me that evil spirits or devils had fastened on every muscle of my body, punishing it so severely as completely to stop the circulation of the fluids & Satan himself held me so close by the throat that I was gasping for the last time. Doubtless it would have gratified the prince of the power of the air if he could have strangled me. But the Lord suffered him not. I had long desired that I might be the first (<u>next to the Twelve</u>) to set my feet on a foreign shore to carry the fullness of the everlasting gospel to the honest in heart. We anchored in the Mersey & took to the small boat & hauled to the shore. Elder Kimball first landed, next Elder Hyde, myself & E. Goodson. Yes we were the first who landed from the Garrick after a prosperous voyage of 20 days from N. York, & we sought the first opportunity to unite our hearts in thanks to our Heavenly Father for his protection.

July 22 Went to Preston & put up at private lodgings in Wilford St.

July 23 Sabbath. Brother Heber opened the mission (in Mr. James Fielding meetinghouse) followed by O. Hyde.

Aug 2 Elders J. Goodson and W. Richards, Elders of the Church of "Later Day Saints" arrived in Bedford, Aug 2, 1837 direct from Preston from whence they were directed by Elder HC Kimball and O. Hyde (two of the Twelve) with instructions to proclaim the Gospel of Jesus Christ, and the Lord willing, build up a Church of "Later Day Saints" in Bedford. After repeated preachings, teachings, warnings and testimonies to the people Mrs. Ann Braddock, Mrs. Ann Lee, Rhoda Coleman, Ann Brown and Caroline Braddock were Baptized.

September 11 Brother Goodson wishes to know if I have any objections to his going to Preston.[2] & I said, "I have none." For I feel it to be the will of God though I feel my want of wisdom & experience in God's house to manage the work of God in this strong hold of Satan. I will humble myself as a Little Child, believing that God will lift me up & prepare & strengthen me for his work. I desire to know nothing but Jesus Christ & him Crucified until he comes.

Sept 18 Kept this as a day of fasting and prayer that God would restore me to perfect health, give me humility & meekness, wisdom & the Spirit of Prophecy & wholly prepare me for his will & service & that he would make known to me his mind & will about the people of Bedford. 4 P.M. much refreshed by the Spirit of my Father.

October 1 Sabbath meeting morn at Bro Smiths, having been moved by the Spirit for a week to attack Satan in his strong

---

2. John Goodson left Willard alone in Bedford after a time together as companions. Willard himself had been a member for only nine months.

hold. I this day preached repentance and baptism to the congregation at St. Pauls Church as they came out of the door at 1 o'clock.

Nov 9 Lodgings surrounded through the night by 100's yelling &c.

Jan 1 [1838] Baptized Sarah Lavender. Prayed that I might baptize one soul per day on an average the present year—with some assurance.

Feb 16 Received a letter from Preston that I must prepare for home in one month & answered it. Previously I had had no idea of going with the brethren this Season though it gave me not an anxious thought. My father thy will be done.

March 22 Jennetta Richards came in the room & I walked with her & Mrs Parker to Ribchester, & attended meeting with Bro H. and K. at Bro Clarks. While walking with them down the fell I said Richards was a good name. I never want to change it, do you? Said I to Jennetta. "No I do not" was her reply & I think she never will.

April 6 Preston. Letter from America containing the death of my mother.

June 27 Jennetta came with Bro. K. in cart. Was with her much of the time as she lodged at Sister Daorus & had a most interesting & delightful visit for which I praise my Heavenly Father. It was all his doings. He shall have the praise. Gave her the Wedding Ring. We acknowledged each other husband and wife & sealed it with our mutual kisses. My Heavenly Father sanction it in heaven & bless our union to the fulfillment of the design for which marriage was instituted for Christ's sake. Amen and amen.

Sept 24 Married to Jennetta at 8 in the A.M. Most truly do I praise my heavenly father for his great kindness in providing me a partner according to his promise. I receive her from the Lord &

hold her at his disposal. I pray my heavenly father he will bless us forever. Amen.

Oct 3 Arraigned before the Mayors Court, Town Hall (with Sister Dawson) for the murder of Allice Hodson[3] (alias the word of God & testimony of Jesus Christ). An evil spirit prevailed in court. & no defense was permitted—discharged.

Oct 7 S[abbath] 9 Cut off. Powers of darkness raged.

Dec 31 2 years since I was baptized. Great are the events which have transpired but those of these next two will be greater.

July 16, 1839 Heber John born 5 minutes past 4 p.m.

Dec 1 S[abbath] Awoke much distressed at the state of the Church particularly in Preston. The bed shook under me. Called Bro. Fielding to pray with me. Eve began to eat.

Dec 17 Heber John 5 mo. old up to the present time has been a sound healthy child, blessed abundantly of the God of Heaven, of a lovely disposition, never angry—a smile for every one, the image of his father. On this day began to be distressed & worrysome. Called the Elders.

Dec 18 Shewed 2 spots on his arm

Dec 19 Many spots on him of the small pox, & continued to break out more & more till he was very full.

Dec 28 Heber John while lying on Sister Susannah's arm or lap where he had been for an hour or two & I had been drowsing. I arose suddenly & gave him some drink for he was very thirsty & would turn his head from side to side to reach the spoon when he suddenly closed his eyes & mouth & ceased to breathe, with a smile on his countenance, at half past 4 a.m. Immediately laid my hands on his head & uttered a short petition, & ran to Jennetta who was in bed & asleep, & told her I did not know but John was

3. Willard had given her a blessing for her health, but when she died, he was accused of casting an evil spirit on her and causing her death.

dead, but she seemed but little surprised for the Lord had shown her the previous night by dream. We immediately returned to John but he appeared quite gone.

Jan 13, 1840 Bros. Woodruff & Taylor & Turley arrived from America & I wrote immediately to Pres. Fielding, Manchester.

Jan 17 General Council. Present. Bro. Fielding, President, Theodore Turley, scribe. Wilford Woodruff, John Taylor, Hiram Clark & Willard Richards—when it was decided Elder Woodruff & Turley should go to the Potteries & Taylor & Fielding to Liverpool; Clark to Manchester with Bro. Clayton & Bro. Richards go where the Spirit direct; & that the seven Elders communicate with the Presidency at Preston once a month for the time being; & that Elder Richards write to Bro. Wright & Mulliner in Scotland. Adjourned.

Feb 16 S Visited Walkerfold & received very kindly.[4]

Feb 23 S Got the Church together. Settled all their difficulties & they promised they would attend meetings & have faith future. They had had no meetings for some weeks. P[reache]d to them & left them quite comfortable & returned to Preston.

Apr 5 S Returned to Preston, found letters from Jennetta, Bedford & Bro. Woodruff blessing me to come down to Hereford immediately.

April 8 Went to Chatburn, & Walkerfold. Quite exhausted and Jennetta's father kindly offered me to stay all night for the first time since marriage, which I thankfully accepted. The brethren having given me sufficient to pay for my clothes. God bless them for it. Amen.

April 9 Much refreshed I returned to Preston at 4 P.M. and

---

4. Jennetta's parents lived in Walkerfold. They had opposed her marriage and had never before invited Willard to their home.

found Bro. Brigham Young and H. C. Kimball in my room, who arrived at Liverpool on the 6th inst[5]—1st day, 11th year of the Church, with P. P. Pratt, O. Pratt, Geo. A. Smith and Reuben Hedlock.

April 14 Council of the 12 when Willard Richards was ordained to the Apostleship. O my God I ask thee to enable me to execute the duties of this office in Righteousness even unto the end, with my brethren the Twelve, that we may ever be of one heart & one mind in all things to be found of thee in Thy Kingdom in the name of Jesus Christ, Amen.

April 15 General Conference of the Church.

April 25 To Manchester. Found Bro Parley. Got some Prospectuses for Millennial Star.

May 22 Visited at Malvern Hill with Bro. Woodruff.

Oct 8 Council of the brethren. Voted that W. Richards take charge of the paper; resume our proselyting efforts to London as soon as consistent &c.

Oct 9 O. Pratt started for Edinburgh.

Oct 11 S Heber John born 10:15 a.m.

April 20 [1841] We went on board of the ship Rochester. There being B. Young, H. C. Kimball, O. Pratt, W. Richards, W. Woodruff, J. Taylor & G. A. Smith of the Twelve. 120 Saints in all and 160 other passengers.

April 24 It commenced at midnight blowing a gale from the S.W. All head wind. It blew away our fore sail. We were all dreadfully sick. But few of us got out of our berths during the day.

April 25 Head winds. Sea mountain high. Ship pitching, all wet and sea sick. Eat nothing but a baked potato in two days that we vomited up. Spent a sick night.

---

5. In this context, "inst" ("instant") means "this month." This convention is used throughout the journals.

April 26 Two years ago this day the Quorum of the Twelve held a Council in the city of Far West and started on their foreign mission, and we are now on our return. Had a still night.

April 28 Strong West wind which soon rose to a Tempest and storm. Sails were mostly taken in and reefed up and while the ship was pitching tremendously, the ropes began to break that held out pile of baggage in the cabin which was endangering the lives of many but through the exertions of W. Richards, Woodruff and others they were soon secured. As W. Woodruff and W. Richards were stacking upon the aft quarterdeck, viewing the raging of the tempest, We shipped a heavy sea. Richards escaped it by being under the bulwarks, but Woodruff got drenched in water. This is 17 days in succession that we have had strong head winds.

May 19 Anchored off Quarantine passed inspection.

May 20 Landed at North River NY. Staid at Pacific Hotel with Jennetta.

June 30, 1841 Emetic. Packed my trunk. Jennetta emetic.[6]

July 22 Ascended the summit of Ramah Cumorah. Blessed & ate some cake cheese & Dried beef—Knelt before the Lord in thanksgiving & Prayer. Read Cowdery description of Cumorah. Searched for cave 18 or 20 trees. 6½ Left the Hill. Arrived at Palmyra 8.

Aug 16 Sunrise landed at Nauvoo.

Sept 5 S. Joseph preached on morn. Hiram P.M.

Nov 28 S. Council of 12. with Joseph at Brigham's. Law of Tything &c.

Dec 13, 1841 Was appointed Recorder and commenced

---

6. Willard left Jennetta and Heber John with his family in Massachusetts while he went to Nauvoo to prepare a home for them.

writing. Directed Bro Decker to remove the Saints from Warsaw & gather affidavits of their treatment.

Dec 23 Commenced writing <u>Proclamation</u> to the Nations.

Dec 25 Christmas eve visited & dined at Hiram Kimballs with B. Young. H. C. Kimball, O. Pratt, W. Woodruff, J. Taylor & wives. H. Kimball gave each of the 12 a Lot of Land & supper of turkeys.

Jan 13, 1842 Left Bro Brigham's and began to board with President Smith.

S. July 24 With Dr. Bernhisel [in New York] contracted for Lithograph of Nauvoo Map.

Nauvoo Nov 20, 1842

Dear General [James Arlington Bennett]

I will give a synopsis of important transactions.

We presented the petition of our beloved friend Gen Joseph Smith to our new Govr Thomas Ford, praying that he would recall the writ & proclamation of his Predecessor—Gen Carlin, for the arrest of Petitioners. The Governor feeling a delicacy & persons not responsibility in the care, called on his council, 6 judges, Supreme Judges, all of which decided that all the proceedings against Joseph were illegal as the affidavit of Lilburn W. Boggs stated that Joseph Smith was accessory to the fact & was a citizen of Illinois, but did not state that he had been in Mo. or that he had fled from Justice—3 of the Council advised the Gov to recall the writ &c—& 3 advised that Petitioner be liberated on Habeus Corpus before the Supreme Court.—& the Gov. decided accordingly—leaving the case precisely where it was, except, the assurances we received that if the Petitioner would make his appearance before the Court he should be set free, &

an assurance from the Governor that he should be protected from all violence going to & from & before the court.

Gov. Ford in his Inaugural address cited the attention of the Legislature to the Nauvoo Charter, as a subject of notoriety & discontent in the state, because the Mormons had so many privileges—This brought the subject before the Legislature & bills were introduced in both houses for amendments, when Mr. Smith our Representative in the House & Mr. Davis our Senator moved an amendment by adding all other city chargers of this state, both bills were referred to committees. What think you—Mr. Councillor—of the Constitutionality of Legislative repeals to Perpetual charters?

Now, Dear General, as I have taken the liberty to ask you one question, permit me to introduce one or two more for your consideration—as the properties of the Mormons has been confiscated by & to the State of Missouri, & we have sought all the redress from the Courts of said state, which the nature of the case will admit, with no success—and as we have applied to the executive of the Union & by him referred back again to said courts, what are your views of the Constitutionality, Practicability & expedience of bringing a suit in the United States Court against Missouri,—for the recovery of our properties?

Dec 1 Began to Record history.[7]
Dec 9 Started for Springfield. 34 miles.

---

7. Willard had been appointed recorder and in 1842 was also appointed Church historian and secretary to Joseph Smith.

Tuesday Dec 13 8 A.M. Arrived at Globe Tavern, Springfield 3 P.M.—staid over night.

Dec 14 Visited Trumbull Sec State. Saw Ford, Governor & Esqr.

Dec 15 Visited Senate & house—saw Judge [Stephen A.] Douglass at statehouse govern in council with Judges 3 for 3 against Gov. discovering Joseph.

Dec 21 Interview with Joseph—read many old letters—& commenced finishing letter to Gen A. Bennet. Appointed private Sec & Historian.

Dec 24 Made entries in the Recorder's office of Money's collected while in the East. P.M. read history with Joseph & walked with him.

Jan 4, 1843 at Josephs trial.

Jan 5 heard Decision of Judge Pope.

[In a letter to Gen. Bennett]

We live in a country of news and new things, & when we can get nothing new, sometimes use the old over again so we will take Missouri once more for by intelligence just received, she has succeeded in capturing our friend O. P. Rockwell and is holding him custody to await trial for the shooting of Boggs. We are assured of his innocence, and shall offer him no exertion to give him a fair trial & procure his acquittal. Rockwell was imprisoned in St. Louis jail on the 6th inst and remanded from there to Jackson County on the seventh. . . . Query whether the trial shall be before the Judiciary of Mo. or on Habeus Corpus before the U.S.C.C.? We have some evidence here, to show that J. C. Bennett is actuated by malice & revenge, and he is the principal witness—it is necessary to destroy his testimony in the case. . . . Gen. Smith is anxious that you should appear at the trial, and wishes me to inform you of the fact, believing your testimony in the case to be of the utmost importance; which, together with your united energies will be sufficient to break down all prejudice, destroy all intrigue, & insure an honorable ~~acquittal~~ discharge . . . Rockwell is innocent & must be saved.

Apr 23 Meeting, twelve commenced their mission to build temple.

Jun 29 Wrote City ordinances.

Aug 4 Read proof Doc [&] Cov.

Aug 12 Appointed City Recorder. Council ½ day.

Sept 15 1st daughter born, Rhoda Ann. 3 o'clock P.M.

Nov 4 Wrote letter for Candidates for Presidency. Eve saw Joseph with Taylor. Read letter & copied to 5 candidates for presidency.

Nov 20 P.M. began to move from the store to the Prophets old home.

Dec 31 Home. Jennetta baptized for Joshua & James her brothers, Ann and Elizabeth, brother's wives. I was baptized for Mary Ann Fay, Nancy Parker, Levi Morton & Susan & Mosely. Meeting eve. Lecture on tatling &c. Sacrament

Feb 21 [1844] Quorum of 12 eve. 8 men rode out to go to Oregon

Nauvoo, Feb 23, 1844
[To John Whitmer]

Sir: Your letter of the 8th of January to W. W. Phelps came in to our beloved Brother Joseph Smith's office this day. As you mention something about the Church records it becomes necessary to reply. We have already compiled about 800 pages of Church history (Large Demi.

closely written one page probably contains about 4 times the amount of matter of 1 which you ~~kept,~~ wrote.) which covers all the ground of which you took notes, therefore any thing which you have in the shape of Church history would be of little or no consequence to the Church at large.

> Yours Respectfully, Willard Richards
> Recorder and Historian for the Church of Jesus
> > Christ of Latter Day Saints
> Mr. John Whitmer, Far West, Mo.

Willard Richards, ca. 1845.

Willard and Jennetta Richards with son, Heber John. This daguerreotype was made at Lucien Foster's studio in Nauvoo, Illinois, March 26, 1845.

"I was Baptized at
Kirtland under the hand of
Elder Brigham Young December 31" 1836 after the Sun
had Set in the West. ⊕

From this time I enjoyed
uninterrupted peace of Mind
& continual improvement of
bodily health until the eve
of the 6" of March 1837 when
I was ordained to the Office
of an Elder in the Church of
"Later Day Saints" under the
hand of President Beman &
Council, at his house,

Carthage jail 8 oclock june the 27th 1844

Joseph & Hyrum are dead. Taylor
wounded not very bad. I am well
Our guard was forced as we believe
by a band of Missourians from 1 to
200 the job was done in an instant
and the party fled towards Nauvoo
instantly this is as I believe it.

the citizens here are afraid of the
mormons attacking them. I promise
them no!

W. Richards —

N.B. The citizens promise us protection
alarm guns have been fired —

John Taylor

Willard Richards's letter from Carthage, Illinois, June 27, 1844.

June 27

3.15. P.M. The guard have been more
severe in their operations — threatning among
themselves or telling what they would do
when the war does over — one would
sell his farm and move out of
the state if Smith stood. — Taylor
sung. "poor wayfaring man of grief —"
Hyrum read from Josephus

4. clerk changed guard. —

4.15. Joseph commenced conversing with
the guard about Jackson Co &c —
& Hyrum & Dr. Richards — conversed some
till 5.15: — 5.20 = Stigall = returned from
town and said Markham was
surrounded = by a mob & had gone to Nauvoo
and supposed that they would be soon in the jail
Joseph said after supper we will go in. — Stigall
went out. — and Joseph. said to Dr Richards — if we
go in the jail will you go in with us. — Dr.
answered — Br. Joseph you did not ask me to cross the
river with you — you did not ask me to come
to Carthage. — you did not ask me to come to
Jail with you — and do you think I would
forsake you now. — But I will tell you what I
will do — if you are condemned to be hung for
treason I will be hung in your stead
& you shall go free. Joseph you cannot. —
Dr. said I will. —
before the jailer had come
in his _____ come in to bring some water

& said the guard wanted some wine
Joseph gave Dr Richards 2, 1/2 dollars - to
give the guard - but the guard said one was
enough & would take no more. - Gaurd
immediately sent for a bottle of wine, pipe & 2
small papers of tobacco, - & one brought them
in soon after the jailer went out, Dr taffs
the bottle presented a glass to Joseph. he tasted
bro Taylor. tasted the Dr Foster. - gave the bottle
to the guard, - who tuned to go out, when at the
stairs top. some one below called him 2 or 3
times. he went down - a little rattling
at the door. - the cry surrender & discharge
of 3 or 4 arms - followed instantly, - Dr opened
an eye by the curtain - says a 100 arms were
around the door. - Joseph Hyrum & Taylors
coat well off - Joseph sprang to his coat for
his 6. shooter, Hyrum for his single barrel -
Taylor for Mortons stick cane - & Dr for Taylors
cane - - all sprang against the door - the
balls whistled up the stair way - & in an instant.
one came through the door - - Joseph Taylor &
Richards - sprang to the left - Hyrum back in front
of the door - & snapped his pistol. - when a ball
struck him in the left side of his nose. fell
back on floor saying - I am a dead man
Joseph discharge his 6 shooter - in the entry
reaching round - the door coming continual
discharges came in the room, - 6 shooter missed
fire 2 or 3 times, - Taylor sprang to leap from
the east window - was shot in the window

Brigham Young, ca. 1850. He was Willard Richards's cousin who converted the family to the Church.

Heber C. Kimball, ca. 1850. He was Willard Richards's mission companion in England.

HEBER C. KIMBALL
1847-1868

BRIGHAM YOUNG
1847-1877

WILLARD RICHARDS
1847-1854

THE FIRST PRESIDENCY
1847-1854

Willard Richards,
ca. 1850.

Willard Richards,

Chapter 2

WILLARD RICHARDS &
FRANKLIN D. RICHARDS

MARCH 1844 TO MAY 1844

WR **Mar 4 [1844]** O. Council eve. First Presidency, 12 &c. Arlington Bennett nominated Vice Prest. Wrote him a letter.

Nauvoo, March 4th 1844
Dear General
I have recently mailed to you "Gen Smith's Views of the Power and Policy of the Government of the U.S." which were drawn forth in consequence of his Friends selecting him as a candidate for the next Presidency, which he very reluctantly acquiesced in—and, it seems would <u>not,</u> only to support a favorite maxim, "The People must Govern." . . . Gen Smith says if he must be President, <u>Jos Arlington Bennet must be Vice President</u>. To this his friends are agreed. Agreed in every thing (and in this commit our power). Consequently your name Appears in our next paper, as our candidate for our Presidency of the United States. You will receive our undivided support, and we expect the same in return, for Gen Smith for the Presidency. . . . Open your mouth wide, and God shall fill it. Cut your quill & the ink shall flow freely. Commence at your own mansion and stay not till by some popular route you reach Nauvoo. And if you preach Mormonism it will help your mission.

All is right at Nauvoo. We are now fitting out a noble

company to explore Oregon & California and making great exertions progressing rapidly with the Great Temple, which we expect to roof this season. On the 6th of April is our special Conference at Nauvoo. From that period our Elders will go forth by hundreds or thousands and search the land, preaching religion & politics—and if God goes with them, who shall hinder? Who can withstand their influence?

Most respectfully

W. Richards

* Dear General if glory honor & power founded on righteous principles are desired by you, now is your time. You are safe in following the counsel of that man who holds communion with Heaven. And I assure you if you act well your part, <u>Victory is the prize.</u>

WR **Apr 7** 10,000 people special conference

WR **Apr 16** To hunt cow; get load wood; eat breakfast; give license; visit sick; load plank; go house, Temple; get 11 window frames, 2 door frames. Load stone. 4 loads brick. Made mortar to commence forms. Gave license. Had a conversation.

WR **April 26** Dr. R. D. Foster told me I was another Damned Black hearted villain & had mind to seduce his wife &c—attended court. Foster, Higbee, & Chas Foster fined 100 dollars each.

WR **Apr 27** I prosecuted R. D. Foster for Slander.

FDR **21 May 1844** Mission to Europe.

WR **May 23** 10.20 minutes adjourned Municipal court. 1 P.M. took the Indians to Mansion back Kitchen—interview with Joseph. 3 dance in door yard.—soon after messenger arrived from Carthage—told me an attachment for me. would be here soon. I walked over to the prophets.—and staid all night—walked out with prophet about 10 eve.

WR **May 27** To Carthage with Joseph—to hear his trial on perjury and adultery returned.

WR **May 30** Court. U.S. vs Joseph Smith on Habeas Corpus.

Chapter 3

WILLARD RICHARDS

JUNE 1844

Jun 10 [1844] To garden. 2 kegs nails from St. Louis. 10 A.M. in City Council till 1.20 P.M. 2.20 to 6½ investigating the merits of the Law party & the Nauvoo Investigator Expositor establishment destroyed this eve.

June 18 Tuesday Legion called out.

Mayors Office Nauvoo
June 20th, 1844
Dear General [Bennett]

Yours of the 14th of April was received at a late date, a multiplicity of business, on account of the peculiar state of affairs has prevented a reply til now. Your views about the nomination of Gen Smith for the presidency are correct. We will gain popularity and extend influence, but this is not all, we mean to <u>elect him</u>, and nothing shall be wanting on our part to accomplish it. And Why? Because we are satisfied, full satisfied, that this is the best or only method of saving our free institutions from a total overthrow.

You will discover by this days extra "Nauvoo Neighbor" and previous papers, which I shall forward with this, that we are already being surrounded by an armed Mob, and if we can believe a hundredth part of their statements, we have no alternative but to fight or die. All the lessons of Missouri's murders are crowding thick upon us, and the citizens of this county declare in Mass Meetings "No peace, till the Mormons are utterly exterminated from the earth."—And for what? A band of thieves, counterfeiters, bogus makers, gamblers, debauchers, murderers, and all that is vile established a printing press in this city, for the purpose of carrying on all their hellish plans, & overthrowing every principle of righteousness, and after publishing a number called the "Nauvoo Expositor" filled on every column with lies & libel the most dark and demonical it were possible for men or demons to invent, on the earth or in the shades of Gehenna; calculated to destroy every chartered right to our peaceful city, & constitutional principles to our nation—being destitute of any vestige of truth & without one redeeming quality, either in their paper or the characters of its publishers—the City Council on the 10th inst, ordered the press and fixtures to be abated as a nuisance, which order was executed by the proper authorities without delay, without voice, tumult, or confusion. The proprietors immediately evacuated their houses and the city. And the night following fired one or more of their buildings—just as they did in Missouri thinking to rain the Hue and cry that Mormons had done it and by that means bring a mob on us without a moments delay, but our vigilant police, discovered the fire and abated that also. Chagrined at their disappointment, and drunk with madness they next, went to Carthage the County Seat and headquarters of Mobocracy & swore that Joseph & about 7 others had committed a riot, & sent a warrant for their apprehension. They offered to go before any magistrate in

the vicinity and answer to the charge. The officer would
not consent, but would take them to Carthage. They had
threatened their lives at Carthage and did not consider
it safe to go thither, and prayed out a writ of Habeas
Corpus from the Municipal Court & were set free. This
only enraged the mob the more. And another writ was
served by A county Magistrate, in the vicinity, not a
Mormon, before whom they were brought, and every
exertion made to convict them, but the Magistrate discharged them. This did not satisfy them, they are determined to have "Jo" Smith brought before themselves for
trial, at the headquarters of Mobocracy—swearing that all
they want is to get him out of the City & they will shoot
the "Damned Rascal." Ammunition and men are passing
the Mississippi from Mo. to Ill. And the Mob is collected
by hundreds at different points in the County, swearing
everlasting vengeance. Where their oats and writs will end
God knows. We have sent messengers to the Gov, but had
no returns, & shall dispatch messages to the Pres. U.S.
next boat. . . .

> Willard Richards
> Gen Jas A. Bennett

June 22 Took many affidavits.—10 eve. Taylor & Bernhisel
with letter from Governor. Had consultation little while & determined to go to W[est] and lay the matter before Gen. G Joseph,
Hyrum & Dr. Richards

June 24 6½ a.m. started for Carthage 20.20 mi. Arrived at
Fellers 4 mi from Carthage. Met Cap Dunn with an order from
Gov. Ford for the state arms of the Nauvoo Legion. Joseph coun-
tersigned the order and returned with all the com[pany] to N.

Got the arms and sent to Carthage same day. Starting about 6 & arriving at Carthage about 15–12 night.

June 25 11.15 we were warned that the Warsaw Troops were nearby—of their own accord. 12 before 1 o'clock P.M. intelligence was given Joseph that the Laws, Higbees & [name missing] were going to Nauvoo to plunder. Gov called at our door with some gentlemen, & Joseph informed him. 2.30 Gov communicated that he would send a company to Nauvoo to cooperate with the police in keeping the peace & call on the Legion if necessary.

Law read was stated by Reid to belong to Civil, not criminal cases. State insisted to have a commission crime acknowledged. Court asked if the parties admitted there was sufficient cause to bind over—and the council admitted there was sufficient cause to bind over—with cognizance in common form. Court acknowledged the admission and ordered cognizances at 5 P.M. Most of the brethren left for Nauvoo after Joseph Smith, John Taylor, William W. Phelps, Hyrum Smith, John P. Green, Stephen Parry, Dimick B. Huntington, Jonathon Dunham, Stephen Markham, Jonathan Holmes, Jesse P. Harman, John Lytle, Joseph W. Coolidge, Harvey D. Redfield, Porter Rockwell & Levi Richards had given bonds, 5 in cash bond, 15 in all, with sureties in the sum of $500 each—$7500. About ½ part of the brethren left for Nauvoo and Joseph and Hyrum went into the Govnr Room and spoke with him, the Gov had promised an interview. After a moments conversation, Gov left for a moment to order the Capt of the Guard to give the brethren some pass. At 8 constable Bettisworth presented a Mittimus as per copy filed, to convict Joseph and Hyrum to Jail. We remonstrated and he waited till about 9 when we heard by Mr. Wood that the Gov had convicted & Capt. Dunn escorted Joseph & Hyrum & W. Richards, and JP

Green, Stephen Markham, Dan Jones, Dr. Southwick, Lorenzo Wasson, & John Taylor—to jail.

We have been received by the Jailer, M. Stigall and first put in the criminals cell but he afterward gave us the debters apartment, where we all slept from ½ past eleven till 3 in A.M.

Thursday June 26th, 1844 Joseph sent to his Counsel by message that he wanted a change of venue. Till 8 Joseph and Hyrum had conversation with Jailer Stigall. Said last week Wednesday they were calculating to have made an attack on Nauvoo and they expected 9000 troops, but there was not 200. They had sent runners to Missouri and all around the counties. 8½ Markam and Jones return, said the Gov was taken by surprise last eve and was very sorry. Was afraid we would think he had forfeited his word.

Gov came here to enforce the law on all people. Gov expressed his feelings about the destruction of the press. Joseph spoke of imprisonment in Mo. Joseph also spoke of the Constitution. We were willing to pay for it, if it were intended to resist the Gov of the State. Firmness, if people believed they were answering to defend themselves, it was all right. ¼ past 10 Gov. left after saying that the prisoners were under his protection. & probably they would go to Nauvoo.

Thursday 27 June 1844,—Jail 5:30 arose. 7. Breakfast. Gov Ford went to Nauvoo some time this forenoon so reported. 10.30 Sent request to the Gov. by Jones, for a pass for private secretary—Dr. W. Richards. 11.20 Jones returned, with Dr. Richards' pass. Could not get one for himself. 11.30 Almon Babbit arrived. Read a letter from O. Cowdery.[1] 3.15 P.M. the guard have been more severe in their operations—threatening among themselves

---

1. If this letter is still extant, it has not been found. One wonders what message came from Oliver Cowdery on that fateful day.

or telling what they could do when the war was over. One would sell his farm and move out of the state if Smith staid. Taylor sung "Poor Wayfaring Man of Grief." Hyrum read from Josephus. 4 o'clock changed guard. 5.20 Stigall returned from town and said Markham was surrounded by a mob & had gone to Nauvoo and suggested that they would be safer in the jail. Joseph said after supper we will go in. Stigall went out, and Joseph said to Dr. Richards. If we go in the jail will you go in with us. Dr. answered—Br. Joseph you did not ask me to cross the river with you, you did not ask me to come to Carthage. You did not ask me to come to jail with you—and do you think I would forsake you now. But I will tell you what I will do—if you are condemned to be hung for treason, I will be hung in your ~~place~~ stead & you shall go free. Joseph you cannot. Dr. said I will.

. . . The guard, who turned to go out, when at the stairs top, some one below called him 2 or 3 times. He went down—a little rustling at the door. The cry surrender & discharge of 3 or 4 arms followed instantly.

Dr. glanced one eye by the curtain, saw a 100 armed men around the door. Joseph, Hyrum & Taylor's coats were off. Joseph sprang to his coat for his 6 shooter, Hyrum for his single barrel, Taylor for Morton's cane—& Dr. for Taylor's cane. All sprang against the door. The balls whistled up the stairway—& in an instant one came through the door. Joseph, Taylor & Richards sprang to the left. Hyrum back in front of the door and stopped his pistol—when a ball struck him in the left side of his nose, fell back on floor saying <u>I am a dead man.</u> Joseph discharged his 6 shooter in the entry reaching round the door casing. Continued discharges came in the room. 6 shooter missed fired 2 or 3 times.

Taylor sprang to leap from the east window—was shot in the window.[2]

> Carthage jail, 8 o'clock 5 minutes P.M., June the 27th 1844
>
> Joseph & Hyrum are dead. Taylor wounded not ~~fatally~~ very bad. I am well. Our guard was forced as we believe by a band of Missourians from 1 to 200 the job was done in an instant and the party fled towards Nauvoo instantly. This is as I believe it. The Citizens here are afraid of the Mormons attacking them. I promise them NO!
>
> W. Richards

Friday June 28, 1844—At Day break to eat breakfast, before which Gov arrived and Gen. Deming. Gov. said it should be investigated, saw there was a great responsibility resting on him &c, &c. Said he would send a messenger with an express for Dr. Richards. Wrote an order for Nauvoo to defend themselves. Went on public square advising all to disperse—& the Mormons would come to burn the town. At day boards were nailed together to carry the bodies in—about 8. Dr. R. started for Nauvoo with Mr. Hamilton, Samuel H. Smith and guard of 8 soldiers detached by Gen. Deming & were met by the citizens of Nauvoo on Mulholland St.

---

2. The account in his journal ends at this point. He left a blank page after it, probably intending to complete the narrative later, but it remained blank. In a letter to his brother on August 10, Willard wrote: "I stood by them & saw it all. Mr. Taylor was badly wounded with four balls & his watch was hit with the fifth and left the hands pointing 5 o'clock 16 min. 26 sec. P.M. The lower point of my left ear was shot off and the side of my cheek & head about an inch and a half."

Nauvoo Sunday June 30th 1844, 6 P.M.

Beloved Brother Brigham Young:

For the first moment we have had the opportunity, ~~and~~ by request of such brethren of the council as we could call, we write to inform you of the ~~present~~ situation of affairs in Nauvoo and elsewhere.

On the 24. inst Joseph, ~~&~~ Hyrum. & thirteen others went to Carthage and gave themselves up to ~~the~~ Robert F Smith the Justice of the Peace, on charge of Riot, for destroying the "Nauvoo Expositor" press & apparatus. 25th were exhibited, by Gov Ford, to the troops assembled, like Elephants. Gave bonds for appearance to court, were arrested on charge of Treason—committed to jail without examination. 26th brought out to the court house, contrary to law, for examination. Returned to Jail till witnesses could be procured. 27th a little before six P.M. the Jail was forced by an armed disguised mob, from 150 to 200. ~~in five minutes or less~~ the guard was prostrated, Hyrum shot in the nose & throat & two other places only saying "I am a dead man." Elder Taylor received 4 balls in left leg & left wrist and hand. Joseph received 4 shots 1 in right collar bone, 1 in right breast, & 2 others back, leaped from the east window of the front room & was dead in an instant. I remained unharmed. The bodies were removed to Nauvoo on the 28th & buried on the 29th. Elder Taylor remains at Hamilton tavern yet, better, we heard today. Warsaw [and other] villages were without inhabitants—as in an instant, they ran for their lives lest the Mormons should burn & kill them suddenly. The wicked flee when no man pursueth. The excitement has been great, but the indignation more terrible. a reaction is taking place and men of influence are coming from abroad to learn the facts and going away satisfied, the <u>Mormons are not the aggressors</u>.

You now know our situation, and the request of the council is that the 12 return to Nauvoo. The lives of 12 more are threatened with deadly threats. It has been suggested by the council that of the 12 approved, Prest. B. Young, Heber C. Kimball, Geo. A. Smith, Wilford Woodruff, and Orson Pratt return immediately, & Wm Smith, whose life is threatened with all the Smiths. John E. Page, Lyman Wight, P. P. Pratt, and Orson Hyde spend a little time in publishing the news in the eastern cities and getting as many in the Church as possible. This is for you to decide.

The Saints have borne it with great fortitude & forbearance. They must keep cool at present. We have pledged our faith not to prosecute the murderers at present, but leave it to Gov. Ford—if he fails, time enough for us bye & bye. Vengeance is in the heavens. We have been in close quarters some time. Money & provisions scarce. Will the eastern brethren contribute to our relief?

Gov Ford has taken away the state arms from the Legion.

Your families are well for ought I know. I have not been able to get any means for myself or anybody else.

The Council consider it best for all the travelling elders to stop preaching politics. Preach the Gospel with double energy & bring as many to the knowledge of the truth as possible.

The great event of 1844 so long anticipated has arrived—without a parallel since the birth of Adam.

Jackson & his ~~hellish~~ gang will try to waylay you coming up the river if not before. Look out for yourselves.—

The saints have entered into covenants of peace with the Governor & Government offices, not to avenge the blood of the Martyrs, but leave it with the Executive, who had pledged the faith of the State for their safe keeping. The elders cannot be too careful in all the world, to keep from saying anything, to irritate, and vex the Gov. &c. for at present we must conciliate, it is <u>for our Salvation</u>. The Governor has appeared to act ~~honestly~~ with honest intentions we bring no charge against him. Will wait patiently his proceedings in the matter. Let the Elders keep cool. <u>Vengeance rests in heaven</u>.

Yours truly as ever

W. Richards

Chapter 4

WILLARD RICHARDS & FRANKLIN D. RICHARDS

JULY 1844 TO MARCH 1854

FDR **4 July 1844** The anniversary of our national independence of the United States of North America. Newspapers report excitement at Nauvoo.

WR **Sunday July 7, 1844** Meeting at stand. Richards advised brethren to go out on harvest; to go on with the temple—to make work in the city &c.

> Nauvoo Illinois U.S. July 9th 1844
> Elder Reuben Hedlock.
> Presiding Elder of the Church of Jesus Christ in England, and the Saints in the British Empire.
> Beloved Brethren:
> We embrace this, as the first opportunity, to communicate to you, one of the most signal events, which has ever transpired in the history of the Church. God had reserved unto himself, a peculiar people for the last days; who would not only be zealous in good works, but who should be purified as gold in the furnace seven times, and who would have to endure through faith and patience, in all long suffering. For some Months past, we have been troubled with the wicked proceedings of certain apostates in our midst, who have striven to overthrow the Church and produce trouble & anguish in the Mind of every

virtuous being; but their designs having been frustrated by the wise & Judicious Management on the part of the prophet & the Saints. These apostates reckless of all consequences made a deadly thrust at our overthrow.

Considerable excitement prevailed in the neighborhood, to allay which, they voluntarily gave bond for their appearance at the next session of the Circuit Court: their Voluntary & Noble conduct, should have satisfied every Mind: but certain individuals of the basest sort, swore out a writ a for treason against the Prophet Joseph—& the Patriarch Hyrum Smith—& they were thrust into jail <u>without trial, without examination without any legal counsel, or procedure</u> on the 25th of June; where they remained till next day—when they were brought before the Magistrate, that a day might be set for, their examination. They were immediately remanded to prison, where they remained until the 27th, when but few of their friends were permitted to see them. Between 5 and 6 o'clock P.M. of that day—a company of 150 or 200 armed, disguised & painted Men rushed upon the guard, who were set to watch the prison door—overpowered them, rushed up stairs into the entry adjoining the room where Joseph Smith & Hyrum Smith were, & John Taylor, & Willard Richards sitting with them to keep them company. As soon as the mob arrived at the head of the stairs, they fired through the door & shot Hyrum in the face, who fell instantly exclaiming, "I am a dead Man" the mob instantly forced open the door with the points of the bayonets, & commenced an indiscriminate discharge of fire arms, upon all in the room.

Mr. Taylor in attempting to leap from the window was shot & fell back in the chamber. Joseph in attempting to leap from the same window, was shot, & fell on the out side about 20 feet descent. The mob gathered instantly round him and again shot him.

Joseph & Hyrum, Received each four balls & were killed instantly. Elder Taylor received four balls, in his left wrist & left leg, is doing well & is likely to recover.

Dr. Richards was marked on his left ear & cheek— otherwise remained unharmed, the whole scenery occu- pied only two or three Minutes when the Mob fled rapidly toward Warsaw. The bodies of the Murdered men, were removed to Nauvoo on the 28th were buried on the 29th.

This event has caused the deepest mourning among the Saints, but they have not attempted to avenge the out-rage. They have said they would leave the event with the governor & if he failed, with God.

Now beloved brethren, we say to you all, as we say to the Saints here, be still & know that God reigns. This is one of those fiery trials, that is to try the Saints in the Last days. These Servants of God have gone to heaven by fire, the fire of an ungodly Mob. Like the prophets of ancient days they lived as long as the world would receive them. and this is one furnace in which the Saints were to be tried: to have their leaders cut off, from their Midst and not be permitted to avenge their blood. God has said vengeance is mine.[1]

The Murder of Joseph will not stop the work. It will not stop the Temple. It will not stop the gathering. It will not stop the honest in heart from believing the truth, & obeying it; but it is a proof of the revelations we have

---

1. A draft of the letter included this paragraph: "This will not retard the work. We are now building the temple at Nauvoo & the Saints are more engaged than ever to accomplish it, knowing the blessings which they are to receive therein."

received from heaven through him. He has sealed his testimony with his blood, He was willing to die—& desired only to live for the sake of the brethren.

Two better Men than Joseph & Hyrum Smith never lived. Two better Men God never made. But they are taken away by the hands of assassins, & of the foolish things of the earth God will raise up others to comfort & lead his people, & not one item of his word can fail. We, alone, of the Quorum of the Twelve Apostles, are here at this time to write to you; the remaining ten are in the Eastern States preaching the Gospel, & we expect them soon to return, & as soon as God will we will write you again.

Proceed onward with all your labors as though Nothing had happened, only preach Joseph Martyred for his religion; instead of living, & God will pour out his Spirit upon you & hasten his work from this time.

Be humble, prayerful watchful, & let not the adversary get any advantage of one of you, & may the choicest blessings of Israel's God rest upon you, & abide with you, that you may endure faithful in all tribulation & affliction, & be prepared to be gathered unto Mount Zion & enter into Celestial glory is the earnest prayer of your Brethren in the New & everlasting Covenant. Amen

Willard Richards

John Taylor

P. S. We would have said that while Joseph was on his way to Carthage, and on the prairie, he said to friends around him. "I am going like a lamb to the slaughter; but my mind is calm as the summer morning. I have a conscience void of offence towards God & towards all men." Joseph also said to his friends "I am going voluntarily to give myself up, and it shall be said of me that I 'was mur-dered in cold blood.'"

FDR **8 July 1844 Mon** The papers report Joseph and Hiram shot. The people believe it.

FDR **10 July 1844 Wed** Found them troubled much with fearful apprehensions for the Prophet's life. Succeeded in some good degree in dispersing their anxious fears and strengthened them in the unbelief of Newspaper falsehoods.

FDR **11 July 1844 Thursday** Spent a few hours visiting the different parts of the city reading the news, which confirms the death of Joseph and Hiram.

WR **Sunday, July 14, 1844** 10 A.M. many people at the stand. P. P. Pratt preached. Dr. Richards prepared a fishing Co. to meet at 8 next morning at Council Room; also—proposed that trustees should be appointed as soon as the Twelve returned and could call a special Conference. 6. Several Councilors came to the council chamber to investigate the choosing Trustees. But decided to wait until the Twelve arrived.

FDR **25 July 1844 Thurs** Here I found the first intelligence direct of Joseph's and Hiram's Martyrdom. In a letter from Jesse Fox to his brother John Fox, neither of them members of the Church, saying that Nauvoo is in tears. O Father extend thy po-tent arm and shield thy Saints from further harm. Enable them in thee to dwell and know thou wilt do all things and [illegible] to thy Saints.

FDR **27 July 1844** Got papers from Nauvoo, dressed in mourning, stating the circumstances of the assassination of Joseph and Hiram.

WR **Tuesday July 30th** P.M. Samuel H. Smith died.

WR **Saturday, August 3, 1844** Elder Rigdon arrived from

Pittsburgh. Pratt and Richards invited Prest. Rigdon to sit in Council at 8 next Morn which he agreed to.

WR **Sunday, August 4, 1844** Rigdon was engaged with a lawyer and could not attend Council. 10 A.M. Elder Rigdon preached, large congregation. Delivered a message from the Lord that the Church must choose a Guardian &c. Text. My ways are not as your ways &c.

P.M. [William] Marks made an appointment for a meeting on Thursday for the Church to choose a Guardian. Dr. Richards proposed waiting till the Elders return, and told the Saints to ask wisdom of God. Marks said—Rigdon wanted the meeting on Tuesday, but he put it off till Thursday that Elder Rigdon was some distance from his family and wanted to know if this people had any thing for him to do. If not he wanted to go on his way, for there was a people 1000's and 10,000's who would receive him; that he wanted to visit other branches around & this fruit. Pratt, Geo A., Dr. R & Taylor had Council and agreed to meet Rigdon next morning 9 o'clock.

WR **Tuesday, August 6, 1844** 8 eve. Bro. B. Young, H. C. Kimball, W. Woodruff, O. Pratt, L. Wight arrived home.

WR **Wednesday August 7, 1844** The 12, 8 of them, in Council at Bro. Taylor's. 4 P.M. Meetings of High Council & 12 simultaneous at the 70's hall 2nd Story. Prest. Rigdon spoke. "Joseph sustains the same relation to this Kingdom as he had ever done. No man could be the successor of Joseph. Kingdom to be built up to Jesus Christ through him. Revelation still. Built up to him. Murdered Prophet head of this . . . you are consecrated a spokesman to Joseph as you have been. You shall speak for him. Church not disorganized. Our head has gone. We might have diversities of feeling &c. If the people want me to sustain this plan I want it on principle that any individual shall advantage it for himself. That the man should be a spokesman until Joseph Smith himself shall descend as a mighty angel, lay his hand on his head and ordain him & say come up and act for me. I have discharged my duty and desire what you command me."

B. Young: "Must have the voice of the Church in conference. All the authorities of the Priesthood. Did not care who lead the Church. How often has Joseph said to the Twelve I have laid the foundation and you must build thereon. I cannot build otherwise." Proposed a conference on Tuesday next of the Church and said to the brethren.

FDR **7 August 1844** To Mr Tifts in Ellisberg 20 miles. Here I found a letter from the Quorum of the Twelve calling upon all the official members of the High Priesthood to return to Nauvoo.

WR **Thursday, August 8, 1844** Signey Rigdon preached in the A.M. 2 P.M. Special Conference. Twelve unanimously voted by the Church to stand as First Presidency of the Church &c.

WR **Friday, August 9, 1844** Council at B. Young's. 1 P.M. B. Young, H. C. Kimball, A. Lyman, G. A. Smith, W. Woodruff, P. P. Pratt, O. Pratt, W. Richards & 11 others. Prest. Young proposed righting up the Quorums.

WR **Monday Aug 12th, 1844** 10 A.M. the Twelve. Voted that B. Young, H. C. Kimball & W. Richards district the Continent & appoint Presidents over the different districts and manage the general affairs of the Church.[2] Voted that the general Superintendency, direction and control of the organizations in England and Keys in England of Brigham Young, President of

2. These three brethren were considered the first presidency of the Church, even though the First Presidency as such was not organized until 1847. The division of the earth into geographic regions with a member of the Twelve overseeing the affairs of the Church in each one continues today.

the Quorum of the 12. Voted that W. Richards go on with the History of the Church & be supported.

WR **Sunday Aug 18, 1844** B. Young preached A.M. about leaving this place. Counseled the Saints to stay and build up the Temple, City, &c.

WR **Monday Aug 19th, 1844** I called on Emma for the New Translation of the Bible. She said she did not feel disposed to give it up at present.

FDR **Thursday October 3** Went with father to Br Brigham Young's. Found uncle Willard Richards present. I ascertained by Pres Young that he had sent a word of council by Elder Orson Pratt from Boston (hoping it would reach me at New York) making it optional with me whether I should proceed to England or return home, saying that I should be blessed in doing either. This counsel caused me to feel uneasy when I found I was not especially counseled to return, on account of those who had contributed to assist me. But, Pres Young assured me that it was all right and I endeavored to feel so. I felt it was good to mourn with the people of God for the irreparable loss which not the Saints only but the world at large had sustained.

WR **Tuesday, Jan 7, 1845** 11. The Twelve met to consult about sending to California & to the Churches to call in teams, &c.

WR **Wednesday, Jan 8th** 10 A.M. Family meeting of Phinehas Richards and relatives at 70's Hall.

FDR **Wednesday January 8** The next day being January 8 a meeting of the family of Richards, Youngs and Havens met at the Seventies Hall. Here we had a fine time. Learned new things, one of which was that the Smith, Kimballs and Goddard families had been all traced back to one stock and that but 2 or 3 generations back of our Father Goddard. Here we learned also that the right and power to hold the Keys of the Kingdom was by Blood. This caused my bosom to swell with joy for that I was a Branch of so excellent stock. I pray thee O God the Eternal Father to enable me so to live that I may never dishonor so good a parentage, neither reproach thy holy cause, but may I so overcome the evils of this world which encompass me that I may be admitted to the enjoyment of all the blessings of thy glory and enjoy a rich foretaste of thy goodness while here in the flesh. Of our company were Mother Smith, Uncle John Smith, 2 of the Twelve, 4 or 5 Pres's of Seventies, 4 High Priests &c. Indeed I beheld in embryo a Kingdom. This was "the first family meeting of the kind that has been held in this dispensation that I have heard of."

WR **Thursday, Jan 30** On history. 2 p.m. Gen Council of the Twelve, City & High Council & 40 police at Masonic Hall concerning repeal of charter & election on Monday next.

WR **Friday, February 21** History. Noon Bullock quit writing History (812–838, 27½ pages or 6 pages per day.) and went to costing the amount of losses in Mo.

WR **Tuesday, Feb 25** History. Rumor said that Young & Kimball were prisoners in Carthage jail. At dusk Council at John Taylors—W. Richards, Taylor, JE Page, Geo A Smith & others did not believe the report, but considered it prudent for 6 or 8 to go out & Hosea Stout & 7 other old police started at 9 o'clock. Arrived at between 2 & 3 next morning.

WR **Friday, Feb 28, 1845** History. Finished writing 1838.

WR **Saturday, Mar 1, 1845** Council of 50 at 70's hall. A committee of 9 appointed to visit different places & investigate the situation of the people & report. Legislature had confirmed the doings of Prest. Joseph Smith as Trustee in Trust &c. Prest. Young called, read a letter he wrote to Prest. J. K. Polk.

WR **Friday, March 14** History. Prest. Young proposed that

Deacons be appointed to take care of the poor, in every neighbor-hood with Bishops at their head; and a meeting of all Bishops and their counselors be at Music hall on Monday eve next to organize.

WR **Saturday, March 15** 10 A.M. Council at Trustees Office. The 12, Seventies committee & architect agreed to put all their help on the Temple. Build a drain for the font; a wall on the south side of Temple block, keep 3 crains going &c.

WR **Wednesday, March 26, 1845** History. 10. went to Fosters Daguerrotype with Jennetta and Heber John.

WR **Tuesday, April 1, 1845** History till 11. Brigham, Heber, John Taylor, Geo A. & Bishop Miller from Ottowa called. 12 be-gan to read History at 42nd page, 47. 3 p.m. Young, Kimball & Smith commenced reading till dark 118 pages. All left. 8 read till 10½=180 pages. Young, & Geo A. retired for home. Police Stout went with him.

WR **Thursday, April 3, 1845** Revising and adding to History, which had been read before the President.

FDR **Thursday April 3rd** Thus I terminated a journey of 1060 miles. Preached 11 times. The object of this mission was to collect tythings & donations for to build the Lord's House. It was at the appointments on this mission that the private seal of the Twelve was instituted and myself the bearer of One. On this mission I obtained about $475.00 for the Temple, 300 of which I Brought in with me. The $175 remainder in sheep, cows, wool, wagons, &c. will come on when the grass will admit of their be-ing driven.

WR **Thursday, April 10** Prayer Meeting at my office. Prayed for rain. It has been very dry for some time; abundant harvest; a curse on Sharp, Fosters, Laws, Higbees &c; blessings on the Saints & our protection from enemies.

WR **Saturday, May 10** History. Examining letters to send to the Governors of the different states & Pres. Polk which were written in March & dated in April from 24 to 30. Signed this day by Brigham Young, Willard Richards, NK Whitney.

WR **Saturday, May 24** 6 a.m. the Twelve assisted in laying the corner stone—or cap stone of the NE corner of the Temple. The Cap Stone. Music by the band & Hosanna, Hosanna, Hosanna to God & the Lamb, Amen, Amen, & Amen 3 times. Sister Jennetta very sick. JE Page, Geo A Smith went to lay hands on her. Long investigation & Brannan was restored, to full fellowship in good standing. Wm Smith was ordained Patriarch to the whole Church of Jesus Christ of Latter Day Saints and to preside over the Patriarchs. All of the Twelve were present laying their hands on him except W. Richards who wrote the blessing.

WR **Monday, June 9** Jennetta remains sick. Have had my clothes off but once since the 24th of May. About this time I wrote Father & Mother Richards, the last letter Jennetta ever helped dictate to her friends.

WR **Tuesday, June 24, 1845** 9 a.m. Young, Kimball, Geo A Smith read history in my room. Gen. Deming shot Dr. Marshall in Carthage Court House. The band came under the window at Jennetta's request, which elated her very much—near 12 o'clock night.

WR **Wednesday, June 25** 9 a.m. Council in my room. 6 p.m. the 12 at Masonic Hall with police & Wm. Smith. Wm read his letter, explained and wanted to know if he had no right, to council the police, wanted the 12 to say so &c., & he would carry on in peace, & if he left & the Smith family, the Priesthood would go with them &c. Prest. Young stated the police were civil affairs, & it was not his right to council the police & he (Young) was not dependent on Wm. S. for his Priesthood—& would not be moved about by him. His priesthood came through Joseph &c.

WR **Wednesday, July 9** By Jennetta's bed, very weak. Kneeled & prayed and laid hands on her three times & I gave her encouragement as I felt & she said "How can I die under such prayers?" 15 minutes past 10 a.m. Jennetta stopped breathing, but continued warm & we continued to bother her 12 hours. Began to grow cold and bloat. Continued to bother till 2 next morning. Sister Wilcox & Lucy Clayton watched & I slept in the room on the floor.

WR **Thursday, July 10, 1845** Sister Durphy, Sessions, Rhoda, Ann Fox, Lucy Clayton & Sister Wilcox dressed Jennetta & put her in her coffin about sunset. Heber said, "Pa will you bury Ma in the garden. If you do I can bear it, if you do not, I cannot bear it." I told him I would bury her in the garden.

FDR **July 10, 1845** I with my family witnessed the interment of Aunt Jeanetta Richards.

WR **Friday, July 11** At dinner Rhoda Ann spoke out very pleasantly and said "Ma is gone away, She is gone to see Uncle Joseph & Hyrum & my little brother." I wept for joy to think of the happy meeting of Jennetta and Heber John.

WR **Monday, July 14, 1845** P.M. visited Temple. Went on Tower with Bro Young &c. Bought 6 shooter revolver rifle—$45.

WR **Wednesday, July 16, 1845** Council at my office agreed to disprove of the brethren selling their grain to their enemies— but store it in Nauvoo. Young & Kimball rode round the City to raise teams to drive 100,000 ft of lumber for the Temple.

WR **Wednesday, July 23, 1845** Arose & prayed at 6. Wrote history till breakfast time. 9. Bishop Hunter called to see about hiring Emma's land. At 11 met the Council at Trustee's office. At 12 advised Hunter to enquire terms of Emma. At 4 Hunter said he could get no definite terms. Her mind was different at different times. Sometimes to stay here & keep the Mansion, sometimes to go to Quincy and hire out the whole, &c.

WR **Thursday, July 24, 1845** 4 p.m. Prayer meeting. After which the Quorum agreed to take no more snuff & tobacco for 6 weeks.

WR **Saturday, August 2** Had 2 preachers & a Sioux Chief for company. Sioux Indian requested us to stop among them. Sioux are formed into bands—thinks they have some 50 or 60 acres of buckwheat, peas, beans & turnips—a little early corn and 1000's of buffalos, deer and elk, antelope, foxes, sausage, cereal. Live in tents mostly. Timber as here. Pike, pickerel, catfish &c. Plenty of streams. 300 Lodges, 2 families to a lodge, 10 souls to a lodge, making 3000 inhabitants. Follow buffalo up and down Mo. River—300 miles. Prest. Brigham wrote to Mother Smith. She might have the new carriage.

WR **Sunday, August 10** Prest. instructed to council the Quorums to bring 1/10th of their grain & all things raised & that agents be selected to go abroad to gather tithing.

WR **Friday, August 15, 1845** P.M. prepared a map of Nauvoo & Temple for [Sheriff] Backenstos to carry to Springfield to get copyright in the name of "Brigham Young, President of the Church of Jesus Christ of Latter Day Saints". Also, Title page of the "History of the Church of Jesus Christ of Latter Day Saints"; also, the "Law of the Lord" & "Biography of Joseph Smith, the Founder, First Apostle, & President of the Church, by Brigham Young, President of the Church of Jesus Christ of Latter day Saints."

WR **Monday, August 18** About 10 Pres. Young called for the seal of the 12—on his way to the Temple. H. C. Kimball, John Taylor, Geo A Smith were present. Wrote all day on January History, 1843. Strained off the cask Elder berries for wine. 7 eve went with Elder Kimball to Prest. Young's to get him to read history.

WR **Friday, August 22** Corrected history. P.M. re-wrote the history of Zions Camp in Co. with Geo. A. Smith till 6 o'clock.

WR **Wednesday, Aug 27, 1845** 12 noon Council assembled. PP Pratt present gave a relation of his mission. Had been absent about 9 months. Visited the branches. Each preached one short sermon, to pay tithing, build the Temple & gather. Few Saints East. Some will come from every place where there is any. Have attended to government of the Churches. The branches East are weak in men and means & growing weaker. Prest Young said it is all good. Something about California cut & dried, a regular organization to make California an independent Country at a set time. Candidate for President selected. One year from next month there will be a regular Governor of California. Voted not to print the notice of Wm Smith's visit to the Eastern Churches & that it is wisdom for him to remain here.

WR **Sunday, Aug 31, 1845** Voted that Brigham Young be next Gov. of California & Heber C. Kimball vice Gov. At dark went to Wm Smith's to see his sick child. Found Young, Kimball, Geo A., Taylor, & Geo Grant. Heard Wm tell about his wife who had left him &c.

WR **Monday, September 1, 1845** B. Young and Geo A. Smith were in revising Camp of Zion &c.

FDR **Saturday 13** In the office. Brother Langely had been in their camp and found out their intentions of the mob which are not to raise only as many as are needed to burn &c with till they shall drive the Saints all into Nauvoo. Then make a general rally from the other Counties and across the river and drive or kill us. But we have no fears. <u>There is a God in Israel.</u>

WR **Sunday, September 14, 1845** 7 P'd. [Prayed] 8 Prest.

Young & Council came in with Sheriff Backenstos who said he had been to Lima & could not get enough help to quell the mob & had come to Nauvoo to get 2 or 3 hundred men for a posse to go to Lima to stop the mob burning grain &c. Council decided that he had better issue a proclamation from Carthage calling on all law abiding citizens to help him & let the Mormons alone—only such as are suffering from the mob. Father Morley, Solomon Hancock &c were present & said the mob had burned some stacks of grain at Lima. Decided to send a messenger to Quincy, St. Louis &c to get rich men & merchants to buy & rent our building so as to help us to Oregon, & save our buildings after we are gone.

WR **Tuesday, September 16, 1845** 7 P'd. 9. Prest. Young & Council came in. It was reported that Backenstos was driven out of Carthage yesterday & fled to Warsaw. President Young proposed to send a company to Prairie Branch & surround Williams & company & destroy him—root to branch. Some objections were made. Prest. Young 2nd proposed to send the mob a delegation & agree to leave here in the Spring, if they will let us live in peace till Spring. Richards in favor. Woodworth spoke in favor, also Kimball, Geo A. Smith, John Smith. Voted to quit the Nauvoo House & all hands go on the Temple. Prest. Young moved that we offer our property to the Catholics—voted.

FDR **Tuesday 16** Mr. Gridley, took a letter for Sheriff J. B. Backenstos. Little past noon the Sheriff arrived barely with his life, having been chased by the mob and in saving his [life] O. P. Rockwell caused Franklin A. Worrell to fall from his horse. He was put into the wagon and carried off hastily. The wound was fatal.

WR **Wednesday September 17, 1845** Bedell of Warsaw brought in telegram that Frank Worrell was shot & died, the one who was shot by the sheriff yesterday. Prest. Young moved that the Sheriff appoint every faithful man a deputy & take writs for all them whom names are reported of the mobbers as found in the Sheriff's papers.

WR **Thursday, September 18, 1845** A letter from Backenstos requesting 800 men posse & 4 cannon to watch the rivers and secure Warsaw. Voted to fire the big gun at 5 o'clock tomorrow to alarm the brethren this signal being previously agreed upon in case of alarm.

WR **Friday, September 19, 1845** Some 600 men under arms assembled on the square east of Gen. Miller's. Formed a hollow square & Gen B. Young addressed the officers & instructed them to encamp on the ground and assemble at the raising of a flag from the Temple. Laid hands on the wounded men. Andrew H. Perkins came in said he was told by two anti-Mormons, Col. Freeman presiding meeting at Carthage, voted they wanted peace and would give peace if the Mormons would give bonds of all their property to leave by the first of April next. Give up all the persons who there were writs against.

WR **Monday, September 22, 1845** Mr. Bedell said there was a division of sentiment among the anti's. Babbit said the committee of Quincy who went to examine were satisfied the anti's fired on their own meeting &c. Mormon population had no knowledge of any meeting till it was all over. Did not send the news to Warsaw till next day. No Mormon has ever disturbed an Anti-Mormon meeting. Prest. Young said it was testimony by the Saints waiting and not resisting when their houses were burned.

WR **Tuesday, September 23, 1845** Found Prest. Young & Kimball at the Temple. Went to see the upper room. Floor nearly laid. Received a letter from Col Markham that 2 baggage wagons are wanted at Carthage & several persons viz. C. Rich, John

Taylor, Daniel Spencer, Stephen Markham, W. W. Phelps, Orson Spencer, J. Dunham, W. Clayton, Willard Richards, Edward Hunter, R. Cahoon, A. Cutler, D. Huntington, John Scott, Hosea Stout are wanted at Carthage to be tried for treason, & we concluded to go tomorrow.

WR **Wednesday, September 24, 1845** Arrived at Carthage court house 12:20 minutes in the Justice office of the Court. We found that Col Markham had been tried before Barnes & EA Bedell, Justices of the Peace & acquitted. While waiting for the Court, went to see the jail—where Joseph & Hyrum were shot. 2.25 minutes the Sheriff called our names as fellows Charles C. Rich, John Taylor, Daniel Spencer, W. W. Phelps, Orson Spencer, Wm. Clayton, Willard Richards, Edward hunter, Reynolds Cahoon, Alpheus Cutler, John Scott, Hosea Stout—who were present. Sent before Esq Barnes & Bedell who cleared us all. No writings brot. Backman appearing vs. us & he did not know one of us. Andrew Burnham came in said he was in Warsaw to day to get some grave clothes. Several little squads. Williams at their head. Said 4000 were coming in from the north, that they were going towards Lima. Moved by Prest. Young that all the teams for 4 miles proceed immediately to gather all the wheat, goods and families at one point, then at another &c till all are in Nauvoo.

WR **Monday, September 29, 1845** 1 p.m. Quorum in my room. 2 p.m. committee of the California Co. came in. Saml Bent read the names he had selected for California.

WR **Tuesday, September 30, 1845** Arose at 7, breakfast, P'd. 8. went to 70's Hall. Council 50,000.

OP Rockwell came in said 2 officers were in town & troops on the prairie. Soon he returned to say Gen Hardin's troops were on the public square & his staff Major Douglass was at the Taylor's waiting to see the Twelve. Council adjourned to Saturday

9 a.m. & the 12 went to the Taylor's. Saw Judge Douglas & Backenstos. Douglass requested the 12 to go & see Hardin. At 12 I rode up with Young & Kimball, others in other carriages. Met Hardin & his staff who read his orders from the Governor to come here & keep the peace if he had to put the county under Marshall Law. Said he had come here to search for 2 men who had been missing—& stolen goods. The last had been arranged. We retired to discuss & Hardin marched his troops to the Temple, Masonic Hall, & Nauvoo House home and made search for prisoners & dead bodies, and then camped on the south of the City.

WR **Wednesday, October 1, 1845** Council with Gen Hardin, & Major Douglass. Prest. Young, Kimball, Pratt, Taylor, Geo A., Lyman & Father Smith. Gen Young asked the gentlemen their feelings as friends & neighbors. Their feelings about our properties for removings. Gen Hardin said he would do all in his power by counsel & to keep us. Approved of our location at Vancouver Island. Judge Douglass said Vancouver Island is claimed by the United States. Felt sure there would be no government objection to it or Oregon. Gen Hardin said he was satisfied we intended to remove but has not the assurance we can go. Property cannot be sold.

WR **Saturday, October 4, 1845** Prest. Young advised the speakers at conference to avoid reference to mobs, troubles &c., that we are going cheerfully &c.

FDR **Saturday 4** Today the windows are all in the Temple, the seats arranged and all necessary preparations made for the Conference to be held in it. A part of the inscription was put to its place today viz: <u>The House of the Lord</u>.

WR **Sunday, October 5, 1845** To meeting at 10. First time since 12 returned after the death of Joseph. First meeting in

Temple. P. P. Pratt spoke on the great sickness in this place and wished the young men & women to go & see the sick as they have wood & cut & put on the fire, &c. Clerks read the names selected by the Twelve to go in the 1st Company about 130.

3 p.m. singing, prayer by Geo. A Smith. W Richards called out the 1st Co. Prest. Young said if any wished to withdraw from this Co. they could withdraw. Are all willing to help remove the poor to their utmost? Every right hand was raised. Elder Richards offered a prescription for the sick that every one from abroad bring a chicken, duck & goose to the poor & the sick.

WR **Monday, October 6, 1845** Prest. Young said the first business of conference was to try the authorities & Father Smith called B. Young, HC Kimball, O Hyde, PP Pratt, O. Pratt which were accepted & Wm Smith was called up but objected to by PP Pratt. A vote last. John E Page, Willard Richards, Wilford Woodruff, John Taylor, Geo A Smith, Lyman Wight—Almon Babbit objected. HC Kimball requested the case might be suspended & his case was laid over. A Lyman was nominated & carried. Wm Smith was presented as Patriarch of the Church—not carried. Willard Richards was appointed, as Prest. Young stated that Joseph Smith appointed Willard Richards as Historian. Voted. Voted to take all the Saints with us to the extent of ability by property & influence. Voted unanimously. George A. Smith prophesied that the Great God would shower down means to accomplish this thing to the fullest extent.

FDR **Wednesday 8** Mother Smith Addressed the meeting about an hour in a very excellent manner. Said she had concluded to go with the Saints to their new home. The Saints then by her request unanimously agreed to bring her bones back and deposit them in the sepulcher with the remainder of her family. Pres.

Young said he should demand from Sister Emma the bones of Br Joseph and place them there also.

WR **Nauvoo October 14, 1845**
Dear Brother William Richards

Jennetta died on the 9th. of June, she was confident that she would have lived could I have been with her in the first of her sickness, and I should have been, had we lived in a land of liberty, but this was not the case, Mobocracy bears rule in these United States, and honest men's lives are not safe by night or day—at that time it was necessary for me to keep out of the way of a Mob Constable, who was wanting to drag me before a Mob Magistrate, on a Mob trial, that they might serve me as they did Joseph and Hyrum, under these circumstances Jennetta sickened and died; and I thank my God that she has gone where Mobbers can Mob her no more. When Spring opens we design to remove this great people West of the Rocky Mountains, where peace and plenty dwell, where he who owns the air, owns the Land also; and where God can have the privilege of ruling over his own, a privilege which he cannot enjoy in this "land of the free, and home of the brave" without having a mob at his heels.

FDR **Saturday 29** Tonight the Twelve hold a council in the Temple, the suite of upper rooms being completed and carpeted & furnished. I have learned of some who are to accompany me to England agreeable to Pres Young's notification to me of July 14th last. Uncle Willard tells me my time is now short in this country.

WR **Monday, November 3** Felt sick & prostrate & lay down till noon, during which time I dictated a line to Pres. Young requesting the Council to return to my room, they having left on account of my health.

WR **Sunday, November 9** No public meeting this day. The floor of the first story in the Temple having been taken up to put in new timbers, the sleepers which were put in at the commencement of the Temple having become rotten. The brethren of the different emigrating companies assembled in and around the Temple and received instruction concerning the emigration.

WR **Thursday, November 13** Council decided that mother Smith should be furnished with wood & flour, with food & clothing. After dinner I went out in the woods with Pres. Young to Stephen Markham's who was cutting and carving wagon spokes. We helped him to cut and saw a while and fired at a mark with his rifle—about 10 rods. At the 2nd shot, Pres. Young hit the pin that fastened the 2 inch paper to the tree.

WR **Saturday, November 15** I dictated an "Epistle to the Saints" to be read at tomorrow's meeting.

An Epistle to the Saints

All those who have letters, or documents of any kind in their possession, which in any way relate to the History of the Church of Jesus Christ of Latter Day Saints, are requested to leave them with the Historian before tomorrow evening.

All Elders who have been out on Special Missions within two years, and have not reported themselves in writing, are requested to do so before tomorrow evening. Every Individual who may be in possession of any fact, circumstance, incident, or event, or transaction which they wish recorded in the General History of the Church will report it in writing before tomorrow evening.

The Historian wants all Books, Maps, Charts, Papers,

Documents, of every kind, name and nature, and all information that may relate to, or have a bearing in any wise upon the History of the Church, before him, in his office, within twenty four hours.

Important Items of history have frequently been presented at too late an hour to gain an insertion. Therefore I would say, that the History is written up to the year 1843 and the Documents now wanting, are for the years 43, 44, and 45 but if any of the brethren have any items of valuable history of any date, they may hand them in, and they will be filed away for future use.

WR **Sunday, November 30** The rooms in the Temple were dedicated.

WR **Sunday, December 7** I went to the Temple at eleven o'clock and remained until dusk. Had the sacrament for the first time in the Temple.

WR **Wednesday, December 10, 1845** Pres. Young labored constantly to complete the arrangements of the rooms, preparatory to the endowments. The brethren commenced their washings and anointing about 5 p.m.

Messrs. Whitney and Miller—Trustees.

Agreeable to conversation with Bishop Miller I forward you this Bill—for travelling I shall need an easy carriage on the Eliptic Spring, high enough to stand in, and wide enough, to lie across for my family—capable of conveying six or seven persons, besides the driver—with an able and steady span of horses, harness, chains, fetters, and all necessary fixtures for moving, and feeding, and prevention of theft.

Two able yoke of Oxen, attached to two light Waggons, and all necessary coverings and fixtures. One set of Plough Irons. One Axe. One Hatchet. One Hammer, One Handsaw, Two Gimlets—different sizes; The necessary quantity of wrought nails—Iron, Steel &c., Two Cows, 1 Beef, 3 Sheep, A Bit Stock and set of Bits, and all such things, and eatables as are necessary, and cannot be produced by the labor of a family.

If the Trustees will please to provide the above articles against the time of need—I will endeavor to as fast as prosecute my labors as fast as my health will permit
Willard Richards

FDR **Saturday December 13 1845** We received our washing and anointing in the "House of the Lord" in the attic story. I pray thee my Heavenly Father, in the name of Jesus Christ thy Son, to impart unto me from henceforth that portion of thy good Spirit which shall enable me to keep inviolate all those sacred obligations which I am placed under by virtue of the endowment this day conferred upon me, for I feel myself blessed beyond measure in being called upon so soon to enter in while many of my Brethren who perhaps are more worthy than I are delayed. Help me O Father, I pray thee, to be as forward to do good to my fellow men, especially those who are of the household of faith, as thou has been to bestow upon me these precious blessings of thy "Holy House", and may they have the savory effect upon my vessel to sanctify it, and make it a vessel of honor, fit for my Master's use. Yea, O God, may I be faithful unto the attaining of the fullness of these two priesthoods and have the power thereof unto the renewing of my body and may my companion also be sanctified by the same means and each of us understand and perform our duties to each other well, that the bond of union may become perfect and never be Broken. May we both keep close mouths, faithful spirits, and observe all things pertaining to the

Oath of the Priesthood and be found faithful therein and never fall, but rise in intelligence until we become fit for the presence of our Father in Heaven all which blessings we ask in the name of Jesus Christ.

FDR **Sunday December 14** For the first time I partook of the Sacrament of the Lord's Supper in the "righteousness of the Saints" in the Lord's House and again attended meeting in the afternoon at 2 o'clock with those who were not prepared with white. A rich time to any soul. By invitation of Pres Young [and] I spent the week in the Temple and several nights in helping to bestow that which I also have received upon others. Jane also spent 4 or 5 days with me there in assisting to sew &c. A precious week to us both.

FDR **Sunday December 21** Jane and myself both of us unitedly enjoyed the Lord's supper in the Lord's House clothed in the "righteousness of the Saints" a blessing most precious to each of our souls.

WR **Tuesday, Dec 23rd** At 10 p.m. took Alice L . . . h by the [shorthand writing] of our own free will and accord mutually acknowledged each other husband & wife, in a covenant not to broken in time or Eternity for time & for all Eternity, to all interests & purposes as though the seal of the covenant had been placed upon us for time & all eternity & called upon God & all the Holy Angels & Sarah Long . . . h to witness the same.[3]

FDR **Saturday 27** Also in office doing errands &c for Uncle Willard's folks. No endowments given on Friday or Saturday on account that the US Deputy Marshall Roberts was here with writs for the 12 and had been several days. Spent Christmas in giving

---

3. Available records do not indicate that Willard and Alice were sealed in the Nauvoo Temple. Some time later Alice married Moses Whittaker and later still, George D. Watt.

the Saints endowments and with some of the Quorum of High Priests offered up prayers in the whiteness of the Saints. A happy day for a Christmas and I feel as though the present that I have received at the hand of my Father in Heaven was a Christmas present indeed.

FDR **Thursday January 1, 1846** Very rainy. Mud deep. I went to the Temple. Assisted to give the blessings of the Temple to 92 persons among whom were a company in the evening of Young relatives. . . . Sister Livona Smith was my partner in a "double French four". In the course of our recreation, Pres Young called the company to order and addressed them saying that it was the mind of the Spirit that there should no one of the company occupy the floor anymore for dancing in that Holy Temple of the Lord who was not willing to abstain from & not meet with the wicked in any of their recreations but those who were willing to do so might continue to praise the Lord in dance in His Holy House—and according to the blessings. And addressing himself to his daughter who was in the room and had been in the dance he said: _____ You can not mingle again with the wicked in their vain amusements without incurring the frowns of a father who holds the Keys of the Priesthood, and you will have to feel his indignation if you do.

FDR **Monday & Tuesday 12 & 13** I spent in Uncle W's service & on Tuesday evening I went to the Temple. Called in to the President's room (No 1 attic story). Found that Evan M. Greene, who had been his clerk was ill and unable to serve, and while sitting by was requested to assist in recording which I did & the President (Brigham Young) wished me to come the next day which I did and continued to write the labors of sealings as long as the ordinances were administered in the Temple in Nauvoo. Much of the time writing from morning until midnight and sometimes until 2 or even 3 o'clock in the morning. Seldom getting an opportunity to go home to see my family. Of the things of which I wrote there I will only write here that they were the sealing ordinances of the Lord's House and belong to him or those who hold the Keys of the Kingdom & is one of the books out of which men will be judged. For the privilege of assisting in this part of the endowment I know not how to be so thankful as I desire.

FDR **Friday January 23** Jane Snyder & myself were made husband and wife by the ordinances of the priesthood in the Lord's House by H. C. Kimball.

WR **Saturday, January 24** I went to the Temple at eleven this morning and returned about 3 p.m. Bro. Longstroth & his wife called at 4, and had much conversation with them.

WR **Sunday, January 25, 1846** At ten o'clock I went to the Temple & after some ordinances of anointing &c the following were adopted into my family viz:

Ellen Partington—	Preston, Lancashire, England	Sept 16, 1834
Stephen Longstroth	Langcliffe, Yorkshire	"
Ann Longstroth	Arncliffe, "	"
Thomas Bullock	Leek, Staffordshire	Dec 23, 1816
Henrietta Bullock	" "	Feb 13, 1817
Lucy Caroline Bullock	Farrington, Lancashire	March 21, 1820

WR **Monday, January 26, 1846** About 11 I went to the Temple with Sisters Sarah & Nanny Longstroth and remained until near four p.m. when we returned home.

FDR **Saturday January 31** The anniversary of Jane's birthday. Brother James Mc Fate presented me his daughter Elizabeth and Jane gave her to me at the Alter. The ordinance was then passed upon us by Pres. B. Young.

WR **Sunday, February 1, 1846** I was in bed all day very sick. Moses Smith preached in the Temple advocating [James J.]

Strang⁴ and was completely used up by Orson Hyde & others. He and others were cut off this day, by acclamation.

WR **Tuesday, February 3** Brothers Player & 2 others altering Jennetta's grave. Busy preparing for my journey to the West. The Coffin was also opened and the whole family looked at the corpse which was but little decayed.

FDR **Sunday February 8, 1846** Was this day performed the last ordinances which were performed in the Lord's House in Nauvoo & the closing prayer made at the Altar by the 12. I dissected the altar, carried the records to Pres. B. Young and saw them carefully deposited for the journey; then accompanied Pres. B. Young in his carriage to the Temple.

WR **Monday, February 9, 1846** Gave F. D. Richards a certificate for employment in the Trustees office. At almost half past 3 the roof of the Temple was on fire. An alarm was immediately given when the brethren marched steadily to its rescue. I went and called on the brethren to bring out all their buckets, fill them with water and pass them on. A line was formed and the buckets passed in quick succession. The fire raged near half an hour. It appears to have been caused by the stove pipe being overheated while drying the clothing in the upper room. At the same time that the Temple was on fire, a number of brethren were crossing in a flat boat, when in their rear a man and two boys were in a skiff in a sinking condition, on account of being overloaded and the unskillfulness of the steerer. They hailed to the flat boat, who

---

4. Strang was an early member of the Church who vied for leadership of the Church after the martyrdom of the Prophet Joseph Smith. When those efforts failed, he formed his own church and eventually gained several thousand adherents, who lived on Beaver Island in Michigan. He purported that he received revelations and translated plates. He was murdered in 1856. Some of this followers later became leaders of the Reorganized Church (now Community of Christ).

soon turned, and rendered them assistance, as soon as they had got the three on board the flat boat, a filthy wicked man named ( ) squirted some tobacco juice into the eyes of one of the oxen that was attached to Brother Thomas Grover's wagon which immediately kicked and plunged into the River dragging another with him, and as he was going overboard he kicked off one of the side boards which caused the water to flow into the flat boat. They steered to the shore as quick as possible and as it reached before the men could all leap off it sunk to the bottom. Several of the brethren were picked up in an exhausted condition. Two oxen were drowned & a few things floated away and were lost. The wagon was got out of the River with its contents damaged, in a short time after.

WR **Tuesday, February 10, 1846** The following documents copied into this Journal pertain to a contract between AG Benson of New York for Amos Kendal and others of one part; and Sam Brannan of the other, to settle Cal[i]fornia on shares.

Brother Young:

I have received positive information that it is the intention of the Government, to disarm you, after you have taken up your line of march in the Spring, on the ground of the law of nations, or the treaty existing between the United States and Mexico "That an armed possee of men shall not be allowed to invade, the Territory of a foreign nation." I thought it my duty to let you know that you might be on your guard. I declare to all that you are not going to California, but Oregon, and that my information is official. We have chartered the ship Brooklyne and that Mormons are going out in her, and it is thought that she will be searched for arms, and if found taken from us—and if not an order will be sent to Commodore

Stockton on the Pacific, to search our vessel before we land. My company now number about 175 people. I chartered the whole ship, put her in the market and have already obtained one thousand dollars worth of freight for the Sandwich [Hawaiian] Islands, and a good prospect for more.

(signed) S. Brannan

New York, Jan 26, 46

Dear Brother Young:

Hastings and Capt. Sutter will go with me, and no mistake the country is ours, we shall have a strong and ruling party in this country that will back us politically and commercially. I shall select the most suitable spot on the Bay of Francisco for the location of a commercial city. You must never admit that you are going to California till you reach the South Pass, and then you must rush right through. This is the council on the part of the Government. When I sail which will be next Saturday at 1 o'clock, I shall hoist a Flag with Oregon on it.

(S. Brannan)

WR **Sunday, February 15, 1846** Very fine morning, snow 3 or 4 in deep. With my buggy lashed behind & tent poles & arrived across the River about 2 p.m. Appraised the Templ. Went where was Prest. B. Young & about 50 loaded wagons & carriage. B. Young would not go on till all who were going at that time were ready—we started about 4. Traveling very bad. About 4 miles out came to a hard hill and Prest. Young would not go on till he had seen all the teams up laboring with his own hands. Left the hill at dusk & arrived at Sugar Creek camp about 8. All in conference in camp—9 mi.

WR **Monday, February 16, 1846** Prest. Young was very

busy in organizing his camp ground on the east side of Sugar Creek. About 10 walked up the valley with Amasa Lyman & W. Richards, where they united with him in prayer & he read to them a part of a communication he had received 2 days or nights previous. Then returned and resumed his organization activity— the part of a father to everybody.

WR **Wednesday, February 18, 1846** 10 o'clock before noon, Prest. Young called the brethren together & instructed the Capts of 100's to raise money in their respective companies and send for tent ends and wagon covers & informed the Pioneer Company that it would be their duty to prepare roads, look out camp grounds, dig wells when necessary and ascertain where hay and corn could be purchased for the camp that if the brethren could not bring their minds to perfect order they had better leave the camp and he would have no feelings against them; that every family must call on the Lord night & morning at every tent or wagon and we shall have no confidence in the man who does not; that the police would be night and day guard; that every Capt of 10 would keep one man on watch every night.

WR **Monday, Feb 23, 1846** Council in Dr. Richards' tent 10 a.m. Prest. B. Young, PP Pratt, O Pratt, W. Richards, George A. Smith, A. Lyman, Bishop Miller & captains of hundreds had conversations about moving the camp. They agreed to pass up the Divide which is a piece of land dividing Des Moines from the Missouri River. Henry G. Sherwood was appointed Pioneer commissary to search out grain and provisions for the camp. Capt Markham was instructed to send a company of pioneers forthwith to find a camping ground between Sugar Creek encampment & Bonapart Mills. This evening Pioneers returned and reported a good camping ground 10 miles from this and corn plenty at 18¾ cents—12½ cts, being the market price at Sugar Creek, Montrose,

&c. This afternoon _____ Savage and some others came into camp. They told Elder Kimball they had been informed that the Twelve wished to investigate Strangism. Elder Kimball told them it was a lie. Strangism was not worth investigating.

WR **Tuesday, Feb 24, 1846** At 7 p.m. Fahrenheits thermometer stood at 12 degrees above zero. Mississippi frozen over above Montrose.

WR **Wednesday, Feb 25, 1846** Prest. Young retired from the meeting and went to distributing his grain among the needy.

WR **Thursday, February 26, 1846** At 6½ a.m. the Thermometer stood at 2 degrees below zero. The weather being so cold it was not considered prudent to remove the tents of families as had been contemplated. The Historian had about been mostly confined to his bed since his arrival in camp with a severe coff and unable to write but has dictated this history from his pillow for the pen of William Coray, scribe as may be seen by his hand writing commencing on the 17th instant.

FDR **Monday March 2** Commenced to labor on the Temple, had an excellent place, good bench and screw & father Stiles gave his chest of tools into my charge and I was thereby enabled to go ahead with work in the joiner department.

WR **Tuesday, March 3, 1846** 7 A.M. 23 degrees. Prest. Young paid $5 dollars in silver for purchases at this encampment. About 9 the camp was called together when Prest. Young told them that he wanted the Pioneers to go ahead and prepare the roads by cutting & trimming trees and filling up bad places &c & the Guard to carry axes instead of guns & help the teams that it is not for the Guard or Pioneers to order the teamsters that he did not want a man along who was not willing to help in every place. The guard have to watch but we will help them—for men can not work night and day. We want every man to quit this camp who can't quit swearing. You had better go now, if you don't, the law will be put in force by and by. I felt insulted yesterday by one of PP Pratt's teamsters who would not let me pass his but hindered me unnecessarily. Some times men must not crowd upon each other. Ox teams must give the road and let horse teams pass. When we got properly organized no two teams must come within 2 or more rods of each other. The camp voted that Prest. Brigham Young should be there leader till they all got together. The Prest. directed the Pioneers to go ahead, the Band to follow, followed by the ox teams and the remainder to go out in order according to their number.

wr **Thursday, March 5, 1846** Prest. Young moved on with his Co. about 10 o'clock and fording the Desmoines just below the Bounapart Mills about 2 feet water and passing up the west bank a short distance arrived on the border of the Prairie about one o'clock p.m., having traveled over a <u>very muddy</u> road, frequently the wagons sinking to the axle trees in the mud.

wr **Sunday, March 8, 1846** We must divide & arrange the camp so that a part might cross the mountain to the great Basin soon enough to plant this Spring; that we must ascertain how many men can go forward from the camp leaving their families somewhere on the road, so as to travel with all speed, that 300 men were wanted for the expedition. Many other things relating to the prosperity of the Saints were investigated, particularly the tooth ache.

wr **Monday, March 9, 1846** 10 a.m. the Twelve met in Council & wrote Orson Hyde to stay at Nauvoo & dedicate the Temple, if the Twelve did not return.

wr **Tuesday, March 10, 1846** Richardson's Point. The band gave a concert in the court house at Reosaugua this evening & cleared $25.70. Were treated with the utmost kindness

& attention by the citizens and invited to come to play again tomorrow evening.

WR **Thursday, March 12, 1846** Richardson's Point. About 7 Levi Stewart arrived from Nauvoo, bringing about 34 letters for individuals, one from O. Hyde to Prest. Young, of the 10th inst., stating that he baptized Luke Johnson, Sunday, 5 p.m.; that Wm Smith had returned to Nauvoo, that John E. Page was preaching for the Strangites &c.

WR **Wednesday, March 18, 1846** Richardson's Point. Bro. G. Staley arrived from Nauvoo bringing letters. One from Rufus Beach to Prest. Young dated 7th Inst, also verbal in telegram that an agent of Wm Smith had demanded the keys of the Temple; that Elder Orson Hyde had returned & printed a long revelation on Strangism. The guard expected an attack on the Temple from the Strang & Smithites. Wm had stated that he would be giving endowments in the Temple within 2 weeks.

WR **Sunday, March 22, 1846** In the p.m. several of the brethren forgetting it was the Sabbath went out on a hunting excursion with very little success, notwithstanding there was plenty of deer, turkey, duck, elk &c in the vicinity. Prest. Young said he wanted a new leaf turned over & if there was not, a scourge would come upon the camp. We must give more attention to keeping the Sabbath & quit shooting & trading & not pass it off carelessly as any other day. For he knew it was wrong.

FDR **April 2, 1846 Thursday** Today I am 25 years old & feeling thankful that my life has been spared & that I have been the favored object of my Heavenly Father's kindness in nameless ways & that many times in a peculiar manner, I felt to call together the strength of my family & commemorate the death of our Lord & offer up the signs & pray in the most holy order that from henceforth we may be the better able to do the will of our Father who is in Heaven.

WR **Friday, April 3, 1846** Shoal Creek Encampment. At 12 noon steady rain commenced & continued the most of the afternoon. The carriage & a few of the wagons arrived at a Hickory Grove, about 1 miles east of Shoal Creek at 2:30 p.m., distance of 12 miles from Miller's encampment or 21 miles from Shoal Creek. The other wagons continued to come on till after dark, excepting Pres. Young's heavy wagons were scattered 8 miles back & Dr. Richards 4 wagons, some 3 or 4 miles back, all of which stayed in the prairie over night, leaving the Dr. without tent or food, except he was kindly fed by his neighbors, his family sat up in the carriage during the night. He lay on the floor of Pres. Young's Omnibus.

WR **Monday, April 6, 1846** Hickory Grove Encampment. Pres. Young was out in the rain all day arranging the wagons, hitching tents, chopping wood and so on—until all were comfortable. The Dr. working in his shirt sleeves & flaps through the rain until he was perfectly wet to the skin, some time lying flat on the ground holding down the tent while the pins were driven.

WR **Sunday, April 12, '46** Locust Creek Encampment, Middle fork. Pres. Young stated that he was satisfied that they were taking a course that would prove salvation [of] the camp and the Saints, that were yet behind. Said he: "I don't think that there ever has been a body of people since the days of Enoch placed under the same unpleasant circumstances that this camp have been where there were so little grumbling and murmuring as we have had & I am satisfied that the Lord is pleased with this camp, but there has been some things done which were not right. We calculate to bring destruction upon us if they are not stopped, but they will be removed. There are men among us who are passing counterfeit money, and have done it all the time since we left Nauvoo, and there are men among us who will steal and these things must be stopped. When we once get properly situated so where every man will have plenty, there will be no more need to steal, and if a man does steal when he has no need, the law will be put in force. Some plead our suffering from our enemies and say they are justified from stealing from our enemies because they have robbed us. But suppose we suffer men to take this course what effect will it have. It will destroy the Kingdom of God. From this time forth I caution the brethren to watch those who pass counterfeit money and when they find them, we will take care of them and not let them go to the gentiles, to bring destruction upon us."

WR **Friday, April 17, '46** Rolling Prairie Encampment. Late in the evening 2 of Bro. Boswick's children of Co. No 6 were buried at this point. One of them having died the day previous, the other about 12 today, both of the measles. There are many cases of the measles in camp and some cases of the mumps—but generally of a mild feature. Prest. Young said I have one thing more to say to those that go over the mountains, that they may expect to be allowance to ½ lb flour to each person per 24 hour. How many will murmur at this. I expect some will turn strangiley and run off to ____. I can do very well on 8 ounces of flour per day, with milk but there are some that will not abide council and would eat and destroy their provisions in half the time and when they would get hungry, brake in provision boxes and if they could get influence enough would raise meeting in the camp and curse the 12 & gods but to guard against such evils. I propose that every man's provisions be under a commissary and dealt it out to them. Don't any of you be trouble, because you may have the diarreah. It will be the salvation of this camp as far as health is concerned. And some men that cannot walk a mile will before we get through our journey walk 20 miles in a day, and there is Dr. Richards, the Historian who has need to be poultice all over to keep life in him—will before we get to the pass on the mountains, skip and run like a boy, with gun on his shoulder running after deer, elk and buffalo. GA Smith who could scarcely ride on horseback when he started, can now skip into the wagon like a boy.

FDR **Saturday April 18** I worked at the Temple as usual. Got 6 dollars cash of the Trustees.

WR **Monday, April 20, '46** Pleasant Point Encampment. Weather fair and pleasant. At 10 forenoon Council assembled at the stand according to previous appointment. Pres. B. Young, HC Kimball, PP Pratt, O Pratt, John Taylor, W. Richards, GA Smith and others to the amount of 48 in all. When GA Smith arrived in council, a general whispering and talking disturbance in the council, which caused Pres. Young to move that any person or persons who shall hereafter interrupt the council while in session by talking, whispering or doing business of any private nature shall be deprived of the privilege of council hereafter until the Council see fit to admit them back again & their names recorded accordingly. Seconded and carried unanimously.

FDR **Wednesday April 22** I accompanied Br Van Cot to Br Kidds hoping to sell him the cattle but they were so old he did not wish to buy them. I drove them and the sheep into town & P.M. went to the Temple. Found the hands having a little merriment. Today the joiner work of the worshipping court of the Lord's House was finished. Br Jesse K. Nichols engaged Philo and myself to come the next day [and] help in the painting department, he being boss of the painters.

WR **Sunday, April 26, '46** Camp Garden Grove. Some have

started with us and have turned back, and perhaps more will go yet, but I hope better things of you brethren. We have set out to find a land of resting-place where we can serve the Lord in peace, we will have some here because they cannot go further at present, but can stay here for a season and recruit, and by and by pick up and come on, while we go a little further, lengthen out the cords and settle a few more, and so on continue until we can gather all the Saints and plant them in a place where we will build the House of the Lord in the Tops of the Mountains. But let any person turn from us and go back to Nauvoo, because we have allowed them. They shall hunger and thirst and will yet take more comfort in a eating a cold peace of Jonny-cake with us, than what they now do with all the dainties and luxuries that they have horded up & taken away. The Lord will bring every person to their covenants, either sooner or later. If it must needs be that they serve a probation in Hell. No one can get around his covenants, his solemn obligations must be redeemed. When the camp went up to Missouri, it was considered a great move, but it is nothing to compare with this, and he that will stick and be faithful through this campaign will always rejoice, and shall be crowned with laurels of victory. I know that we can live upon much less provision than what we have formerly been accustomed to. I have seen around the tents in this camp provisions wasted, beans and corn scattered, a plate full of meal or flour sitting in one corner, or spilled by the children, pieces of bread kicking around, and nothing but waste all the day long. It is eight years to day since the Twelve leave of the Saints on the foundation of the house of the Lord at Far West Missouri to go to the Nations of the earth. Previous to that time, Joseph had this mission in contemplation, viz, to find a location west of the Rocky mountains. Whenever Joseph spoke upon this subject, he proposed to send a company of young men as Pioneers to seek a location and raise a crop previous to sending families.

WR **Monday, April 27, '46** Camp of Israel, Garden Grove. At 9 President Young, Elders Kimball, O. Pratt, PP Pratt, Richards, Taylor & 9 others and seven others of the Council of YTFIF [Fifty] met in Council at John D Lee's tent. The council decided to sell the temple at Kirtland and at Nauvoo & all other public property of the Church and help the poor Saints move West. The Council considered that the Temple would be of no benefit to the Church unless they possessed their private dwellings and if the time should come that they should return and redeem their inheritances they could redeem the Temple also. That a sale would secure it from the judgments and mortgages of unjust claims for debts, mobbing fire &c more effectually than for the Church to retain it in their own hands. Bishop Whitney had some doubts as to the propriety of selling the Temple. President Young related a dream he had the previous night, which is in substance as follows. I saw myself employed in the service of an aged man that was a Lord superintending and managing the whole affairs of his dominions (assisted by the Council) among which I instructed some responsible things to be done which I considered actually necessary, notwithstanding the Lord had not instructed me to do so. By and by the Lord came to me smiling. His hair was white as the pure wool. I told him what I had done & asked him if I had done right. Pausing for a moment, he turned to me with a smile on his countenance, said you have done well. But whether Bishop Whitney's doubts were removed or not, after hearing the dream, voted to sell. The Council wrote Elder Hyde their decision.

FDR **Tuesday April 28** At the Temple as usual till in the afternoon went up stairs to the attic story as per invitation of Br Hyde. On being assembled it was deemed unsafe to occupy the room, the company was so numerous. After mature deliberation, Br Orson Hyde dismissed the company & all. All dispersed leaving the cake & wine still on hand. The Temple hands felt much disappointment and went to their homes (rainy). This afternoon while together, Br Hyde told me that I was a drafted man, <u>appointed by council in camp to go to England immediately</u>.

FDR **Friday May 1, 1846** Having been appointed last evening by Br Hyde, I was at the door this morning at 9 o.c. A.M. to assist in seating the congregation. Tickets of admittance $1.00, there was not a large congregation. Elder Hyde offered a dedication prayer & Elder Almon Babbitt delivered a sermon. Only one meeting today. Elder dismissed the congregation with a general invitation for all to attend on Sunday, saying there would be no meeting on Saturday.

WR **Saturday, May 2, 1846** Garden Grove. Pres. Young was employed about 4 hours in chopping and scoring some white maple logs to make board to fit his wagons for the mountains. The Historian walked down to the bridge to see him labor.

FDR **Sunday May 3rd** This forenoon I assisted to seat the congregation which was large. All could not get in. Elder O. Hyde preached. It was an interesting time. Elder Wilford Woodruff preached. It was voted today that if the council in camp concur therein, we think the Temple had better be sold to help away the poor Saints. During recess, at noon, those who were before selected to go to England were requested to gather together at the west pulpit to deliberate upon the matter, which they did. Today seemed to me to be the consummation of what the Saints have anticipated for more than 5 years & the Spirit seems to testify that the offering is an acceptable one to him who commanded it to be built, & the Satisfaction of feeling that we & our dead are not rejected is a consolation to the faithful of the Priesthood that is almost unspeakable. For the last 2 or 3 weeks Jane's health has been so very poor that she has been unable to sit up any of consequence and could not enjoy the dedication with the rest of us. She begins, however, to sit up a little. May her health increase until she is able to endure the fatigue of the journey.

WR **Thursday, May 7, '46** Garden Grove. Pres. Young had a horse bit by a rattle snake. Bro. Daniel Hendrick's horse died which was probably bitten the evening before. Many horses have been bit in the camp. Only 2 have died and it is believed that their death was occasioned more by over-doctoring than by the bite. Several of Elder Kimballs beasts have been bit. He has done little for them and they have soon recovered.

FDR **Wednesday May 13, 1846** Went with Br Samuel to Br J. L. Heywood's. Got our "credentials" of which the following is a copy:

"To the Presidency of the Church of Jesus Christ of Latter-day Saints in England. Greeting. Bros Hedlock and Ward.

"The bearer of this letter is our much esteemed and worthy Brother, Elder Franklin D. Richards who is also of the High Priesthood. We have been directed by the President & Council of the Twelve in the Western Camp of Israel to send him unto you as a true and faithful laborer in the Kingdom of our God, to assist you in dispensing the word of life to the people of your Country.

"He is instructed to labor under your direction & Presidency. The private seal of the Twelve having been taken west, we are unable to affix it to this letter. We beseech you to receive this, our worthy Brother, and render unto him every necessary facility that you may be able to in order that he may be a blessing to you, to the cause & to himself; and that he may answer the expectations of his Brethren who send him unto you in the name of our Lord Jesus Christ."

WR **Thursday, May 21, 1846** Mt. Pisgah, Potawatimie lands. Prest. Kimball stated that "the time had come for the brethren to decide whether the Twelve should go on or stay & let others go on; the Prest. Young & others had had to double teams all the way from the farm here & they could go so no longer, that he would rather go back into the vineyard & preach, convert the people & raise means than proceed in this manner; that the Twelve brought out provisions for a year but they had fed it to the camp—the brethren who came out without means. The people have stripped the Twelve and not the Twelve the people." He wanted it published to the nations that unless the people let the Twelve go and find a place the Church will lie scattered. A motion was made that the brethren outfit the Twelve for the mountains, a part voted in favor and a part did not vote either way. [President Young reported the] rising of 800 men [who] reported themselves without a first night's provisions; that he had a years provision for his family, but had fed it all out & now if the brethren will continue to tie our hands so that we cannot find a resting place our enemies will inquire—where is Zion? Don't know. & where is your gospel? You have none. Bishop Whitney & Wm Clayton & the Artillery & public stores have not teams to go on neither has Dr. Richards, the Historian & the Lord's house must be established in the tops of the mountains, where the people may gather, the Saints receive their endowments & the Lord hide Israel while his indignation shall pass by. Prest. young called on those who wanted to help to give their names.

WR **Saturday, May 30, 1846** Mt Pisgah. Pleasant morning. About 10 a.m. President Young, Kimball, PP Pratt, O Pratt, John Taylor, Geo A Smith, A Lyman, W Richards, Father John Smith, Wm Clayton, Wm Huntington, Ezra T. Benson, Charles C. Rich, Daniel Spencer, O Spencer, NK Whitney in carriages & in horseback rode out North on the prairie about 3 miles. Formed a square with 2 tents. Dressed in their Priests Garments & all kneeled & prayed.

WR **Sunday, May 31, 1846** Mt. Pisgah. Bro. W. Richards said he had borrowed a fish hook & had forgotten the one he borrowed it of & inquired of the owner.

FDR **Thursday June 4** Feeling unwell, I continued in bed until late in the morning & was called up by Mr. Harrison Brooks inquiring about my place. After a short conversation I accepted the offer of 2 yokes of oxen, a wagon with a jackscrew, chain & whip—for a 2 story Brick house & an even acre of land which my neighbors considered one year ago worth five hundred dollars. I now get what I could by with 125 dollars at most. The oxen and wagon being barely enough to enable me to get my family filled for their journey. If I may be prospered to borrow some Money with which to buy provisions & repair the wagon, so that they may have the prospect of going without suffering to the wilderness where I hope & pray that we may realize an hundredfold as the promise is. I spent the day in going to the office for the deed & power of attorney which I gave the trustees to sell my place for which they charged me 75 cents beside the expense of getting it acknowledged before the justice myself. This seemed rather hard since Br Brigham Young said before the public congregation that it would cost the saints nothing, only a little time to do it, and he advised them to do so which was the cause of my doing it.

FDR **Thursday 11** Got Br Graham Coltrin's wagon and moved my family across the river, family cows and oxen save one yoke of steers which got away from the landing, and arrived on the west bank at 12 o.c. night. This morning Br Edward Hunter loaned me $5.00. Took my note.

WR **Saturday, June 20, 1846** Musketoe Creek. About

10 a.m. Pres. Young, Kimball, O Hyde, PP Pratt, O. Pratt, J. Taylor, W. Richards & their families with the band & many others from the camp started for the Indian Agency at Trading Point & about 12 stopped at Major Mitchel's, the Pottawatomie US Indian Agent. Many Indians & others were assembled. Half Day & Hoby, 2 chiefs were introduced to the Presidency & band. After a few tunes, the Presidency, Ladies & band dined with Major Mitchell, 12 at a table, 6 tables. Then music & dancing & song by Bro. Kay till about 6½ when the party started for home. A lady from Leavenworth told Bro. Lewis that Boggs started with a Co. of emigrants for Oregon, heard that 4000 Mormons were on their way & for fear they would find him to kill him he had returned home to Independence, Mo.

WR **Thursday June 21, 1846** Musketoe. Government has provided that Emigrants may stay where they cannot go through to the mountains. It is a law of the camp from the proper tongue, that all dogs shall be chained during the night or from sundown till 7 next morning. If any dog is found worrying sheep it may be shot without trial. Voted unanimously. Some member of the company passed a price of bogus to the Potawatomies on the Nisha Botany & the Indians took an ox from the next company & killed it. Prest. Young decided they did right.

FDR **Tuesday 23rd** This day we nearly completed the wagon. Put on the last coat of paint but could not get the w. over the river this night on account of the ferry. I find that after making some tent poles I owe him one dollar, the payment of which he deferred till my return from England.

WR **Saturday, June 27, 1846** Musketoe. Motioned by GA Smith & 2nd by John Taylor that John E. Page be cut off from the Quorum of the Twelve Apostles. Voted Unanimously.

WR **Sunday, June 28, 1846** Musketoe Creek. Bro. Chintman

came up from the Trading Point & said 2 US Officers had arrived to enlist the Mormons to go & take Santa Fe & if they did not enlist should consider them as enemies & treat them accordingly.

WR **Tuesday June 30, 1846** Musketoe Lewis at Head Quarters informed the council Capt Allen of U.S. Army had arrived on the hill & wanted volunteers. Young, Kimball, Richards &c in O. Pratts tent. agreed it was best to meet them in the morning & raise the men wanted. At 12 noon Pres, Young addressed the assembly wished them to make a distinction between this action of the Government. & our former oppressors. Is it prudent for us to enlist to defend the country, The U.S. if so all are ready to go. Capt Allen said that he was a representative of the president & he could act till he could notify the president. & the president was bound to ratify his actions, doings or indemnify for damage and that the president might give permission to travel through the Indian country—& stop wherever & whenever Circumstances might require. 1½ Capt Allen left & the Twelve continued to converse on the good prospect before us and they wanted to get 500 men to go. Voted that Prests Young & Kimball go to Mt Pisgah to raise volunteers. Prest Young said he would start in the morning. Prest Young. said the Cos must be organized.

WR **Tuesday July 7, 1846** The brethren counted & reported 205 Waggons at Mt Pisgah which with three on the road & at Head Quarters made 1805 waggons.

WR **Saturday July 11, 1846** Muskusaka or Fox Island of the Sac___ Prest. Young told him [Poorsheek], "come over the mountains & see us with your men & hunt for us & we will make your men blankets, guns. powder. Cloth &c."—Poorsheek said he would like to go.

WR **Monday July 13th, 1846** Mo. River. Cloudy. 8 rain

commenced, heavy shower till 10 o'clock, then pleasant. Brethren began to assemble according to appointment.—Col Kane & Capt Allen were present about 11, at ¼ before 12 Major Hunt began to call out the first co of volunteers, Prest Young was in council with Col Kane in Woodruff's carriage, conversing about the state of the nations, Prest Young told Col Kane the time would come when the Saints would support the government of the U.S. or it would crumble to atoms. Prest Young, who requested that families should not be mentioned today, but men must be enlisted & it is right they should enlist & there is no time for argument it is for our salvation in time certainly. & we want 500. & we can do things that no other people can do—build temples out of nothing because we build them out of nothing & we can raise 500 good active young men from among the old men & boys. We want 500 men right here.

WR **Wednesday July 15, 1846** Mo River. Elders Kimball & Richards & the remainder of the 12 to get the soldiers together & instruct them how to behave &c on their expedition, wear their temple garments, & prove themselves the best Soldiers. Soldiers can tarry & go to work when they are disbanded & the next temple should be built in the Rocky Mountains, & he wanted the 12 & the old brethren to live in the mountains where the Temple is to be & where the brethren will have to come to get their endowments. Prest Young said he would prophecy that the time would come when some one of the Twelve or a high Priest would come up and say can't we have a temple at Van Couvers Island, or at California, &c &c, but it is wisdom to unite all our forces to build one house in the Mountains.

WR **Thursday July 16, 1846** Council Bluffs. At 5, the Quorum kneeled before the Lord in prayer led by Prest Young then arose & laid their hands on Ezra T. Benson. & ordained him a apostle in Church of Jesus Christ of Latter Day Saints with all the Keys & power & blessings pertaining to the Apostleship in the Church & kingdom of God in these last days.

WR **Friday July 17, 1846** Mo River. If you stay here you must send back teams & bring up the poor,—& fulfill their covenants they made in the temple never to cease our exertion till all were removed. Prest. Young said the soldiers must leave their wages for the benefit of their families.

WR **Saturday July 18, 1846** Pigeon Creek Mo River. Prest Young said the Captains must be fathers to their companies, & in their Cos. manage the whole affair by the power of the priesthood, and you will have power to preserve your lives & lives of their Cos. & escape many difficulties. Would not be afraid to pledge his right hand that every man will return alive if they will go in the name of the Lord & pray on every morning & evening in every tent. You will have no fighting to do.

WR **Friday Aug 7. 1846** Place of enquiry. Col Kane wished to know our intentions. Prest Young said we intend settling in the Great Bason & those who go by water settle on St Francisco. We would be glad to raise the American flag. We like the constitution but are opposed to mobocracy. We will not live under such Governors & Judges as we have. We are willing to have the banner of the U.S. Constitution float over us. If the Government of the United are disposed to do us good, we can do them as much good as they can us. Col Kane said Gov Boggs had been working against you in Washington I suppose. You would like a territorial government. Yes Sir was the president's reply. English emigrants will probably settle at Van Couvers Island. Col Kane proposed that we send Prest Polk a resolution of thanks for what he has done & let him know that we [must] have a pledge from Prest Polk that he will defend the Mormons in a territorial government;

by the strong arm of the law. Col Kane asked whether we believed in conversing with the Lord bodily; Prest Young replied No. but in vision. by the Spirit.

WR **Sunday Aug 16, 1846** Cutler's Park. Meeting opened & addressed by O. Pratt. The reason why we have changed our council so often is because the people did not abide the best counsel, which was given us by the Spirit. The best council was for the church to fit out a company to go with the Twelve over the mountains, but as they were dilatory and failed to do this, we would not forsake them but give the next best advice. So that no one has a right to find fault with the council for changing their advice, from time to time. It is unbelief that causes all our whining.

WR **Friday August 28, 1846** Cutlers Park. About 9½ the council, Prest. Young & all at the camp assembled in a double tent with the Omaha chiefs & braves and after shaking hands smoked the pipe of peace. Logan Fontenelle the interpreter being present; the principal chiefs & about 80 of the Omahas being present & the High council & several of the brethren.

WR **Monday Sept 7, 1846** Cutlers Park. Col Kane walked to Elder Young's camp and received patriarchal blessing under the hand of Father John Smith. Dr Richards was engaged in writing to Prest. Polk. Two Letters—to Trustees at Nauvoo, one to introduce Col Kane; the other to apologize for not writing till they send him a clerk. One to Hyde, Taylor & Pratt, Liverpool for a copying press. One to Stephen Longstroth, St Louis. One to Ann Braddock St Louis. One to C. C. Rich, Mt Pisgah; & Wm Garner; & 1 to R C Richards, Kirkpene Eng—which he closed about 3½ A.M. next morning.

WR **Wednesday Sept 9, 1846** Cutlers Park. Dr. R. called on Jane Richards saw little Wealthy who was sick & Elizabeth

McFate, was very sick. 12 teams were reported by the Marshal ready to go to Nauvoo & remove the poor. Prest. Young proposed to raise teams by donation to bring the poor out & then give them the teams & offered 3 yoke &c. & then proposed to have the brethren go after haying & work all winter bringing off the poor & working to help themselves—& thus many teams may be wintered without eating hay here with very little hay & they can go one or two months hence.

FDR **Wednesday September 9** At 8 o'clock found Bro Cyrus H. Wheelock. Bros Taylor & Hyde had sailed for Liverpool the day before. After dinner went to the Post Office but found <u>no letter</u>, nor even paper from any of my folks and they were to write to New York in time for me to get it before or by the middle of August, as we thought to sail by that time when we left home for some season. I feel very thoughtful & solicitous for their welfare.

WR **Monday September 14th, 1846** Cutlers Park. Wealthy Lovisa, daughter of Franklin & Jane Richards, died in Co 2nd and from 4 to 9, Dr. Richards was mostly engaged in comforting the friends & making preparations for the funeral.

WR **Tuesday Sept 15, 1846** Cutler Park At 4 took Jane Richards & her Mother & Mary Richards with Wealthy L. Richards corpse 3 years old, & went & buried her on the bluff east of the Turnip patch.

FDR **Tuesday September 15** On coming down from my bed, Behold! Elder P. P. Pratt was there. He told me that Jane had been confined & lost her little babe & was when he saw her about 15 of August, getting comfortable & was able to ride. He met them on their journey towards Council Bluffs.

FDR **Thursday September 17** After dinner I went to the East River & bespoke our passages on the "Queen of the West", second cabin except Bro Pratt in 1st cabin. His fare $80.00, and our $22.50 cts.

WR **Wednesday Sept 23, 1846** Cutler Park. Cloudy. This day the camp began to move on their new Location for winter quarters. Part of Prest Young's division including Dr Richards & others & Prest Woodruff & Prest Kimball arrived late in the day.

WR **Sunday Sept. 27, 1846** Council Plain. Pleasant, wind south. morning Dr Clinton came into the Post office with a Paper, the Mo Reporter, which gave an account of some of the mob proceedings at Nauvoo, Pope & other counties in Illinois.

Thursday: 2 week mob encamped on Woodbury place near Hunters farm. We lay as in ambush.

Friday: Undertook to come in on Laharpe were met & pitched tents on Laws & Hiram Smiths.

On Saturday made a stand on White St. 120 min. Mob 42 cannon ball we 36. Lost 3: Wm Anderson & son & Norris, Whitehead & Durphy & one more wounded. Quiet Sunday. We fired cannon. They returned it on Monday & Quincy committee on Tuesday to make peace. Proposition refused on both sides. 10 on Cook & Quincy Committee to abide decision. Mob demanded immediate surrender. We made propositions. Wednesday eve, we disbanded & finding 3 P.M. Saturday goods all gone, we left as they came in. Suffering of the brethren &c on the west bank caused tears from the mob couple of guard. 1200 strong. Lynched 8 men when laboring. Many have staid in Nauvoo unwilling to leave the poor in the hands of the mob. Every man in the battle ascribes the victory to Israel's God. Robert Smith shot through the neck—another gen officer wounded. Came up to camp to tell the story & get teams. Camp has been praying for the saints in Nauvoo. The camp here are near well nigh worn out & if we draw cuts with the brethren there we would get the longest cut. Care nothing about the temple. The Almighty may do as he pleases with it. Saints have gone to Mo cannot stay there. The saints must assemble. The Lord will have dominion over his & the devil over his. We have teams, but no more men to spare, Is it wisdom to send word to Trustees to sell the temple? Geo W Harris & John Smith volunteered to go across the river & see the council & get teams to go after the poor. Voted that the temple & all church property in Nauvoo be sold as opportunity shall present to the Judgment of the trustees, the avails to be appropriated to helping the poor as circumstances shall demand. & we shall council from time to time. Tomorrow morning 7. oclock will send for Temple Bell.

FDR **Sunday October 4th** Wind from the Southwest most of the day & increased towards night. I kept the berth all day till the Brethren told me we were experiencing a regular gale, which was about 7 o.c. evening. This announcement so animated me that I immediately dressed and went above Decks where I beheld a scene supremely grand. The Captain and his mate, both in water proof suits, each with their speaking trumpets, by the rapid use of which they could scarcely make themselves heard from one mast to another in passing orders from the Captain to the sailors, so boisterous had the tempest now become. This was a scene of terrific grandeur, such as I had wished to see. The winds howling through the rigging made music on as many different notes as there were ropes of different sizes & seemed as if by their melody to move the clouds with their stirring strains in Jehu like velocity, while the sea seemed to catch the enthusiasm and became enrapt in the ecstasy of joy. Now these two great elements of nature seemed to plead with each other in such awful tones of eloquence as if contending for their respective rights to our gallant ship. Even and anon the "Queen of the Mist" would arise upon the summit of a mighty billow as if to bid adieu to the valley regions & rise aloft, then again would descend as if destined for the bottom of the sea. The winds and waves by their stirring appeals inspired even the close minded Irish & Yankees with such heart felt liberality that many even divided their food out of their mouths with the finny offspring of the sea & scarcely reserved enough for their own immediate use. For myself, I held on a hat with a hand over each ear to prevent the winds making them ache. Took my position top of the lifeboat & gazed & heard with admiration & delight while the powerful intonations of our Orators caused my head to ache with their accents and I retired to my room to spend the remainder of a Sabbath evening in meditating upon the solemn and impressive occasion of divine service which I had just attended.

WR **Tuesday Oct. 6. 1846** Winter Quarters. Esqr Babbit said the Mob had possession of the city. Had got most of the brethren's guns. Had defaced the Temple, only one store open. Many had gone to Burlington, St Louis &c. Had paid about $50,000 debt. 25 or 28,000 was yet due. & could sell the church property for $125,000 wanted nothing for his services.

WR **Thursday Oct 15. 1846** Winter Quarters. South wind. It was currently reported that the Indians were killing 2 or 3 oxen per day. Cattle are yet very much strayed. Prest. Young has about 14 head missing & Dr Richards about 30 oxen & cows &c. About 4 P.M. Elder Woodruff was brought home, badly hurt by the falling of a tree. About 8, Prests Young, Kimball & Richards called on him thinks his breast bone is broken.

FDR **Thursday October 15** Elder Hyde suggested Samuel & myself for 2 Scotland conferences, but it was not Decided on. He [Brother Hyde] asked Bro. Wheelock whether Samuel or I was the best man. After much hesitation, he replied: "I think Bro Samuel will make the best Sailor."

WR **Sunday Oct 18. 1846** Winter Quarters. Prest Young spoke of the Omahas killing our cattle & the ⅓ part of the brethren here the rest don't know it was Sunday. Complains of the brethren not resting Sundays. Counselled not to feed the Indians or let them in their tents, are not to be converted this winter. "Not many generations shall pass away." Indians will steal with one hand while you give them a loaf of bread in the other. Go no further than I tell you & it will have a good effect. If driven to it we can build a fence around our tents, gathering of cattle.

FDR **Thursday 22** Winds and waves were silenced by command.

FDR **Monday November 2** Today my little daughter Wealthy, if she lives, is 3 years old. May she live and realize all that has been promised in her blessing by Apostle Heber. May her life & health be precious in thy sight & may Thy Spirit direct her mind in the way of that which is good.

WR **Saturday Nov. 7, 1846** Winter Quarters. Dr. called on Bishop Whitney & asked him for 1 Doz packing boxes. He said they were engaged. Dr. told him he had no place to keep public Records but in the bottom of his waggon & must have some help but the bishop gave him no encouragement.

FDR **Sunday November 22nd** Felt very solicitous about my family yesterday & today while the cold wintry winds are howling about me & I wonder if they are sheltered from the still more piercing winds of the cold, bleak prairies. O Lord my Heavenly Father, I do entreat Thee, do not leave them to suffer, but mercifully order their way before them that their lives and health may be precious in thy sight, that they may live long to experience much of Thy goodness and glory on the earth among the children of Zion; for we have given ourselves as living sacrifices to Thy cause.

WR **Thursday, Decr. 3, 1846** Dr. Richards sick in bed but arose before noon & was about the rest of the day. According to previous invitation to the Twelve, High Council & others, the brethren assembled and covered his house with Straw & put on it about 45 loads of dirt. By which they took out of the side of the hill, near the head of Cutler Street, preparatory to a Sawpit.

WR **Sunday Decr. 13. 1846** The Twelve remained in Counsel for about an hour afterwards. Brother Luke Johnson was also with them & stated that all but one who were engaged in mobbing, tarring & feathering Joseph & Sidney, in the town of Hiram, Portage Co. New York, had come to some untimely end, & the survivor Carnot Mowon had been severely afflicted & was the one who dragged Joseph out of the house by his hair. Dr. Denison prepared the Viol for Joseph, supposed to be aqua fortis. Dr. went to the Office—asked Bishop Whitney for a packing box, which the Bishop gave to him without asking a question.

WR **Tuesday Decr. 15. 1846** Fontenelle found 73 dead (Omahas) & the Sioux carried off all their goods principally old men women & children & 2 or 3 Warriors.

WR **Thursday Decr. 17th** Dr. Richards spoke of the bushels of papers, now in his possession that are not now filed, & of the need of a place to gather them & arrange them for future history. A man must have his mind free, who writes a history that is to last for time & thro' all Eternity, & not burthened with other cares. W. Woodruff says this is a subject that will benefit the whole Church & Kingdom of Go—when I heard Joseph speak I could not rest until I had written it down in black & white—I am now in one of the most important eras of the world—the people ought to keep a strict eye upon the historian—I feel deeply interested in the books out of which I am to be judged—it is the duty of High Counsel to let the Dr. have a box to put the papers in, to find wood, beef &c—this is to be a book of books—I rejoice that we have a ready writer—let the Dr. go to work & save the Church History.

WR **Sunday Decr. 20. 1846** The Saints assembled at the Stand at the ring of the bell & were addressed by Prest. Young for the space of two hours. The grand features of the address went to show that there was iniquity in the Camp of Israel, that some of the brethren indulged in laboring on the Sabbath, some in swearing, others in taking the name of God in vain, daming their brethren, profane & unkind language, stealing hay &c. refuse to pay their tithing or assist the poor—& other similar evils & instructed the Bishops to get up meetings in their several wards where the Saints might assemble themselves together, confess their sins, pray with & for each other, humble themselves before the Lord, & get up a Reformation that all should learn to exercise themselves in the principles of righteousness & that those who receive the Holy Priesthood did not abide their Covenants & walk uprightly before the Lord & before the brethren & deal justly. He would rather cross the mountains with the Twelve & not another person with them, than be accompanied by a set of wicked men & those who continued to lie & steal & swear & commit iniquity & follow the camp would have their heads cut off for that is the law of God & it shall be executed & I swear that I will not live amongst & all whether they belong to the Church or not & will not assist the poor, shall be cast out—if the Saints will reform & act upon the knowledge which they now possess—flood gates of knowledge will be to them & they will be filled with light & intelligence—but if they do not repent—the gates of knowledge will remain closed.

WR **Dec 22. 1846 Tuesday** Winter Quarters. Letter from O. Cowdery Nov. 14. 1846.

WR **Tuesday Decr. 29 1846** Winter Quarters. Prest Young asked shall the 12 travel together or in the Pioneer company? Shall all the 12 go next Spring—We want to make a pattern for the camp. Those who are going want to know it & prepare. Those who tarry want to know & prepare for a farm. O. Pratt motioned that the Twelve do not go in pioneer Co.—Prest Young said the pioneers were to find a location to put in crops this season & described the order of building & location.

WR **Thursday Dec 31. 1846** Winter Quarters. Adjourned till next Sabbath at 6 o'clock to meet at the Octagon—the names of Octagon, round house, tabernacle, windmill, Potatoe heap, Apple heap, &c were occasionally applied to Dr. Richards house. This was written at 11 oclock P.M. near the close of the year 1846.—the Weather this Winter thus far has been very mild, so that there has been very little crossing of the Missouri at this point—the health of the brethren at Winter Quarters is better than at any previous time—a greater spirit of love peace and union prevails, and prosperity attends the labors of the Saints. The Seventies have established a manufactory of Willow Baskets & several other factories are in successful operation & many individuals in Camp are engaged in making baskets and several loads are already for market. Missourians are asking from forty to fifty cents per bushel for Wheat, whereas they would have been glad to have taken 18¾ or 20 cents had it not have been for this encampment of the Saints.

FDR **Liverpool, January 4th 1847**
Dear Brother Franklin D. Richards
Sir, by the suggestions of the Spirit of God & those suggestions confirmed by the concurrent voice and

counsel of Elders Pratt & Taylor, you are hereby notified and called to come to this city. In consequence of the death of Elder Orson Spencer, you are chosen to preside over the Church in England, Scotland & Wales, Ireland, &c. But before you can act in that capacity, you must come here and enter in at the door by our blessing and confirmation. This letter from under our hands does not authorize you to act in this high and responsible calling until you have received a confirmation of this appointment under the hands of the authorities of the Church here.

FDR **Friday January 8** This is the anniversary of the birth of my Martyred Brother George Spencer Richards, who had he lived till today would now be 24 years old. Found Br Hyde writing his valedictory address to the Saints in which he wrote of my appointment to the <u>editorial and president of the Church</u> and placed his mantle on my shoulders in token as he wrote. He blessed me and cheered my heart but, O Lord, how shall I do this great thing and glorify thy name?

FDR **Wednesday January 13** By a N York Herald we learned that the Ship Brooklyn had landed her passengers at San Francisco and met a welcome reception from the settlers.

WR **Thursday January 14, 1847** Prest Young commenced to give the Word and will of God, concerning the emigration of the Saints & those who journey with them. Prest Young continued to write the word & will of the Lord. President Young retired to the octagon & finished writing the "word & will of the Lord" & Dr copied, closing about 1 next morning & after reading the piece, Prest went home.

WR **Saturday January 16, 1847** About 11. A.M. Prest Young called on the Dr, & informed him he had called the High

Council to review the "Word & will of God" which has lately been written. Jed M. Grant: since the death of Joseph have believed that the keys of Rev. were in the church. when I heard that read I felt a light & joy, satisfied that the Holy Ghost had dictated the words. Prest Young proposed that E. T. Benson select 1, 2, 3 or more men to assist him & Erastus Snow to take the revelation across the River East. & to Mo and up & down this camp gather the Saints & organize a Co. also. O. Pratt. W. Woodruff, do the same. also A. Lyman & G. A. Smith call brethren to their assistance and do the same, that the brethren of the council disperse among the different ward meetings on the morning. About 4 P.M. the 70s, High Priests & Prest. Brigham Young, Geo. A. Smith, A. Lyman, W Richards, E. T. Benson present. Dr read the "Word & will of the Lord." &c. The 70s voted unanimously to receive it as Revelation. Then the high Priests, were called upon by Prest B. Young & all present voted unanimously to receive it. The house was very full & Prest B. Young addressed the assembly to show that the Church had been led by Rev. just as much since the death of Joseph as before & said that Joseph was a great & good a man and as great a prophet as ever lived upon the Earth, Jesus accepted. Joseph received his apostleship from Peter & his brethren & the present apostles received their apostleship from Joseph.

WR **Jany. 16, 1847**, Camp of Israel, Winter Quarters
Mr. David Fairbanks
Bishop of 2nd Ward
    Complaint has come to me that Sister St. John whose husband is in the Army, has been destitute of Wood or the Chopping of Wood, one or both, either of which is equivalent to no fire during most of the last cold snap—I request you to look to this and see that no such case exists

in your Ward—whether they be Sisters whose husbands are in the Army, or poor of any kind for there is wood plenty in this Vicinity, and men and teams to draw and cut it.

Willard Richards

WR **Wednesday Jany. 1847** Winter Quarters. Sarah, Wife of Willard Richards was delivered of a Son named Willard Brigham at 30 min: after 3.

FDR **Saturday January 23** At 4 o.c. P.M. soon after I had returned to the office, Elder Spencer came and after an introduction and a joyful reception, I accompanied him to the Custom House. We spent an agreeable evening at the office asking many questions about my family and the Camp of the Saints; but was deeply afflicted to learn that my little Daughter <u>Wealthy Lovisa Richards</u> was dead; and that my family had all been sick.

WR **Sunday 24 January 1847** The Will of the Lord was not brought to the people until it had been taken to all the Officers— have Joseph or the Twelve done like J. J. Strang? No! the people have got to ponder over them & ask the Father in the name of Jesus—they then acknowledge it—it then becomes a law.

FDR **Monday January 25** I went to the office. Found 7 or 8 ship letters for Elder Pratt and 1 for Elder Taylor. None for any other of the American Elders. Went to the Post Office and inquired at the Ship Letter Office, & at the Strangers window, where I found 2 for myself and 1 for Br Samuel. Went to the office and read my letters which detailed the sufferings of my wife, the birth & death of our only son Isaac Snyder [Richards] on the 23 July 1846, also the protracted sufferings from diarrhea, fever, chills & fever, and sore eyes, of our only daughter, Wealthy Lovisa Richards; and of her death on the 14th of September, being 2 years, 10 Months and 12 days of age. The account of her sufferings, the woman like patience with which she bore them and the termination thereof by Death; together with the sufferings of my wife & the multiplicity of care and sorrow attendant upon the loss of both son & daughter to her in my absence, call for the tears from my eyes in rich abundance. I spent about an hour giving vent to my feelings in that way, then wrote summary of the contents of my letter and sent it with Samuels letter to him in Glasgow Scotland. Attended to the commonplace business of the office during the day.

WR **Friday 29 Jany. 1847** This evening the Choir met at the council house & enjoyed vocal & instrumental music & dancing.

WR **Tuesday Feb 2. 1847** From 6 to 8 the Dr. chatted with Prest. Young on the cause of the sickness & deaths in the Camp, the situation of Israel, Zion, the world &c during an hours conversation not a soul was present.

WR **Friday Feb 5. 1847** Winter Quarters. About 5 the Twelve & Ladies visited the Silver Grays, Pic. Nic. & were about the time of their refreshment, which consisted of pies, cakes, bread, meat, parched corn & cold water furnished from their Several baskets placed on a table & passed round to those who could not come at the table. The house was very full. After supper the evening was spent mostly in dancing. Conversation & reading the Word and will of the lord by Wm Clayton. The Band was present.

WR **Sunday Feb 14. 1847** Winter Quarters
[letter to Col Kane]

The Indians have stolen many of our horses from the rush bottoms & killed many cattle, consequently it will be impossible for as many to go forward in the spring as otherwise would, but we shall not be wanting in devices to take off as many as possible. Though had all our cattle lived we should have been far from having a sufficiency to remove all who have been driven from their homes, without the opportunity of making sales & procuring an outfit.

P. S. Feb 19 Since writing the above, an express has arrived from Fort Pueblo, on the Arkansas stating that 170 of the "Mormon Battalion" (sisters & Laundresses) had returned to that place. About 16 had died, the remainder recovered or convalescent. The express was from a detachment of the sick who left the Battalion on the 12th Nov, 280 miles on their route from Calafornia, and within 60 miles of Alpasso, in Chewawa. They were on half rations and expecting to take said city by storm & procure provisions. Before the express left Santa Fee, news believed to be correct, but not official arrived that the Battalion had taken possession of Al passo without firing a gun & had taken winter quarters in the city.

FDR **Thursday February 18** I received a letter with the word that Br Samuel was broke out with the small pox. By train reached Br Samuel about 11 A.M. Found him in bed having the small pox thoroughly, though not in its worst form.

WR **Monday 22 Feb** At 2 P.M. the Twelve & Gents met to learn to dance in the Council House.

WR **Tuesday 23 February 1847 Winter Quarters** Went to the Council House at 10 this A.M. The Bishops feasted the Poor of the Camp in the Council house—the Tables were abundantly loaded with the good things of the Camp—and not only did the fragments fill Twelve Baskets. but according to computation there was "a Cord" of Fragments left (22 Baskets full, not touched) whereby the families of the Poor can be supplied during this inclement Season of the year. Five & a half tables full for 120 ladies—& also about 66 Bishops councillors & Band—Total No. feasted about 300.

WR **Sunday Feby. 28. 1847** B. Young s[ai]d—I want the Bishops see that the property of the people is not destroyed by water—leave your Sod houses & go into your Wagons & Tents—youl be healthy, but if you live in the Sod houses youl Sicken & die—a Week last Wednesday I was taken sick, suddenly, & could not get back to the bed—when we get thro' the Vail we can talk how I felt—I felt like death grappled with me—I spoke I had been where Joseph & Hyrum were—its hard coming to life again—I went into another world & recollected what I saw—but it went away Again—next day I was on the bed & fell asleep I saw Joseph. He sat in a room in the S W—at a brilliant window. I shook hands & kissed him a many times & asked why we are not more together. He sd, we shall be separated a little season but you will by & by. He sd do you be sure to tell the people this one thing—the whole of the bre[thre]n—it is all important that they keep the Sp[irit] of the L[or]d. Teach them to humble themselves & keep the quiet Spirit—& get His Sp. & sd. how it wo[ul]d descend & reflect upon man. They can know the diff bet[wee]n the Sp of the Ld & the enemy—the mind of man sho[ul]d always be open to rece[ive] all the Sp—& rece the Sp of the Ld. The Sp of the Ld wod bring peace joy happiness. Take away strife, malice, hatred &c. When the still small voice comes it will teach, instruct, reveal. If they do that—they will see that they r just where they were organized bef they took tabernacles—he showed how they were organized & he showed they were organ[ize]d perfectly from Adam to the latest gen. but darkness had cov[ere]d the p[eo]pl[e] & they don't know what to do. Every person's heart will be perfectly prepd to rece the station organ'd for him. He was at the edge of the light. It was darkness where I was. He sd you must go. I turned into the dark & woke up. I know it was the Sp of Joseph. I actually went into Eternity last Wednesday week, & came back again.

WR **Saturday March 13. 1847** The following Questions were asked, & answers given—

1st. Shall there be a council left here? Yes. Presidents & Captains of Companies, & when they leave, appoint others.

2nd. Shall the houses be put on a line, & this place picketed in? Let the people decide.

3rd. Shall they pay one tenth of their labor for the poor? Yes.

4th. How much ground shall each family have for a Garden? Let the Council control this matter.

5th. How much bread stuff to each person that follows after the Pioneers. Not less than 200 lbs.

6th. Shall the brethren labor unitedly, or every man for himself? Unitedly, & every Captain of 10 oversee his own Company.

7th. Shall a record be kept how every man occupies his time? A record shall be kept.

8th. What plan will be the most beneficial to preserve crops, and other property from Omaha aggressions? Take care of them.

9th. May not every family have a garden of their own, independent of public fields? Yes.

10th. Shall a guard be kept up at Winter Quarters after 1st. Emigration? Council that a guard be kept up, & the people pay them.

11th. Shall we take all the Widows, or only Women whose husbands are ahead? Take the Women whose husbands are in the Army, and as many more as can fit themselves out.

12th. Shall Thomas Bullock be the Historian of 1st Emigration Co.? Yes; fit him out, and take him along.

17th. The Temple Bell to be rung every morning to wake all

up, then have prayers, breakfast, prepare teams, at the second ringing of the bell, in 15 minutes afterwards, start for their days journey.

18th. Whenever there is a Company of 75 men, with 18 months provisions, may they come on with or without their families? Yes, until the 1st Septr but they must not expect assistance from those who are ahead.

WR **Sunday March 14. 1847** [Pres. Brigham Young] I now say to all who profess to have the auth'y of the H. Priesthood they ought to repent of their heart wanderings—& dig about themselves—& not be negligent in duty in serving the Lord—return unto the Lord—get the Holy Ghost & keep it—pray for me & my bren that we may carry off the K[ingdom] of God—we must not indulge in negligence, slothfulness, coldness—if we have a little power seek for more—have visits from Angels—Who has faith? We are apt to trust in the arm of flesh—we must trust in the Almighty—& have faith to say to the sick be healed—or the sickness depart from this habitation—live for it & we will have it—we r looking for glory immortal and eternal lives—got at it that we may turn away disease from the camp—that we may live & redeem Zion. This is what we ought to live for & obtain—We have to work & labor—pray that we may live to do a great work in the Earth—pray for me—hang on one to another—never slacken your exertions dont give it up—I say hang on—& dont give it up—be wide awake—have your hearts open & know what you ought to do all the time—I feel all the time like Moses—I would to God that all these my bren were Prophets Seers & Revrs then live to them & glorify our Far. in Heaven.

FDR **Thursday March 18** Got a "Herald for Europe" giving an account of the war and the doings in Congress of a bill being before to grant $3,000,000 dollars for the President to effect a reconciliation with Mexico, with which nation they (the United States) were then at war. Upon this bill the North and South were at loggerheads. The North do not wish for a further accession of territory, unless slavery in the same should be inhibited and resolutions from two Northern States were before to that effect and John C. Calhoun was the Champion of the South, he offered resolutions counter to those from the North and he and the North were both determined to have these resolutions acted upon before acting on the three million bill and <u>upon these slavery and antislavery resolutions appears now to be pending the existence or dissolution of the Union.</u>

WR **Wednesday March 24th 1847** Prest. Young told the Council that if a brother Shot an Omaha Indian for stealing, they must deliver the murderer to Old Elk to be dealt with as the Indians shall decide, & that was the only way to save the lives of the Women & Children.

WR **Monday 29 March 1847** Dr. busy preparing his Wagon for Pioneering—The Sun set, having the appearance of dull Silver—Wm. McCarry gave a Concert in the Council house—Prests. Young, Richards, Kimball & Benson present—after his variations—dancing commenced & kept up till after midnight. Elizabeth McFate Richards died about 11 P.M., wife of Franklin D. Richards.

FDR **Monday March 29** I spent the day in my room, tolerable free from pain. [in different ink, added later:] "Elizabeth died just before 12 tonight in Camp."

WR **Thursday April 1, 1847**
Winter Quarters April 1, 1847
Mr Stephen Longstroth.

I go with the Twelve & others, to find a stake of Zion, leaving our families here, expecting to return here next fall, to spend the winter and take them on next spring, one year. I wish you were all here this spring, raising grain, but as this cannot be, I wish you well. & shall anticipate a chat with you next winter.

I sent a team for yourself & family last fall, I received for answer that you were at St Louis, & that the team was offered to Bro Mons Whitaker & family on condition that they would ride with a widow who had no other mode of conveyance & that Alice wanted to come, but Mons would not come unless they could have a waggon to themselves. All I know, is, I did what I could, and only write this as a reply to Sister Ann's letter on this subject that she may understand I was not in fault & would have been glad to help them forward, & will yet if opportunity presents. Heber John & Rhoda Ann Jennetta, are well & have been most of the time since they left Nauvoo, And my family are now pretty comfortable. The health of the camp is as good as could be expected. No late news from the Battalion. The Saints in camp are happy.

Be diligent, patient, & persevering. and so live as to cherish the whispering of the small still voice & it will always lead you right.

WR **W. Q. Apt. 13th. 1847**
Mr Logan Fontenelle, or his Brother, Interpreter
Dear Sir.

Three days since my light sorrel, genteel built mare, left our Camp about six miles North of the ferry on the East bank of the Elkhorn, either strayed, or taken by some of the Omahas, and I confidently believe that she is somewhere in your neighborhood and I wish you to forward the beast to me by the Bearer Mr Joseph Murdock so that I may receive her this evg. If you cannot do this, but should find her on the morrow, send her to our Camp on the Platte bottom or near the Elk horn ferry so that I may get her by Thursday morning to put into my team and I will pay you $5, & you will oblige your friend

Willard Richards

P. S. The mare has a streak of white in the face of considerable length & the shoulder is rather high with a Bunch on one side & switch tail.

FDR **Good Friday April 2nd** I find myself this day, living on the earth while a sore famine is vexing this nation, Great Britain, & causing all the European Nations of the Continent to stand aghast with the prospect of want before them & some of them, England and France in particular, are suffering from hunger, and importing her Bread stuffs, while the Land of Zion is the only land that affords food for exportation, to which the poor who have just means left for to get away with, are going by 100's & 1000's to America, leaving the suffering, destitute & wealthy to remain. At present, so great is the suffering that one paper from Ireland states that from 20 to 30 die daily from hunger in that immediate vicinity; and that the most lucrative business is coffin-making; and that many are buried without any; and often lie a week after death without interment.

FDR **April 15** 5 letters from the Camp. 2 from Jane to myself, including a scrap from Father informing us of the Death of our Brother Joseph W. Richards at Pueblo on the Arkansas River on the 19th of November, 1846. In the words of one of the Twelve, he has gone to wear a Martyr's crown & I hope to be a blessing to Brother George. May the Spirit of the Lord be upon our Mother & Father & enable them to bear these afflicting dispensations and feel willing, if necessary, to give up all their sons to the Lord. Brother Joseph was not so tenderly attached to me as might I would have been, but that we were separated when he was very young & I, 17 years, for 5 years. He was a good boy. While young was fat and stout, but during our absence he grew tall and slim and was very obedient and for a year or two before he went in the Battalion, was sick much of the time & but feeble when he left the Camp to go to California as a drummer from Council Bluffs or Fort Leavenworth. When he was about to die, he said he was very tired & wanted to rest for awhile & requested one of the Brethren to Seal him up unto Eternal Life. <u>The second of our Father's House a Martyr to the cause of God in the Last Day.</u>

    WR **May 22**

6.15

9.20 Dr. arose

10.30 & 30

11.37 noon

1.45 move

4.10 passed Poisoned Bluff

6. half night _____ River[5]

    WR **28 May** Rain 9.20 Prest Young called ( ) to his wagon & said he felt that the camp would fail in their mission unless they repented had written what had ___ constrained by the Spirit—16 lines. The danger of falling into the hands of Spirits inimical to our souls, is greater than that of mob.—did not care to write any more. If the camp stop in the morning & repent, &c. If they will not—I had better they would return back. It is in vain for this camp to go any further to find a location for Zion unless we go with pure hearts.

    WR **June 21**

2.50 Independence Rock

---

5. Willard's journal is very cryptic regarding the daily log of the pioneer journey, as may be seen here.

6.30 Devil's Gate

FDR **Friday July 2** One year ago this day I left my wife and family & exchanged the parting kiss with them. With their recollection was associated many tender & endearing reflections, both of <u>sorrow & joy</u>.

WR **July 12 1847 Monday** Branch Bear River

12.50 Halt—Prest Young stopped sick

WR **July 21, 1847** Leave directions in a crotch of a stick—turn to the right ascend a steep hill—descend thro an aspen forest—cross a small creek. In 4½ miles from the dividing ridge is an excellent Spring—a good camping ground (camp here)—we turned to the right ascend steep hill, pass over to another small creek. Travelled 14 miles in 13 hours.

Kanyon Valley July 21. 1847

5 forenoon

Brother Orson Pratt

Yours of the 20 Inst. we received last evening about 5 oclock having arrived at the place of its deposit; we were very glad to hear from you, in proof of which, we send you this our ansr. by Express.

We left bro. Young day before yesterday, a little above the Ford on Weber river his health was improving but was not able to travel as fast as the Camp. We came on our way 13¾ miles, encamping just above the Kanyon on this Creek—Yesterday morning Father Sherwood was unable to travel & we left him with 3 Wagons. & we arrived at this place having cut considerable brush & made other improvements on our way. Brothers Kimball, Woodruff, & Benson, & 8 or 10 Wagons tarried with brother Young, we expect they are coming on leisurely. No Eastern Mail since you left.

Prest. Young gave us his views concerning a stopping place in the basin, by saying, that he felt inclined for the present not to crowd upon the Utes until we have a chance to get acquainted with them and that it would be better to bear toward the region of the Salt Lake rather than the Utah, & find some good place for our seeds & deposit them as speedily as possible, regardless of a future location without wishing to dictate your course, we will briefly say, that our feelings would be gratified & we think that the views of Prest. Young & Council would be carried out the most perfectly, by your continuing to prosecute the route as you have hitherto done, until you arrive at some point in the basin, where you "could hear the Potatoes grow," if they had only happened to have been there; then let all your mechanics, even to the rough hewers, be employed in fitting up plows while all your horses & mules should be employed in small companies in scouring the country in every direction so that by night you will be able to get a tolerable good report from the various companies & begin to judge where will be the best spot to put in the Plows & we hope to be there to hear the report, as we anticipate we will not be more than one day behind you, and we expect the whole camp will be on hand in a day or two following. The time for planting is fully come, & we feel anxious to make every move that would facilitate the Potato crop, it matters not where it is—the Prest. thinks the Utes may feel a little tenacious about their choice lands on the Utah, & we had better keep further north towards the Salt Lake, which is more of a Warlike or neutral ground, & by so doing we should be less likely to be disturbed & also have a chance to form

an acquaintance with the Utes; & having done our planting shall select a sight for a location at our leisure.

Wishing you prosperity in every good work. we most
cordially subscribe ourselves.

Your brethren with all due respect
Willard Richards
George A. Smith

WR **July 22, 1847** Pass thro' the Kanyon, making an entire
new route & camp in view of Salt Lake, 7¼ miles at 6 p.m. From
the entering of Pratt's Pass near Weber River to its end in view of
Salt Lake is 35 miles.

Great Salt Lake Valley
July 22, 1847
Pres. Young

Enclosed we send you a synopsis of our travels since
we left you the morning after the departure of the second division of the camp. Father Sherwood and Brother
Dewey were too sick to travel and the wagons they were
with together with Father Cases' stopped by the way.
Since that the remainder of those who were sick have
been recovering. We found some hills very steep and
some of the road very rough though we consider it not
bad for such a mountainous country. The brethren have
done a great deal of labor on the road and there is much
more that ought to be done. We would gladly have left
a good road for our Pres. and his company to come over
but after so many wagons passing we presume you will
find some repairs necessary, and should you find it very
bad we hope you will look upon our labors with a ___
eye for we have tried to do the best we could. The 2nd
company overtook the 1st this forenoon. Since that we

have opened a road thro the Kanyon where it is uncertain whether man or beast had ever had before unless it was a bear or a rattlesnake, for we saw a bear's back and killed 2 rattlesnakes and one since we arrived in camp. We are now about 4 miles within the long sought valley and while the camp were making a road through the Kanyon this day, brothers Pratt & Smith and 7 other horsemen explored the valley north of this as far as possible for lime and met the camp on their return at this point. They report some beautiful creeks north of this about 3 miles, whence we propose to remove in the morning and prepare for planting. A short distance north of that point, the soil becomes very barren warm hot sulfur poison & a variety of other springs abound. They passed through one extensive forest of greasewood, the tallest of which they were able to see without the help of glasses and the best computation they could make without instruments was 6 inches high. The forest was very dense and several miles in extent. Timber can hardly be said to be scarce in this region for there is scarcely enough of it to be named and sage is as scarce as timber, so that if you want to raise sage and greasewood here you had better bring the seed with you from the mountains. In many places the grass, rushes &c are 10 feet high but no mire. Mammoth crickets abound in the borders of the valley. There are some sand bill cranes and Hawks feed abundantly and of the best quality. Water in the creeks passably good. We hardly need enter into particulars at this time as we anticipate you will be here in a day or two and be able to see for yourself and see much more than we have had time to look at. Our prayers are in your behalf continually that you may be strong in spirit & body & come to us speedily

& if you have a word for us before you arrive we shall receive it joyfully. Bros Kimball, Woodruff, and Benson are also remembered by us as & while we anticipate a speedy meeting with your whole camp, we subscribe ourselves your brethren in Christ.

Most affectionately and respectfully

Orson Pratt

Willard Richards

George A. Smith

P.S. the bearer has been with the exploring party today and is also acquainted with the road hither.

FDR **Saturday August 14** Jane writes me of Elder Littlefield being on the way. She alludes to Elizabeth's death. This is probably my Dear Elizabeth whom God gave to me in his Holy House. It is precious to learn that Jane is well, though death should rob me of every other relative. O Lord, why should she be taken from me? When we separated we fondly hoped to live and enjoy each other's society for many years to come. But, Father, I own thy dealings just. Thy blessings had been more than my desserts, but I did not know that thy goodness never fails. I fear I should feel Thy hand was against me, but now I trust that in this also Thou wilt reveal thy hidden stores of goodness and blessings. Yet how insuperable must they be to counterpoise the deep wounds of separation and death of our dear companions and tender babes. . . . Qualify me for every trial through which I must pass and let Jane be one with me.

FDR **Friday August 27** This morning I awoke from a dream in which I seemed to have been with Pres. Brigham Young in the Temple at Nauvoo. We [word missing] Saturday opposite each other with our feet in a clear lovely pool of water & we conversed together. He asked: "Brother Franklin, would you accept of it if

I should appoint you one of our Quorum?" I replied: "Brother Brigham, I always have accepted and as far as I could obeyed every appointment that has been given me and I always intend to do so."

FDR **Monday September 6** I went up into the Hall with the Brethren and saw them dance with their deportment or bearing. I would not have known but they were highly respectable people of good character, but I was assured they were most of the females strumpets & kept themselves for that purpose and that the gentlemen were many of them sons of wealthy parents who rather they would live there than to marry, unless they could marry a few hundred so as to have it called respectable. It did seem painful to look upon them in that point of light and I could not find even the shadow of a desire to partake of their enjoyment, but felt exceedingly anxious to be pure before God and true to my covenants with him & my <u>wife</u> that a crown of Celestial Brightness may adorn our Brows and the joy of our hearts be unsullied when we meet & together share the pleasures of righteous matrimonial life. O Lord, grant me this in the Holy Name of the Lord Jesus Christ, and thy glory as well as ours increased thereby. What a pity that they who lead this life are the most beautiful part of the community.

WR **Sept. 17, 1847**
Platte River, 110 Miles West of Fort Laramie, return
   Pioneer Camp of Israel,
Brother Miller,

    Your letter of April 21st to Prest. Young was received in Camp a few days since, about 300 miles West of this, & read to the Council who did not think it necessary to make any reply as they had answered all your previous letters in which they had given you Special council relative to your duty; but thinking that it might be desirable, on your part, to know that your letter had arrived, I take up the subject as an Individual, & shall briefly express to you my own views of yourself, your course & the circumstances with which you are surrounded, as you have made them manifest in your letters.

One of the most important items which you introduced in your letters, as you appear to consider it, is the case of William Smith, who, you say, wishes to be restored to his fellowship & standing in the Church, & yet it appears that his private & particular feelings have been committed to you in Confidence & yet you have expressed that confidence to a third & uninterested party. & upon this point I will ask you one question; If you are the only Individual who has been able to touch "the main Spring of William Smith's heart" & that "Confidentially, and you have betrayed that confidence, how could you expect that any Council instituted for the Salvation of Israel would act upon such testimony alone, in deciding such an important matter?" and if not, how could you expect or reasonably demand an "immediate," "frank," and "Impartial" answer, to such important query, & of such a council? I sincerely wish William Smith well, & I know my brethren do also, for I have often heard them manifest it, but I do hope that he will not do himself the injustice to deprive his.

I remain Your well wisher, friend & brother in the everlasting Covenant.

Willard Richards.

FDR **Wednesday September 22** Bro Singleton slept with me. I was very wakeful. Had much of the Spirit in meditation about the state of the Saints in Liverpool & other things.

FDR **Thursday September 23** This P.M. I smoked part of a cigar and threw up my supper to pay for it.

FDR **Monday September 27th** Jane's letter detailed <u>sickness & death of E. M. F. R.</u> She made her exit on Monday night a few minutes before 12, March 29; was sensible to the last. Told Jane repeatedly she believed her breath was going to leave her; and the last time told her to hold the candle which she did and saw her fall asleep.

FDR **Wednesday November 3rd** Met the Brethren in Council of the Branch. [Bath] at my room at 8 o'clock and continued together till near 11 o'clock. Examined the list of members. Find a dozen or more members names whose whereabouts and standing are unknown. Gave instruction about the records duties of the officers. Decided about a 'singing book' affair and advised the Brethren, strengthening them in their callings. They consist of 1 E, 2 P, 2 T and 2 Deacons beside myself.

FDR **Monday November 8th** As I walked I meditated upon her who shares my choicest love; who partakes with me in my highest hopes for the future. The Lord grant that health, peace and sufficient to prevent suffering at least may be her portion. While I pensively muse upon her condition and my own, now at 8 o'clock A.M., she may be now dreaming of walking with me, or sharing my company under some pleasing circumstances as I did hers the other night. The more I see of the world, the more I love her, the higher I prize her, and "the wonderful chain of our union is tightened, the longer it is stretched". <u>May she and I forever be one. Heavens first blessing to us both.</u>

FDR **Saturday November 20** Bro LOL wrote me of there being 2000 Saints converted in the Society Islands by Bro Addison Pratt; also that Pres Polk's Lady with Ex-Pres Madison's Lady have got up a magnificent tea party for the benefit of the Mormons in the wilderness; and that most of the influential ladies of the Capital are engaged in it. Let the Presidents wives feed my Queen while I must be absent on thy work.

FDR **Monday December 6th** To Ledbury on foot and over hills and dales, as well as through mud and rain (Herefordshire the natural way), 7 miles. Bro Brigham Young has preached in the same room and also Uncle Levi Richards. It seems good that I may travel after the Apostles and ministers of the Everlasting Gospel and preach in the same places, the same comforting things by the same comforting Spirit of God. Good folk. Uncle Willard has preached here and Elder Woodruff also.

FDR **Friday December 31** This morning before I was out of my bed, the postman handed in a letter from Brother Thos Bullock at the Camp, giving an account of the journey and adventures of the Pioneer Company to the Salt Lake—detailing some of the distresses of his family and others in Nauvoo, the barbarity of the mob and the tender mercies of a Father in Heaven in feeding the saints in their last extremity on quails which he also described. There was also described in the letter, a small portion of the city plot as laid out by them containing the Temple block and some contiguous blocks—on one of which were written Fathers, Uncle Levi's, Bro Samuel and my own names as being each on the lots designated for us. No of lots 5, 6, 7, 8 of block. In contemplating the labors and duties of the past year, I can discover wherein I have done things which again under the same circumstances, I think I would not do. Also things which I did not do which I think I would if again under the same circumstances do, but in all these things, I feel and humbly trust that a kind and merciful God will patiently bear with my errors of inexperience forasmuch as I was suddenly exalted to such an eminent station of such immense responsibility. During the past year the intelligence of the death of my two children and of Elizabeth McF. Richards reached me and I have sought diligently to know why this should be, but I know no cause on my part, but the Lord gave and he hath suffered them to be taken away from the evils to come. May these and all my sacrifices be accepted and placed in the balances that all my errors may be forgiven; that both I and my family may stand approved before Thee without rebuke unto the ends.

FDR **Wednesday January 5th [1848]** I accompanied Br Samuel, John Banks and several of the Saints to the Metropolis of London, where I spent about a week in visiting different of the Saints and the public places of amusement; such as British museum, Madam Tussauds Wax works, British National Gallery of Painting, St. Paul's Cathedral, Westminster Abbey, the famous tunnel under the Thames, the wire suspension Bridge over it; Old Westminster Hall, where were 5 courts in session; and where Charles 1st was condemned for treason; the House of Commons, St. James Park and Palace Royal and The Bloody Tower whose tragic scenes adorn the History of England at almost every page. They are the amassed magnificence, wealth, antiquity and Pride of the British Nation from the days of William the Conquerer till 1849 and almost every item thereof has been dyed with <u>human blood.</u>

WR **Winter Quarters 12 January 1848**
To Mr. James Lavender
Dear Brother,

I avail myself of the present opportunity of sending you a few lines, to inform you that I am in my ordinary state of health as also my family. I have been on to the Mountains last Summer and with the rest of the Pioneers have found a home for the Saints, even a hiding place where Israel may rest secure and protected while the overflow scourge of Jehovah shall go forth to make waste, and vex the nations, and having a Brotherly feeling for you & your welfare in the kingdom I thought I should tell you that the way is now open for Jacob to go home and help establish that kingdom which shall never be thrown down nor given to another people; but which will extend from sea to sea & from the river to the ends of the earth. Come then dear Brother and help us to build a house to the Lord where we can enjoy the communion of Angels, learn the plan of salvation, and be enabled to go through the gate into the city and take our posterity with us. I shall expect to see you here by the 1st of May ready to go west with the Company who will start then. We have issued a general Epistle to all the Saints scattered abroad throughout the earth copies of which will be issued through the Union, & if you are desirous of hearing it, & no Elder should come your way with it, you can send to Bro Nathaniel H Felt, St. Louis Presiding Elder, who will doubtless forward you a copy.

    Am Your Bro in the Gospel of J C
        Willard Richards

WR **Winter Quarters 8th Feby. 1848**
Nanny Longstroth, Beloved wife,[6]

    Yours of the 19th of Decr. is received which I acknowledge with much pleasure, and rejoice to find that you are firm in the faith and desirous of getting away from Babylon. I have written to your fa[ther] to come

---

6. Willard and Nanny had been married in Nauvoo, but because of her youth, Willard agreed with her parents that she should stay with them until later. At this point, she desired to leave St. Louis and join him in the journey to the Salt Lake Valley.

here as early in the Spring as possible and to go hence to the Great Salt Lake City and as you wish to know I will inform you that is your destination also and in 2 months at most I expect you will be here perhaps at April conference. I expect to see you soon. Shall say but little. My health is not very good, but expect a few years residence at the Lake will perfect that which was commenced for me last Sumer. I can most cheerfully respond to every sentiment of your letter and am pleased to see that dutiful regard you manifest for your parents for it is a true maxim that a dutiful daughter bids fair to make a dutiful wife. Comfort your parents & do them all the good you can & I pray the Lord to bless you & I bless you let peace never depart from them. Be faithful in all things and a fulness of blessings shall be multiplied unto you for ever & ever even all blessings which your Soul can desire. Sarah joins in kindest love to Nancy & Alice.

I remain forever your affectionate husband,
Willard Richards

FDR **Sunday February 20** The printed Epistle arrived announcing the appointment of the First Presidency at the Conference held in the tabernacle at the Hollow i.e. Kaneville, and giving further instruction about opening emigration &c. etc., about the Pioneers to & the valley &c. During the day I was introduced to the Master of the "Carnatic", Capt Wm McKenzie by Br Cyrus Wheelock (who with Andrew Cahoon were my councilors as we were suggested by Elder Spencer to the Co and by them appointed by vote), as the President of the Company. I had conversation with him about ship rules, the Parliamentary code being posted at the descent of both hatches. I found him a very affable man and ready to allow us any internal rules of order which might not infringe upon the ships rules, seemed pleased at our religious inclinations. At evening when the company were ready attend to prayer, I sent him an invitation to meet with us if he felt inclined which he did. I laid before the Co. the necessity of observing the rules of the ship with other general remarks and introduced the Capt to the Co., requesting him if he had anything he would like to communicate, to do it freely. He said I had said all that he would if he were to speak and merely seconded my remarks. The Co. sang a Hymn and I prayed during which the Capt kneeled by my side like a Brother. I felt liberally the Spirit of grace and supplication, and all seemed to feel well when we separated. It is no small care to have charge of such a company at sea. During a rough time all are more or less affected by seasickness, quite a peevish complaint naturally, after which constipation of the bowels generally ensues according to the degree of sickness, which prevents recovery and appetite. I had to go around like a hospital [Dr.] daily and enquire into their health and prescribe for each case separately.

WR **March 21, /47 10 eve**
Beloved President

Bro Stewart brought a few letters from Huntsakers, but left many & all the papers. By him & the papers from St Louis—We learn of the sanction of peace or New Mexico with Mexico by the Senate. the U.S. taking Texas, Santafee & Calafornia, & paying Mexico $20.000.000.

England has some fears of an invasion from France. Sicily is in a Revolution. Yucatan has petitioned the U. States for admission into the union. Canida is on the fence not knowing whether to petition U.S. or go alone to independence, at least so says report.

I am somewhat weary having to be my own clerk. I remain Respectfully

W. Richards.

FDR **April 2, 1848** I find it necessary to keep a sharp watch lest too much intimacy spring up between the sailors or even the Mates and some of the females of the Company.

FDR **Monday, April 17** The health officer came on board and with the most cursory observation, without going between Decks, remarked to the Capt: "You have got an uncommon respectable lot of passengers this time" and after the usual civilities with the Capt., left.

FDR **Thursday 20th** Capt McKenzie in getting his papers permit &c, of the Custom House obtained a permit for me and my entire Co. gratis which otherwise would have cost each family the trouble and expense of procuring Permits to have their luggage examined and passed by a C.H. Officer. I kept a good look out and when the Custom House Officer came on board, I obtained an early introduction of the Capt., which accomplished, I introduced him to a "Bottle of Brandy" with this instruction that he should treat any of his Friends that might call aboard respectfully at my expense. This finishing stroke of gentlemanly civility on my part, inducted me into Mr. Kirkland's good graces and saved the company the trouble of overhauling much stuff, and probably not less than £100 for duties which, had their things been examined, they would have had to pay; but as it was, not a trunk, chest, box, barrel or bag was examined; but as fast as they were raised out of the Hatch, the officer affixed his Mark until all were on Deck. I never before considered the worth of a bottle of Brandy.

FDR **Tuesday, May 9th** As W.Q. [Winter Quarters] is to be evacuated soon, Jane had moved her things over the River and was living in her wagon by her sisters. On the approach of the boat, she made ready and came over but I had by this time, got the business so arranged as to go up in to the town and met her in the street. Did not know her till I came directly up to her. Took her into my arms and kissed her. Yes it was her as she looked, and as she felt, solitary and alone in her feelings, bereft of her darling Wealthy after almost dying herself to take care of her; having not yet then recovered from the dreadful time of confinement with her second child while birth was premature. This birth of our first-born son was on _____ and _____ East of Mount Pisgah and _____West of Nauvoo. The boy lived but a short time and was buried at Mt Pisgah. I will here note the names of the following persons who distinguished themselves by their kindnesses to her during her <u>extreme affliction</u> in which she was given up to die. Wealthy was now sick and needing constant attention. She continued getting worse, better at short intervals till on _____ she died and was buried—the first corpse in what is called Cutlers burying ground. She was first attacked with dysentery as early as first of July on Sugar Creek where I left them to go to England. Then took the chills with it and became very low till a short time before she died became blind entirely.

Winter Quarters and vicinity will be forever remembered as the place where the Furnace of the Saints afflictions was heated seven times hotter than it was wont to be; by all those who were blest to feel its purifying effects. Here the Saints were literally worn out, used up and consigned to their graves in scores; and hundreds by disease, fatigue, destitution and every ill of exile. The scurvy or black leg caused the death of many. The winter too, was unusually severe, and many suffered with cold, and indeed for the want of all things, gave up the Ghost. Fathers, Husbands, Brothers or Sons, to the number of 500 having gone in the Mormon Battalion by order of the Government to serve in the Mexican War. My Brother Joseph W. Richards, youngest but Henry, went in Company A as Drummer and died at Fort Pueblo on ____.

At this meeting, I asked Bro Brigham about going to the Valley. He asked me my circumstances. I related them. He replied if that is all you have got, I guess you'll have to stop and help Br. Benson and George A. travel and preach about in Pottawatomie, Co. I told him if it was consistent, I felt very desirous to go, having been so long absent from the Church and I thought I could obtain sufficient to get off with of some of my Friends, if it was advisable. He then told me if I could to do so and rig up as soon as I could.

WR **Winter Quarters Indian territory 16 May 1848**
Dear Brother [George D. Watt],

    As I am on the eve of my departure from this place for the mountains, I thought I would write Brother Watt a few lines. We are taking as much provisions this year as will sustain us until we can raise more—tho' we have heard from the valley this week, their letters dated 6th March, informing that they had sown 860 acres of Fall wheat & were intending to plant & sow in Spring crops upwards of 7000 acres—Climate very healthy air clear & pure, Water excellent. They have found different kinds of earth, clay & sand which makes excellent plaster, with which they plaster their houses inside & out.

WR **Winter Quarters 25 May 1848**
Brother Randolph Alexander,

    I am informed by the by that Brother Bird Barnet late of Tennessee is now at St. Josephs Mo, and that he is stopped there for the present and is not going over the mountains this summer. Now I want to state in a few words to you my situation, and the situation of the Camp. Prest. Young has left for the Horn on his way to the mountains, and Bro. Kimball is nearly ready to start. Their outfit which is far less than it ought to have been has taken all the surplus funds from this viccinity, and many of the Brethren have stayed behind, and furnished them their means to go on, and the company that has gone with them. I have been sick for sometime and unable to attend business, having previously spent my all in going to the mountains to find a location last season, & for the relief of the Camp & other ways. Thus you see I am left here sick and destitute with instructions from the President to call upon the Brethren wherever I can find them who have the means to help me to an outfit, and I am informed that Brother Barnet has some means in his hands, & I want you to go down and see him as you are well acquainted with him, and state to him my situation, & ask him to loan me $1.000 till he gets to the valley. I do not ask him to give it to me, he shall have it again to his satisfaction, but my health, my life, & the cause in which I am engaged, all demand immediate relief, for I am sinking & have never been well in this climate. The church requires of me to go to the valley as soon as I can, but if I cannot go West I must go East for a change of climate.

> I remain your Bro. in the New & Everlasting
> Covenant,
> Willard Richards
> near Huntsucker's ferry, Mo.

WR **Decr. 12. 1848**
Great Salt Lake City, Great Basin, North America
My Dear Colonel [Kane]

In my last ex-party from Winter Quarters, you learned some of my individual views concerning a petition for a Government in the Basin, and my partiality for an original State Charter, and in that we should all be agreed, did circumstance permit—But that must be waived for the present, however reluctantly; and while our petition goes forth for a Territorial Government, I am instructed by the Council to give Col Kane such information concerning the situation and wishes of the people as will enable him to act in wisdom and decision, on the Petition, let the action of the Government assume whatever shape it may.

It has long been the voice of Mobocracy and Governmental misrule, that we are a peculiar people, and cannot exist in an organized government with others, and so we wish this voice to echo until the proof is doubly manifest. In aid of this testimony, we have retreated from State to State, before the blood and carnage that have every where followed us, until we find ourselves in the midst of the adamantine Mountains and desolate wastes, so drear and desolate, cold and barren, that not more than an acre in a thousand, Yes, in all probability, not more than 1 in 100,000 can ever be made to produce either fruit or grain for the sustenance of man, while, at the same time, we are about 1000 miles from Civilized man; and although this small Valley is one of the best situations known to us, in the whole territory petitioned for, by far the greater portion of our Crops, have this Season been destroyed by frosts, and Mountain Crickets more dreadful than the Locusts of Egypt.

Already it is whispered, (true or false we know not,) that Congress has organized Western California into a Territorial Government; and that we are, or are about to be annexed thereunto; But this can never be; or, if it is, it can never accomplish its intended object. What would be the natural result of such a Union? The same as in former days, when our Governors, Judges, and Legislators lived at a remote distance; and were alike ignorant of our wishes, necessities, true character; and the principles of virtuous honesty, and righteousness. It is said that falsehood travels the world over while truth is buckling her sandals. This has often been verified, when some fawning sycophant, disappointed office seeker, or fiendish mobocrat, with but one leg, and that perhaps a wooden one, astride have taken umbrage at their folly's failure, and astride the promentory of some long eared gentry, join the steeple chase at midnight; and leaping o'er the bounds of time and space, with lightning speed, informs his Excellency, Lilburn W. Boggs; or his Excellency, Thomas Ford, alias, his Excellency, the Devil, that the "Mormons are the most corrupt and lawless people on the face of the whole Earth; and our Nation will be destroyed if they are not put down." We wish Congress to be advised definitely, that that can <u>never be</u>; that this people will never consent to be governed by any man who does not live in their midst, who is not familiar with their daily wants; and who can be influenced by foreign falsehood to practice corruption and death upon us as heretofore. <u>Our Governor whoever he may be, must be as one of us; living with the people</u>—And so must our Judges.

Should it be necessary, at any time, we wish Congress to be advised that we shall not accept a piccayune Charter; or one combining half penny principles; but we want a charter that is noble in principle, and exalted in its operations—Yes Sir, we want one that is calculated to exalt the character of men, and that is worthy of the most enlightened people. It has been customary hitherto, most generally, when any public functionary has been sent among us by the authorities of the Nation, that the Individual selection has been of such a character, as to destroy the influence he otherwise might have had among us; but the time has now come when it is doubly desirable that such things should be done away.

The true spirit, the justice of Republican Government consists in securing equal rights & privileges to all its citizens; hence the declaration of the 9th Art. of the U.S. Constitution, "No preference shall be given by any regulation of commerce or revenue to the ports of one State over those of another." This commercial revenue or tariff on imports, being raised without partiality from the different States, and applied to the support of the General Government, gives an equal claim to all for protection: but if one of the States had no products or articles of export and yet paid duties on imports where would be the equality? Were that state possessed of equal wealth, today, with her sister States. Yet having no home products to barter for foreign Merchandize on which she is obliged in part or whole to depend for subsistence, her ready stock must [be] exhausted, and the land be vacated, or the inhabitants perish with on any supposable the annihilation of that State must be the final and the higher the tariff the more speedy the dissolution. Here then is a supportable case, which if it actually existed, would cause the letter of the Constitution to operate in opposition to its Spirit; but happily no such supposition is realized by any of the States. For no people would be so foolish as to settle in such a state or on lands that would produce such results, unless compelled by superior power, or combination of circumstances presenting the most fearful alternatives. So that the spirit and the letter still agree; but more happily still, that said declaration refers only to the States, and has no bearing on the Territories thereunto belonging, for here is a large territory without produce sufficient to sustain its inhabitants.

Not so with any other Territory of this nation; or that could scarce be named on the earth. Almost every country has some natural product as means of immediate resource. Western California abounds in wild cattle & horses, which furnish heavy exports of Tallow, peltry, hams, & pack animals, and although the country is but just merging into civilization, rich mines of gold, silver, quicksilver &c are extensively worked, and a variety of grain grows spontaneous.

Not so with our proposed territory. The Bison deserted this region some 20 years since. There are no wild cattle & few or no wild horses; no spontaneous grains, and not so much as a chalk or coal pit, towards the mineral kingdom, has been discovered in all this region of country, so far as we know, even wood for fuel is very scarce, and what there is, is almost inaccessible. We have obtained salt sufficient for our consumption, partly by vaporization, partly by boiling the water of the lake, but were it ever so plenty it would be of no value for export— salt, in the ocean, is too plenty. The natural and artificial products of Western California & Oregon, are easily exported to the ocean by the various Rivers that intersect their valleys and prairies at convenient distances; while this territory is deprived of this advantage; while almost every article consumed among us is by import, at an advance by cartage, from one, to one & two thousand per centum Ad valorum; and no exports; & no prospects of any exports, for a long time, if ever. Although we have been robbed of more lands & property in the United States than all the soil of this proposed territory is worth, and although thousands of valuable lives have been sacrificed by Mobocracy, and their carcases have been buried in the western wilds, or have been the prey of the wolves & the vulture, & their bones lie bleaching on the prairies & in the forests, we make no plea on this score, but leave it with our friends to do as they please; We are almost as secluded from the world as though we were on an island in the midst of the ocean without ship or plank, and on account of our terra-isolated situation Justice demands for us, <u>free soil</u> & <u>free Tariff</u>, until such times as the Electro Magnetic—Telegraphic—railway & canal shall favor our approach to some foreign market, or until this age of improvements, shall devise some speedy & safe method of scaling mountains, traversing impassable deserts, & annihilating distance without the aid of human sinew.

We are better acquainted with the wishes and necessities of the Petitioners than and, any other class of men can be; and we also know the hearts of the rulers of and the nation better than they know themselves, and, our charter granted and the President, wishing to exercise his privilege of nomination in a way to secure those good and wholesome feelings which are necessary for any man to possess, in securing his claims to a righteous influence over his constituents, will want to know the choice of the citizens of Deseret—and we support the name Brigham Young for Governor, Willard Richards, Secretary, Heber C. Kimball, Chief Justice, Newel K. Whitney & John Taylor Associate Justices, Horace S. Eldridge, Marshall; Daniel H. Wells, Attorney General; Albert Carrington, Assessor & Collector; Newel K. Whitney, Treasurer, and Joseph L. Heywood Supervisor of Roads. We suggest these names in the fullest confidence—to be used so far as it is the presidents perrogative to nominate. Our highly esteemed brother and mutual friend, Doct. John M. Bernhisel, who is duly delegated as the bearer of our Petition, will present this letter to Colonel Kane, and co-operate with him in all things in bringing our cause before the Government.

With a grateful remembrance of past favors, and The warmest friendship and unshaken confidence, in-behalf of the council, I have the great pleasure, Dear Sir, of committing our Petition & wishes into your hands, & once more, & forever subscribe myself your friend.
God bless Brother Kane.

> Willard Richards
> Colonel T. L. Kane
> Philadelphia

FDR **February 12, 1849** Ordained into the Quorum of 12 Apostles by HCK, BY, AL, WR, JT, PPP.

WR **Gt. S. L. City Feb 20th 1849**
Bro Shoemaker,

A few weeks since, I sent a Messenger to you, to get

me some Corn. I received for answer that you had none to part with.

I have been on rations of 4 ounces of Flour per soul, per day, since I arrived in the Valley, having nothing more of bread stuff, only as I could get a trifle of corn occasionally, & have that only to last me till an early harvest, with 20 Souls I feed. My feeble health deprives me the privilege of seeking bread in person, & from the same cause I am short of provisions, independent of the Valley.

Again I sent a Messenger to you two days since to buy some Corn, & received for answer by my Messenger, "Has the Dr. no Corn?" "No, not a bushel." "Has he no Flour?" "Yes a very little," "Then let him eat his flour," was your reply.

Now, bro. Shoemaker, will you be so good as to inform me, if it is more healthy for a people to eat all fine flour this week, or month: & the next three months eat nothing but roots, or corn, (provided they should be so fortunate as to get any) than it would be to mix their flour & meal, and have a portion of each daily? Or when you have Oats & hay, do you feed all your Oats to your horse before you let him have any hay? And then give him hay only, at that season when he has to labor the hardest?

If this be the true Gospel, I want you, Bro Shoemaker, to be so good as to inform me, which of the Gods it was that called & ordained you to be a Prophet, & Revelator, Bishop & Dictator, to, & over, me & my household, to give me this information, & for my good, to withhold from me those fruits of the Earth which my Heavenly Father has caused to grow for the benefit of all his children?

Now with your keen perceptions in prophetic vision

you must be aware that I need 30 bushels of corn to make me equal with the rest of the people of the Valley, in rations at 3/4 per pound, per day; or about 50 bushels to make me one pound per head per day, which would come nearer the actual standard, for no one can reasonably suppose for a moment that there exists in this Valley less than 16 ounces of bread stuff per day for each soul, until a reasonable harvest.

I am not seeking for a pound a day, but will be content with the established or current rations, and that my mind may be relieved from a daily, hourly & unnecessary burden of searching after a peck of corn, to prevent starvation, instead of attending to the more important duties of my calling, I send unto you, this the third time, & say, Brother Shoemaker, In the name of Jesus Christ, Sell me twenty five bushels of corn, for I have need of it to help me in my masters work. Therefore deny me not, & give me your answer in writing, (stating your terms, when I can get &c.) that it may be deposited, with a copy of this letter, in the sacred archives, as a testimony in your favor, on the day of final Reckoning.

I am your Bro.
Willard Richards

FDR **June 20th Wednesday** Jane gave birth to our second son at 15 min to 10 p.m. Been making fence all day.

FDR **June 28th Thursday** Our little boy, whom we called Franklin Snyder Richards was blessed by Pres. Willard Richards in presence of a few Friends just before a good supper.

FDR **Friday July 20th** I accompanied Brothers P. P. Pratt, Erastus Snow, Levi Hancock and Henry Herriman on to Ensign Hill and made some preparation for the next morning at which place at 6 o'clock, Pres. B. Young, the 6 Members of the 12, 3 Presidents of the 70's with Father ___ consecrated the Hill for the erection of a Standard thereon, a place of prayer and the giving of Addison Pratt his Endowment, which was then immediately bestowed upon him and the company left at 9 A.M.

FDR **October 6th Saturday** Appointed to England.

FDR **Sunday Nov 4th** Had a fracas killing a buffalo and camped in a storm of rain which turned to snow.

FDR **Monday Nov 5th** We run out of snow and met a man from Virginia having in Co 2 ox teams and 17 men. Rather a cold hope of passing the mountains with such poor teams and so late. Camped at Devil's Gate.

FDR **November 12th Monday** About 200 Cheyenne charged upon us while at dinner. We 35 of us saved all of our horses and confronted them with out any loss. This grand defeat rather chagrinned them. That night the Crows stole about 20 horses from them and Reynolds the trader, which kept them busy while we got out of their country.

WR **Gt. S. L. City. Nov 20. 1850**
Dr J. M. Bernhisel
Dear Sir,

It is our wish that the Indian title should be extinguished, and the Indians removed from our Territory or Utah? We answer yes, and that for the best of reasons, because they are doing no good here to themselves or anybody else. The Buffalo had entirely vacated this portion of the country, before our arrival; the Elk, Deer, Antelope & Bear and all eatable game, are very scarce, and there is little left here. (abeting the white population,) save the naked rocks & soil, naked Indians & wolves. The first two we can use to good advantage, the last two are annoying & destructive to property & peace, by night & by day; and while we are trying to shoot, trap & poison the wolves on one hand, the Indians come in and drive off & butcher our cattle, & steal our corn on the other, which leaves us little time between the wolves & Indians, to fence & cultivate our farms; and if Government will bye out and transplant the Indians, we will endeavor to subdue the wolves, which have destroyed our cattle, horses sheep & poultry by hundreds & thousands.

But even this will be no easy task for us, situated as we are, in the midst of hills thousands of miles in extent, and beasts for wolf prey scarce, except around the settlement; when deep snows come over the earth, they come down in droves, and devour all before them, till their voracious appetites are satisfied, then skulk to their burrows till hunger warns them out to another bloody banquet; Thus during the mist of midnight when the marksman's eye is dim, have we lost stock enough to sustain all the inhabitants of Deseret for a long time.

Is not this alone bad enough for pioneers of the wilderness to contend with? Most certainly, but worse, by far, are wild men than wild beasts, for they possess not only the cunning & ferocity of the beast, but by trade with Hucksters, Licensed or unlicensed, & by robbing & killing the mountains travelers have become possessed of many excellent fire arms, which, added to their native bow & arrow, make them a fearful foe, insomuch that emigrants to California are not safe, except in large companies, well armed, added to close watching, and even then are liable to be divested of all their teams in a dark or thoughtless moment, as many travellers have experienced the past season.

Do we wish the Indians any evil? No, we would do them good, for they are human beings, though most awfully degraded. We would have taught them to plough & sow, & reap & thresh, but they prefer Idleness & theft. Is it desirable that the barren soil of the mountains valleys should be converted into fruitful fields? Let the Indians be removed. Is it desirable that the way should be opened up for a rapid increase of population into our new State or Territory also W California & Oregon? Let the Indians be removed. We can then devote more time to agriculture, raise more grain to feed the starving millions desirous of coming hither.

For the prosperity of civilization; for the safety of our mail Routes; for the good of the Indians, let them be removed; at least, from the interior of the country, now destitute of game to sustain their shrunk sinews to some remote part; suppose on the borders of the wind river chain, where fish, at least, a part of the year, buffalo abound; or on Snake river where are fish and game; or on Mary's river, where, also are fish & game; or on the eastern slope of the Sierra Nevada, between the Northern & Southern route to California, where no white man lives & forests & streams are plenty; or on the western slope of the Sierra Nevada, above the dwellings of the whites, if there be space, so as not to interfere, and where Elk & other game are abundant; or any other point of compass, more congenial to their good.

Should the proper authorities think it best to gather them on the east of the Rocky Mountains, in the vicinage of others, hitherto gathered in like manner, and by their teachers, farmer & missionary teach them agriculture, the arts & sciences & religion they would improve faster, being thus removed from old hunting grounds, knowing as many of them do now, the value of bread, then they would be glad, be instructed in this region, where they have been accustomed to hunt and long remembered explain to would be constantly brought to mind by daily observations.

Not wishing to dictate the Modus Operandi, or place of their removal, we submit these few suggestions to your disposal, with full assurance, that the sooner the Indians of this country are removed to some better country & instructed properly, the better for them, the better for Deseret, the better for California, the better for the Union, the great whole of the nation.

With the greatest respect, we subscribe ourselves your friends &c.

FDR **January 18, 1851 Saturday** I applied to the magistrates again for the license which with the accompanying papers were immediately made out and I was instructed to appear in court to obtain the official signatures which I did and was detained from two or three hours but affected my purpose and am now a passenger Broker or immigration agent for the Saints.

WR **Wednesday, Feby 19th 1851** Cloudy & cold snow fell 3 in through the night. Major Grant & 25 men gone to Toola Valley after missing horses.

WR **Sunday Feby 23rd 1851** Clear day, thawing. Meeting at Bowery. Prest. B. Young spoke. Dr. R attending Amelia who is very sick. Amelia Richards died about 7 P.M.[7]

---

7. The journal notes that Amelia gave birth to a son on February 20. He died two days later, on February 22, and Amelia died February 23, probably from complications of childbirth.

WR **Monday March 10th** The Brethren preparing the Temple Block for to work on.

WR **Saturday April 5th** Clear warm day. Prest B. Young sick. Concert in the Bowery. Dr R at office all day.

To Dr. J. M. Bernhisel

We would respectfully suggest the establishing of the following Post routes, Post offices, and the appointment of the following named Postmasters for the said offices respectively, to with:

From Great Salt Lake City, north 20 miles, Davis post office, Davis County, for Postmaster, John S. Fullmer, Thence north 28 miles to Ogden post office, Weber County, for Postmaster Isaac Clark.

From Great Salt Lake City West 30 miles, Bensons Mills post office, Tooele County for P.M. Ezra T. Benson.

From said City, South 12 miles, sand plain post office, for P.M. John D. Lee, thence south 34 miles, Prove Post Office, Utah County for P.M. Isaac Higbee, thence south 20 miles Ptetetnete post office, Utah county, for P.M. James Pace, thence southeast 65 miles, Manti post office, San Pete County, for P.M. Isaac Morley.

And from Petetenete post office, south westerly 190 miles to Centre Creek post office, Iron County, George A. Smith for Post Master.

It requires the establishment of the above routes and offices for the accommodation of the public.

We would therefore recommend that contracts be let for carrying the mail weekly upon these respective routes. We also suggest that a monthly mail go from Centre Creek to Cahoon Pass 450 miles, Cahoon post office, Amasa Lyman post master. Thence to San diego Post Office California 150 miles. There is a good wagon road the whole distance, which can be travelled all seasons of the year. We further suggest James Little, Charles Decker & John M. Lytle as mail carriers to Centre Creek & all the intermediate post offices—& Ephraim Hands to carry the mail from Centre Creek p.o. to San Diego, who are all well acquainted with the mountains, Indian customs, and are used to camping out, and are well qualified for the business. And we wish the necessary mail bags, to be forewarded, all of which is respectfully submitted. We remain respectfully yours &c.

Willard Richards

My Dear Colonel [Kane]

I have fondly anticipated that before another mail I would have found time to re-read your friendly messages and have a response, according to my feeble ability, worthy of their author, and the circumstances which called them forth; but, alas! The old story once again, the mail will soon close, I have been on my back a day or two from a sudden cold; and the most I can do for my worthy friend is to let him know I have not forgotten him. . . .

Immediately after the murder of Joseph & Hyrum Smith, a great excitement was raised, fearing we should take vengeance on the murderers; and at the same time Eye witnesses voluntarily offered me their services, for the conviction of the murderers, to all of which I replied, in behalf of our community, that we should enter no prosecution, nor attempt any trial of the murderers, or even receive the testimony of witnesses of which to report, that if they had ought to report, they might do it to the Governor, of Illinois, who was there in the vicinity, or to the proper authorities of state, and that the Mormons would have nothing to do with the matter. President

Young, and most of the principle men in the Church were absent at the time I gave the above pledge, all of which was sanctioned by them, on their return, and the same has been faithfully adhered to, by us, to the present time. Those murderers were tried at Carthage, Ill, by Court & Jury of their own selection, proved guilty, and acquitted; the Mormons had <u>nothing to do with it</u>. The minutes of that trial, at length were taken in phonography, <u>are yet in existence</u>. Time will determine what disposition will ultimately be made of them. All these events transpired in full view of the fact, that no nation on record, ever punished the murderers of God's Prophets. And that the United States would no more punish the murderers of Joseph & Hyrum, than the Jews did the murderers of Jesus. It was necessary that the events connected with Jesus should be left to the decision of the Jewish nation, to prove them, and open the way for their expulsion, from the land of their nativity, & be scattered among all nations; which punishment they have sorely felt to this day; and it was just as necessary, that the punishment of Joseph's murderers, should be left to the U. States, that they might convict themselves by their own acts, and prepare themselves for their final overthrow, which as assuredly awaits them, as the word of Jehovah is here. And that blood is the legal price of blood, and because that President Young has declared this fact, in his office, and calling, as a faithful minister of Jesus Christ, he has been trumpeted to the world, by whoremongers, drunkards, liars, hireling priests and omnibus editors as an enemy to the government; a plotter to overthrow the nation and every falsehood that men, and the meanest of devils could invent, have been resorted to, to blacken his character otherwise to gain an influence in the public mind, and thereby eventually, fix the damming stain & sin of Treason on Brigham Young, the Prophet of God; the same as they tried on Joseph Smith. But Joseph died without a stain, and so will Brigham if he dies at all; for there is not a greater, truer & more substantial friend to the Government of the United States, on the whole earth, But the faults of rulers and wickedness of the people, he will tell them of, and if they repent not, they will have to be their own folly. And should Brigham cease to declare the wickedness of men in high places & low places, he would cease to be the leader of Israel, and God would raise another who would make the proclamation, just as he raised up Brigham when Joseph was killed. And what did the nation, or the people gain? And what would they gain by a repetition? The only gain for any man is by obedience to the warning and learning to do right. I have long known Brigham Young in public & private and am assured that no man has the disposition or ability to sustain the government of the U.S. than himself and every word I ever heard him utter, which could be centered into hatred to the government, was spoke with special reference to the wickedness of the rulers of the government, and he has in every instance upheld the Constitution and laws of the nation and all men who have executed those laws in righteousness and is bound so to continue to do & ____ disposition, but by his Religion, they in government always at his post in any emergency. Have not his acts always proved these facts? They have!

Relative to the Spiritual wife doctrine, I demure until I get a definition, until I understand what is meant by the term, for I discover it used by various individuals with as various significations. If the signification be literal, and "spiritual wife" means spiritual wife as a spirit, I can truly say I am in favor of the doctrine; for, at different periods of my life, I have had three wives, all of whom have died; their bodies are inanimate, and any relation thereto, may not be of any practical utility previous to their Resurrection, their spirits are animate, existing in the world of spirits, and, for ought I know may be of that class which are called "ministering spirits, sent forth to minister to those who are or shall be heirs of salvation"; and if this be their office and calling, who knows but that I may, at times, be a blessed recipient of their ministrations; and as they are my wives still, and though their spirits are in the spirit world, are they not my spiritual wives? And when their temporal bodies not in their graves, shall arise spiritual bodies in the Resurrection, and their spirits & spiritual bodies are united in the Celestial world, as their spirits & Temporal bodies were in this, they will be all spiritual, they will be my wives still, and most assuredly I shall then be in possession of spiritual wives. And are not their spirits as spiritual now as they will be after the Resurrection of their bodies? Certainly! And they being mine now, as they will be then, are my spiritual wives now as they will be my spiritual wives then. Thus I freely acknowledge that I have spiritual wives, and wish that all men were disposed to be righteous enough to enjoy the same blessings.

If the term "Spiritual wives" is meant to signify having more than one wife living, in these mortal tabernacles at one time, the phrase itself is a misnomer, and includes its own refutation, and I need say nothing for or against. The Saints have the same foundation and ground work for their faith concerning marriage, as have had all Christian nations since they have been in possession of the Bible, to wit: the Old and New Testament. And any truth established therein I can, and do believe, and this is the faith of all the Saints; and if any highly esteemed friend wishes an hours social chat on the general principles of marriage, as taught by those authorized to teach, in those sacred Records referred to, I will be most happy to meet him, any time, when he shall please to give me notice; but, I am admonished that I am weary, and fear your patience will be wearied before you have read this hasty scroll. I must, however, add my fullest approbation of your course, in all your cross fires with Editors & Presidents.

God bless Colonel Kane
    W Richards
    Coln Thomas L. Kane Esqr
    Independence Hall P.A.

P.S. Secretary Harris took with him all the funds designed for the Territory ($29,000) and the Legislature directed the Marshall to draw on the U.S. Treasury for all funds needed for the support of the Government.

FDR **May 29 Thursday** I closed a bargain with Mr. William out in the 16 Princes St., Red Lyon Square, to print 5000 Books of Mormon and stereotype them. Deliver it and all with paper, press work, hot pressing, composition, etc., included 496 pounds 16 shillings.

FDR **October 5, 1851** Spent the day after Breakfast and signing the articles of lease for the depot. With Brothers Snow and Kelsey at Connaught Terrace in Council and prayed about Bro Wheelock's case and about the state of things in Liverpool. It is reported that Church Clergymen have got Jane Yates, who was turned away by Sister Rodgers, and got her to testify to many things highly disreputable and perhaps criminal against me. This is like a dagger in my heart. I have endeavored to walk uprightly before my God and his people all the Days of my life, and have maintained a reputation without spot or blemish hitherto and in nothing could I be so deeply wounded in my feelings as to have my character injured in the sight of God's people.

FDR **December 7 Sunday** In the evening I presented the subject of Tything for to build a Temple in G.S.L. City.

WR **Great Salt Lake City, Dec 29, 1851**
Mrs. Mary McMinn,
Beloved Sister

Could I throw any light in the particular subject to which you referred me, in those letters, it would give me peculiar pleasure, but the history of my genealogy, for the last century, has been far more vague than I could wish, for I love my kindred, and would be happy to know of their locality and welfare.

Some time in the latter part of the last century, my father's (Joseph) eldest brother, (William) located himself in Hinsdale, on the Green Mountains, in the western part of Mass. And raised a numerous posterity of whom, Hiram & Walter & Harriet remained in that vicinity, the last I knew, Achsa, wife of Solomon Bixby, removed, a few years since to Vergennes, Vt. William, Ira and I don't know how many more removed many years since to Western N.Y.—& John to Milwaukie, Mich, some 20 years since. All the names of that family I do not recollect, and the children, grandchildren and Gt. Grandchildren would doubtless make a great party, before this.

My father's younger brother (Thomas) lived, most of his days in Brookfield, Mass. In the course of his life had three wives, one of whose name was Lucy, the others I do not recollect if I ever knew. I was young while he was in his prime, and being at some distance, I knew but little concerning him, yet I recollect that he had a daughter named Mary, and my mother told me that she nursed Mary at her own breast, with me, because her mother was sick, or died, which I do not recollect, she having been carried through the country many miles to be with my mother. Uncle Thomas had a son named Curtis, and many more whose names I do not recollect; and daughters, if I ever knew. I cannot recollect how many, but I will recollect my cousin Willard. He was about my age, and I met with him twice, if I mistake not after we had arrived at a portion of manhood; but so diversified has been my scenery, for the last twenty-five years, that even to give a particular description of his person I could not, neither do I know where he has been located for the past 20 years.

Dec 19th 1851
Willard Richards / GSL City
To Mrs Mary McMinn

WR **January 29, 1852**

My dear Colonel [Kane]

To give an idea of the apathy that prevails throughout the whole organic structure of governmental proceedings, I will simply state that the Blanks for taking the census of Deseret for 1850, arrived here a few days ago. In arithmetical Ratio, according to the amount of labor to be performed, when might the census returns reasonably be expected? ~~Without any definite estimate~~ we may suppose about 19 hundred & 50; and if we had waited the result of said census, on which to predicate the organization of a Territory, at what time would the organization have been

153

completed? About 5000 years hence, or about as long as it will take Congress to build a railway, or lightning Rod from her Capitol to her colonies & states, if she goes about as fast as she has done.

One Question more? Consider the Utah Indians; existing in the most unique manner, in their habitat and customs, selling their women & children taken in battle, & their own flesh too, from individual to individual, from family to family; from clan to clan, from tribe to tribe, and from the nations to Mexicans and others, as slaves forever; consider these same women & children, offered at sale, for a pint of corn, in any, and all of the organized countries of Utah, daily, with the knowledge of the fact before the Citizens, that if the child or woman was not bought in twelve hours, more or less, said woman or child would stone or have its brains dashed out against a rock, or roasted alive, or tormented in some more inhuman manner, by its owner or conqueror or parent; and at the same time, Our good old mother has reserved to herself the exclusive right of nourishing her own copper colored babies, and would impose a fine of five hundred dollars on the Mormon citizens who should have the audacity & rascality to pay a pint of corn for said Indian woman or child to save its life, or cause all the property of said benevolent Individual to be confiscated; and for what? Good heavens, for what? Just because some philanthropic soul has paid a pint of corn, or 2 gills of wheat for an Indian child, that he knew was destined to death's torture without remedy, if he did not do it, he must pay $500 or have his property confiscated; and he became a vagabond on the earth & die with hunger, in the mountains, a thousand miles from no place; and why? Because he had the feelings of humanity, and tried to save the life of a mother's child whose skin is tinged with copper and by the purchase trading it to life & salvation and give it its freedom forever.

Have the citizens of Utah emenated as they have from the most enlightened societies & nations under heaven, become so sordid & devilish in their feelings, as to suffer the brains of a fine promising child to be dashed out in their presence, rather than give a quart of wheat for said child, because the laws of the U.S. would make it slavery; and all their property must be confiscated because they have been trafficking with the Indians contrary to laws made & provided; and that too in the midst of civilized society, of organized Territory & Counties? If they will, thus look on martyrdom, and not lend the helping hand, it is time for hell to lend a helping hand. But what will you do. The U.S. laws are against salvation of life in this thing. And Utah has no authority from mother to make laws to the contrary.

My dear friend, forgive my scribbling, many a truth is spoken in jest, as the saying is, and some had better be spoken in jest than not spoken at all, Time and strength admonish me to leave the field at 2 A.M. January 29, 1852.

W Richards
Colonel Thomas L. Kane, Esqr
Independence Hall, Philadelphia, PA.

WR **May 3rd 1852**
Great Salt Lake City, U Ter
Dear Bro. Benson,

We received your two letters on the 30th ultimo which were forwarded yesterday morning, along with some other dispatches to Prest. Young, by an express;

he having started on the 22nd of the same month, with
a number of the brethren, including Bros O. Pratt,
Geo A. Smith, W. Woodruff, DH Wells, and others for
the most southern part of the Territory, to find a place if
possible to locate a settlement where cotton and grapes
could be cultivated to the extent that would supply our
whole community. Your letters contained News cheering
to the heart of every saint and which gave us unfeigned
satisfaction to know of the general removal of the Saints
from Pottowatomie and of their ability in this respect
which only answers our expectations. But you have not
informed us of how many are going to walk the plains
this season, with wheelbarrows, and handcarts, the number of whom you are requested to communicate to Prest.
Young immediately as upon this depends in a great measure his going out to meet the coming companies and this
information should be obtained if possible by his arrival
from the expedition alluded to, which is expected to be in
the month of June next. Ninety-three persons at our late
Conference, bravely and generously volunteered to meet
the travelling saints with teams and provisions, who are
also contemplating to start in June, on which account also
we should be correctly advised as to the number coming,
for if, as may be inferred from your letter, that few will
venture across the plains on foot, trudging the hand carts
&c, such a large preparation of relief will not be needed,
and those coming with wagons, and with teams can trust
in them for succor as heretofore, and the labor of those
who will not be so required to go out is needed and can
be used to much greater advantage in our midst; than
in leaving their homes of industry, their fields, and their

crops to return to the earth, in order to go and assist those who are able to help themselves.

It would be well if on receipt of this, you would get a list prepared of the names of all those who are coming, with the strength of each mans team, arranged under the heads of the different Captains &c, so that we could know what to do in regard to giving assistance. This from your past experience, you know would be very desirable to all in these vallies.

Conference was held in the New Tabernacle, which had been finished for the purpose and was dedicated the first day, Tuesday, the 6th of April; and when these brethren in the public assembly thus volunteered, as also on the previous, and following days on which the Conference was held, from Tuesday to Sunday inclusive, such an outpouring of the good spirit from God was manifested, such union, love and joy beamed in each countenance of that vast assembly, with the manifestations of the Holy Ghost. From press of business I will close praying my heavenly father to shower upon you his choicest blessings in the name of Jesus Christ, Amen.

Thos. Bullock

W. Richards

Great Salt Lake City May 3, 1852

To Elder Robert Campbell

All is going well with us in this peaceful valley. Public & private buildings are continually being erected, the foundation of the wall around the Temple Block is dug, and a general vote was taken at last Conference to commence building a Temple the coming Spring. The Saints are made fully alive and energetic in the great work of the Lord than ever. Many have paid their tithing, up to the current time, and the store house of the Lord is full. We are glad to hear of the rapid progress of the work of the Lord in Europe, and the diligence and faithfulness of the Elders, in doing their duty. There is a large emigration expected this season. Several hundred are coming across the plains, with Hand Carts, and Wheel barrows, and Prest Young intends to go out and meet them; ~~as also a great many for the Gold mines.~~ It is the intention of building an office this summer and when finished, the records of the Church History will again be unpacked and proceeded with, which will require the aid of a number of clerks.

As we have seen in times past, when the Church has been persecuted, and lied about, she has always took a long stride onward, and ever will do so. Therefore, the enemies of the Church are unwittingly building it up, instead of, as they suppose drawing it down.

God bless you—farewell

Ever your friend,

W Richards

FDR **Saturday May 15th, 1852** Brother E. Snow and I had been in close and fervent conversations upon many subjects pertaining to our missions and our ministry and the Great blessings of our Heavenly Father upon us and our labors; and in the course of our chat he said: "Brother Franklin, if I should ever let down a stitch, or make any misstep, or if [you] ever should see me likely to get wrong in any way (the Lord forbid that I should), will you be my Friend and help me to recover, get right and go ahead again and will you counsel me, steady me and help me along that I may not fail but continue to the end and obtain my crown?" I answered: "I feel that I can say from my heart that I will and with the more cheerfulness for I fervently desire of you the same favor.

I feel that without the aid of my Brethren, I shall not be able to triumph to the end and with them inherit the Brightness and fullness of our Hope. Do you feel willing to promise me that you will be my Friend and watch over me and give me a word in season if you see you can prevent me going astray, or if I should get astray, stretch our a hand to Bring me back into the right way?" He answered me that he would. I thanked him sincerely and told him I should record it, that it was not a vain thing with me.

WR **Great Salt Lake City May 31, 1852**
Hon J. M. Bernhisel,
Dear Sir

I have hinted to the department that our mountain mails are not safe without the best of India Rubber bags. I will suggest to you, and if you have the leisure, please converse with the Department on the propriety of furnishing safety bags of India Rubber, or Gutta Percha to lash on each side of coach & mules, while swimming mountain streams. This is the cheapest and safest method I know of to accomplish the safe keeping of the mail. The last mail was wet by the Coach, which was water proof in Hull, being capsized, had there been air bags on the sides, the mail would have come dry, and if the department does not furnish those bags, they will not be furnished. They cannot be had here. No mail from California these 2 months, a very probably supposition that the carriers have been killed by St. Mary's Indians.

WR

FDR **Thursday June 17** A very warm day, wet and sultry. Early this morning was called to the bedside of a very rich man who has the cholera. How appalling its scourges. Spent considerable time with him. Got much exhausted. Last night he supped with us, tonight he is a corpse. His son is very ill. How awful the ___, the sights & crampings of the cholera.

FDR **Tuesday June 29** Hunted till 12 p.m. for my cattle and got under way & went through to Jackson's Point. Tonight had a most terrific thunderstorm I got no sleep for mosquitos & storm till 3 a.m.

FDR **Saturday July 24** Anniversary of Pioneers entry into the valley. A horrid days drive. Flies woeful indeed beyond all I ever before saw. Horses bloody all over and covered with blotches.

FDR On the **19th August, Thursday** About 3½ p.m. we were met by the Brethren with teams and fresh melons and vegetables for our comfort, just before we came down into Big Kanyon. As each man recognized his relatives their joyous shouts from over-flowing shouts made the high hills and valleys ring with their manifestations of joy. It was indeed a happy time of meeting. Camped near the east foot of 2nd mountain and on the Friday at 2 p.m. arrived in the valley and about 3½ p.m. met my three wives in my residence, or the residence of my first wife. All well in health and happy in spirit—as joyous as they knew how to be. My heart was full to overflowing & I felt my soul satiated with increasing and unbounded goodness of God to me & mine.

FDR **Friday September 3** This day is rendered notable for the arrival of Capt. A. O. Smoot's Co in the valley. Pres. B. Young and W. Richards with the band and several of the municipal authority went out to meet the Co. I took my wife and son and daughters, my father and mother, also Pres. Willard Richards and went out and met them near the mouth of the Kanyon. The procession was received by the firing of the cannon and camped on Union Square.

Today the Snake and Walker's band met to talk, smoke and make a treaty. Walker came into the ring with his tomahawk on, when the Snake chief snatched it from his belt and threw it furiously away.

FDR **Sunday September 5** Attended meeting and heard Elder Orson Pratt deliver the <u>first public</u> lecture upon the subject of Patriarchal matrimony or Plurality of Wives. This Holy and glorious doctrine is a precious meal of food to the people of God. How searching in its nature, opening up an immense field for contemplation on the doctrine of Eternal Lives.

This p.m. Thomas Bullock read in the ears of about 2500 people who crowded the tabernacle the Rev (revelation) upon the subject given in July 1843. This is the first time I ever saw or heard it notwithstanding it has been 9 years, known by most of the Twelve. Polygamy corruption, lasciviousness and an open charge of all fleshly indulgence is the leading argument in all nations where the gospel has been preached against the truth. It is fully admitted throughout most of all the British Conferences that plurality is practiced in Zion and this is the time to reveal it to the world.

WR **Gr S. Lake City Oct 30th 1852**
My Dear Doctor Bernhisel
  With the receipt of yours of Sept 9th I have to acknowledge the renewed obligations you have laid me under, in procuring <u>a commission</u> to print the Laws of the 1st Session of 32nd congress &c, <u>Dated Sept 1st</u>. And, though I am ~~obliged~~ compelled to return the commission, unaccepted, for good and substantial reason, I am none the less obliged to those noble & generous feelings that prompted the procural.
  Reasons for returning the commission.
  1st: The dollar per page will not pay for the paper to print on.

2nd: The dollar per page will not pay for setting the type.

3rd: The matter would crowd out the column of the News. More important matters or what would be more interesting to most subscribers & injure the subscription list.

4th: The matter would be no accommodation to the Editor for he has more matter before him continually than the News will contain.

5th: I have paid 10 times as high for type setting as it costs in N. York & other works in the office in proportion, and paper is worth 4 or 5 times as much here as in the Eastern Cities. And these means necessarily prevent my accepting your kind offer, & most Respectfully return you the Commission.

> Most sincerely,
> Your Bro. W Richards

WR **Gr S.L. City June 21, 1853**
Brother Hinman

I understand there is an anxiety among some of the brethren to secure some of the grass or hay from my lot on the bottom, on the supposition that it has been surveyed more than a year, and is not fully fenced. Consequently think or pretend to think that according to an act of the Legislature of Utah at their first session; but this is quite a mistaken idea, & I wish the brethren to understand it so that neither they nor myself may have any trouble about it.

It is well known that I purchased the right of possession, or secured the survey of said lot, 90 or more acres, for the purpose of securing hay to support teams necessary to carry on the business of my mills, that there is no more grass there than I need to support my teams in hay, that I have cut said grass annually; that the lot is partially ditched, & design to complete the fencing as soon as possible; that I have been taxed for all my improvements in Davis county, and have the same legal right to the improvement and occupancy of said lot & all the avails thereof, as I have to my mills, houses, gardens or cash in pocket.

The Legislative law referred to (date of which I do not recollect, 1st printed volume) has no reference to such lots. The Legislature understood that there were individuals who were having large tracts of land surveyed for no other purpose than to hold possession, till they could get a handsome sum of some immigrant Brother or other person & thus make a good speculation out of nothing at all, & to prevent that speculation the Legislature inserted the clause in the law referred to.

I have never yet been prosecuted by law or gospel ordinances, neither have I prosecuted any one on the earth, & so far as I am concerned would rather give 500 acres of land than open a suit. But should we all sit down in silence, and let Saints and sinners openly & designedly set at defiance all law, all right, all Justice; & rob us of the means of living, we may well offer our lives a sacrifice at once, or give up at midnight, as we have hitherto been forced to do, and find a place of safety where we can. But O! where shall we find it? I know of no more Rocky Mountains for the Saints to flee to for protection against oppression. Therefore, I wish you to teach, instruct & pray the brethren, (if there be occasion) to let the grass, which my heavenly Father has give me, through my exertions alone, & not force me to appeal to the court of heaven for justice.

You will make use of this letter, as you please, or as the nature of the case may require.

Wishing you peace, health & prosperity, with all the Israel of God; & praying that the unity of the Spirit may be preserved by all who profess to be Saints, I subscribe myself your brother in the New & Everlasting Covenant
W Richards
Richards Mill, Davis, Co., U.T.

FDR **October 18, 1853** Mother Wealthy Richards died at 15 m to 6 A.M. She was born in Richmond, Mass September 6, 1786. Married same place February 24, 1818. Monday next day, took my seat in the House of Representatives for fifty days.

WR **Eds Room, Dec 8, 53, 11 p.m.**
Bro. Brigham Young,
Most Dearly Beloved Brother,

After my best wishes for yourself & household, for whose good I labor & pray without ceasing, and an apology in brief, for saying, I wished someone would burn your chair and give you a better one, having had all the blood of my lower extremities palsied for an hour by sitting on a thing <u>called chair</u>, which every valley mechanic <u>ought to be ashamed</u> of, even in name, when such a hoggish fellow as myself, of less than 300 comes in contact; and of which a musketoo would not be proud, unless he wanted to sit cross legged. I proceed to answer the question you gave me on parting this eve; which, if I recollect was substantially "How do you like it?" referring to the new alphabet[8] & characters then before us.

---

8. This is his final letter to Brigham Young in response to Brigham's question about his opinion of the Deseret Alphabet characters.

My answer is <u>I like it—well</u>, because I believe the Committee & Regency have done the <u>best they could</u> to the present time, and I think they have done much to promote a unity of sounds, whereby we can communicate our ideas without so much writing & printing as hitherto; but, I still feel that the thing which we are after, which we all desire, is not as perfect as it may be, if we continue our labors.

The bringing forth of the <u>various sounds</u> that have been presented before the board, I consider of incalculable benefit, and the <u>combinations</u> of those sounds, but they are not yet <u>quite perfect</u> to my ear. By conversation, questioning, &c I discover improvements going ahead in these things every evening. And I regret that I could not have been present all the time to have heard more.

Now Beloved Prest. Excuse me for my plainness—if I have spoken amiss pardon me, for you know when I speak, I speak what God or the Devil gives me. There is no half heart about this boy, never was, and God grant there never may be.

I would have said more, by way of explanation, but I am weary, have other letters to write, before I retire, and beg your favor to let explanations come at a future moment.

May God, my Heavenly Father, who ruleth in the Heavens, Give my God on the earth wisdom & Revelations to conduct all the affairs of his Kingdom just as he would have them, & build houses, and plant vineyards, & cultivate fields & gardens & make him & his family comfortable & happy, till the Son of Man & the Ancient of Days shall appear in our midst, & may Heber & Willard be one, undivided with him forever, is the daily constant prayer of your Bro.

W Richards

FDR **March 11th (1854)** At 9½ A.M. Br Willard Richards died. [Later, in another journal, he wrote:] Uncle Willard died. I helped to do the needful in preparing for his interment. Mourning in Israel. A great one, an Apostle, is departed.

Chapter 5

FRANKLIN D. RICHARDS

MAY 1854 TO FEBRUARY 1882

Wednesday May 3, 1854 Started at dawn. Went to and crossed the Kaw Kansas River. Fed & [bathed] crossed the Mo. Line about 4 p.m. Passing many former inheritances of the Saints & mobbery, crossing Blue and Duck creeks. Arrived at Independence at dusk.

Thursday May 4 Before Breakfast went to the Temple spot. After went again with Bro Fred Kesler, also to the store of Br. Gilbert, printing office of Br. Phelps, &c., etc. How precious is the spot where the glory of God shall be revealed.

June 3 Saturday This a.m. sea more quiet and I arose early at half past 7. Discovered the Irish Coast. About 10 passed Tory Island. The stillness of the sea enabled us to run much nearer the coast which gave us a fine view of some places. Passed Giants Causeway, London Derry, Belfast Lough, Maiden Sisters & Copeland Lighthouse at dusk.

June 4 Sunday Arrived in the Mersey at 7½ o.c. and went to Anchorage. Got the customs past & on the loading stage where we met Brs. Samuel, Linforth, Turnbull in waiting for us.

Thursday September 21 Pleasant most of the day. German seas sublimely rough, but not magnificently grand just enough to keep up retching and prevent eating. Three agreeable cabin passengers and a jolly captain are the company.

Friday 22 I arose at 8 a.m. We were in sight of land on

our right and had our pilot aboard. Capt says we are 60 miles off Hamburg which is 70 miles from the mouth of the Elbe. Beautiful are the lawns and everglades, and on the Danish side, the palisades, villages &c. which ornament the river.

Tuesday September 26 Renewed my ticket of residence and got my passport. Visa for Kopenhagen.

Sunday October 8, 1854 At 2 a.m. steamed down the Elbe and about 9 passed the outer bar into the Sea. Had a wind from the little off the larboard beam which allowed of setting all sail, and which also steadied the ship as she rolled much, being light— scarcely any freight and but 10 passengers. We proceeded very agreeably, fair wind and beautiful weather continuing till we came into Grimsby Dock.

On Sunday **July 29, 1866,**[1] while present at a two day's meeting in a large Bowery on the public square in Springville and seated on the stand at its extreme left, President B. Young beckoned me to him. I went and sat down by him. He asked me how I would like to go on a mission to England. Said he would like to have me do so & that he believed it would be a great blessing to me. I told him I knew no choice about such things. If it was his wish that I should go, I would do so, though to human calculation it seemed difficult. I asked him if I should make ready to go in the Fall. He said he reckoned I could get ready & be off in four or five days.

Sunday August 12 Attended meeting at Bowery & spoke a short time in morning. After meeting, attended Prayer Circle and received my blessing. Set apart for my mission to Europe. Historian's Office, H. C. Kimball, D. H. Wells, Wilford Woodruff, G. A. Smith, and Geo Q. Cannon having their hands

---

1. There is a break of nearly twelve years in Franklin's journal. It is likely that he wrote during that time, but the journals are lost.

upon my head with Pres. B. Young. He said: Bro F. D. R. in the name of the Lord Jesus Christ and by virtue of the Holy Priesthood, we lay our hands upon your head to bless you and set you apart for your European mission. Inasmuch as you are called to go to England, and to other countries or wherever the guidance of God shall lead you on a mission to preach the Gospel of Life and Salvation, the Gospel of the Son of God; we dedicate you and set you apart to this end, and pray our Father in Heaven to pour out his Holy Spirit upon you and to fill every particle of your system with the same. At the close of the blessing, Pres. Young said: "There, Bro Franklin, is there anything more that you desire, just write it and live for it."

Tuesday Sept. 11th 4 o'clock a.m. at Liverpool, making per ship's log, 3066 miles; from New York to Omaha 1500 miles; Omaha to Salt Lake 1000; Salt Lake to Liverpool 5566 miles by our route in just 28 days of which we were detained five days and 8 hours which makes that we performed the journey in 22 days and 16 hours traveling time.

Monday October 29th While yet in bed with Bro. A. Miner, the Postman handed in a letter from Franklin telling me of Jane's serious illness of Diphtheria—but at writing, September 29th, slightly better. This accounts for my earnest feelings of anxiety for her for a long time back. O Lord, heal her, I pray thee, and make her well and sound speedily. Let also thy servant Brigham be led to send her over here to live with me awhile if it can be consistent with thy holy will & for our best good.

Tuesday December 11 The Elder from Neath testified that of 10 cases of cholera among the Saints, all were healed by the laying on of hands of the Elders and it had become common for the Doctors, when they could do no more, to tell their patients there was only one chance left for them—that was to call the Mormon Elders which several did do and were healed. Some went about inquiring for oil, "Mormon Oil", common oil would not do—thus the great mercy and blessing of God through his ordinances has become proverbial even in the mouths of outsiders.

Monday December 31, 1866 Br. John W. tells me in a letter from B. Y. Jr that J. W. Young is expected to return to Utah next summer and that I am expected to take charge of the mission. Johnny voluntarily said he meant to write his father and ask if Jane might not come out and stay with me during my mission.

Although I almost shudder at the thought of possibly having to take charge of the mission, still my heart overflows with gratitude to God for his everlasting kindness in this great manifestation of confidence and kindness to me and I pray with all the yearnings of my nature that He will give me grace by the presence and power of the Holy Ghost to do all things well while on this Mission; that if I am not sufficiently chastened and humbled to secure a free and full pardon for all past imperfections and the full fellowship of the Holy Ghost—that he will carry on the work until I am, so that I may from this day forth live nearer up the measure of my calling as an Apostle than I ever have done.

Sunday January 6 [1867] The vessel was put on her course to Rotterdam, 200 miles. The wind being from the South, the sea was worst kind for sickness, being what is called "cross" or "chopped seas" and I took the full benefit of it being sick and vomiting severely at short intervals all day.

Monday January 7 Went on up and arrived at Rotterdam at 10:30. A passage of 45 hours which normally is performed in 17 or 18 hours. It is built in the form of a triangle, one side resting on the right bank of the Mense. It is a very neat city of 110,000 inhabitants. Every street is a canal. No stranger, traveler could walk the streets or sidewalks without being impressed with its singular neatness. After passing through Hague, Leyden and Haarlem, we arrived at Amsterdam about 3 hours of ride on R. Road. The place is named from its situation on the Amster and the dam necessary for its existence, hence "Amsterdam". It has 260,000 inhabitants, of which 35,000 are Jews. The State Church of Holland is <u>Calvinistic</u>. Holland or the Netherlands has been subject to several dreadful inundations by the sea. In one instance in 1570, an inundation destroyed 100,000 persons.

Saturday January 12 Awoke about 6 a.m. from a dream of visiting with my family at home. Felt assured of letters soon. When Bro. Wideborg awoke, he said he had also been having an excellent visit at home in Utah. Got our luggage past the custom house officer and left per R. Road for Copenhagen, where we arrived at 10 a.m. The Danish papers say the Lower House of the American Congress has passed a Bill for the Impeachment of President A. Johnson.

Tuesday January 29 I took a good stroll through the town while Bro. Widerborg hunted up some of the Saints. In Sweden there is no protection by the law for the Saints, but the spirit of human progress and the almost universal desire for religious liberty give us great sufferance. Still we have to be careful not to get up any excitement or attract special attention, else we might be arrested and sent out of the Kingdom as Bro. H. C. Haight was when he came over to hold Conference in Malmo in 1857. To avoid this we stay at hotels and only go to the Saints meeting—which must not be at the same hour as the Lutherans hold meeting or we should be seen to be ousted. The Lutheran being the State Church.

Wednesday February 20 Received a letter from Uncle Willard's family Nanny,[2] the first from them since I left home.

Friday March 22 Being permitted to peruse a letter of Instructions from the First Presidency to B. Young Jr. en route for Europe. I find it directs that, as no teams will be sent to help Emigration this year, those who come, must come through on their own means, and should come together. "Every effort should be made to impress upon the Saints in Europe the importance and necessity of paying their Tithing."

Monday April 1 At the office getting the Journal of Discourses forwarded. Read Semi Weekly Telegraph. The political nature seems to be in pain about Utah. The U.S. Govt knows not what to do with us and seems to be negotiating with Nevada to let them the job. The Telegraph treats the whole matter very facetiously in fact it appears more and more as though labor pains were coming on which might result before long in the birth of a State.

Tuesday Jun 4 At 6:30 left and took rail at Ludgate Hill Station for Paris about 360 miles 2d class, £2-6-0. Arrived at Paris at 6 p.m. and took room at Grand Hotel, 459 on the 4th floor, 131 steps up. After wash, dinner at Palais Royal Restaurant, went out to exercise. As Brigham and I were passing from the Palais Royal to "Rue de Rivoli" we came into it near the Imperial Palace and found a concourse of people aligning both sides of the street and numerous police keeping the track clear—on inquiry we learned the Emperors were expected and taking as good a position as we could, we waited a few moments, then came first a detachment of Lancers, second, the Imperial Gala Carriage containing the Emperor of France, Emperor of Russia, the

---

2. Franklin had married Nanny and they had children together, but he continued to refer to in this way.

Empress of France & Grand Duchess Marie. The first 3 I knew by their photographs. They were talking and laughing merrily. The Czar is a very pleasant man and looks goodly—quite different from Napoleon 3d who is more stolid & dull. We returned about 4 p.m. and passed near where the Czar was shot at by the Polander Berezowski.

Monday July 29 Since before the missionaries commenced to arrive, I have felt much concern as a wise and discreet appointment of them to the proper fields of their labor and during all last week arranged one after another as made manifest to me and this morning I was enabled to complete the work as appeared satisfactory to myself when I got the Elders and the Brethren of the office together and read them over in the hearing of all present and asked if anyone thought of any alteration that could amend the matter when all expressed themselves perfectly satisfied as the appointments were read.

Sunday September 15 Health much improved but still not substantial. I attended meeting morning and heard Brs Preston and Penrose. Evening I spent an hour in a very pleasant instruction and edifying manner preaching to the Saints in the love of the Truth. All present felt the happyfying influence of the Holy Spirit, Saints and strangers. I feel to thank and praise the Lord for the dying love of a crucified and risen Redeemer.

Sunday September 22 After supper I spoke extensively to the young Elders and Brethren about a proper import of their time— how they could while on their missions, treasure up knowledge of various kinds and improve themselves very much for all their future life, felt it continually gushing out of my lips from the fountain of my heart by the promptings of the Holy Spirit and the love I have for them.

Sunday September 29 Attended meeting in the morning,

heard Elder A. Miner preach. Spent the afternoon in bed, having had but little sleep for several nights on account of Fleas, which I brought home when I went out to conference. Last night finished killing them and today I get rest. 9 pages of Journal of Discourses proof to read.

Tuesday October 22 Found awaiting me a note from "The Royal Bank of Liverpool."

> Sir, I am requested by the Directors to inform you that this company has been compelled to suspend its operations.
>
> A meeting of the shareholders will be held tomorrow to take into consideration the course to be adopted with reference to the liquidation of its obligations.
>
> Meantime, craving your forbearance, I remain Sir,
>> Your Most Obedient Servant,
>> H. H. Withers, Manager
>> Liverpool, October 22, 1867

This gave us the deepest concern, and we all, Preston, Penrose, Miner and I talked of it, and of the uncertainty of all human institutions, and of the growing uncertainty thereof. I examined myself to know if I had been, or could have by any means the means of it, or why, if the disaster must occur, I was not warned of it in some way; and spent much of the night meditating on it. Although it seemed threatening news with £2178-9-6 of the Church and individual monies in it still,[3] I could not feel that consternation of mind which I expected to feel, neither could either of the Brethren feel so. I drafted letter to President

---

3. In the United Kingdom, for centuries before decimalization on February 15, 1971, monetary values were written in pounds, shillings, and pence.

Young giving the facts so far as I was in possession of them. I first opened the account with the Royal Bank of Liverpool in 1850 or 1851 and the Church as seen fit to continue it with them ever since. Up to last week its credit was so good that persons suspecting that other banks did in some instances close their accounts and transferred them to the "Royal Bank". How can any one not intimately connected with their operations know which or whether any of them are safe, even the shareholders were as "taken aback" as I. O, Lord, help me wisely to do whatever I may do to recover these funds and secure them to the proper owners.

Tuesday December 10 At Birmingham, stopped and dined and went to Liverpool. Found a pile of letters awaiting my attention, among others one from Brother Karl G. Mazer, informing me of his very interesting visit to Dresden, seeing Br. Martin whom I baptized in October 1855 when I baptized Mazer and Schonfeld. I thank that Lord that he has presented the spark of truth, which I was enabled to kindle there, and I hope the same may yet prove life unto life to many.

Wednesday December 18 Samuel Longbottom and Frederick Hansen called to see me. They are known as Josephites, the former on a mission to this country; the latter to Denmark. They have with them copies of, as they say, the new translation of the Old and New Testament Scriptures as rendered by the Prophet Joseph Smith. Longbottom having 2 copies, I got one of them. Whether the book is the genuine translation or not, I felt it important to get one of them and see what it is.

Sunday December 29 Spent the morning studying the scriptures and comparing the old with the New Translation, which latter adds much to the plainness of their rendering in many places.

Sunday January 19, 1868 After evening meeting, Bro. John Davis, a Priest and John Teneday, an Elder, called on us in their capacity of Teachers, approaching their duty with considerable reluctance. I bade them feel free here as anywhere, which they endeavored to do and we spent a mutually profitable hour.

Sunday February 9 News from the States anything and everything but encouraging for reunion of North and South.

Tuesday March 24 Found C[eleste] R[oberts], a young sister of 17 years waiting to see me, to narrate the case of her father's family and to see if anything can be done to secure their emigration. Her parents were baptized twenty-two years ago, and her father was a very faithful Elder—baptized scores, perhaps hundreds into the Church—was for years a presiding Elder of Ki . . . Branch—but when in Br. _____'s administration, often spoken of here as the reign of terror, he made tithing a test of fellowship. Br. Roberts being so very poor he could scarcely support his family, considered he had no tithing to pay and was cut off. They have lived at Waterloo, no meetings, and lately have moved into town and the children by the influence of the mother are going to meetings. Celeste has quite lately been baptized & helps her mother to keep the fire of the Spirit alive and their faith from dying out. It seemed to arouse my whole nature to listen to her story of their trials, and the feeling came over me that her Father must be reclaimed and they all go to Zion together as a family of Saints. O Lord, help me to effect it in the manner of Jesus. I humbly pray thee, that Bro. Roberts may be saved and realize a reward for all his former diligence.

Saturday March 28 P. R., husband and father of the sisters that called on Thursday came in and renewed his acquaintance with me. He has been in the Church, was baptized 23 years ago & has baptized many into the Church, but was cut off by _____ for not paying what he thought was sufficient tithing. He came very humbly into my presence & feelingly acknowledged his unworthy course, received my instructions with gladness and before leaving set next Tuesday to be re-baptized with three others of his family. He seemed to go away relieved & happier. I felt that he was the one of the 100 that wandered from the fold & that there is joy in heaven over his return more than over the 99 that went not astray.

Sunday April 5 How blessed I am to have received the Holy Apostleship, only 3rd person from Peter, James and John. What marvelous truth—that they conferred it on those who conferred it on Brigham & Heber and they conferred it on me.

October Conference [1868] Bro. Brigham Young Jr. was set apart to the Council of the Twelve, G. A. Smith, 1st Counselor to the President and this was the first time that the 12 Apostles and the First Presidency have met together for 32 years in their entirety. The last meeting previous was held at the house of Heber C. Kimball in Kirtland. Pres. Brigham Young prayed with us and we had much pleasant conversation.

October 9th Met with Council of 50, where near $70,000 was subscribed as capital for Mercantile Cooperative Institution.

October 24th We had the Constitution ready and presented it to the School of the Prophets where it passed without loss of a single section.

26th November I had also a very liberal flow of the Spirit in delivering two discourses to a well-filled house at Farmington. I also find that the Mill is stopped and sadly out of repairs.

Sunday January 10, 1869 Attended meetings at Tabernacle and at Council prayers it was decided that I be appointed to go and live at Ogden; take charge of and preside over that Stake of Zion & be elected Judge of Weber County and that B. Y. Jr. be Mayor of Ogden City.

Saturday February 20 This morning received official notice of my election by the Legislature to the Office of Probate Judge for Weber County.

Monday February 22 Pres. Loren Farr invited me to stop with him till I could provide a home, in welcoming also to ride to Ogden with him. W. R. Smith, S. W. Richards and Joseph Woodmansee signed my bonds as security. I got my certificate, & on application to the Hon. Higgins obtained a Commission as Judge of Probate for Weber County.

Friday April 30 Called at Farmington on way and saw and kissed the children and their mothers, and arrived home at 12 night. Found Franklin sick in bed.

Saturday May 8 Evening met with City Council and was elected one of 4 Committee to go to the Promontory on Monday next at connecting the rails and driving the last spike.

Monday May 10 Went as delegate with L. Farr, C. W. and J. B. H. Stenhouse to Promontory, Summit Co. to attend the ceremony of laying the last tie and rails connecting the U.P. [Union Pacific] and C.P. [Central Pacific] Rail Roads into one. Appointed and authorized by the City Council of Ogden. I was and we were cordially entertained by Gov. Stanford and his Friends of the C.P.R. but the men of the U.P.R. scarcely noticed us. I handled the Golden Spike that was struck twice with the silver hammer by Gov. Leland Stanford, and which two blows discharged the guns in San Francisco and Chicago.

Monday August 2 Walked a mile and voted the ticket for Deseret and Utah. Myself Rep. For General Assembly & for Terr. Legislature; my son F. S. R. for County Recorder. Dr. Ezra Williams called and vaccinated Emily, Josephine, William H. Jenne, Lorenzo & Charles for Kine Pox.

Wednesday October 6 Attended Conference in the New Tabernacle morning and evening.

Friday October 8 At Conference all day. P.M. spoke about 20 minutes & found it very laborious to speak in such a tone of voice as to make myself heard by the immense audience which filled the house. At 7 p.m. assisted the Twelve & First Presidency to set apart the 160–170 Elders who have been called to go on Missions.

Thursday March 24, 1870 Wrote some on report of Pres. W. Richards Estate. Franklin very sick, diphtheria.

Sunday Jun 5 After deliberation and prayer, it was decided that Jane would feel better to stop and take care of our dear little Grandson. In all my travels to preach in the Territory I have never been able to take her with me since 1853 when we went to Iron County together.

Monday Jun 20 Pres. Young gave me a suggestion about my public speaking. Wished me to become an Orator as I should have to stand before the great ones of the earth.

Wednesday Jun 22 Franklin Young called on me about genealogy and how to get up the Young' Family.

Monday July 25 It still seems as if the Bishop and Pres. Farr were heedless of quarantining the Small Pox. At 2 p.m. attended the City Council and pushed the work of quarantine as far as possible, while all seemed determined to do as little as possible in that direction. I went with L. Farr to the grove selected for quarantine—a beautiful place and comfortable in a shady box elder grove, 1¼ mile East of Ogden City.

Saturday August 20 Spent most of this week in helping F. S. R. execute deeds for N. Ogden town site and in getting out lists of names for genealogy of kindred for baptism for dead.

Wednesday December 21 Spent the morning reading Abbott's Life of Christ. P.M. called on father Stickney who is failing and not expected to live long with us. His wife presented me of a copy of the first edition of the Book of Mormon, which I prize highly. Paid bill for 4 kegs of nails, $31.71 at Co-op.

Friday December 30–Saturday December 31 At home with Jane who was very sick, distressed and apparently dying, all day. At night Br. Thomas Wallace came and Sister Wallace also. After long struggling and oft repeated administrations, Jane seemed little or no better. Wallace and I went to separate places and had secret prayer. When we returned, I asked him if he felt any backing down from promises of life and health for Jane. He replied no. I told him, "nor I neither"; and we laid our hands on her head. He prayed &c., then I prayed, rebuked and prophesied, and she seemed better immediately. This was some two or three o'clock in the morning. Jane continued to feel better through the day and night and until Sunday, and still on Sunday—causing us great joy and gratitude to God. During the closing hours of the year 1870.

Wednesday February 8, 1871 Wrote W. B. Toune of Boston inquiring after some 8 or 10 works on Genealogical history. O Lord, help me to do a good work for the dead as well as for the living.

Thursday Jun 8 After Breakfast went to the Endowment House, where I saw and heard 682 Baptisms for our Dead. Father, Samuel, Levi Willard, Maria Adelaide and myself were baptized about 100 times each for Richards and Dewey Families. Closed soon after 5 p.m.

Monday December 25 At home today except to walk through the street and see the drunkenness, Blasphemy and fighting, the most and worst that I have ever seen on a Christmas day in Utah during all our stay in the Territory. Several arrests were made by the officers of the Peace. Dined at home on a fine fat goose with the portion of my family living with me and felt thankful.

Friday February 9, 1872 Was very busy in the Session from about 9 a.m. until after 4 p.m. Maintained an argument on an "Act Amending City Charters" against several members who opposed the right to tax for Education.

Thursday April 4 Was elected Speaker of the House of Representatives of the Legislature of the Proposed State of Deseret and entered upon the duties.

Saturday December 28 Examining records nearly all day with fair success. I am blessed in searching out genealogical matter and I hope to help many to a knowledge of their Father and Mother that they may be baptized, confirmed and do other works for their redemption.

Wednesday February 12, 1873 Spent the day in copying-transcribing names of Richards Race and Genealogy to go into my new Family Record which Deseret News Office is getting for our Family.

Sunday May 4 A.M. listened to an excellent discourse of Pres. B. Young. P.M. attended meeting and attended Council of 12 and Presidency. Father, Uncle Levi and others were designated to be ordained Patriarchs.

Tuesday May 27 Morning in the office. P.M. attended with my family the N. York and N. Orleans Menagerie and Circus who perform this p.m. and evening. Saw a man handle a sea serpent 21–2 feet long and a woman handle and put around her neck two African Boa Constrictors 8 feet long each; saw a man go in and discipline two lions and a leopard quite severely and come out unhurt; beside equestrian performers, acrobats and canines.

Saturday July 19 Attended Priesthood meeting. Heard reports and spoke quite spiritedly about the increase of

Free-Loveism and of Licentiousness generally among us—seductions and abortions increasing, &c.

Wednesday September 10 This was a week of great anxiety to me about Brother Samuel's business relations with the President & his liability to be cut off from the Church; also how to close the probate business of the Estate of my late Uncle Willard Richards.

Wednesday February 4, 1874 Went and staid with Karl G. Maeser who I baptized 19 years ago in Dresden, Saxony.

Friday February 13 This evening I went with Joseph F. Smith and about a dozen other members of the Legislature and took supper with Samuel H. B. Smith and with Sister Warren Smith and her son Willard, who were at Haun's Mill massacre when my Brother George Spencer Richards was killed with some 16 others and buried in the well—to me a very interesting visit.

Wednesday March 18 Worked awhile at the genealogy of Hinckley and read, rested, and took it easier. Health poor and threatening, stormy, snowy day. Did not attend prayer circle. At evening Sister E. R. Snow and Zina Young arrived and attended meeting with the young people at City Hall and I did not feel able to attend.

Saturday May 2 This a.m. Pres. D. H. Wells and Geo. B. Wallace arrived by first train. 2 Days Meeting. Our first instruction publicly in the United Order and Pres. Wells gave us a rare excellent discourse this forenoon. Tabernacle was <u>full of men only</u> all day.

Sunday May 24 Went by U.N.R.R. to Willard City where I met Pres. Lorenzo and Erastus Snow and met with the people of that place in two meetings in which the United Order was presented; generally received and the place organized. Br. Erastus goes on with Br. Lorenzo to help him organize Box Elder and part of Cache County.

Friday August 14 Today Br. William Sawyer commenced to record the names of those for whom we have been baptized into our Family record book of Baptism for the Dead—Richards Family. I spent the day starting this work of recording and waiting on such as called on official business—feeling thankful to see it commenced and anxious to have it so done that it can be approved and accepted by the family and by all concerned. Commenced to Record Baptisms for the Dead in the Family Record Book.

Friday September 11 Spent most of today on Hinckley genealogy and nearly completed it.

Wednesday October 21 Completed compiling the lists of between 900 and a thousand names for Baptism for the Dead.

Thursday November 12 Deseret News says Bro. George Q. Cannon was today arrested and admitted to bail $5000 on an indictment for polygamy.

Tuesday January 5, 1875 While lighting the fire was called to go and administer to Bro. Augustus Bartlett. He seemed to be dying, but continued till midday. Pres. Jas. Parry called by request and I directed selections of young folks from his District for their Endowments. Father David Nelson called about Mother Griffin's death. Br. Wilson called about his orphan grandchildren and homes being found for them. Pres. F. A. Hammond asked counsel about sheep herding and cheese factory. Br. Lorin Farr called and talked over about arrangements of Junction grounds and starting a shovel and spade factory.

Friday January 15 Hunted up several Church works for my bookcase, viz., "Evening and Morning Star" and "Messenger and Advocate" &c. Found a scrap of Revelation from Prophet Joseph where that Lehi and his family started from and landed in Chile about 30 degrees So. Latitude.

Saturday January 30 Called at Deseret News Office and then to Heber John's and Willard's where I had a very satisfying chat with them and Willard as Attorney of Record, consented to the settlement of the business of the estate on the first fair terms that we have talked of.

Wednesday February 17 Today closed the administration of my Uncle Willard's Estate—almost 21 years since his death, and near 18 years since I was appointed to the responsibility.

Sunday February 28 After the rest getting to bed, Jane and I spent till nearly one o'clock in the parlor talking over the hardships and trials of life.

Thursday March 11 Went to City and found that the President was before the Court for contempt and was hearing a motion of appeal argued; but which the judge J. B. McKean would not notice and ordered Pres. B. Young to prison 1 day and $25 fine for contempt. I rode out to prison with him in Bro James Townsend's carriage and staying an hour or more. Some 200 Brethren in arms camped in the school house near the Penitentiary.

Saturday March 13 Went to President's Office and in presence of Geo. A. Smith, B. Young Jr., A. Carrington, spoke to me about the late Ogden City Election blaming me severely for not getting Louis Farr elected. Then, about the business of my Uncle Willard's Estate, particularly about the lot on which the boys live in City. Then, about the distressing affair of the Hand Cart Companies, and wound up by saying that he was not angry and asked me to have dinner with him, which having just eaten, I declined. At close, he said "Franklin, you know the truth and you do it".

Monday March 22 While at supper received a telegram from Robert Campbell that Sister Ann Dalby Richards, my wife, was dead and funeral to be tomorrow at 2 p.m.

Wednesday April 7 Arose at 7:30 a.m. and went directly to Elder Woodruff's where I was received cordially. Had much chat about the genealogy of our kindred &c. Took Breakfast there and went with him to Conference.

Sunday May 23 Listened to Elder Erastus Snow who spoke in Ogden Tabernacle 1 hour and 1 minute—all very interesting but rather lengthy.

Friday Jun 25 Manti. spent forenoon in looking about with the President to view the situation around for a spot to build a Temple on the Temple block and on Quarry Hill.

Thursday July 8 Spent the morning in a very interesting visit with Pres. Geo. Q. Cannon and Bp. Herrick on the commencement of our work of reform and re-baptism in Weber Stake of Zion to commence with our Priesthood Meeting next Saturday when some of the Twelve will attend.

Wednesday July 21 I read the 14 Rules of the U[nited] Order and each agreed to adopt the same and I baptized in the Weber River my wife Jane S. Richards, Joseph A. West, Josephine West, Lorenzo M. R., Kate Frough, Charles C. Richards, Clarissa Jane Marsh and Mary Ann Marsh "for the remission of their sins, the renewal of their covenants and the observance of the 14 Rules read in their hearing."

Friday October 1, 1875 After a visit to the Woolen Factory, went on to Cove Creek Fort, kept by Brother Ira Hinckley. Here we were made very comfortable.

Thursday November 25 Went to depot and saw our delegate Geo Q. Cannon off for Washington. Attended meeting at 11 a.m.

in Ogden Tabernacle and <u>delivered the first Thanksgiving Sermon at the First Celebration of that National Holiday in Ogden</u>.

Friday January 28, 1876 Went to City with Bro. Herrick, Thomson and also with Br. Penrose. Called on the President at 2 p.m. to talk over about the last municipal election of Ogden. But he did not wish to hear much and stopped each of us. He blamed all[,] but I being the Presiding Officer of the Stake he censured me the most severely.

Sunday April 30 Preached in the Ogden Tabernacle, subject: the Temple, with peculiar interest and power of the Spirit. This morning I set apart Elders Oluf Hansen and David W. Davis to missions in Europe, taking their genealogies for Historian's Office.

Monday Jun 5 Went by first train and with my sons at Farmington George F. Richards and Ezra went to City. They received their endowments. I attended with them.

Saturday October 7 Attended Conference and Convention. 12 met in Council at President's Office to see if endowment shall be discontinued in Endowment House when the Presidency goes South to dedicate Temple.

Thursday November 9 My left eye is so bad that that I can do but little—get and read the newspapers reports of the election returns. The presence of Small Pox is such that one feels as if he were in the valley of death—its shadows surrounding.

Thursday November 16 How sad, gloomy and sorrowful this dreadful scourge makes all to feel, as we walk the streets of Ogden it seems like the Valley of Death.

Sunday November 26 Still prevented public meetings. I held meeting in my house of my family in Ogden, and organized into a United Order arrangement and felt much blessed in setting my house in order so far. All eat together at 7:30, at 12:30 and at 5:30 or 6 p.m. and prayers at 7:20 and 6:30.

Friday December 22 City Council raises the quarantine restrictions on Public Assemblies, but it is presumptuous to hold meetings, parties or any kind of assemblages.

Wednesday December 27 Returned by first train to Ogden in a snowstorm with my son F. S. R. Summit County Rail Road sold to U.P.R.R. which kills all spirit in Saints to build more Rail Roads.

Monday January 1, 1877 New Years day of 1877. At home all day, read some, meditated much and with a grateful heart for mercies past and present, contemplated the onerous condition of the human family—American and European Countries and the very threatening prospects of a great national war or a state of anarchy unless God interpose to prevent. A time of suffering and judgment as promised and signs of times portend its approach. The condition of the Church is very significant and highly suggestive in studying our condition before God and the Angels.

January 2, 1877 Saint George. The basement and lower story of the Temple were dedicated yesterday at one p.m. Elder Wilford Woodruff offered up the dedicatory prayer of the font room and basement, Elder Erastus Snow of first main room, and Elder Brigham Young, Jr., of the sealing rooms. President B. Young spoke about twenty-five minutes with great power and effect. Two hundred and thirty persons were present, among them most of the bishops and presiding elders from the neighboring settlements. Correction—by an error in the copy of a dispatch published yesterday, from St. George, it was stated that 230 persons were present at the dedicatory services of certain portions of the Temple. It should have read 1,230.

Saturday February 10 A.M. Wrote several notes to enquirers about their genealogy.

Thursday February 15 Went to City, arriving about 7:30 a.m. Dr. Groves examined a defective tooth. Cleared it out and filled it with a paste which caused severe pain till while at Elder John Taylor's the blessing of God delivered me.

Friday March 30 Went to St. George. As we came in sight of the Temple it appeared majestically grand—its whiteness seemed so chaste and pure. Arriving in town Pres. John Young conducted us to the Temple where his Father, the President, received us all and took us up into the main court where we heard the instructions lecture and as the people came through we saw many acquaintances.

Wednesday April 4 Attended the two days meeting in the St. George Temple and occupied a seat in the pulpit at the East End occupied by the Presidency of the High Priests Quorum in that Stake of Zion. Joseph F. Smith sat in the same desk, also Charles C. Rich. B. Young, Jr., occupied part of time a chair in the aisle.

Friday April 6, 1877 Conference opened. I attended and occupied the same seat each day. Several missionaries were called, among others, Franklin S. Richards to go to Europe.

Thursday May 17 Went with the Company on to the bench and saw the spot determined upon for a site for the Logan Temple.

Friday May 18 The weather not having turned cold. The snow soon went off and just before Noon a Brother took us in his wagon (Lorenzo Snow, Joseph Young and myself) up to the South East corner of the Temple Spot where each of the Twelve present (after Pres's John W. Young and Daniel H. Wells) threw out a few shovels full of dirt. The Pres. B. Young Sen[ior] remained in the

Buggy. At Meridian, 12 M [noon] Elder Orson Pratt proceeded to offer up the Dedication prayer, after which President Young made an address to those assembled. Sitting in his Buggy, in which he gave the people till 3 years from next October in which to complete the building of the Temple for Dedication.

Saturday May 26 At 9 I received the President and company, who, with John W., Geo. Q. Cannon, Geo. F. Gibbs, Bathsheba Smith and Zina Williams and son put up with us. The President seemed to feel happy all over inside and out—was very humorous in his discourses, which was of a high order of sentiment.

Sunday Jun 17 Went to Farmington where we met Pres. B. Young, J. Taylor, E. Snow and G. Q. Cannon there to reorganize the stake of Zion for Davis County, and assisted to ordain the Presidency of Stake. President Young narrated the finding and losing a chest of treasures and the circumstances attending the return of plates to Moroni in a cave in the mountain where quantities of records were seen. Laban's sword and other matters. The sword taken from the wall and laid on the plates unsheathed and the saying that it should not again be sheathed until the Kingdoms of this world have become the Kingdom of our God and His Christ. I staid at Farmington, at Nanny's.

Wednesday, August 29 This morning went up to the President's bedside—and between 9 and 10 was sitting with my hands on his head. John W. Young requested Bishop Elijah F. Sheets to anoint and me to seal the anointing with several others, which we did. At the close he said, "Amen" as distinctly as either of us, and added "that's all right," and seemed to breathe easier—the last I heard him speak. Immediately after John W. Young requested I meet with the President's family and household in the large parlor of the Lion House and held Family Prayer with them. Several prayed besides myself.

Tuesday, September 4 Went by the 5 a.m. train to the City. Met with 9 of the 12 and with counselors John W. Young and Daniel H. Wells at 10 a.m. in the Endowment House, a comfortable and retired place. Came to an understanding on the question of responsibility and authority to guide the Church. It was determined and settled to devolve upon the Twelve, the 2 counselors assisting. John Taylor was sustained as President of the Twelve and Council.

Thursday, September 6 Was appointed today chairman of committee on preparing the new [e]ddition of the Pearl of Great Price for the press. Richards, Cannon, Young, and Carrington were said committee.

Wednesday, September 12 With the rest of the counsel I called on General Thomas L. Kane and felt blessed in my interview with him. He thanked me for my expressions to him and seemed pleased and gratified therefore. In Council I reported my labors on Pearl of Great Price which was accepted.

Monday, September 17 At 7 a.m., all hands left by a Special train for Logan where we arrived in good time to form in procession for the laying of the Corner Stones at 12 noon. I assisted to lay and then prayed on the Southeast cornerstone of this Temple.

Wednesday, October 3 Council decided to revive the Perpetual Emigration Fund Company operations and present the importance of its operations to the Conference and propose a collection of its outstanding dues. Orson Pratt spoke of his position and change of position in the Quorum and declared himself satisfied. Council elected Elder John Taylor, Trustee in Trust with the Twelve and 2 counselors.

Sunday, October 21 At 9 rode out with Pres. John Taylor and viewed a piece of land at the Schoolhouse in the Lane for University site for Weber County.

Wednesday, October 24 This p.m. the Council approved the Trustees conclusion to donate 5.2 acres of land in Ogden for University purposes.

Tuesday, October 30 I attended meeting of the Relief Societies of Weber Stake in Tabernacle. The society's report that over $10,000 passed through their hands, and that they have on hand over 500 bushels of wheat.

Sunday, November 11 To Coalville for conference. I spoke an hour and a quarter or so on tithing, honesty in all things, Perpetual Emigration Fund interests for gathering the poor; intemperance and the introduction of saloons into our towns and settlements execrating those who do it. Also dwelt upon the opening of Endowments sufficient for Sealing, and etc. Joseph F. Smith said he never heard me speak with so much of the Spirit before.

Saturday, December 15 Charley and I viewed the Temple and new Tabernacle and went into their walls and through the architects and stone cutters shops—returning by late train.

Tuesday, December 25 This being Christmas Day, I spent it at home in quiet with my family. The threatening weather arouses my ill feelings and I must stay in—meditating, writing, reading, feeling thankful for the many favorable changes that have occurred since last x-mas and especially that before departure of Pres. Brigham Young, he came to know how he was mistaken in his apprehensions and suspicions about me and affairs in Ogden and Weber.

Friday, December 28 Went to Farmington and spent the day with my Uncle Willard's family.[4] Nanny who has been in bed 3 weeks past, and is gradually mending. Rhoda was very sick day

4. Franklin's plural wives who had been sealed to Willard.

before yesterday, but better today. I visited with them and dined with Mary and her children.

Tuesday, January 8 [1878] Spent most of this snowy day in studying the Revelations and making notes of the same on various of subjects. I thank thee, oh Lord, for the light granted me in the study of Thy Holy word. Do thou grant me the Spirit in the power of the Holy Apostleship that I may by the Holy Ghost feed and edify Thy Saints with the Bread of Life in all my public ministrations.

Sunday, January 20 On account of the presence of smallpox in Ogden, no conference yesterday nor today. We held meeting in our house. This Branch of my family being all present—I gave instruction, prayed and effected arrangement with all the children to arise at a given signal in the morning, have our prayers and breakfast with more method and regularity.

Thursday, January 24 Met with President Taylor, Auditing Committee and Brother Briggy Young.

Wednesday, February 13 At President's office, spoke and heard <u>10 rods</u> in the Telephone, separated by partitions into other apartments. How wonderful the discoveries that are being made—some have heard <u>sweet music 70 miles by this invention</u>.

Tuesday, February 19 Last night I received a very convincing manifestation of the condition of children after their death and after Resurrection. How good the Lord has been to strengthen my Faith and to instruct me in many points of Doctrine.

Thursday, March 21 Cousin Stephen L. Richards came in, first time I have seen him since his return.

Wednesday, March 27 By vote of Council was instructed to present and make application to Logan City Council to purchase the Temple Block.

Thursday, April 4 Fast Day. I expressed my uneasiness that we had no safe that we could occupy with effects of the present Trustee in Trust. President Taylor concluded to order a safe for Deeds and Records. The church has 3 safes but all are occupied and filled.

Monday, April 22 President John Taylor, Wilford Woodruff, Orson Pratt, Lorenzo Snow, E. Snow, FDR, Brigham Young Jr., Joseph F. Smith and LJ Nuttall considered the subject of best mode of preserving Church property from Escheating to United States under the active July 2, 1862, when the forms of deeds and declaration which we have received from general Thomas L. Kane through George Q. Cannon and Brigham Young were adopted.

Tuesday, April 23 For $10,000 President John Taylor conveyed to Angus M. Cannon and he to Orson Pratt, that Deseret Publishing Property, paper mills, printing office. Also for $19,000, the social hall and museum to L. W. Hardy and he to John Henry Smith.

Saturday, June 1, 1878 I weighed 168 pounds on scales in Brother Layton's store.

Sunday, June 23 The distraction of the people has led to raising of several vexed questions which by the aid of the Holy Spirit I was enabled to answer clearly to the understanding of all the Elders present and the congregation as well.

Friday, July 12 Also wrote Little, Brown and Co., inquiring after other scarce Genealogical works for the Church. Made some examinations of Genealogical items for others.

Wednesday, July 24 31 years ago the God of Israel Brought his Exiled People to these vallies where he has given us liberty and power to make homes to ourselves and families and here to gather and garner the Saints, and build up His Church on the earth.

Wednesday, July 31 Council at 2 p.m. I reported on the impracticability of issuing Tything Currency as the Internal Revenue is 10 p.c. [percent] on all issued or re-issued which is unbearable. The ZCMI is calling in its issue, also the United Order of Brigham City.

Friday, August 9 A file of N.E.H. and G. Registers arrived from Lowell, Mass. yesterday. I opened them last night. The commencement of Genealogical Library for the Church. Spent some time with Franklin arranging.

Friday, October 4 This afternoon while Pres. Taylor visited the Fair, I had a cast taken of my mouth so as to have some teeth fitted to my gums.

Thursday, October 10 This morning between 4 and 5 o'clock. I dreamed of and saw Uncle Willard come into my room, I being in bed and quite ill (as was really the case). As I saw him entering, I raised up and told him that I had been thinking of him for an hour or more and had been over to the other house (where his family was) to see if they had heard from him. He kneeled on the bed by my side and putting his arms around me hugged me to him with much apparent affection. I was so interested that it awoke me, and it was a dream. He had on the same overcoat with a fur collar on it. I have seen him wear it often.

Sunday, November 3 Superintendent to Charles O. Card applied for counsel about and engine for to hoist material on Temple. It was favorably considered and action deferred for President. To October 1, 1878, contributed by Cache Stake, $58,578.99; Bear Lake stake $21,242.95; Box Elder stake, $14,449.04; other donors, $27.61. Total equals $94,298.59.

Thursday, November 14 Pres. Taylor and I set apart and blessed Hon. Geo. Q. Cannon for his Congressional mission.

Saturday, November 16 Jane has the diphtheria unmistakably. We use bacon, mustard and gargle often with chlorate of potash and swab the back of and about the palate and tonsils with the nitrate of silver.

Saturday, November 23 Dr. Heber John Richards says Elder O. Hyde's difficulty is in depositing too much fat which retards the circulation and induces dropsy—that if he had him in control, he would reduce him about 40 lbs and make quite a man of him yet.

Wednesday, December 25 This morning I made an address to our little Grandchildren explaining why it was Christmas— what made it so—and enjoining certain observances upon them till another Christmas, when they marched in to see the illuminated tree while Charles served as Santa Claus Agent to distribute the Presents.

Tuesday, January 21, 1879 Evening at Eliza R. Snow's surprise party in Lion House with about 100 others. Jane and I dined with Eliza and Pres. Taylor and others.

Tuesday, February 18 Sister E. R. Snow and Jane organized the Young Ladies and Primary[5] of the 3rd Ward and today the same in 4th Ward.

Thursday, April 3 Heard Delegate Cannon report affairs at Washington. Democrats wish Utah to renounce Polygamy and come into the Union.

Monday, April 14 Put in box in So. East Cornerstone [Manti Temple] with the books, papers and coins. At Temple Hill with 9 of the 12 helped and after laying Corner Stones, spoke shortly.

Wednesday, May 7 Council appropriated 100 beef cattle, 1000 bu wheat and perhaps $1000 for the Logan Temple. Am exceedingly weary tonight.

Monday, June 16 at the Depot bade Br. Reynolds adieu for

---

5. The organizations for children and young women were under the direction of the Relief Society.

a time for the Gospel's sake—he goes to State Prison at Lincoln Nebraska. Pres. agreed with Richards and Williams to do legal business $1000 each per year and expenses.

Saturday, June 28 Franklin came down this a.m. Read and compared Dr. Bernhisel's copy of the Prophet Joseph's New Translation of the Scriptures and put it into Daniel, the copyist's, hands to make a clean and complete copy. He did about 10 foolscap pages today.

Sunday, July 6 Baptized Charley Wang who lives with Lorenzo and confirmed him. The first known Chinaman baptized.

Wednesday, July 9 We learn that warrants are out for Trustee and Executors.

Sunday, July 20 Joseph F. Smith gave us the thunders of the Lord for our slackness in duty, Sabbath breaking, Sunday bathing trains, mortgaging our property and homes.

Friday, July 25 All appears as if the wicked were given power over the Saints again and old time persecution were being renewed.

Thursday, July 31 Imprisonment for Contempt deferred till tomorrow. Joseph Standing's corpse arrived.

Friday, August 1, 1879 The wealthiest Brethren in the City offered themselves for bonds to keep Trustee and Executors out of Prison. But, they being sent for, went to Court. The Apostles all went. Trustees counsel got the liabilities reduced from $161,000 to $99,000 and odd. Commitment amended and filed. Trustee is impressed to give the promised bond or go to prison. Rudger Clawson detailed the assassination of Joseph Standing.

Thursday, August 14 Called a few minutes at the Penitentiary and greeted Executors Cannon, Young and Carrington, also Br. George Reynolds.

Tuesday, August 26 This forenoon Joseph F. Smith and I compared Copy of manuscripts obtained of Dr. J. M. Bernhisel through Dr. Sharp, Dentist, purporting to be a Copy of Joseph Smith's corrections and revision of the Bible—Old and New Testaments—which he obtained of Emma Smith after Joseph and Hiram [were] assassinated, about 1844 or 5 and which Bible accompanying properly marked constitutes the "New Translation".

Saturday, September 6 Met with 10 of the 12. BY and WW absent. Had very interesting time speaking around upon the duties of Bishops and the powers of their calling and office; also attending to appointment of a First Presidency as altogether uncalled for and unbefitting the present feeling and condition of the Church. The 12 ought first obtain a full unity with each other and people first.

Wednesday, September 10 Dreamed seeing Pres. B. Young. He requested me to see to Genealogy. Pres. Young urged by attention to Genealogy.

Tuesday, September 30 Yesterday Rudger Clawson called and was blessed to go to Georgia and testify in the case of Murder of Elder Joseph Standing.

Thursday, October 9 I got off early and by 3:40 went to Ogden. At home with Jane and the family. How good it seems and I give thanks to my Heavenly Father.

Sunday, November 30 I occupied the afternoon in speaking on learning and listening to the voice of the Spirit. Isaiah 30:21 "The voice at thy back saying this is the way, walk ye in it, when ye turn to the right hand, and when ye turn to the left."

Saturday, January 3, 1880 I derive great satisfaction from a careful study of the Laws of God to man in every age so far as can search out from all History, sacred and profane. The Law of God through Moses to Israel anciently I find to be rich and replete with excellence for them in their day even to the withholding of the Covenant of Priesthood from the 2nd Tables of Stone on which the Lord repeated his Law to His people.

Wednesday, January 14 Attended Council of 12 about a loan of $2000 to help complete the Assembly Hall—granted. Went to Assembly Hall. Met architect, committee, and painters about the finishing work and painting.

Tuesday, January 20 Pres. Lorenzo Snow called at the Office and consulted with Pres. Taylor and myself about expediency of passing the Women's Rights Bill—now on the table of the House. At Pres. Taylor's request went to Legislative Hall and requested Br. Penrose not to call up that Bill today.

Sunday, February 1, 1880 I spoke 55 minutes—Temple building by Tything only free will offerings; warned them against special doctrinal hobbies.

Thursday, February 5 Hubert Bancroft of San Francisco has written invitation for Professor Orson Pratt to visit and make his house a home while on the History of Utah, with him in California. This seems an opportunity to put ourselves right on the page of History before the world.

Friday, February 6 Dr. Carnahan pronounces our apprehensions true that Willard has Scarlet Fever and Diphtheria.

Tuesday, February 10 . . . Willard was worse. I found him suffering terribly in his head and at once anointed his head copiously and prayed with Faith. He became immediately quiet and spoke. Eyes looked brighter but with difficulty got accumulations out of his throat or swallowed anything. I carried him about and we did all we could to alleviate his sufferings and watched his pulse wax and wane. They held out to an extraordinary extent until 3 to 5 minutes past 12 noon he drew his last breaths and rested in death. We all gave up to an overflow of tears, although we all wished him released from his sufferings.

Sunday, February 15 I talked with my sons about the importance of attending meeting of Quorum and Sunday punctually. They see and feel the importance of it.

Monday, February 16 Pres. Taylor handed me letter and Revelation from Elder W. Woodruff in which he says "The Lord met me in the wilderness and communed with me. It was on the night of January 26, 1880 in a shepherd's tent" and he sent the Revelation, which I read. His letter was dated January 26, 1880.

Sunday, February 22 Bro. Moses Thatcher who arrived in the City yesterday presented the scheme of Mexican Government and Emilio Biebuyck for Emigration of Colonists into Mexico and colonization. Copy of contract read discussed.

Tuesday, March 2 After breakfast went to the office. Looked through stationery room where we found Records 2 & 3, Law of the Lord, Vol 1 had been found there a day or two since and in it we found that particulars were given of organization of 1st Relief Society on 17th March, 1842 in the Lodge Room, Nauvoo by Joseph and helped by Eld. John Taylor. Also, original manuscript of Book of Mormon was deposited by Joseph in Corner Stone of Nauvoo House when he laid it October 2, 1841.

Thursday, April 1, 1880 Considered call of Council of 50 and found about 30 names of members living and that about 20 have died since last sitting in the spring of 1869. Considered some names to fill the vacancies caused by death.

Sunday, April 4 The revelation received by Elder Woodruff January 26, 1880 was read and remarks were made by President Taylor, Woodruff, Snow, FD Richards, C. C. Rich and voted to receive the Revelation as the Word of the Lord to us.

Tuesday, April 6 Pres. Taylor presented his views about

appropriating relief for the poor through Church direct, through
P.E. [Perpetual Emigration] Fund, through transfer of wheat by
Relief Society and by various other means.

Wednesday, April 7 This day the large Tabernacle was filled
and the hearts of the people were made to rejoice by the Relief
offered the poor from the PE fund. The Church, the Relief
Societies and the other means offered for relief of the poor and
distressed—by forgiving of debts, distribution of cows and sheep
and wheat. These transactions thrilled the people with gladness,
thanksgiving and praise.

Thursday, April 8 Pres. Taylor wishes each of the Twelve
present to speak and bear their testimony before the Conference.
At Conference at 10 and each spoke as reported, bearing their
testimony to the truth of the work of God on the earth in which
we are engaged.

Sunday, April 18 Read Circular of the Twelve Apostles on
remission of PE Fund in indebtedness—some $800,000; back
Tythings $75,000; Cows, sheep, loanings of wheat and general
liberality among the people each to all.

Sunday, May 9 Borrowed 5 cents of a lady and forgot to
hand it her again. This annoyed me. Have not her address and
know not how to make restitution.

Wednesday, May 12 Good night's rest. Breakfasted early and
all 5 of us took train for Palmyra where we put up at Palmyra
Hotel. Hired a livery team and went to "Cumorah", "Ramah";
then to Manchester and called on Dr. J. R. Pratt, M.D.—
Manchester, Ontario Co., N.Y. He told me he could put his hand
on the manuscripts which Martin Harris lost in an hour if it was
needed. Called on Chapman at the farm where Joseph saw God
and Jesus and the Visions of his Latter-day work.

Thursday, May 13 Jane and I rode out to Whitmer farm.

Whitmer place is about 3 miles from Waterloo and we paid $2.00 for the team and driver and were back before dark. The remembrance of what has transpired here is marvelously wonderful to contemplate.

Friday, May 28 We went on to Richmond. To grandparents graves and where I used to tend Saw Mill, Cider Mill, Shingle machine and distillery where I first read the Book of Mormon; near where I was baptized; where I was born and went to school and knew my earliest pleasures. Visited the burying ground. The house I was born in and Grandfather Dewey's are long since burned.

Monday, May 31 Visited interior of the White House. Felt no inclination to be presented to Mr. Hayes.

Thursday, June 3 Went to Florence and then with much difficulty found near about the spot where little daughter Wealthy Lovisa and Cousin Eliza Ann were buried. We placed a post near the spot of Wealthy and Eliza Ann's graves as could be determined.

Monday, June 7 Towards evening went with Franklin and Charles to driving Park and saw them practice on the Bi-Cycle.

Friday, June 18 Bancroft's answer to O. Pratts of the 10th inst. arrived which approves the method proposed to supply the material for "History of Utah". Elder Pratt is so very feeble he says I must go to San Francisco with the Book, Documents, etc., and give the oral information. Pres. Taylor approves.

Friday, July 9 Weather much cooler here. This morning presented my letter of introduction to Mr. Hubert H. Bancroft and had a lengthy pleasant conversation. I feel encouraged by his candor and fairness that he will give us a reasonably fair History. Returned to Hotel and went with Jane to Baldwin's Restaurant where we got our dinners for a much more reasonable price, making a good meal for 25 or 30 cents.

Monday, July 12 Mr. Bancroft took us directly to his house and offered us a room, which we accepted. Spent p.m. giving dictation, taken down in Phonography of myself and life labors.

Wednesday, July 14 This evening Mrs. Bancroft and Mrs. Victor interviewed Jane on the subject of Plurality of wives at Mr. Bancroft's. Jane did nobly.

Sunday, September 5 Soon the special from the East arrived with President RB Hayes and wife. Secretary Ramsey, General Sherman, and Sweet—4 cars in all, was presented to President Hayes by delegation George Q. Cannon and on our way to City he came and spent half-an-hour in chat with us.

Thursday, October 7 Statistical report was read by GQ Cannon giving total representation: Stakes in America 113,828 souls; European Mission 11,682 souls; all on Earth reported 127,451 souls.

Saturday, October 9 Council at 6 p.m., at which the 12, except E. Snow and B. Young who were absent came to a vote to organize the First Presidency and voted Pres. J. Taylor and he nominated GQ Cannon and JF Smith for his Counsellors. All carried unanimously.

Wednesday, October 27 Pres. Taylor gave the 2 candidates a very interesting and impressive charge when with all hands on his head Pres. Taylor ordained FM Lyman and in like manner W. Woodruff ordained JH Smith and set apart members of the Council of Apostles. Voted that Heber J. Grant be President of Tooele Stake.

Wednesday, January 19, 1881 Lorenzo Snow opened by prayer when Pres. Taylor presented in prayer the names of many who have been the persecutors, betrayers and murderers of the

Prophets and Saints in this dispensation and who now are laboring to deprive us of our rights as citizens before the law.

Sunday, January 23 Quarterly Conference. Pres. JF Smith followed about 15 minutes setting forth Government in this Stake of Zion and telling the Presidency of the Stake that I was the man for them; to seek Counsel and Advice of Br. FD Richards.

Friday, January 28 (   ) Tells brethren that Joseph F. Smith instructions last Sunday were incorrect—that I have no more right to advise here than any other of the Twelve, or than he has to go anywhere else and give Counsel.

Sunday, February 27 George continues at school in the City and is doing well in the Deseret University.

Wednesday, March 16 The determined vindictive spirit of two of the Nihilists who threw the 2 bombs that killed the Czar of Russia on Sunday indicates most clearly how deep seated is the spirit of rebellion, revolt and revolution in the hearts of the over-ruled, the oppressed.

Thursday, March 24 Bp. McQuarrie called about David McKay of Huntsville for Mission.

Wednesday, April 6 I will here say or state that I was voted accepted as one of the Twelve Apostles, As PE Fund Director, as one of the Auditing Committee and as Counselor to Trustee in Trust.

Monday, April 11 I had a painfully interesting and unpleasant visit with Jane on our relations with Charlotte[6] and her children. They have wounded her so deeply that it is difficult to overcome her feelings.

Thursday, April 14 Called on President's Office. Had a very pleasant conversation with him on the subject of Atonement[7] as

---

6. Charlotte, one of Franklin's plural wives, was disaffected and unhappy.

7. President John Taylor was writing his book *The Mediation and Atonement.*

decreed and wrought out by our Lord Jesus Christ. I found several scriptures for him, and he desired some books, which I have and intend to bring him next time I come.

Friday, April 22 Cooler and windy weather. I wrote GQC giving extract of a Revelation by Joseph of the course of Lehi to Chile in So. America.

Monday, May 9 Wrote HH Bancroft and completed a parcel of Books to him—gave him a good refutation of the Mountain Meadow Massacre—referring to "Utah and its people" by Hon. Geo. Q. Cannon.

Friday, June 3 At 2 p.m. was with First Presidency at closing Exercises of Deseret University and opened with Prayer. My son George F. Richards of Farmington received certificate of proficiency in English Language and Literature. Very interesting exercises where will these young people be next decade from now?

Thursday, June 9 I attended Quarterly Conference of the Relief Societies of Weber Stake in the Ogden Tabernacle at 10 a.m. I read account of first organization of Relief Society in March 17, 1842 &c, and made a few remarks about the societies and associations being the true legitimate remedy for our hoodlumism in our settlements.

Saturday, July 9 On way to Post fell in with Dr. Wm McIntyre who informed me that Br. Joseph Wm. Richards died at Pueblo of being poisoned with Ivy badly, that his case was let to run till it got into the blood and absorption into the system caused his death; . . . Joseph was a good honest boy and was highly esteemed and his death deeply lamented.

Tuesday, August 2 I wrote in my Record the account of number and duration of missions which I have performed, which shows that to October 1, 1868 I had been absent on distant missions 12 years less 14 days.

Saturday, September 17 Pres. Taylor informed me that he had an article on the Atonement of our Lord, Jesus Christ about ready to read to the Apostles, perhaps next week.

Monday, September 19 Bells toll. I went to Herald Office and learned that President Garfield died 10:30 or 10:35.

Saturday, September 24 This morning met with the Presidency and others of the 12—except Brother Lyman has gone home—and listened to remaining chapters of Pres. Taylor's Book on the Mediation and Atonement of our Lord Jesus Christ. Spent some time in conversation on that and correlative subjects—about 4 hours.

Monday, October 31 Fillmore to Meadow & Kanosh. Kanosh is very sick and are indulging in bestial drunkenness by liquor obtained from men professing to be Brethren.

Wednesday, November 9 At St. George. Spent the day with the Brethren of our Company in the Temple and listened to the instructions thereof. Only one Temple on Earth. 174 persons received ordinances, some for themselves but many for their dead. Much of the Holy Spirit dwells there and all the people of St. George feel it.

Wednesday, November 30 During this Journey we have traveled not less than 850 miles and I have delivered 32 discourses in public meetings; been blest with good health all the way and with an unusual measure of Spirit.

Tuesday, December 6 Went to Farmington. Joseph F. Smith and I laid hands on Nanny who is very ill. I spent afternoon visiting and instructing my son George.

Thursday, January 19, 1882 Wrote also Dr. JR Pratt, M.D. of Manchester, Ontario County, N.Y. asking for Town History of Manchester with Topographical map of same; also, offering to pay him for the sheets of manuscript got away from Martin Harris, "a little something."

Friday, February 10 An Article in DE News of 7th inst. induced me to obtain a Bottle of HH Warren's "Safe Kidney and Liver Cure." I find the testimonies of its efficacy are indeed marvelous. I am inclined to try it.

Wednesday, February 15 Voted that I get together material in vindication of Pres. B. Young and the Church against the charge of perpetrating the "Mountain Meadow Massacre."

Thursday, February 16 Spent much of the day getting up material about "Mountain Meadow Massacre." Br. E. Snow and Pres. Woodruff consent to make affidavits of what they know of Pres. B. Young's ignorance of the affair until after its accomplishment. Spent some time searching records.

Friday, February 17 The Edmunds Bill passed the Senate yesterday is all the talk yesterday. How much will the wicked be allowed to oppress us?

Chapter 6

FRANKLIN D. RICHARDS &
GEORGE F. RICHARDS

MARCH 1882 TO DECEMBER 1899

FDR **Thursday, March 9** About noon went to the Endowment House and sealed George Franklin Richards and Alice Almira Robinson at Altar.

GFR **March 9th 1882** Was married to Alice Robinson of Farmington. Rented two rooms of old Lady Thompson of the 16th Ward at $5.00/00 per month and moved in on the 9th inst.

FDR **Saturday, March 11** Enjoyed much of the Spirit of my calling in teaching the people doctrine and morality.

FDR **Wednesday, March 15** At 3 Council met again and status of our City Councils and County Courts considered. Voted best for Brethren in these being Polygamous to resign and place to be filled by other faithful men so as to retain controlling power against possible disabilities created by Edmunds Bill. Pres. instructed Franklin & I and we went to Ogden reconstructed the City Council and County Court leaving only Mayor and Judge polygamous because these bodies have not the power to fill by appointment—2 changes in Court; 6 in Council.

FDR **Thursday, March 23** Edmonds Bill. About 3:45 this afternoon it was announced to me that the Edmunds Bill had been signed by the President of the United States and so became a Law of the Land. Law to punish for Polygamy and to turn the Territory of Utah over into the control of our enemies.

FDR **Tuesday, April 18** At City. A pleasant day. While in bed read 5th of President Taylor's Book on Atonement. O that my soul might be enlarged to comprehend and to appreciate the nature and the power of the Atonement wrought out by our Lord Jesus Christ for the Redemption and Exaltation of my soul in His Church and Kingdom. Father in Heaven grant me thy Holy (Spirit) that I may. I ask it in the name of Jesus. Amen

FDR **Friday, May 12** Got water pipes in our home.

FDR **Sunday, May 21** My soul melts with gratitude to God for his kindness in giving me his Spirit in teaching the people and in opening up the visions of my mind on doctrinal subjects.

FDR **Wednesday, May 31** Pres. Taylor wishes me to notify Church attorneys to meet next Monday and deliberate on the Policy to pursue in our Election affairs as affected by the Edmunds Bill. Also, about How best to protect our public property from sequestration or confiscation by Government.

FDR **Thursday, June 1, 1882** About 5 p.m. called on my son Geo. F. Richards. Viewed the shop where he works. Spent 2 hours or so.

FDR **Saturday, June 3** 44 years ago today I was baptized by my father Phinehas in Markham's Creek in Richmond, Berkshire County, Mass.

FDR **Tuesday, July 4** We got along well with our work while Uncle Sam's hired men—the Governor EH Murray and others of his ilk were holding forth their special Eagleism in Liberty Park and many people forgetting the heat thought they were very happy in celebrating the glorious fourth with men who were ready to plunder of the last vestiges of our religious liberty.

FDR **Wednesday, August 9** At 3 p.m. met in Council with Taylor, Woodruff, Wells, B. Young and all felt to make the best legal resistance we can.

FDR **Sunday, August 13** If Gov. Murray and his clique

undertake to spring appointments of new officers upon us—or if commissioners arrive and undertake any new policy—I want all the business of our office in good shape.

FDR **Saturday, August 19** Got statement of Emigration completed of people from European Countries to America by our Church Agents at L[iver]pool and Copenhagen. Totals show that to the close of 1881 not less that 232 ships have brought out from those countries to American shores. Seventy three thousand and sixty six souls and never has there been a wreck of any one of them. 73066 souls.

FDR **Sunday, August 20** Talked with Franklin. He thinks I better be absent a few days.

FDR **Friday, September 15** All are wondering what will be the decision of the judges as [to] the validity of our women's suffrage law. Registration is going finely.

FDR **Monday, October 2, 1882** At 3 p.m. met Mr. Jas. N. Kimball and a pilot reporter at Court House when Mr Kimball presented his Commission from the Governor and requested very respectfully that I should turn over the Records, Files, &c, &c, belonging to the office of Probate Judge to him, which I as respectfully declined to do stating the I considered myself to be the legal incumbent until my successor should be elected and qualified.

FDR **Friday, October 6** FS and I went to the Office of the Bennett, Harkness and Co., Attorneys.[1] There Mr. Marshall Greenman served me with a writ of Mandamus—returnable on the 10th Inst in First District Court at Ogden, to show cause why the writ shall not be made peremptory and require me to

---

1. FS and, later, FSR are the initials of Franklin D. Richards's son Franklin S. Richards, an attorney.

turn over the Records, Files and property of the Office of Probate Judge of Weber County to Mr. James N. Kimball.

FDR **Tuesday, October 10** E Snow and M Thatcher were appointed to arrange for a refuge in Mexico and go via Colorado and advise them.

FDR **Thursday, October 26** . . . Also filling the vacancies in the various quorum of 70's & the true status of the "Seventy"—whose decision is equal to that of the 12 Apostles. Who are they?—and delivered the same to Pres. Taylor. On adieu the Presidency advised me to be sharp enough to keep out of prison if possible.

FDR **Monday, October 30** At 10 Decision as in "Ogden Daily Herald" Judge Emmerson overruled the demurrer and ordered "Preemptory Mandamus". Set 2 p.m. to hear application for appeal to Supreme Court on the Territory. Telegraphed FSR at Provo of decision, also Pres. John Taylor.[2] At 3 p.m. case argued and appeal granted. Received telegram this forenoon that Judge Hunter, decided in his cases to sustain the Demurrer and deny the Writ of "Preemptory Mandamus". Thanks praise to God of Israel that he is not ready to turn us over to our enemies notwithstanding all unworthiness.

FDR **Sunday, November 26** Conversation turned whether we could name or accept any terms or conditions of Statehood.

FDR **Monday, November 27** Considered the points and concluded on no Compromise.

GFR **Dec 17, 1882** I was appointed assistant clerk in the 3rd Quorum of Elders of the Davis Stake of Zion in a meeting held in the vestry. Immediately after, I wrote 17 letters to delinquent members of the Quorum.

---

2. As an attorney, Franklin S. Richards led efforts by the Church to plead through the courts the unconstitutionality of the Edmunds Act.

FDR **Monday, January 1, 1883** At home in Ogden. FSR is a delegate to Congress from the Territorial Convention to try for admission as a state. Joseph A. West, our son-in-law is an Elder, a missionary in London and presiding over that conference. Lorenzo is County Clerk, Charles is County Recorder and Deputy County Clerk, and despite Mandamus case pending, I am still Probate Judge. The boys are a wholesale mercantile firm with a credit standing—A-1. I am blessed in my labors as one of the Twelve Apostles. Jane presides over the Relief Societies of Weber County. Josephine presides over the Primary Asso. of Weber County.

GFR **January 27, 1883** Cleaned out the stable and hauled three loads of manure onto the old field. Parched corn and read from Mark Twain Roughing it Abroad & Art and Etiquette of Making Love.

FDR **Saturday, February 10** At one in the Supreme Court. Decision of 1st District Court affirmed. Judge Hunter dissented. Application for appeal and Supersedeas consented to by Mr. Kimball.

FDR **Thursday, February 15** At Harkness' office I executed a Bond in duplicate for a supersedeas of $2500.00 if they can get the judges or either of them to approve it. This will complete— with the citation—the appeal to the US Supreme Court as far as can be done here.

GFR **Feb 23rd 1883** My 22nd birthday. Attended priesthood meeting where my name, in company with others, was presented and sustained as home-missionary in the Davis Stake. Rode Minnie over to Frank's and on returning she (the mare) fell throwing me headlong into the mud. Spent the evening at home.

FDR **Thursday, March 1, 1883** Supreme Court Territory decided Appeal allowed. Supersedeas Bond of $2500.00 approved.

A grand triumph not only for me but for the whole of Utah Terr. and adverse decision might have turned over our whole territory over into the hands of our enemies by ordering out present officers and putting in the Governors appointees—some 200 or more.

FDR **Thursday, March 15** Too little snow in the Mtns, there can be but little rise in the Rivers this summer. A merciful providence sent Spring early. The farmers are getting their crops in while the ground is wet and good.

FDR **Wednesday, March 21** Calling at President's Office I found Pres. Taylor narrating his experience in Carthage jail. The first time I ever heard him give it.

GFR **Mar 24th 1883** Planted peas. Took stock & horses on bench. Spent the afternoon visiting my Father and talking about the principles of our religion.

FDR **Wednesday, March 28** FSR attended and got minds of the Council to proceed with the suits to test the Constitutionality of the Edmunds Law and acts of the Commission under it.

FDR **Thursday, March 29** Assisted to set apart BH Roberts of Centerville to assist Br. John Morgan in the Presidency of the Southern States Mission.

GFR **April 8/83 Sunday** Got late for conference train. Staid at home.

FDR **Friday, April 13** At 10 met with First Presidency, Pres's of 70's and W. Woodruff, L Snow, E Snow, A Carrington, FM Lyman, DH Wells to consider the reconstruction of the 70's—or reorganization and filling up of the Quorums.

FDR **Saturday, April 14** Council at President's Office and found the same together as yesterday. Heard Geo. Reynolds read the conclusions and directions of the Presidency as to method of reorganizing the Quorums of Seventies and Revelation given today through Pres. John Taylor approving our consideration and conclusion on this subject.

FDR **Wednesday, May 2** Wrote a letter to the First Presidency recommending the translation, stereotyping, and printing of the Book of Mormon in Spanish and asking Trustee to furnish funds therefore.

FDR **Friday, June 15** Had a pleasant and precious chat with Joseph F. Smith and Geo. Q. Cannon about various historical and doctrinal topics. Bro. Joseph F. Smith loaned me a letter of Addison Everett's to him narrating what he heard Joseph the Prophet say concerning the visit of Peter, James and John to him and Oliver in the wilderness on the banks of the Susquehanna River—when they conferred Keys of the M. Priesthood. Letter dated January 16, 1882, St. George.

FDR **Tuesday, July 3** Attended Central Committee meeting at City. Polygamists better not attend the Primaries or be chosen delegates thereto.

FDR **Friday, July 6** The Record of my Case on Mandamus is sent to Washington with docket fee to the clerk of US Supreme Court of $100, to come on in October term.

FDR **Sunday, July 8** Pres. Woodruff stopped to fish a day at Huntsville.

FDR **Thursday, August 2** Met at 3 p.m. to consider a Report from Pres. Cannon upon the subject of the School of the Prophets. After which Pres's Taylor, Cannon, Pres. Woodruff and I made remarks upon the subject. Pres. Taylor evidently aims at a high or higher moral standard in the organization of another school than has been heretofore attained.

FDR **Wednesday, August 8** Pres. Taylor addressed Council at length upon improvements of the Saints—instructing us to teach obedience to Council and preparation for School of the Prophets with much good instruction.

FDR **Saturday, August 25** This p.m. a Cow Boy shot and killed Marshall Burt. He died in a few minutes. The mob lynched the murderer in a terrible manner.

FDR **Tuesday, September 25** Today I had the great satisfaction to hand to Pres. LW Shurtliff his Commission of today's date as Probate Judge of Weber County and to congratulate him.

FDR **Friday, September 28** At 10 I met with Presidency and 7 of the 12. About 11 o.c. the 12 and Counselors met in front room of Historian Building and each one present expressed his views of various matters—Word of Wisdom, social relations and any and all matters affecting good fellowship till noon and then from 1:30 till 5:30 when we all met with Presidency and all accepted and eventually approved for admission to School of the Prophets.

FDR **Thursday, October 11** At 10 a.m. Presidency, Twelve and Stake Presidents met in President's office. After instruction from Pres. Taylor—he asked Zebedee Coltrin, the only one living in the Church who was a member of the 1st School of the Prophets in Kirtland in 1833—related visions of the Father and the Son appearing to them—of seeing the heavens opened and with Joseph and Oliver seeing Adam and Eve on a glorious throne.

FDR **Tuesday, November 20** About 4 o'clock p.m. Pres. LW Shurtliff and his counselors, Flygare and Middleton called bringing with them David McKay, President of the 75th Quorum of 70's. He has been appointed by the Presidency of the Stake, approved by the First Presidency and the people of Eden, I ordained him a High Priest and set him apart as Bishop of Eden.

GFR **Dec 6, 1883** Attended Fast meeting. Went teaching in the afternoon. Spent the evening at home reading the P. of G. Price.

FDR **Friday, December 14** Bro. Robt. S. Watson arrived to take stock of Richards Bros. Good. The boys closed their doors and proceeded to inventory the stock to turn over to ZCMI. This is a vast relief for which I feel to praise the Lord with thanksgiving and rejoicing.

FDR **Friday, December 21** As Lorenzo swallowed it ["a teacup full of mild porridge"] with some effort he turned his eyes upon us and ceased to breathe. His heart had stopped beating without a struggle or a groan at 5 m. past 1 a.m. by the parlor clock. His heart and lungs refused to act any more. Our pent up grief had its full free overflow. We all gave vent. 5½ Months day and night watching had made his afflictions ours. We had desired to take them from him but we could not, only in part. We had shared with him as best we could, withholding nothing that we could command that would contribute to his support or comfort. The fountains of our grief were broken up to their very depths and we took relief in the overflow. I washed the body.

FDR **Thursday, January 3, 1884** I dreamed of seeing Pres. Brigham Young, my father and several others. They all seemed thin in flesh as if they were hard worked and anxious, but they seemed cheerful.

FDR **Wednesday, January 16** Pres. Taylor suggested that I be appointed "Assistant Historian and Church Recorder" which JF Smith seconded and voted unanimous.

GFR **Jan 21st** Lecture by B. H. Roberts. Word of Wisdom: Tobacco oil is as poisonous as strychnine. Tobacco juice will kill a dog, hence we are in danger when we chew tobacco. Smoking brings on consumption. Liquor does not unite with the blood.

One part of the brain governs muscular faculties and when liquour enters it cannot do its duty and the muscles relax.

GFR **Sunday Feb 3rd 1884** Was ordained a Seventy by Seymour B. Young in the Farmington Vestry after being sustained by a vote of the Ward.

FDR **Friday, February 8** Congress is making use of us and our position for party political affect at next election for President. Public prejudice is very terrible.

FDR **Wednesday, March 19** It was decided that Bishops of wards in a stake may be ordained by the President of the Stake when so directed by the First Presidency or Apostleship.

GFR **Mar 19th** Wrote a letter to my father.

FDR **Thursday, March 27** F. informs me that James M. Kimball proposes to compromise or settle Mandamus case of Kimball vs. Richards for $250.00, now in Supreme Court of United States.

GFR **Mar 28th** Visited with my father. The following is a copy of letter written to Robert Campbell in answer to his letter of inquiry.

I pen the following in answer to your letter of the 26th instant.

I am twenty-three years of age, was born and raised in Farmington, Davis Co. I have a wife and one child, have never been on a foreign mission. Financially, I am in poor circumstances at present, being in debt more than four-hundred dollars, and paying interest on a part of the same.

I have no ready means and all the property I have is a set of harness, wagon (both been in use more than five years), six head of horses, a cow and two calves and not quite two acres of land worth from seventy-five and one-hundred dollars.

While I feel that I am poor, I do not wish to let that stand between me and my duties as a latter-day Saint. That which I have is upon the altar and subject to the direction of those in authority, as is also my time and life if necessary.

Your Obedient Servant,
George F. Richards

FDR **Saturday, March 29** After arriving at Ogden, I signed a stipulation or witnessed a stipulation—or in other words James N. Kimball executed a stipulation not to further prosecute the case in which I am appellant and he the Appellee—now before the Supreme Court of the United States, known as the "Mandamus Case"—$250.00 consideration. By the vigorous resistance of this case and success in getting it appealed to Court of last resort the territory was saved from going into the hands of enemies—it being a test case for all other Probate Judges.

FDR **Monday, April 7** Presidency, Apostles, Pres's of Stakes meeting at 3:30 Social Hall. Pres. Taylor gave disquisition of Sec 132, the Eternal Marriage Covenant—all to whom it is revealed must receive it and abide it or be damned. All present voted that they so understood it.

FDR **Saturday, April 12** FSR informed me that Mandamus Case was dismissed in the US Supreme Court on the 7th inst, as per our stipulation.

FDR **Monday, April 14** Slept at Historian building as usual.

FDR **Wednesday, April 16** I asked and Council granted that I turn over and deliver to Historian's Office the collection which I have accumulated of Genealogical Works in my possession. Trustee to pay me what they cost me.

FDR **Saturday, May 10** Pres. Taylor thought I had better

repair at once to Logan and help arrange the consummation of affairs at Temple and in 30 minutes I was off by train.

FDR **Saturday, May 17, 1884** Logan Temple Dedicated. A clear beautiful comfortable day. 1600 tickets issued, that no. of persons went into the Temple. About 1400 present in Temple. Choir Sung dedicatory hymn. Pres. Taylor read the Dedicatory Prayer, it took about half an hour. Choir again sang. Then Pres. Woodruff spoke, then Lorenzo Snow. Congregation standing shouted Hosannah.

FDR **Wednesday, May 21** At Logan received Endowments. I assisted Pres. Taylor to set apart Marriner W. Merrill to be President of the Temple and Pres Cannon to set apart Samuel Roskelley as Recorder, with 8 or 9 other of the 12 and Bp. Preston. I was baptized, the first person in the font, first for my-self then for Uncle Wm. Richards. I got Endowment for George Spencer Richards.

FDR **Thursday, May 22** I went to the Temple, observed their opening of the records, bulletins &c. Pres Taylor and several of Pre[siden]cy and 12 came. Pres. Taylor directed the Recorder Roskelley to insert that the Lord has accepted the Temple and its Dedication; that He is well pleased with our work, and is also well pleased with us.

FDR **Wednesday, June 4** I passed in my account to the Trustee for "Genealogical Library" amounting to $765.14 less $237.25 = $527.89.

FDR **Friday, June 13** Charles Bancroft in his Footprints says Population of Earth is 1,380,000,000. Average of life is 33 years. ¼ die before their 7th year. ½ before their 17th year.

FDR **Thursday, June 26** At 3 p.m. met with Presidency, Twelve, a full Council nearly to consider about how to secure our Real Estate for Confiscation. FSR being invited met with us.

FDR **Friday, June 27** The 12 except M. Thatcher and JH Smith at Endowment House and decided to incorporate companies to whom to deed our Temples as Literary, Scientific, and Educational Properties.

FDR **Sunday, June 29** The company of Emigrants arrived from Europe today. The 2 last companies came through in just about 2 weeks.

FDR **Thursday, July 10** At Logan. Today attended 3 meetings of the Delegates and succeeded in accomplishing a full organization of the "Logan Temple Association" and incorporating the same—according to Law for "Scientific, Social and Educational" purposes; and as a "School of Science" to teach theology, mathematics, astronomy, history, laws, natural science and all true knowledge of Heavens and of the Earth.

FDR **Friday, July 25** Plenty of work and the greatest uneasiness I experience is for that I seem to accomplish so little while there is so much to do, and that needs to be done.

FDR **Monday, August 11** From Richards' Rest in Ogden Canyon to the City. Conversed with Br. Andrew Jensen about terms of and for Service if we should employ him in the office of Historian.

FDR **Wednesday, August 13** Learned further that Elders John Gibbs and William Berry had been killed by the mob last Sunday in Tennessee.

FDR **Monday, August 18** Mr. HH Bancroft called on me about 2 p.m. and spent 3 hours in conversation and explaining his aims and methods in regard to his great work of History on which he is engaged. Also, his views and intentions concerning the History of Utah which he wishes to make satisfactory to the authorities of the church. He left Chapters of history of Utah for me to read and criticize for further revision.

FDR **Friday, September 12** At City. Weather getting warmer. I took Franklin's horse and buggy and Jane, Mr. and Mrs. Bancroft and with them visited the Tabernacle, the Assembly Hall, and Temple, going to the top of the So. East Stairs above the parapet walls. We then rode to and around the Old Fort Block, then to and around the drive in Liberty Park; and dined with Mr. B., family at their Hotel, "The Continental".

FDR **Friday, September 26** Presidency and 12 in City met at Pres Office. Had explanation and decision that those who persist in sending their children to Gentile teachers shall not be recommended to receive the Blessings of the Temple. Pres. Taylor, Cannon, Woodruff, Carrington, and myself met with Sister Eliza Roxy Snow Smith in Gardo House and corrected her views as contained in W. Exponent.

FDR **Monday, October 13** I learned that Judge Zane had issued an order to bring Joseph F. Smith and DH Wells into Court forthwith. Word was conveyed to JFS.

FDR **Saturday, December 6** The Lord preserve Bros Daniel H. Wells and Joseph F. Smith from the hands of their enemies. It is now becoming generally understood that these 2 Brethren are keeping out of the hands of their enemies and that it is their duty to do so—even if they have to visit foreign lands to accomplish it.

FDR **Thursday, December 11** Today SWR called and I arranged with him and Franklin and Henry and through SWR, with Maria that we all go to Logan next Tuesday and attend to being sealed to our father and mother in the Temple.

FDR **Wednesday, December 31** Had a very interesting conversation with Pres. GQ Cannon, about the spies and the surveillance that is being extended over and among us. The job put up by Detective Gilson on CW Penrose and also the visit of a Gentleman claiming to be the private Secretary of President Elect

Grover Cleveland, to Pres. John Taylor concerning our political status as a Territory. Joseph F. blocked by snow on Sierra Nevadas and returned.

FDR **Thursday, January 1, 1885** Pres. T. told me he intended to absent himself for a short time. Wrote Franklin lengthily. A messenger from Pres. Elect G. Cleveland has done his errand to Pres. Taylor and is fervent that Utah must become a state to save bloodshed. Convinced of his sincerity and integrity, B. Young and CW Penrose, will go accredited to Cleveland and further learn of his purposes.

FDR **Tuesday, January 20** SL Herald contains the decision so much desired and now it is adverse. Court won't interfere with discretion given by Legislatures to lower Courts. The Decision of the Court operates on our enemies like the smell or taste of blood does on wolves. They seem ferocious. Pres. Angus M. Cannon was arrested and put under $2500.00 bonds and his family were subpoenaed to appear at 2 tomorrow. Information reached now that warrants are out for Pres. Geo. Q. Cannon, RT Burton, W. Woodruff and the officers searched News Office for CW Penrose. Geo Q. arranged for his safety.

FDR **Thursday, January 22** A good guard is kept at the gates of President's office—that no one may surprise the clerks or anyone who may be in the offices. Pres. GQ Cannon concluded to change his residence to the upper room of the new rich Stable, Center of Tithing Office Block.

GFR **Jan 22nd** Settled tithing, $25.50 for 1884.

FDR **Sunday, February 1, 1885** E. Snow and Pres. Jno Taylor preached in Tabernacle SL City. Presidency went underground tonight.

FDR **Tuesday, February 3** Professor Ellis R. Shipp came with her class of 9 students of obstetrics who all desired to be set apart and blessed for their new studies and vocation.

FDR **Saturday, February 7** I received drafts for the sums of Ten Thousand and 6 thousand, one hundred and twenty ($6120.00) with a letter to committee selected for the purchase of a place of refuge for the persecuted Latter-Day Saints within the confines of the Republic of Mexico.

FDR **Tuesday, February 10** Weber's quota $1500.00 is ready for the "Refuge Fund". Sarah Jane Cannon is still at our house secreted.

FDR **Friday, February 20** Got a letter from Pres. Woodruff, L. Allen. A voice from a man in exile—Bunkerville. Elder OW Oberhansey got off all right but was detected en route and escaped his enemies and came in disguise to tell me.

FDR **Wednesday, February 25** Apostle L. Snow writes that Deputies are hunting him and he cannot come to Council without jeopardizing arrest. The Presidency and most of the Twelve being absent in obscurity to avoid arrest—on account of persecution. I presided.

FDR **Thursday, February 26** Received letters from Pres. Taylor. I wrote the Pres. about several items informing him that I had done and would do what he suggested.

FDR **Sunday, March 8** Spent this beautiful day in rest. My mouth for want of teeth is unfit to speak in public so I take the liberty to rest.

FDR **Friday, March 20** Last night the Marshalls raided home of Pres. Geo Q Cannon and subpoenaed children, housekeeper and school teacher to appear to day at Grand Jury.

FDR **Sunday, March 29** The Supreme Court at Washington has ruled the test oath unlawful and men once in polygamy always so unless relieved by Amnesty from the President. Women-first wives-relieved by death of their husbands and may vote.

FDR **Friday, April 3** At evening and by special train I went with a large number of Saints Elders and Presidents to Logan. HJ Grant brot me memos from the President—that I am to preside at Conference.

FDR **Saturday, April 4** A General Conference in Logan. At 10 a.m. and being the Senior Apostle present it devolved upon me to preside. I opened with remarks about 20 minutes.

FDR **Tuesday, April 7** Wrote President Taylor incidents of the Conference. I feel to thank and praise the Lord for so kindly ordering so goodly a measure of his Spirit with us at Conference and overruling and restraining the Deputies and Marshalls of Utah and Idaho Territories from arresting Elders and from intruding upon the Temple or disturbing Conference.

FDR **Friday, April 10** Received a letter dated yesterday, signed by Presidents John Taylor and Geo. Q. Cannon, approving my course in presiding at the 55th General Conference in Logan. This 55th General Conference is the first in this dispensation at which neither of the First Presidency were present when there was such a Presidency in the Church and this occurrence caused me much concern as to how, I, should accomplish it.

FDR **Monday, April 13** Orson P. Arnold arraigned today plead guilty to the charge of Co-habitation and did not propose to continue the married relation—only to support both wives. Zane fined him $300. No imprisonment.

FDR **Tuesday, April 14** I enjoyed a very pleasant evening in hearing FSR relate his experience while away especially in regard his argument before the Supreme Court of the United States—when he presented in the Rudger Clawson case, the case and position of the Latter Day Saints as he never had opportunity to do before.

FDR **Friday, April 17** Rumors of search for Pres. Taylor led us to secure from the Endowment House such things as could be removed that ought not to be seen.

FDR **Monday, May 11** at Pueblo and to Denver. Having found the oldest inhabitant, Mr. Lewis Conley, now of Alimosa and he conferring with Judge Josiah Smith, he, Conley, Charley and I spent most of the day searching for the Camp ground of the invalids of the Mormon Battallion among whom were my Bro. Joseph William Richards who died in the arms of Brother Caratat Rowe on the 19th day of November, 1846 and whose place of burial I earnestly desire to find. After a patient and careful search we found it out of our reach to discover the precise spot of the graves of our Brethren who were buried here.

FDR **Wednesday, May 27** The Apostles present received a letter from the President asking "Whether he should continue away or return and go [to] the Pen?" After consultation, wide range, I was requested to write a reply and submit to Apostles tomorrow.

FDR **Wednesday, June 3** M. Thatcher reported result of his and BY's visit to President P Porferio Diaz and Secretaries Don G. Pacheco of Interior and Ignatio Maresal of the Foreign Affairs—all desiring that we colonize in Mexico.

FDR **Wednesday, June 10** Pres. Taylor sent word by Geo. Q. to Apostles not to indulge in levity, joking, and frivolity and slang phrases—which all present feel to approve and adopt. Says Pres. Cleveland is anxious to get us into statehood, if not, fears we shall be put under Martial law.

FDR **Friday, June 12** Sent letter from Bishop Hunsaker out to Pres. Taylor by tonight's underground mail.

FDR **Sunday, June 28** I labored with my own folks and with several of the neighbors to stop the visiting and playing that goes on during the Sabbath on my lawn. I am in hopes I have stopped it and thereby perhaps done as much or more good than if I had been at meeting and preached to the people.

FDR **Monday, June 29** Printed letter to JF Smith, Mr. Mack at Box 410 Honolulu Sandwich Islands.

FDR **Monday, July 6** Franklin is with Mr. Kirkpatrick defending Bro. Job Pingree against the charge of Cohabitation—in Judge Power's Court, but the inquisition of Spain nor the Dages of Venice were ever more sure of conviction than these mock courts of packed Juries are.

FDR **Sunday, July 19** At 2 p.m. met in general meeting and spoke an hour or more on the Sacrament of the Lord's Supper— its nature, object and power. In Meditation upon and reading from the 6th Chap of John's Gospel, I received edification of the Spirit and the understanding also, but cannot find language to correctly and clearly and fully convey my ideas to others. The hearers gave close attention and seemed edified. Lord help me so to eat of his body and drink of his blood so that I may have eternal life to abide in me.

FDR **Thursday, August 13** Soda Springs and to McGammon. This morning at the Lane Spring, Capt. Codman asked me to ride with him, Joseph Smith, President of the re-organized Church and Mr. Luff an Elder in his Church, to lower town which I did. He, Joseph, said in answer to questions, that he would be 53 years old next November; his uncle Wm Smith lives in the N. East part of Iowa; his brother David was still in the Assylum at Elgin, Illinois in a taciturn condition—hopeless of recovery. His own residence is 17 miles S. East of Garden Grove, at Lamoni; has never practiced law, but has been Justice of the Peace 10 years in Ills.

FDR **Friday, August 28** At 7:30 Franklin and I went out to Col John A. Winders' farm 3 miles south of Temple where we spent the evening with Pres. John Taylor, GQ Cannon and LJ Nuttall talking over several important items of Church business, court cases and seeking counsel.

FDR **Sunday, October 4** Notwithstanding word arrived that bridges at and near Ogden were being watched by deputies day and night, Bro. Geo. Q. Cannon went on, leaving about midnight in hopes to be at Logan for Conference.

FDR **Tuesday, November 10** Sister Phebe Woodruff died 2 a.m. Spent morning helping Pres. W. to get arrangements for funeral. He confined and cannot go out—his folks come secretly to see him in the back office. He sleeps in my bed.

FDR **Thursday, November 12** I went to my office and put down the blinds to all my windows except one and placed Pres. Woodruff where unobserved he could see the funeral procession of his 1st wife pass on the way to the grave.

FDR **Monday, November 30** Reports are threatening Martial Law for our City.

FDR **Tuesday, December 8** We hear that some of our Brethren in Arizona are killed by Apache Indians. A Br. and Sr. Johnson and 2 brothers Wright.

FDR **Saturday, December 12** Received a letter from Pres. Woodruff with one he received from the Presidency calling on him and the Apostles to raise 100 families more or less to settle in the San Juan Stake of Zion[3] and so preserve the balance of power against our enemies there and in Moab Ward.

FDR **Tuesday, December 22** Bro. Matthew Wheelwright of Ogden called being in jeopardy on both Counts and it was

---

3. This group of faithful, obedient Saints journeyed to San Juan through the Hole in the Rock.

concluded that if search for him continues—he better take a mission.

FDR **Tuesday, December 29** Obtained of Bro. James Jack a draft on New York for $90 with which to purchase a Type Writing Machine and the necessary extras for Historian Office use.

FDR **Thursday, January 7, 1886** Took satchel of Diaries to FSR house for safety.

FDR **Thursday, January 14** Decided best to incorporate Stakes to hold the General Church Property located in those stakes severally and any personal property if the new Edmunds bill shall become law.

FDR **Sunday, January 17** Gave up to rest, all day—was very tired, weary—almost worn out.

FDR **Thursday, January 28** Council. First: how best to dispose of personal property of the Church—to protect it. After, about sending Erastus and Moses to Mexico with Money to purchase a place of refuge.

GFR **Feb 6th 1886** Our baby Legrand was born.

FDR **Thursday, February 18** Apostle John H. Smith, having received a lengthy letter of 24 pages of letter size from his Cousin Joseph of the Reorganized Church, left the letter with me to read, which I retained for several days. It is evident by this, that Joseph has thought to persuade John H. to leave the Church and join him and a few others. Would help divide the Church, &c.

FDR **Tuesday, March 23** Bro. Isaac Wilson who worked for me several years ago, called and offered to be in my stead if I shall be arrested and they will accept him for me in Prison. God bless him.

FDR **Sunday April 4** Ogden to Provo Annual Conference. Opened Conference by a few opening remarks of ½ an hour.

Apostles JH Smith, HJ Grant, JW Taylor were present. I being oldest Apostle present, presided.

FDR **Tuesday, April 6** At Provo Conference. Another fine day. This morning Bp. Whitney occupied almost an hour and a half reading 30½ pages of the General Epistle of the First Presidency slow and with a clear strong voice in the most understandable manner. This afternoon Professor Talmage read the remaining 31½ pages of the General Epistle in some less time. A lengthy comprehensive able paper which seemed to fill up the souls of the Saints with brimful satisfaction.

FDR **Monday, April 12** Today the stone layers began to lay stones on the west tower of the Temple in Salt Lake City.

FDR **Thursday, April 15** Wrote Pres. Woodruff and sent out a paper approving the sale of Church stock in the ZCMI by HJ Grant with a view to put it out of reach of Government plunderers and keep it in the hands of faithful Saints. At 4:15 by train to Farmington and delivered to Aunt Nanny L. Richards[4] a letter from Gilbert Cope and Dawson genealogy—which contains some genealogy of Longstroths. This caused her great joy.

FDR **Friday, April 16** Apostle JH Smith read to me an elaborate reply to his cousin Joseph Smith in answer to his of about 25 pages of letter sheet size received and read to me sometime since. The answer is a masterly production and does Br. John great credit.

FDR **Wednesday, May 5** Elder Stromberg of Grantsville just home from Scandinavian Mission finds all his children 4 or 5 have died [of] Diphtheria while he has been gone.

FDR **Thursday, May 6** A telegram from Washington in

---

4. Nanny was Franklin's plural wife, but she had previously been sealed to Willard, his uncle. His reference to her as his "aunt" evidences his respect for that sealing.

Cypher could not be translated by McKenzie. It was sent out to LJ Nuttall to de-cypher.

FDR **Monday, May 10** Franklin telegraphs = Supreme Court dismisses the Snow Cases for lack of jurisdiction and vacates their former Decision in the Cannon Case.

FDR **Thursday, June 10** Had a very interesting visit with Elder Moroni Pratt—he reports that three cases of disturbing the religious worship have been prosecuted in the Nottingham, Leicester and Bristol with excellent effects in the British Mission.

FDR **Thursday, August 12** Had quite a chat this morning with Mr. Wm. Burke on the porch about the situation generally—especially about Polygamy and our relation with the Government. If we compromise this one tenet of our faith—it will be required of us to relinquish others and indeed every objectionable one—perhaps all.

GFR **Aug 14th** Had a Richards' reunion at Liberty Park where Georgie was taken sick and had to remain in the city for more than a week.

FDR **Saturday, August 28** Reported today that Marshall Dyer has applied to Fort for troops to be in readiness to aid in the arrest of Taylor and Cannon who they expect to find within a week.

FDR **Thursday, September 9** Bro. Hiram Goff just from Penitentiary brought cheering word from Pres. L. Snow.

FDR **Tuesday, September 21** A great trial for me and Sarah not to see each other while yet so near.

FDR **Tuesday, October 5** Rec'd letter of appt. from Pres. Taylor to take Presidency of Conference tomorrow.

FDR **Saturday, November 20** This morning received a very satisfactory letter from the Presidency in answer to mine of day before yesterday expressing appreciation of my labors—approving my course and advising me to continue in my office work so far as I can with safety.

FDR **Wednesday, December 29** Wrote President about a man for the German Mission—Henry Eyring.

FDR **Monday, January 17, 1887** Telegram in Cypher from FS Richards in Washington "are doing utmost defeat bill, hope to succeed, but think should prepare for worst and place tithing and other property beyond reach of enemies. Expect argue case Tuesday or Wednesday. Shall I start home immediately or wait till bill is disposed of?"

FDR **Saturday, January 29** Received letters from Henry Eyring St. George and Ben E. Rich sent out to Pres. Taylor. H. Eyring wishes approval to go to Mexico.

FDR **Sunday, February 6** At Logan Quarterly Conference. We deliberated upon founding a settlement North in British Dominion by Pres. CO Card as directed by the 1st Presidency. How to maintain a legal High Council while 5 or 6 are absent underground, and other items of interest and importance.

FDR **Monday, February 7** Toward evening received a telegraph from Franklin "Supreme Court decided Snow case in our favor and against Segregation." When Franklin's tel. came, I replied "I congratulate you my son, All Israel rejoices in the success of your efforts before the Supreme Court of the U.S. for which all thanks and praise belong to God."

FDR **Tuesday, February 8** We learned that Pres. Lorenzo Snow was escorted from the Penitentiary this p.m. obtaining his freedom about 3 o.c. p.m.

FDR **Friday, February 11** At 6:30 Marshall Dyer and 6 Deputies or aids rung at my door, Historian's office. I had kindled the fire and lighted the gas. I took them through the building, that is Dyer and Vandercook. Rest staid outside. They then went through Gardo House, Pres' Office, Tithing Office and Block, then Temple Block.

FDR **Wednesday, February 16, 1887** This evening Franklin and CW Penrose sent out to Presidency a statement of their views based on the Scott amendment. Can we accept a constitution with a prohibition of Polygamy and Bigamy in it?

FDR **Wednesday, March 9** Pres. GQ Cannon and FS Richards discoursed on the methods to be adopted to effect properly the transfer of authority of Trustee to President and of Property from Trustee to Stake Corporations; and of receiving and paying of "Tithing" to that of "donations."

FDR **Saturday, April 2** Rec'd a letter from Pres. Woodruff replying to Bro HJ Grant's inquiry of him who should be the successor of Pres. Taylor when he vacates the office—a clear and vigorous answer, the Twelve Apostles.

FDR **Thursday, April 7** At Provo General Conference and Fast Day. A very pleasant comfortable day. Bro Oliver B. Huntington of Springville called and I paid him $10.00 to aid in fencing, planting out trees and erecting a memorial to the memories of the dead who are buried in Mount Pisgah burying ground—supposed to be 300 or more. Our little son Isaac Phinehas Richards who was born July 23, 1846 and died the same day was buried there.

FDR **Thursday, May 19** Pres. Taylor is not so well. Tendencies to faintness and suffocation. Can not lie in bed as much as would like to.

FDR **Saturday, May 21** Heavy day's work to set apart 23 Elders for foreign missions give them their instruction, take their genealogies, make letters of appointment.

FDR **Monday, June 13** CW Penrose who arrived yesterday from Washington presented to us proposed amendments to our New Constitution which have been discussed and approved at the Capital—with explanations. All were asked for their views. Many were given. All present voted in favor but 2. Spoke 20 minutes in favor of them.

FDR **Tuesday, June 21** Grand Jubilee in England 50 years.

FDR **Monday, June 27** Spent some time with Pres. Geo. Q. Cannon at Pres' Office—inquired carefully about Pres. Taylor's health declining. Br. GQC has deemed it imprudent to defer longer and has informed the family partly of the Pres.'s condition—legs badly swollen and abdomen considerably enlarged with Dropsy. I asked about Joseph F Smith—is he informed? Br. C showed me copies of letters sent him last April and we conversed freely about propriety of his return.

FDR **Tuesday, June 28** I wrote to Pres. Joseph F. Smith stating Pres.'s condition, and that if he were depending on his counsel as to whether or when to return he would probably never get it. I thought he ought to be made aware of the fact that he might seek his counsel from the source above.

FDR **Wednesday, June 29** GQC read letter from Bp. LG Farrall reporting Northern settlement on Lee's Creek—near Ft. McLeod, Alberty, NW Territory, Canada. 41 souls, 34 horn stock, 45 horses, 8 men with families and 4 without.

FDR **Tuesday, July 26** Guard at outer door of Pres' office tells me at 7 a.m. that GQC and JFS arrived in about 5 a.m. and are sleeping. At 9 o'clock Geo. Q. Cannon informed me that President Taylor died at 5 m to 8 last evening.

FDR **Saturday, July 30** The United States today planted suit in the Terr. Supreme Court of Utah to escheat the property of the Church Corporation and of the PE Fund Company incorporation for three million dollars against Trustee in Trust and his assistants.

FDR **Sunday, October 9** Still at Conference. Vast crowd

occupied the Big Tabernacle. Afternoon LS and I accompanied Pres. Woodruff to the Tabernacle. As we took our seats in the upper Desk for the first time the people recognized him—clapped their hands, shook handkerchiefs and rejoiced.

FDR **Friday, October 21** I packed such papers correspondence &c as are undesirable to fall into Receivers hands with a purpose to take them to Ogden.

FDR **Wednesday, November 23** Going to the Office learned that Receiver Dyer and aids, Pratt and others are at Pres' office urging his claims for Books, Records and any and all property of the late Corporation of the Church.

GFR **Dec 6th 1887** Repaired sleigh and killed two pigs. Commenced reading the Book of Mormon in the evening, read 13 chapters and wrote in my Diary.

FDR **Wednesday, December 19** At Washington DC. Soon went to the old Senate Chamber where the US Supreme Court was in session and saw my son Charles admitted to practice there on motion of his Brother Franklin.

FDR **Thursday, December 20** At Washington. Hon John T. Caine went with and introduced us to President Grover Cleveland. F. remarked we had not come to ask for or urge claims any office, only wished to pay our respects to him. He mildly replied "You are no less welcome for that Gentlemen." I said I believed his recent peculiar message would increase Democrats in the land. He replied Congress left an unpleasant responsibility upon him, which he must get rid of some how. Charlie said he hoped to be able to vote for his re-election for another term. He thanked him and hoped he might. We were brief, others were waiting and we went to next room.

GFR **Dec 31st 1887** Staid in the house all day with the children & mama. Made molasses candy and ate peanuts & candy.

GFR **Jan 4, 1888** Snowed and blowed all day. Joel was taken sick and I was up in the night with him; administered to him and he rested pretty well the remainder of the night.

GFR **Jan 5, 1888** Snow about two feet deep. Was up with Joel in the night again.

GFR **Jan 6, 1888** Friday. Was up all night with Joel who was very sick with cold and inward fever.

GFR **Jan 7, 1888** Windy and cold. Severly cold and deep snow drifted. Joel no better. Administered to Joel. Joel turned for the better at 4:00 a.m. Sunday 8th.

GFR **Jan 8, 1888** Joel continued better, weather severely cold. Kept up a fire all night, but I slept part of the night.

GFR **Jan 10, 1888** Joel still improving. The weather still cold & windy, severely cold. Kept fire all night and water froze in the room where the fire was. We now all of us sleep in the front room.

FDR **Thursday, January 26, 1888** I ate with the Brethren at the Office, a sacred pleasure.

FDR **Thursday, February 2** Telegram from FSR and JTC and Washington for Senate Judiciary Committee "Do you think it is the honest intention of your people or majority of them to abolish and suppress Polygamy?" "Second: by your 'good faith' do you mean that it is merely their intention to prosecute those that violate the provisions of the Con. on that subject?" To be heard on Friday but got deferred one week. Answered and sent lengthily. Pres. Woodruff concluded to let Br. Joseph F. Smith go to Washington to preside and deliberate mode of procedure, means to be employed. Council approved heartily. Voted not to favor a Constitutional Amendment on Polygamy and voted to draw up an enabling Act to use if necessary, but avoid if possible.

FDR **Saturday, February 18** Apostle JH Smith called and talked over the situation in Provo City and Utah County on the Liquor question; its existence, prevalence. It is stated that ½ of the male population of Provo are users, drinkers of alcoholic drinks.

FDR **Wednesday, March 14** President thinks a First Presidency should be appointed at April conference.

FDR **Friday, April 6** At 4 met with the Apostles and took Sacrament of the Lord's Supper—a most interesting time. All spoke and forgave each other. These 15 Brethren ate Bread and drank wine after having asked and granted forgiveness of and to each other. Pres. Woodruff expressed his feelings that the Lord accepted of us.

FDR **Sunday, April 8** What shall I render to my God for all his gifts to me? At close of Conference met with the 12, the Presiding Bishops Preston and Winder and about 20 Pres' of Stakes or Counselors. Pres' WW, GQC, LS, ES, MT, BY, FML, GQC spoke on the present situation of the Saints; necessity of Tithing—its diminution; refrain from teaching Polygamy awhile; necessity of Fast Day Offerings, and other very important items.

FDR **Friday, May 11** I met Pres. WW and GQC to ask the former how my blocking out of material for the Prayer[5] suited him. He wished me to hasten on with it, as time is getting short.

FDR **Saturday, May 12** Spent today in the most diligent application preparing dedication Prayer by Pres. Woodruff's special request. Patriarch _____ asked me how a faithful worthy man could obtain the sealing of a second wife to him. Perhaps in the future I may be able to answer him, not now.

FDR **Tuesday, May 22** Manti Temple. House packed full over 1600 persons before 11 a.m. Sung the opening hymn. FDR delivered Dedicatory Prayer in 43 minutes.

---

5. Wilford Woodruff had asked Franklin to draft the dedicatory prayer for the Manti Temple.

FDR **Saturday, June 2** This morning my son Ezra F. called to see me. I was pleased and thankful to welcome him home from a 3½ years mission in New Zealand. Has done a good mission. Translated the Book of Mormon into Maori tongue. The Spirit of the Gospel is upon him.

FDR **Thursday, June 7** Read over the Article of First Presidency and 12 Apostles contained in the "Desert News" of August 23, 1865 suppressing Mother Smith's History of Joseph Smith.

FDR **Monday, June 18** Heard my son Franklin state the progress so far made with District Attorney Peters in arranging terms for basis of compromise or a stipulation of terms on which to get our case up to the Supreme Court and estop proceedings in law against the Church Property in the Territory.

FDR **Wednesday, July 4** I feel, in view of the fact that our great Nation has turned a legal Mob[,] my patriotism has terribly evaporated, and I had rather rest and help Jane clean house than go to any resorts or celebrations. Our Republic having made laws to plunder and rob us of our property has authorized a Court and asked it to take up $2,000,000 of property, pay it over to a Receiver, an Examiner, and as many of the bitterest Attorneys as they choose to employ and confiscate the rest if they prefer to do so—and this is to suppress and destroy the work of God and of His People in the Earth.

FDR **Tuesday, July 24** At Ogden—Pioneer Day. Viewed the Base Ball Game.

FDR **Saturday, July 28** Went with Jane and Franklin to Brigham City and put up with Sister Minnie Snow in the new Brick house. The owner and builder cannot enjoy his home— Br. L. Snow lives in Br. Bp. Nichols in next block.

FDR **Monday, September 17** Geo. Q. Cannon gave himself up to Marshall Dyer and plead guilty to 2 indictments covering till September 15 and received sentences: 1st 75 days in Pen and $200 fine; 2nd 100 days in Pen and $250 fine. In all 175 days in pen and $450.00 fine. No cost and was taken directly to prison.

GFR **Tooele Oct 19** three horses got in wire, tied blood vessels and sewed up wounds.

FDR **Tuesday, November 6** At City Presidential Election today. Herald this morning states that the Brethren after their terrible struggle in Idaho are permitted to vote. That there is a deputy sheriff at each Poll Box to arrest any Mormon who may attempt to vote and United States Marshal also who is to arrest any officer who attempts to prevent a Mormon from voting. Everything is exceedingly quiet here.

FDR **Thursday, December 13** Went to Penitentiary. Saw Br. Geo. Q. Cannon. Warden Pratt directed Mr. Ward to show my Bro. SW Richards through the new prison—120 cells for 240 convicts; with 223 present occupants. Changes in and out almost daily. Saw Kitchen, Bakery, dining Room, Bath room—work shop—all was neat, clean and well supplied with good work.

FDR **Saturday, December 29** At 12 Noon FSR and DH Wells met here and concluded it undesirable to state as from the Temples the cessation of plural Marriages.

GFR **Jan 3 [1889]** Fasted and attended meeting. Gave 50 lbs flour fast offering. Attended a committee meeting in the evening for the purpose of arranging for a ward sociable in respect for Apostle Lyman who is to receive his sentence, for living with his wives.

FDR **Friday, January 11, 1889** I carelessly afflicted my dear Jane by a slight request that caused her to weep bitterly and me to feel sorry indeed for such inadvertence.

FDR **Thursday, January 24** The Herald of today says a special from Washington yesterday says Mrs. Emily S. Richards delivered a striking speech on suffrage in Utah and the deprivation of women.

FDR **Tuesday, March 19** Elder CW Penrose ventured out on the Liberty Pardon and Amnesty granted him by Pres. Grover Cleveland. Efforts are being made for JF Smith's liberty.

FDR **Monday, April 15** Elder FM Lyman spoke to me in terms of praise and high commendation of a discourse delivered by my son by Nanny, George Franklin at Tooele last Sunday for which I feel very grateful.

FDR **Thursday, April 25** Andrew Jensen's Historical Record which contains the names of the Prophet's wives with their affidavits is causing extensive schisms in the ranks of the young Joseph's followers. They find that he and his mother have lied to them and that Joseph had plurality of wives and no mistake.

GFR **Apr 30** Attended meeting held in the meeting house in commemoration of the Centennial of Our 1st Presidents inauguration (in the U. States). By request occupied 15 or 20 minutes speaking to the people. Attended BASEBALL GAME between Tooele & Stockton boys.

GFR **June 13** Finished reading the History of Apostle <u>Parley Parker Pratt</u>, having read it aloud to my family.

FDR **Thursday, June 20** Counseled Professor JE Talmage to accept the Diplomas offered him as Master of Science and others from a Chicago University.

FDR **Monday, July 22** Pres. WW gave us an exceedingly interesting hour's talk about the great work that is upon us for living and dead. He had between 3000 and 4000 of his ancestors baptized, endowed and sealed for which he felt exceedingly thankful.

GFR **Tooele, Jul 26th, 1889** An Editorial for the Intelligencer

Wherein can we make an improvement that will be the most mutual, and produce the best results? The answer comes to me thus: "in the Expenditure of our Time." Our young men . . . see nothing amiss in spending a large portion of their time standing on the street corner. However it is amiss and is displeasing to our Heavenly Father. Our home, our books, our religion and charity all have more claim upon our time than have the street corners.

FDR **Thursday, October 10** At 10 a.m. met with the Presidency in Gardo prayer room. Considered relative powers and duties of the First Presidency and Presidency of Bishopric in which all agreed that the First Presidency are supreme over all in Church on Earth in all things Temporal and Spiritual. That they can arrange the working details to suit the best interests of all concerned.

FDR **Sunday, October 13** Wind this a.m. capsized D&RG train near Kaysville, none killed as we learn. Several wounded.

FDR **Saturday, November 9** I did a little work on my Records. It seems an endless work to gather up all the data of Birth, Marriage, Death and when, where, by whom all the Church Ordinances were conferred upon any one person of our race and how much more upon all the varied branches of our numerous families. Every item like the drop of water that in the bucket helps to fill it so also helps to make up the Record of the person and of the Family. Oh that I might be enabled to complete such a Record of my Families and generations.

FDR **Saturday, November 16** Patriarch John Smith called with Joseph Smith the son of Prophet Joseph and the head of the "Reorganized Church". Said he held his present position as President by virtue of his Birthright in his Father's family and by his ordinations under the hands of Wm. H. Marks, Zenas H. Gurley, Sr., and John P. Blair. He holds the Doctrines publicly taught by the Prophet at his death but considers Baptism for Dead only permissive under proper conditions.

FDR **Thursday, November 28** At home. Thanksgiving Day. While step by step the Saints are plundered of their liberties they still should be thankful for the Gospel with all its knowledge, Faith, Hope and Charity and that their enemies are yet restrained from violence and shedding of blood; and that Zion is in this best of all lands, and best of all governments.

GFR **Nov. 28, 1889** Thanks Givings Day.

FDR **Sunday, December 8** The Endowment House was torn down soon after last October Conference.

FDR **Thursday, December 19** A Revelation received by Pres. WW on Sunday, November 24 was read giving to those now first hearing great joy as it did the others who heard when first given.

FDR **Sunday, December 22** The warm rainy weather has made the streets a sheet of quagmire. O when shall I be able to again enjoy the liberty of meeting and of labor again? The terrible trouble in my back so long prevents the strength returning as heretofore. To stand a few minutes almost breaks my back, or to sit and write a short time inclining forward. I have to lie down often. O, Lord, if thou wilt be pleased to strengthen me I will endeavor to serve Thee.

FDR **Wednesday, December 25** Franklin came and spent the night with us. He is quite overwhelmed with the amounts and kinds of labor imposed upon him and expected at his hands in the City. The narration of his experience in Washington recently was very interesting indeed.

FDR **Thursday, January 2, 1890** Receiving repeated invitations I went with Jane to an Old People's party in the 2nd Ward meeting house. After incessant persuasion to please others I danced 3 times, which I have not done for many years. I don't feel the Spirit to dance.

GFR **Jan 29** Was informed by Pres. Gowans that I had been sustained by the Stake Conference at Grantsville, held the 26 and 27, 1890 as Second Counselor to H. S. Gowans, President of the Tooele Stake. I met in the evening at Apostle Lyman's where I received instructions from Apostle Lyman after which I was ordained a High Priest and set apart as 2nd Counselor to Pres. Gowans in the Tooele Stake of Zion, Apostle Lyman being mouth. I received a good blessing with many promises.

FDR **Monday, February 17** I am thankful that my sons learn and love to pay their tithings.

FDR **Wednesday, March 12** Pres. Woodruff feels afflicted with the course Apostles M. Thatcher and John W. Taylor are taking about the mining interests they are engaged in.

FDR **Saturday, March 29** At home in Ogden. A beautiful pleasant day. Spent most of today entering carefully and correctly in my Family and Church records all the Temple work done by us during the present week, which I have nearly accomplished.

FDR **Saturday, April 5** Deliberations were indulged in as to the propriety of splitting up the People's Party into Democrats and Republicans—did not conclude to do so.

FDR **Thursday, April 10** Senator Cullum of Ill[inoi]s introduced a Bill in Congress prohibiting any Latter Day Saint from voting, serving as Juror, be elected to or hold any civil office in the Territory of Utah.

FDR **Tuesday, May 13** 360 non-Mormons in Ogden have signed protest to Congress against the Disfranchisement Bills now before it.

FDR **Sunday, May 18** I wrote to JJ Fuller of Provo giving him account that his friends had received Endowments in Nauvoo but no record of sealing—many are finding themselves mistaken who received ordinances in Nauvoo, Endowments only, while they suppose they were sealed also.

FDR **Saturday, May 24** Ogden to Omaha about 1032 miles in about 34 hours or about 31 miles per hour including the stoppings for meals and changes of engines. What a contrast—going over the same Longitude in 1848 with our teams required from July 3rd till October 19th—3½ Months.

GFR **May 29** Three Grand Divisions of Labor for the Saints: 1st Work for the dead.

2nd Raising, providing for and properly teach and educate our children.

3rd Preach the Gospel abroad

GFR **Sat June 7th 1890** Tooele. Weather fine. I attended Stake Priesthood meeting. There were but fifteen persons present. Ate my dinner, which consisted of cream and bread and gooseberries. Entertained the sewing machine agent for a short time who tried to have me buy the Improved Singer for $55.00 Cash.

FDR **Wednesday, June 11** At Philadelphia and for Chicago. A very warm day. I got names of Langstroths and Longstroth from Phil City directory. Visited the Independence Hall and the Carpenter's Hall. The reminiscenses of those halls are intensely interesting to any patriotic American whose father deliberated or fought in the Revolution.

GFR **June 12** George C. came to see me about hiring some money. We conversed upon the principles of Geo. Q. Cannon skipping his bonds to escape the Penitentiary. He, having been suspended for making the assertion that Geo Q. was the biggest Hypocrite in the country. I tried to convince him that he was in error and would better make amends. I told him, his arguments were, in my opinion as foreign to the spirit and genius of the Gospel as are the arguments of the Sectarians in their claim that baptism is not essential to Salvation.

FDR **Tuesday, June 17** After due consideration it was

unanimously decided not expedient to divide into Dems. And Repubs but stick to People's Party principles even if we go down in defeat.

FDR **Thursday, July 10** GQC addressed the Council at some length in stating the efforts being made by Republican Friends to pave the way of Utah into Congress. Spoke of the decision of the Presidency concerning plural Marriage.

GFR **Saturday July 12, 1890** Had my first ripe apple of the season from one of our tress. No worm in it. Shaved and bathed.

GFR **Monday July 14th 1890** I was elected to the office of School Trustee for a term of 3 years. Votes as follows G. F. Richards 48. Total 57.

FDR **Friday, July 18** I paid Br. Niel $40.50 for those who had been receiving Ordinances for our kindred, the last 3 weeks, about sixty dead—the rule of the Temple being 50 cents per day for women and one dollar for men.

FDR **Tuesday, July 22** Spent the morning recording Temple labor and nearly finished that of the immediate line of our ancestors back to the Emigrant Richard Richards who came over in the London Merchant in 1620 and landed in the Jamestown Colony—became member of Burgesses till 1612 or 1613 when he left and was next heard from at Lynn, Mass in 1613.

GFR **Monday Aug 4th, 1890** Tooele at the election I was elected County Treasurer.

FDR **Thursday, August 7** Decided that if the Hedrickites will mortgage the whole Temple Block in Independence, being 8 lots for $15,000 at 6% interest, we are willing. The Presidency shall so permit.

FDR **Wednesday, September 24** At 2:30 attended with 3 First Presidents, at upper room in Gardo House and considered the text of President Woodruff's Manifesto—critically, and the same was unanimously agreed on by all present and we were sorry that Pres. L. Snow could not or was not present.

FDR **Tuesday, September 30** Met in upper front room of Gardo House and after singing and prayer by FML, Pres. Snow addressed the Council and was followed by FDR, MT, and FML, all spoke of the President WW's Manifesto—its reception by the Saints and by the World. How the Lord had suspended the operations of His laws in various occasions; and held the enemies of his Church responsible for the same.

FDR **Monday, October 6** At Conference. Delightfully pleasant day. A day long to be remembered by the whole Church. After reading "The Articles of Faith" I moved their adoption. After reading the Manifesto of 24th of September by Pres. Woodruff, Pres. Lorenzo Snow moved the General Conference approve the same, both which were read by Bp. OF Whitney and both were adopted unanimously. It is indeed wonderful hour. The people are so unanimous on this great question of suspending the institution of plural or Patriarchal Marriage. It is a melting testimony to Pres. WW of the implicit confidence the people have in him and his administration. The Holy Spirit bears indubitable testimony.

GFR **Monday Oct 20th 1890** Tooele Received four copies of Pres. Woodruff's Manifesto through the mail, Pamphlet form, including the proceedings of the Conference meeting held in the forenoon of Oct 6th 1890 at the Tabernacle Salt Lake City.

GFR **Wednesday Oct 22nd 1890** Tooele. We all got weighed. I weighed 165½ lbs.

FDR **Friday, November 21** learned of another child born to my son George at Tooele, and of a relapse of his wife, &c.

GFR **Thursday Dec 4th 1890** Tooele. I fasted and blessed the baby giving her the name of Amy May. Took the baby to Fast meeting and had it blessed there. My donations are $1.00 per month fast offerings, $1.00 per month temple offerings.

GFR **Saturday Dec 13th** Met my father and Aunt Jane at the depot it being Relief Society Conference. Took them directly to meeting. Visited with my father in the forenoon of Sunday. He put up with us.

FDR **Sunday, December 14** At Tooele City. A clear, fine day. I spent the forenoon at visiting with my son George, his wife Alice and their six children. George, LeGrand, Joel, Minerva, Sarah Ellen, and Amy May. I presented Geo. Life and Words of Christ by Geikie, Biographical sketches of my life.

FDR **Sunday, December 21** FSR informed us of his interviews with Pres. Harrison, Secty Baline, Atty Genl Miller, Speaker Reed, and of his experience in the Court.

FDR **Wednesday January 28 [1891]** Pres. W. W. stated the object of this meeting to be to consider the financial condition and liabilities of the Church and its relations to the Sugar Industry; total $280,000.

FDR **Thur January 29** Our Council's Fast Day. The same Brethren in Council. All of the Brethren in Council partook of Lord's Supper. Br. Joseph F. Smith spoke powerfully about our want of respect and deference for each other and bore a remarkable testimony of my trials and integrity to the work of God. Also said "All honor to that man, Brother Richards for his steadfastness in all he had passed through" and much more. Brother G. Q. C. remarked he had noticed with peculiar pleasure that since Pres. B. Young's death in all our deliberations he never had known anything pass my lips that would have been unpleasant for Pres. Young to hear. Much precious instruction, exhortation and explanation was given today.

FDR **Wednesday March 4** Great danger that contention will

drive the Holy Spirit from the bosoms of the Elders who indulge in it.

FDR **Monday March 9** At evening listened just about 2 hours to the most intensely interesting lecture that I ever head by the greatest living explorer that I have any knowledge of. [John Rowland H. M.] Stanley gave us "Incidents of 23 years life as an Explorer in Central Africa." Born in 1841 at Denbigh Wales. His real name is Rowland.

GFR **Sunday Apr 12th 1891** Vernon—Met with the mutual and I addressed them for 30 minutes upon the necessity of a testimony; the ways to obtain such a testimony.

FDR **Monday May 4** Pres. Chas O. Card represented the Church in Canada—50 families, 300 souls, S. Schools, R. Societies, M.I. Asso, and Primaries. Close by Reservation, 15 and 40 miles, of 2300 Blackfoot or Blood Indians, friendly, neither Catholic nor protestant. Get on well with them. Cardston, 800 miles from S.L. City, fare nearly $60 round trip—takes 3 days time for the trip.

GFR **Friday May 8th** Took Alice to the Station on the way to Salt Lake to do some trading. Cheap fare on account of the visit to Salt Lake of U.S. President Harrison.

GFR **Wednesday May 13th** We left here at 5.30 A.M. and arrived in Salt Lake at 10 A.M. Had the buggy repaired. On our way home we were hailed by a trickster who mulched us in the Sum of $20.00. A dear experience but I trust it will be a profitable lesson.

GFR **Sunday May 24th 1891** <u>An Essay</u> (on spirits, free agency, eternal progression)

We expect by passing through the same ordeals as He did to become the same as he is. We were not born upon the earth because there was an earth not peopled but the earth was made for us to dwell upon and as soon as it was made ready the emigration commenced from that world to this. We anticipated coming upon this earth as a mission to perform certain work necessary to be done before we could arrive at the stage or blessed condition of our God. To obtain to the glorious state that our Father had attained was our aim and object. A mark set high but by so many of us lost track of in this life. We were given our free agency to act as we wish and hence show what we are good bad or indifferent. We get our bodies here, which by passing through death we become immortalized, fit to live forever. We form relations here to last for eternity and lay the foundation of our own Kingdom here-after by our posterity. We often lose sight of this most important part of our mission here and only form relationships for time thus failing in this part of our mission. We should not forget the object we had in view of coming into this life. We do not do as well as we know and are too slow in carrying out our good intentions.

He that does his duty, no matter how humble, is the one that has the approval of the Lord. It is not position that will save us but our daily works, not our intentions. The roads to apostasy— Neglect of duty, faultfinding and any thing that drives from us the Spirit of the Lord.

FDR **Tuesday May 26** I met between 25 and 30 of my children, G. Children and Cousins and their children. I had great and unexpected pleasure in relating my early experience to them, partaking of an excellent dinner, and then holding a meeting with them. I spoke to them of my proxy relation to them and of their Eternal Father Willard and exhorted them to constant duty with promises if faithful.

FDR **Tuesday Jun 9** Today the Round Ball on the South East Pinnacle of the Temple in this City was put in place.

FDR **Monday Jun 15** I was attacked with a terrible pain in the upper part of my chest which continued about 2 hours. I struggled against it. Laid my hands on and rebuked it.

FDR **Monday Jun 29** At 11 met other Brethren at the Gardo House. 1st felt deemed advisable that political parties may approach near an equality of numbers. 2nd that in Salt Lake District it may be and is deemed politic to get up a fusion ticket or a Citizen's Ticket in order to defeat the Liberals design to disenfranchise all Mormons.

GFR **Sunday July 19th** There was no [Sunday] school, it having been discontinued to prevent the spread of diphtheria. I read and lounged under the trees until meeting time when Alice and I attended meeting and I addressed the meeting for about 45 minutes as led by the spirit which aided me materially.

GFR **Sunday Aug 2nd** So eager is man to obtain the wealth of this world that he often times sacrifices his good name, his self-respect, his honor and character and even his hopes of Eternal Life in order to obtain it, which in the end proves to be a mere phantom or shadow. Should we be as devoted in our efforts to obtain the riches of eternity we would scarce fail in obtaining them.

GFR **Monday Aug 3rd** My name was on the Republican Ticket for Representative from 9th Legislative District to Next Territorial Legislature. It was also upon the County Republican ticket as County Justice of the Peace for Tooele Precinct. It was also on the Municipal ticket as 1st Alderman for the City.

FDR **Friday August 7** Did little at my Records for the Dead selecting names baptized for to be sealed. It requires the most searching deep and studious thoughtfulness to get strict accuracy for this supremely important labor of Love for our kindred in order that it may be worthy of all acceptation.

FDR **Friday August 14** In a dream, Pres. B. Young, dead, said to me: "I think you might have horse and buggy to get about and perform your duties more easily."

GFR **Thursday, Oct 1st 1891** Sentiments—Tear down the wall of fortifycation against evil and the captor will take you unawares. The strongest fortifications are Humility, prayr and the faithful discharge of every duty.

GFR **Monday Nov 9th** In the evening I attended a lecture delivered upon the Subject of palmistry by Prof. Aulguire and from there to the Wizard Martin's show.

FDR **Thursday, November 12** Recd. Circular of the 1st Presidency of October 31 asking $100,000 to finish the Temple; also no longer necessary to send their recommends to Pres. Woodruff for his endorsement—Bishops and Stake Presidents will do.

GFR **Thursday Nov 19th** In the evening I attended the Y.M.M.I. Ass. and lectured on the habit of gum and tobacco chewing from a physiological and refinement Standpoint.

FDR **Wednesday, December 9** I signed a petition to President Harrison in which the 1st Presidency and the 12 Apostles ask general amnesty for our people.

GFR **Monday Jan 11th** On my way met the returning Rabbit hunters. The Democrats & Republicans having been contesting their claims for championship 408 rabbits killed Democrats claim ahead.

FDR **Wednesday, January 13, 1892** Pres. Snow was uncommonly nice and fine in his instructions to us. Pres. Snow read a Poem by himself on the Sentiment of God and Man.

As we are now,
So once was He,
As He is now,
So may we be.

249

FDR **Thursday, February 25** Talk of April Conf. and placing the Top Stone. I found account of laying one in Nauvoo, May 1845 and handed in to the Presidency.

GFR **Friday Mar 11th** Positions of Trust held by me this date—

1. Second Counselor in the Stake Presidency
2. County Treasurer of Tooele County
3. Member of County Board of Examiners of Teachers
4. Member of Board of Directors of the Tooele City Water Co. and Treasurer of the Company
5. Vice Pres. of the County Republican Committee
6. A member of the School Board and Chairman
7. Employee of AF Doremus @$70.00 per month and conveniences of the place

I was a candidate on the Republican ticket for Representative to the Legislature but was defeated by the Democratic candidate from Bingham.

FDR **Wednesday, March 16** Found Pres. L. Snow on the Train going to City to give deposition concerning Title to Property in Independence which "reorganized Josephites" and "Hedrekites" are contending about before Commissioner of Court.

FDR **Friday, April 1, 1892** Pres. JF Smith handed in Draft of a Telegram from Atty. Williams at Washington concerning Amnesty. MT and JWT declined to sign it. Joseph would see Pres. WW about it.

GFR **Sunday Apr 3rd** I boarded the 8:18 A.M. special train for conference after an experience with a balky horse in a heavy storm.

FDR **Wednesday, April 6** At Gen Conf laying Top Stone of Nauvoo[6] Temple. Weather delightfully comfortable. Was in

---

6. He meant the Salt Lake Temple.

place in upper stand with 1st Presidency and Pres. L. Snow in the Tab. And at 11:15 went out in procession to Platform with the Presidency, Twelve, Patriarchs, the 1st Presidents of 70's, the Choir and the H. Priests, Seventies, Pres' and Counselors of Stakes, Bishops and Counselors of wards, Lesser Priesthood and Multitude. Generally computed there were 40,000 persons on the Temple grounds and about 10,000 more in the surrounding adjacent streets and on the houses. At Meridian, the services commenced and when the Plate and Books were deposited and announced by Architect Joseph Don Carlos Young, Pres. W. Woodruff pressed a Button adjusted at the back of his chair and a bell was heard to ring from the Tower and JDC Young reported the Cap Stone in place. At 4 p.m. my sons Franklin and Charles went with me onto the Temple. Charles went to the top and stood by the Angel statue. I felt too weary to go to the top.

GFR **Wednesday Apr 6th 1892** Attended the Tabernacle and Temple services [and] the laying of the Capstone of the Temple.

FDR **Friday, April 8** Dropped my dime dated 1891 into the slot of the Capstone.

FDR **Sunday, April 24** The Fast Day of next Sunday will be occupied by two meetings and obtaining contributions for hastening the completion of Salt Lake Temple.

GFR **Sunday May 1st** this being the day set apart by the Church Presidency for fasting & prayr I fasted twenty-six hours. Attended the meeting and offered the opening prayr. Meeting held from 10 A.M. until after 2 P.M. and then subscriptions were taken for the completion of the Salt Lake Temple. Funds included promises to the amount of over $700 were raised. I subscribed $50.00. During the meeting Alice at home had severe pains and when I came home I sent for Miss Grace McKellar whom we had previously engaged as nurse and soon after sent for Dr. Davis. At 10:30 P.M. a baby girl was born in a perfect condition.

FDR **Tuesday, May 3** Salt Lake Stake appropriated about $60,000 on Sunday for the Temple.

FDR **Monday, May 16** The importance of a proper education and habits of morality and getting old heads on young shoulders.

FDR **Tuesday, May 24** . . . Deplores the unhappy feeling in Ogden—old time Friends now pass each other in the streets of Logan, a Temple City, and will not recognize each other being now Dems and Reps.

FDR **Tuesday, June 28** Mutually decided for FS and Emily, Charley, Jane and I make ready to start from here on Thursday, the 7th of next Month on a trip to Portland, Tacoma, Port Townsend and to Sitka if the Lord permit on a summer vacation in search of health.

FDR **Monday, October 10** At 10 a.m. met with the 1st Presidency, Twelve, 7 Pres' of the 70's and other Authorities of Stakes and Wards—some 2 to 3 hundred. The first meeting held in the upper main Court of the Temple. An unusual measure of the Holy Spirit was realized and liberal subscriptions were made toward the completion of the building.

FDR **Thursday, October 13** Telegram from a friend in the East was read affirming that Amnesty would soon be extended to us in Utah and that Pres. Benjamin Harrison requested our prayers in his own behalf and for his sick wife who is very low of consumption.

FDR **Tuesday, November 15** In Council with 1st Presidency and FML and JHS gave my approval for Pres. WW to have another thousand dollars to his annual allowance. He ought to be unembarrassed and give his strength to the spiritual concerns of the Church.

GFR **Monday Dec 5th** Snowed all day without cessation. At bedtime about a foot of heavy snow. Notwithstanding the storm I was working out nearly all day. After doing the morning's work I brought in the cattle and fed them in the shed. I went to the depot in an almost blinding snow storm and got 2200 lbs of coal, unloaded it; hauled some wood down from the sheds, made paths about house and yards &c. Spent the evening at home. Played marbles & authors with the children, read a chapter of a love story & wrote in my journal. Still snowing at bedtime. All well & happy.

FDR **Wednesday, January 4 [1893]** We received, ten of our Brethren (separately), a Letter from the Presidency to us and delivered to each, a note from the Presidency with a request for certain amounts named privately to us.[7] Scowcroft and Sons . . . $1000; Richard Taylor . . . $750; Browning Brothers . . . $1000; Wright & Sons (merchants) . . . $1000; Thos. D. Dee . . . $1000; David Eccles . . . $1000. All felt kindly and will do what they can.

GFR **Tuesday, Jan 24th** worked with the hydrant to try and get water it having frozen up and busted.

GFR **Monday Jan 30th** In the evening I read aloud from "Scottish Chiefs" & played a couple of games of checkers with Alice. All are tolerably well, colds excepted.

FDR **Thursday, March 16** Pres. WW proposed a Circular to the people to settle wrongs and be united before Dedication.

FDR **Saturday, March 18** Shaved and clipped and did chores. Dismissed a gang of boys from a convention in my barn.

FDR **Sunday, March 26** The Saints generally are showing a

---

7. This was an invitation to wealthy brethren to contribute to the completion of the Salt Lake Temple.

very renewed interest in reconciling themselves to each other and in being re-baptized for renewal of their Covenants.

GFR **Wednesday Mar 29th** Got recommends for the family to go to the Temple dedication.

FDR **Wednesday, April 5, 1893** Pres. W Woodruff requested the Saints to attend to their private prayers at bedtime for the Holy Spirit to be with us mightily during Conference and the Dedication season. Pres. L. Snow and all the Council (except HJ Grant who is not arrived from Washington) labored with Brother Moses Thatcher till near midnight to enable him to see and feel as the rest did on some points of Fellowship with us and with the First Presidency and succeeded fully; to the great joy of our hearts.

FDR **Thursday, April 6, 1893** Dedication of the Salt Lake Temple.[8] A Terribly windy day. <u>1st Exercise</u>. At 1st Dedicatory services in the Temple, Presidency 3; Twelve 12; Seventies 7; five Presidency of 70's; Patriarchs; Presidents of the Quorums of 70's; Widows of first Presidencies and Twelve Apostles about 185 in number. 300 singers. After anthem, Pres. WW delivered dedication prayer in 36 minutes; Pres. GQC spoke 37 minutes; WW spoke; JFS spoke 11 minutes. Dismission at 12:23 by L. Snow.

GFR **Thursday April 6th 1893** Salt Lake City. Weather threatening in the morning and during the Dedication Services a regular hurricane. I attended the First services of dedication of the Temple during which time a hurricane raged blowing down houses, trees, fences, etc. Had a most enjoyable time.

FDR **Friday, April 7, 1893** At Temple met with Saints. . . . Prest. WW stated his night vision. WW said Joseph Smith,

8. Franklin recorded in his journal the details of each of the thirty-one dedicatory services—plus the five sessions for Sunday School children—including the names of those who offered the dedicatory prayers.

Brigham Young, & J. Taylor had gathered together all the Church of the Firstborn in the Latter-days & the ancient Saints & with Christ in their midst. When we shout, they shout, and the work is more earnest with them than with us because they know more than we do.

4th Service: P.M. L. Snow delivered the prayer in 38½ min. Pres. WW testified to the truth of JFS's remarks and said that Pres. B. Young has twice since his death delivered to him the Keys of this Temple and commanded him to dedicate it. He first saw the dedication of this Temple 50 years ago while in Boston. No one is more rejoiced over these things than the Prophet Joseph Smith.

FDR **Sunday, April 9, 1893** At Dedication, O[gden] to City and return, 74 m.

8th Service: WW said no one was more interested in these services than Joseph Smith, Brigham Young and John Taylor. Hosanna and Anthem as usual. Pres. WW "Heavenly Hosts are near us. The Son of God is among this people." He bore a powerful testimony of Christ's and Joseph's Missions and labors.

FDR **Monday, April 10, 1893** Pres. WW said Christ has charge of the Earth and is in our midst no less because we do not see him than when he appeared in Kirtland and other times.

FDR **Tuesday, April 11, 1893** Noontime, all the Twelve Apostles met in their Room and subscribed amounts for furnishing same, equal to $2000 and HJ Grant volunteered a painting of Nauvoo and its Temple to help adorn the room.

FDR **Thursday, April 20, 1893** A glorious day in the Temple. A drinking glass with Temple etched on, which I took my wine with paper napkin was given me as a souvenir of the occasion.

GFR **Thursday April 20th 1893** I met the Brethren of the Priesthood at the Temple where we heard the voices of the

Apostles & Presidency & held Prayr Circle, the first ever held in the Temple and the largest ever held in this dispensation. Partook of the Lord's Supper and our glasses & napkins were given to us to preserve. A glorious time we had indeed and a spirit prevailed such as I never before witnessed.

GFR **Saturday April 22nd 1893** This day Alice took the four small children, Legrand, Joel, Sarah and Amy to SL City with the Sunday School to see and attend the Temple dedication. I took them to the Depot and met them in the evening. Planted trees during the day. In the evening I shaved and bathed &c.

FDR **Monday, April 24, 1893** Last Day of Dedication services. 31st Assembly: 2:30 p.m. I offered the prayer in 37 minutes. Shout and Anthem. Joseph F. Smith summed up. Found conference lasted just 3 weeks. Held 44 meetings, 62 thousand Saints had attended. Pres. WW stated the Lord had accepted the Temple, forgiven us our sins if we sin no more and have broken hearts and contrite spirits.

FDR **Tuesday, April 25** Much of our time was occupied in listening to the transactions of Directors of the "Mexican Colonizing and Manufacturing Co." . . .

FDR **Sunday, April 30** At 7:45 read Telephone message from AH Cannon, Pres. WW worse and wished me to come by the first train.

GFR **Sunday April 30th** In the evening Bro Lyman used the time and well too . . . on kissing.

FDR **Thursday, May 4** Pres. WW rested well last night and feels comfortable this morning. Paid my donations $100 toward furnishing the Twelve Apostles room.

FDR **Saturday, May 6** To Pres. WW. Found him weak and weary in bed. I named leading incidents in his life and our earlier associations in Gospel labors. He felt that his work here was done. Expects soon to meet with old Friends on the other side and will remember me with others of his Friends here to them there. Said I had always been obedient to God and to his servants—had known me a long time and had no fault to find with me. Blessed me on our separation.

FDR **Thursday, June 8** To City and return, 74 mi. Weather very warm. Pres. GQ Cannon left this a.m. to join HJ Grant in the East and they to London to effect a loan if possible to relieve the Church a large loan on long time and low interest. Pres. Woodruff and JF Smith and several of the 12 attended the opening of the Salt Air Bathing Resort.

FDR **Thursday, June 29** JFS read a statement of am[oun]ts of indebtedness of the Church. No one showed the way out of embarrassments.

FDR **Saturday, July 1, 1893** This trying time is the first day that Bro. Jack has been unable to meet the 1st of each Month the amounts due to those who look to him as paymaster.[9] All this is caused by the worldwide agitation of the "Silver Question". Bro. Jack unable to furnish me any means at present or any one of the 12.

FDR **Friday, July 7** A Cablegram from Pres. GQC says "unsuccessful."

FDR **Sunday, July 16** A very interesting and powerful discourse from Pres. Josh F. Smith on debt, mortgaging homes, economy and living beyond our means.

GFR **Saturday July 22nd** At the priesthood meeting the subject of choosing a Patriarch for the stake was considered. I was

---

9. Brother Jack was the comptroller for the Church. He provided for the payment of the Church's bills and even the stipend received by the members of the Twelve. The Church was greatly in debt at this time, and no one was willing to lend it money.

very much surprised at my name having been presented for a Patriarch but could not oppose the Spirit of the Lord which directed the matter.

GFR **Monday July 24th** After the services we made ice cream and had dinner and went for a ride with team and two seated buggy. The folks retired early but I sat up until nearly 12 o'clock reading the Book of Covenants and Bible. All usually well. Myself enjoying a good spirit having a measurably clear conscience having no enemies that I know of and many friends.

FDR **Wednesday, July 26** My son George F. Richards, who was ordained a Patriarch on the 23rd inst by Apostle FM Lyman spent an interesting half hour in asking information of me concerning the duties of his new calling and ordination.

GFR **Wednesday Jul 26th 1893** While in the city called on my Father and had a chat with him.

GFR **Friday Aug 4th** [after beach party with the ward] Estella tried to thwart our wishes by trying to stay later and acted hateful in trying to have her own way. When I arrived home I gave her a plain un-garnished talking to.

FDR **Tuesday, August 15** With Pres. L. Snow called on the Presidency. All seem well but loaded down with indebtedness and cares.

FDR **Thursday, August 31** The Scarcity of Money renders it difficult for many of the poor Saints to make themselves comfortable for food and necessities. A poor and afflicted sister called related her adversities in trying to sustain her family with her needle—fancies she sees starvation before them. I encouraged her the best I could and she wiped away her tears and went with apparently increased bravery.

GFR **Sept 5** Copy of a letter written from my father with blessings enclosed.

L.D.S. Historians Office, P.O. Box 1676, Salt Lake City,
   Utah, Sept. 5th 1893
To my well beloved son Geo. F. Richards,
Patriarch and Counselor to the President:

   Inasmuch as you are one of the few distinguished persons in Zion who are blessed to have two fathers and both
in the Church, I thought you might like to know something of the blessings that you became heir to through
their diligence and faithfulness in preaching the Gospel,
gathering Israel and laboring to establish righteousness in
the earth. Since you have attained to the Patriarchal office
at so early a period of your life, it may prove profitable
for you to observe and study the spirit of these blessings.
They will nourish and enrich you with the spirit of your
new calling. My son, may the blessing and power of God
make you equal to all requirements made of you, with
love to you and all yours.
                    Yours affectionately,
                    Franklin D. Richards.

[George received copies of the patriarchal blessings of both
Franklin and Willard Richards but did not record them.]

FDR **Tuesday, October 3** Prest. Snow addressed us joyfully
and with assurance that the blessing and help of God will be
equal to all our necessities as it was with Christ our Savior at his
last earthly trials.

FDR **Wednesday, October 11** Bro. Andrew Jensen brought
a copy of John Whitmer's Church History that was refused by
Whitmer when the Prophet Joseph demanded it of him that
1838 in Missouri. I directed Br. Jensen to put it in Type by a Type
writer so that we may have it complete.

FDR **Thursday, October 12** Decided not best for Pres' and

counselors and Bishops and their counselors to put themselves or be put in nomination for Political officers, as it would injure themselves and the Church to do so.

GFR **Satuday Oct 28th** In the evening I attended a meeting of the Republican party to nominate city officers and School trustees. I was named for Mayor to be voted for but declined to accept a nomination. When it came to School trustees my name was proposed and I stated that the only way I could accept a nomination was to have it made by both parties. . . . This statement grew out of the fact that the Presidency of the Church had counseled the Presidency of Stakes and Bishoprics of wards to not accept nominations for political office.

FDR **Friday, November 3** I went with Franklin and heard him report his labors in Washington with Supreme Court, Committees in Congress; various Senators, Sergeants at Arms; Attorney General, Assistant Attorney Genl and Pres of United States to get the "Joint Resolution" restoring personal property to the Church through Congress and approved by Atty. Genl and signed by President Cleveland. Then to Court with Motion to order decree in Utah Court to pay over the amount on Auditation and approval by the Court—exceedingly interesting to us all.

FDR **Wednesday, December 13** Wires say that the Bill enabling Utah to become a state passed the House of Reps—about 4 p.m. today.

FDR **Monday, January 1, 1894** As James Smith is fitting our house with electric lighting, so I ask the very Eternal Father to light up my Soul with the light and Life of His Eternal Favor.

FDR **Thursday, January 25** Pres. JFS reported the Proposition of Principal Kingsbury, Dr. Talmage, and Prof. Stewart, that Church University and Utah University be converted into one and Talmage be Principal.

George Franklin Richards, ca. 1878,
age seventeen.

George F. Richards, ca. 1898, while serving
as a Utah state legislator.

Tooele Stake presidency, October 6, 1891: H. S. Gowens, C. S. Anderson, G. F. Richards.

Left to right: Asenath Richards Grover, Alice Richards Smith, Nanny Longstroth Richards, George F. Richards, and Minerva Richards Knowlton, at Nanny's home in Nephi, Utah, ca. 1890.

GEORGE FRANKLIN RICHARDS.   ORSON FERGUSON WHITNEY.   DAVID O. M'KAY.

The Deseret Evening News *published the photos of three Apostles called in April 1906: (left to right) George F. Richards, Orson F. Whitney, and David O. McKay.*

administered to. I took 6th 5:55 train and arrived in Salt Lake about 9:45 PM. A successful time —

Monday, June 26, 1922.
Home.

I had a busy day at the temple. Sealed 26 couples. Alice, Rie, Josephine, Franklin, and Alice & Joe Tate were each baptized for 20 names, 120 in all.

I went before the Presidency to consult them about the reception to be tendered Sister Edna Smith, the Matron of the Temple. The matter of a successor came up. I told the brethren that I thought it would be well to defer the appointment of a successor to E. J. Smith as it would not then be associated with Sister Smith's release. This was approved heartily. I said, however, that since I had such a good opportunity I thought I might express my thoughts as to a successor to Sister E. J. Smith. So I told the brethren that I thought it somewhat more proper and preferable to have my own wife as an assistant to me in this temple work than some body else's wife provided the brethren felt that she is worthy & capable of filling the bill — The brethren unanimous said she is just the woman for the place, none equal to her and said further that they had already considered the matter and decided upon her. Tears came in Pres. Grant's eyes as he spoke of it.

George F. Richards (front row, fifth from left) with missionaries in the Southern States mission, 1928.

George F. Richards, shortly after his call to serve as president of the Salt Lake Temple, 1922.

PRESIDENT GEORGE F. RICHARDS
Died Aug. 8, 1950 at the age of 89 years. He is survived by 13 children, 61 grandchildren and 89 great-grandchildren.

Death notice of President George F. Richards in the Deseret News.

GFR **Monday Feb 12th** In the evening I read from the Juvenile and helped George with his arithmetic examples and gave Legrand a Patriarchal blessing. George wrote for the same.

FDR **Tuesday, February 13** . . . These tight times. Hundreds of men out of work through the streets daily, their families destitute of food beside those whose wants are not paraded. Many plans are being adopted to raise supplies for the needy.

FDR **Sunday, March 18** About 5 p.m. His Excellency Caleb W. West, Governor of Utah[10] and his Honor Judge Chief Justice Samuel A. Merritt came in and spent the evening in a very pleasant way. Dined with us and our visit tended to promote friendly relations.

FDR **Monday, April 9** At 10 a.m. Presidency, 11 of the Twelve, 7 Pres's of 70's, Pres's and Counselors of Stakes and of Wards, High Counselors and others faithful met in Assembly Hall. Deci[sion] by a Bp. or Pres. of Stake without their counselors is no decision. They must use their counselors. And not make up their decisions alone. If Pres' decisions are not confirmed by Councils a rehearing must be had.

FDR **Thursday, May 3** Voted not to defend in case Josephites vs. Hedrickites trying for Title to Temple Lot in Independence.

GFR **Thursday May 17th** Anointed Legrand's leg and administered to him.

GFR **Saturday June 2nd** Shaved, bathed, went to meeting house to attend Stake Priesthood meeting, which failed for want of attendance.

FDR **Monday, July 16** The Salt Lake Herald of the 18th inst. states that at 11:50 p.m. President Grover Cleveland signed the Enabling Act for Utah's Statehood.

10. Franklin's son Charles C. Richards was appointed secretary of Utah Territory under Governor Caleb W. West.

GFR **Monday Aug 27th** Made crutches for Legrand and put thick wood sole on his shoe.

FDR **Wednesday, September 5** At Pres' Office got from Relief Society's Record at Nauvoo that my Jane joined the Society March 9, 1844 at a meeting held that day in the Hall over the Brick store. Emma Smith presided.

GFR **Sunday Sept 9th** Had splendid talk by Jos. F. in which he denounced Debating Societies, card playing, round dancing, and kindred evils and encouraged the young in good works &c.

FDR **Tuesday, September 25** Spent near 2 hours in Temple and Annex, in Council with President L. Snow about the initial work of our "Genealogical Society and Library of Utah."

FDR **Friday, September 28** With Franklin my son, went to Pres' Office. He is still ill at home. FSR explained to GQ Cannon and JF Smith the New Amnesty that arrived yesterday from Pres. Cleveland that with the New Oath by Commission of yesterday that most can and ought to accept the same and Register, as it clears up all to date and only requires promise to obey the Law and not advise others to disobey it.

FDR **Saturday, September 29** Accepted amnesty and pardon. Registered at Ogden.

FDR **Sunday, October 7** At City. A beautiful lovely day. Great throng at Conference. Pres. WW spoke 20 minutes and told the Conference if he and John Smith could not leave off Whiskey and Tobacco they had better resign their offices.

FDR **Thursday, October 11** Susa Gates called and deliberated how to avoid repetition of the labors for the dead in the Temples.

FDR **October 22nd** Exchanged Cards with Russian Count Gregory Galitzin from St. Petersburg, and with Rev. Francis Laslow, Roman Catholic in the S. Lake Temple by permission of

Pres. WW. I learn Gen Clarkson has also been permitted to pass in and through the Temple.

FDR **Sunday, October 28** What shall I render to my God for all his gifts to me? I feel melted under a sense of His goodness unto me.

FDR **Thursday, November 1, 1894** Clerk GF Gibbs read Articles of agreement for Incorporation of "Genealogical Society of Utah" when it was unanimously voted that the Society proceed and incorporate as contemplated and that Apostle FD Richards be President of the Society.

GFR **Thursday Nov 8th** Took Amy to the Doctor.—Dr. Davis prescribed for her and gave us medicine but did not indicate to us her true condition, I believe though he did not know the true condition. Her nose had bled for several days, the blood had oozed from her lips, tongue and mouth and purple hemorage had set in and made its appearance on the body. About 1 week previous she had jaundice so said Dr. Davis and a few days later had fever and a rash for three days which resembled scarlet fever. She had seemed languid and fatigued but otherwise not very sick. Rested well usually at nights.

GFR **Friday Nov 9th** When I came in at noon from plowing finding her condition no more favorable than the day previous and her nose still bleeding having bled slowly but continuously since early morning we decided to go the City with her. Little did we think when we bid her good-bye at the station that it was the last good-bye in this life and when on the cars Mamma held the baby up to bid us another good-bye poor little Amy sat on the opposite side of the car holding a cloth to her bleeding nose when her poor little arms must have felt like they were about to drop off. She had bled so much, become so weak and was so fearful that the blood should drop. A contemplation of these little incidents causes copious tears to flow, with grief almost un-bounded. After taking the folks to the station I returned to plow and in the evening attended a meeting of the School Trustees un-til a late hour but not so late nor I so tired but that I could bow in secret prayer petitioning the Lord in behalf of our little girl.

FDR **Sunday, November 18** Spoke 1½ hours to a large con-gregation of attentive hearers on the importance of the Law of Tithing and obedience thereto, and the heinousness of the strife that exists between Republicans and Democrats and the abuse indulged in by the parties. Warned Church officers of the danger of showing partiality to either and of losing their influence and power over the people by so doing.

GFR **Saturday Nov 24th 1894** Georgie & I went hunting horses between here and the point of the mountain & through hay field. My horse fell on me and hurt me severely in the region of the ribs and heart. Bathed and retired to bed early.

FDR **Sunday, November 25** While I cannot preach the word to the living I search out the dead and labor for them.

GFR **Saturday Dec 29th** Made inventory of my properties & means, showing my worth at present not including household furnishings to be $8489.20.

GFR **Tuesday Jan 1st 1895** Welcome New Year, may you bring us much to cheer and little to regret. Since I became a man grown I do not remember having been freer from guilt, cleaner and more nearly prepared to meet my Lord than at the com-mencement of this New Year of 1895.

FDR **Thursday, January 17, 1885** The first time for years for-got to be at Council of 12 this a.m. in Temple.

GFR **Friday Feb 8th** Bro Lyman gave us some valuable in-struction & information. "A good public speaker is a calamity in a bishopric. A man slow of speech is much preferred, everything else being equal."

FDR **Thursday, February 14** Pres. WW desired the 12 to bear in mind and intercede with God to open the way and deliver the Presidency and the Twelve from their financial embarrassments.

FDR **Wednesday, February 27** At evening with Jane attended the Relief Society party in the 3rd Ward amusement hall. Large attendance, supper, dancing, speeches &c. Jane, I and Bp White addressed the meeting. I danced first cotillion with Jane. I told them when and how and where dancing originated among the Saints in the Nauvoo Temple and at Winter Quarters—to drive away the envy and melancholy and sadness of our persecutions, sicknesses and deaths.

FDR **Tuesday, April 2** At City. A beautiful pleasant morning. I am 74 years of age today if the reckoning has been kept correctly.

FDR **Thursday, April 4** Spent 2 hours or so considering the Question of getting Suffrage into the Constitution, or not. In Convention Suffrage for Women passed its 3rd reading and remains in the Constitution by vote of 75 to 14 after a strenuous effort.

GFR **Monday April 15th** My son George offered the evening Family prayer for his first time.[11] The first time requested to do so and it was a consistent and appropriate prayer. Splendid.

FDR **Wednesday, April 24** A 2 column account of James J. Strange's Kingdom, his Crowning, His murder, and the Breaking of his settlement on Beaver Island, Lake Michigan.

FDR **Thursday, April 25** Pres. JF Smith says I am chosen to meet with Susan Anthony and ladies of her company and a

---

11. At this time George was a week short of his twelfth birthday.

meeting of them with the ministers of SL City to represent the Church of JC of LDS among them.

FDR **Tuesday, May 14** Suffrage Convention met in Assembly Hall at 10 this a.m. Jane attends. Republican League meets today. At evening attended Suffrage meeting in Assembly Hall. Heard Miss Anthony, Bradford, Stansbury, and Shaw.

FDR **Wednesday, May 22** At 4:30 held a meeting of about 35 of Willard's family and several neighbors. I spoke about their relations to Willard and to me, and bore testimony of his greatness and his worth that he was vastly to be preferred to me in ability and in excellence. Willard's family is increased to about 200 souls by Nanny, Mary and Rhoda having been sealed to me and having children.

GFR **July 7th Sunday** Jos Tate desiring to cut today, I wrote them in answer as follows.

Bro Joseph Tate:
I do not believe Sunday work to be profitable. While I am very anxious to have my grain cut realizing that I may realize great loss by its standing too long, yet, I would not myself cut grain for myself or for any one else on Sunday and since you have the cutting by contract, you may do as you wish in the matter.
Respectfully,
G. F. Richards

FDR **Sunday, July 28** Br. Samuel Roskelly of Smithfield, Logan Temple Recorder, called and said it was talked of running Logan Temple on half time and I told him the people should be aroused to keep the Temple in full work on full time.

FDR **Saturday, August 10** The political elements thicken. Eastern people seem trying to create public sentiment against women voting on adoption of the Constitution and for state officers.

FDR **Thursday, September 5** O[gden] to [S.L.]C. and return. At 11 a.m. met with 3 Presidency in Temple. Discussed "Cocaine" as supposed remedy but an insidious vice; of suicides and their character.

FDR **Sunday, September 8** This morning I was admonished in a dream that my family was not observing the Sabbath properly. I saw several of them at various occupations and the children were playing ball and I was sharply surprised and reproved.

GFR **Wednesday, Sept 18** Alice had all of her upper teeth out while in the City.

FDR **Monday, October 7** JF Smith's remarks that 1 of the 12 and one of the 7 Pres of 70 were not approved—in taking the bits in their mouth and going without counsel were not approved. Created a rumpuss.

FDR **Sunday, November 3** Bro. Goddard introduced me to a Maori chief—Hirini Whanga—who is engaged in Temple labor.

FDR **Thursday, December 12** General conversation about dismissal of CW Penrose from the SL Herald, employment of BH Roberts instead. Presidency think perhaps we may get CWP and start compiling the Church History.

FDR **Thursday, December 19** Various topics were introduced and freely discussed as about Bros. M. Thatcher and BH Roberts line of procedure during last political campaign &c.

FDR **Saturday, January 4, 1896** On entering I was shown a telegram from Gov. Caleb W. West, viz—"Hon CC Richards, President signed Proclamation three minutes past ten, Three Cheers for New State."

GFR **Saturday Jan 4, 1896** This day at 8:03 A.M. or 10:03

A.M. Eastern time, Utah became a State by the signing of the proclamation by President Grover Cleveland.

FDR **Sunday, January 12** Towards morning I dreamed being at Lenox, Mass, where I once spent 3 or 4 Months in school at the Academy when Professor Hotchkiss was teacher; during which I lived with Eldad Post in Winter of 1835–6 and did chores for my board.

FDR **Thursday, February 6** Decided not expedient for Elders to take their wives with them on missions except in special cases, perhaps President of a Mission.

FDR **Thursday, February 13** We spent till 7:40 endeavoring to convince Br. Roberts of some improprieties and grievances perpetrated by him during the last political campaign.

GFR **Sunday Feb 16th** Nephi D____ offered a verbal resignation as counselor to Bishop on grounds that he was a user of tobacco & Apostle Lyman had said at our last Stake Conference that such men in official positions should hand in their resignations.

FDR **Thursday, March 5** At 11 a.m. in Council, 1st Presidency, All the 12 except Thatcher and Lund and the 7 Presidents of 70. The time from soon after 11 a.m. was spent in hearing testimony concerning Pres. BH Roberts as obtained two weeks ago. The conclusion of all was that Br. Roberts be dropped from his Presidency and suspended from the functions of his office as a 70 unless he show repentance and humility and reconciliation. Adjourned at 5:40 p.m. for 3 weeks to give him time to consider and make satisfaction.

FDR **Friday, March 13** Apostle Heber J. Grant came in and read to Apostle Geo. Teasdale, Geo. Reynolds and myself a note from Br. BH Roberts in which he lays aside his stubbornness of opinion and bows to the decisions of his Brethren the 1st

Presidency and the Twelve and six Associated Presidents—which caused our hearts to leap for joy and give thanks to our Father in Heaven that the Spirit had constrained him into the right way of the Lord.

FDR **Thursday, March 26** At 11:30 met with First Presidency, the Twelve except Thatcher, Taylor and Lund, and with the 7 Presidents of the 70's. At President Woodruff's request Pres. GQC stated the object of the meeting of the 3 Councils and asked Elder Roberts to state his feelings and intentions. This he did in a most unreserved and satisfactory manner showing a broken heart and a contrite spirit stating the reasoning of the Spirit with him as the only Male representative of his Father's or his Mother's line in the Church for the redemption of their dead— this overcame him, he broke down with a terrible struggle and conformed entirely to the wishes of the Presidency and Council. All were melted to contrition.

FDR **Saturday, April 11** The "New Manifesto" was read and Bishops were instructed to have it read in all their Wards tomorrow, and to have a vote of acceptance taken, in each ward.

FDR **Tuesday April 14** FSR informed Pres. WW that the Attorney General did yesterday move Supreme Court that our case of Church property be remanded to Utah for final decree.

FDR **Thursday, May 7** The rule for Missionaries is "Without purse or scrip" any deviation is the exception.

GFR **Sunday May 10th** Raining & snowing until noon. The ground must be thoroughly wet. Favorable for dry farms. I have 65 A. lucern & 85 A grain exposed to all this wet & blessing.

FDR **Wednesday, May 13** Pres. WW is up but very poorly. What he sees in the papers sickens him worse than his bodily ailments.

GFR **Tuesday May 26th** Apostle Lyman called to see me. Said

I had been suggested for President of one of the Stakes of Zion but He and my Father did not want to let me go from here.

FDR **Thursday, May 28** After mature deliberation it was decided that the Council of Twelve take up a labor with Apostle Moses Thatcher and learn if he is with us or against us.

FDR **Tuesday, June 23** Got out with assistants help a draft of Reply to Joseph Smith's Article in "The Saints Herald" of June 3rd inst. in which he charges me with changing and corrupting the words of Joseph Smith since his death.

FDR **Wednesday, June 24** This forenoon found the original letter written by Joseph Smith, Jr., Hyrum Smith, Lyman Wight, Caleb Baldwin and Alexander McRae while in Liberty Jail, Clay Co. Mo., which will enable to answer Young Joseph.

FDR **Monday, June 29** Today Receiver John R. Winder made his final report to the State Supreme Court of Utah, in compliance with the mandate of the US Supreme Court, and has turned over to the First Presidency cash, $13,404.30, Gardo House grounds, Historian Office and Grounds, Tithing Office and grounds, The Church Farm, and the Coal lands at Coalville. His report was approved and he with his bondsmen were discharged.

FDR **Tuesday, August 25** Instructed CW Penrose about the Hist of 1856—Hand Cart Company's.

FDR **Wednesday, September 9** Pres. WW very fond of angling, caught 160 of fish in from 1½ hours to 2 hours more or less—delightful experience for him in recreation.

FDR **Tuesday, November 3** Being now nearly 76 years of age and never yet having voted for President of the United States I voted for William J. Bryan.

FDR **Thursday, November 5** Decided to change Fast Day from the first Thursday to First Sunday in each month. It is not known among us when, where or by whom it was first instituted as a Day of Fasting.

FDR **Thursday, November 19** At 10 a.m. the Apostles met and considered the case of Moses Thatcher. After which, it was decided that he be severed from the Council of the 12 Apostles and that he be deprived of his Apostleship and other offices in the Priesthood and that the same be published in the DE News. Every member participated. A sad and sorrowful days labor for us.

GFR **Sunday Dec 6** This being the first fast under the new order of the Church, 1st Sunday in the month I & most of the family fasted until 5 o'clock p.m.

FDR **Tuesday, December 29** Both WP and RGW Roads grant Rev. Jane S. Richards a Clergyman's Permit for 1897, and RGW has given me an annual pass between all points of its roads.

GFR **Sunday Jan 17 [1897]** Read the Moses Thatcher episode pamphlet.

FDR **Sunday, February 7** I also called on a lonely afflicted widow of the Prophet Joseph Smith named Mary E. Lightner who is very deaf, sight feeble, and weak in body. I presented her a Doc & Cov. in large type. She presented me a copy of the 1st edition published in Independence, Jackson County, Mo. I esteem it very highly.

FDR **Monday, March 1, 1897** Attended the refreshing exercises of President Wilford Woodruff's 90th Anniversary of his Birthday. He spoke 23 minutes to a packed audience.

GFR **Monday Mar 1st** Attended Pres. Woodruff's 90th birthday celebration in the Salt Lake Tabernacle. Shook hands with Pres. Woodruff & wife.

FDR **Thursday, March 4** Lengthy talk about the numerous

unmarried young women and men in Zion and some urgent reason for special cases of Marriage.

FDR **Friday, May 28** Today Apostle HJ Grant suffered terribly from appendicitis.

FDR **Saturday, May 29** This morning Bro. Grant submitted to an operation for removal of the "Appendix". Extraordinary suppuration and commenced mortification confronted the surgeon, Dr. Joseph Smith Richards and occupied one and ¾ hours.

FDR **Thursday June 3** Prefer putting the B Young Statue in Center of Street Corner of East and South Temple Sts.

FDR **Wednesday, June 30** Spent the morning preparing my oration for tomorrow at placing corner stone and Box of BY Monument. Herald states there have been 83 train robberies in 7 years, 73 killed, 58 wounded.

FDR **Saturday, July 17** I also looked among the stables in rear of Little's Row where FSR was born; and where his mother was raised from the dead in 1849 soon after his birth, when the honored and loved Daniel Spencer laid on hand and blessed her.

FDR **Sunday, July 18** Andrew Jenson reported his 2 years and 2 Months around the world in a very hasty and lively manner getting history of missions in all Pacific Islands. Egypt, Palestine, Damascus Asiatic and European Mission. Brought over more than 1000 of Record Books of the various mission founding.

FDR **Sunday, July 25** At home tired and weary. A pleasant comfortable day. I thank the Lord from my heart that there is such a Day as Sunday in the land. I felt to possess it as a day of Rest, and I did eat but lightly and slept most of the day and night. The Lord blessed me in obtaining a measure of rest to my weary soul. Read but very little. My eyes needed to rest, my head need it and all my nature. I admired the wisdom of God in ordaining the 7th as a day of Rest and that He rested from His labors, the 7th Day. If He rested. He must have [had] knowledge and wisdom when to stop and how to limit, their toil.

GFR **Sund. Aug 15** I read from Des. News of Aug 14, 1897 an account of the Moses Thatcher trial by S. L. Stake High Council his compliance and also a 10 page letter from Bro. Roberts to Bro. Thatcher.

GFR **Sat. Oct 2nd 1897** Bro Lyman instructed Prest Gowans & his counselors to catechize high councilors, Bps and counselors in regard to their tithing & keeping of the word of wisdom that he might be able to vouch for them.

FDR **Thursday, October 21** Long deliberation about methods of calling the numerous Elders for their various missions and certifying by the Bishops and Presidents of Stakes to their moral, social as well as their financial standing.

FDR **Tuesday, November 2** At Ogden, City Elections. A very pleasant day. The Parties, political are badly disintegrated—Democratic, Republican, People's Party, Washakies, Dem. Silverites, Rep. Silverites, McKinley Goldbugs, Bryan Silverites. I took the liberty to scratch and make up a ticket of such names as I felt willing to vote and did not inform my Friends nor my family who I voted for.

FDR **Sunday, November 7** Addressed the Theological Class giving my testimony of manifestations which the Lord has favored me with, mentioning the Pillar of Fire and the healing it appeared and gave to me in the early part of the Raid [the time in the later 1880s when federal officials aggressively enforced anti-polygamy legislation].

FDR **Monday, January 3, 1898** With Presidents WW, GQC, JFS investigated about the Breast Plate found in the box with the plates about an hour.

FDR **Monday, January 17** Read my Address as President of the Historical Society of Utah.

FDR **Sunday, February 13** The Ogden Standard of today details the plot of Tom Sharp of Carthage, Squire McCauley of Appanooce, and JB Agnew of Pantoosee and its execution in the burning of the Nauvoo Temple.

FDR **Wednesday, March 23** H. Priest Geo. B. Wallace spent ¾ of an hour in happy visit reminding each other of our early experiences in the Church, and of my Ordination [as] an Apostle by Heber C. Kimball, BY, and WR in his (GBW's) house in the Old Fort, February 12, 1849 where Councils were held in which CC Rich, L. Snow, E. Snow and I were ordained.

FDR **Saturday, April 9** Select Priesthood meeting. At 10 a.m. General Meeting [of] all the Priesthood in Big Tabernacle. About budget retirement and reform, also a per cent that is appropriate to Temples and various objects; also Tithing of 1897 exceeded 1896 by $90,000; Pres WW, origin of indebtedness—confiscation by Govt. and charged for rent of our own property. If our debts were paid today would be willing to die tomorrow. Four Temples cost about $6,000,000.00. Thought if the Priesthood before him will make an honest effort we will get out of debt and overcome.

GFR **Sat. Apr 16th** The House of Representatives in Congress has passed resolutions of war with Spain & the Senate are considering similar resolutions. The President has ordered troops to the front and the Queen of Spain is in a mood for war, both countries have made and are making extensive preparations for war by the purchase of war ships &c. War seems inevitable.

FDR **Monday, April 25** Congress declares War today as having existed since the 21st. New York City is under War regulations, only entered by sea in day time.

FDR **Friday, April 29** Presidency informed me that they had decided to reduce their receipts from the Church this year to 20 percent of the allowance hitherto from the Church. I expressed a desire to do the same if I can manage it. Some will have to draw full up, others quite less.

FDR **Thursday, May 5** Pres Snow asked if a person whose greatest fault was using Tea or Coffee could be recommended to the Temple. Each case to be decided by its merits and direction of the Spirit. If refused for Tea or Coffee then for eating meat?

GFR **Thu June 9th** Went to the temple. Sister Helen Miller was endowed for her daughter Edna Moselle [dead] and stood for her in having her sealed to me.

FDR **Sunday, June 19** At home in Ogden. I am tired, tired weary and worn outside and inside and I avoided all unnecessary labor and care and appropriated the day for rest to my body and mind.

GFR **June 26** In morning wrote following for Y.P. Paper: Marriage.

> Marriage was ordained of God. Nothing is more honorable than honorable marriage. The first great command of God is fulfilled through it. The blessings of Moses of Abraham and of all the Prophets and patriarchs of former days who received their blessings direct from God are received through this principle. The earth was made for Gods children as a dwelling place. We are his elect people through whom the faithful spirits desire lineage. Our unions should be such as would entitle us to bear the souls of the most noble of Gods children unborn.

FDR **Friday, September 2** Informed me of Pres. Woodruff's death in California at 6:40 this a.m.

GFR **Thurs Sept 8th** Attended the funeral services of Pres. Woodruff at Salt Lake City in the Tabernacle.

FDR **Friday, September 9** At city. At 10 met with the Twelve Apostles, Counselors Cannon and Smith resumed their former· seats with the 12 as Lorenzo Snow, FD Richards, George Q. Cannon, B. Young, Josh F. Smith, FM Lyman and 14 in all of us after singing "Zion Stands with Hills Surrounded." Earnest and able prayer by FM Lyman, then Sung "God Moves in a Mysterious Way." Some precious talk, heavenly sentiments. Resolved, that the Council of Apostles accepts the Presidency of the Church and sustains Lorenzo Snow as its president. Each spoke.

FDR **Tuesday, September 13** Council in President's office—14 Apostles present. Elected Pres. Lorenzo Snow 1st President. He chose GQ Cannon 1st, and JF Smith 2nd Counselors; Pres Snow Trustee in Trust and FD Richards, President of the Twelve Apostles. With the other 13 sat at CR Savages for our likenesses in group [photograph].

FDR **Monday, October 3** Had an impressive Dream teaching me to shun every appearance of evil—I felt the mortification of a suspicion.

FDR **Tuesday, October 4** I [spoke] to the Quarterly Council of Apostles. The Lord has given me the hearts of these Brethren. He also gave me words of inspiration for their edification. The first day I presided in the Council of Apostles.

FDR **Monday, October 10** To President's office where the First Presidency and 11 Apostles laid their hands on Rudger Clawson and President L. Snow ordained him an Apostle and into the Council of Apostles. Pres. Snow with 14 hands on his head was set apart and blest by GQ Cannon; then Pres Snow and 14 set apart and blessed Geo. Q. Cannon as his first and JF Smith as his 2nd Counselor. Then Pres. Snow directed Geo. Q. Cannon to bless me as President of the Twelve Apostles, which he did.

FDR **Tuesday, November 1, 1898** Arrived at Ogden 1030 miles. About 3:30 p.m. arrived home. I feel overflowing and melted down with gratitude to my Heavenly Father who sent His Angel of mercy and helped us, and delivered us from our terrible adversaries that threatened Jane's destruction, but the Lord gave us that we prevailed and she came home passenger instead of freight. And she accomplished all she was sent to do at "National Council of Women's Congress."

GFR **Tues. Nov 8, 1898** Election day: My election to the Legislature is almost assured. I stand 864 to J. C. Delamare's 848 and the Deep Creek precinct only to hear from.

FDR **Monday, November 14** Bro. Orson F. Whitney called about working on the "Church History" when Br. CW Penrose shall leave it to edit the "Deseret News".

FDR **Monday, November 21** Pres. Snow thinks we may have to issue Bonds to raise Money and will consult &c.

FDR **Wednesday, November 23** We deliberated on the importance and propriety of issuing Bonds by the Trustee to sell to our people or any by which to raise Money and pay off our indebtedness. It was unanimously voted to issue five hundred thousand dollars of 6 per cent bonds, payable in 10 years or in 5 if desired.

FDR **Sunday, December 4** It was shown me in a dream that every son and daughter of God had the right privilege and blessing to avail themselves of the ways of means to overcome and escape the ruin of sin and Satan's devices for their destruction if they were determined to lay hold and avail themselves of it.

FDR **Sunday, January 1, 1899** At home, 2443 Lincoln Avenue, Ogden. Fast day. Bless President Lorenzo Snow with Wisdom, light and love and show him the way out of all embarrassments that beset him in his presidency and Trusteeship of Thy Church.

GFR **Mond. Jan 2nd** I consulted Dr. Stephen & Dr. Jos through the Phone and called in Dr. Phipps. Treated [daughter] Lucena with mustard baths, sponging off and cold water injections and gave teas and throat medicine etc. Continued bad all day & night.

FDR **Tuesday, January 3** Visited Pres. Snow. Condoled with him in the burial of a daughter and a wife during recent holidays. Referred to new debts coming to light says there must be an auditing committee appointed.

FDR **Sunday, February 12** Was ordained 50 years ago today an Apostle—have lived to see a whole Quorum, was then youngest, am now the oldest and President of Council of Apostles—what hath God wrought!

FDR **Tuesday, April 4** Afternoon I spoke of the Masonic Organization in Nauvoo and some of the circumstances which led up to the Prophet Joseph asking of the Lord and obtaining promise to restore that which was lost, indeed to Restore all things which enraged the high officials of the Mystic Order so that the National Grand Conclave expelled or cut off all the Mormon Masonic Order from their fellowship.

GFR **Tues. Apr 4th** At prayers all the family present by request. Alice was mouth in prayr, the first she ever offered in my hearing though she prays in secret and with the children in my absence.

FDR **Wednesday, April 5** President Snow narrated a case of urgent entreaty for a plural Marriage by one proposing to go to Canada &c. He refused any permission or encouragement.

FDR **Saturday, April 8** President Snow gave a very interesting discourse on the importance of getting out of debt by stopping to make debts and live within our means and thus become honest, honorable, and worthy to be trusted with the use of means; as there will come a time when vast amounts of money will be had; and must be handled to profit and advantage to the work of God and His People.

FDR **Sunday, April 9** Pres Snow called on me to speak. I occupied 47 minutes with edification to myself but my voice was rather weak and I did not make the vast audience to hear so good as usual.

GFR **Monday Apr 24th** I called at Utah Lumber Co& perfected arrangements to sell their material. Two cars of lumber ordered.

FDR **Monday, June 12** At 10 a.m. met with the Priesthood of Salt Lake Stake and General Church Authorities. President Snow presented the law of Tithing and urged its renewed consideration and its faithful observance.

FDR **Thursday, June 15** Decided to have next Fast Day a meeting of Presidency, 12 Apostles, 7 First Presidents of 70's, Patriarch, Pres' of Stakes and bishops all together in the Temple to receive the Word of the Lord on Tithing.

FDR **Thursday, June 29** Neither of us can tell where the Book of the Law of the Lord is since its loss and burial in the Raid.

GFR **Sund. July 2nd** I went to the Temple in Solemn Assembly at 10 a.m. & got out at 7:20 p.m. Tithing was the subject discussed or talked by the Presidency & Apostles & Church Bishop.

FDR **Sunday, July 30** Stake Conference at Ogden. Pres. LS spoke nearly an hour giving the people the importance of Tything and its proper payment with necessity therefore. P.M. Several Apostles and Bp Preston occupied the time on the one subject. Pres. Snow arose at 10:30 and presented the leading topic for consideration—Consecration, Tything. Referred to Saints' experience in Missouri and its consequences and gave warning of results of disobedience. Read some from Sec 64 Doc & Covenants, explaining some points in progress of his talk. Read also from D&C sec 104 on page 105—might have been redeemed even now, but did not use their Money as required by the Lord. If by purchase, great blessing; if by blood—O how terrible the consequences. Made the application. Read Sec 119, Tything; surplus property; Temples; Foundation Zion; debts of Presidency; &c etc—that the land may become Zion unto us. Explained 53 minutes.[12]

GFR **Sund. July 9th** At meeting I spoke 25 minutes upon the Subject of Tithing. Apostle Lyman spoke upon same subject and in the course of his remarks said no plural marriages are being solemnized in the Church. No one in this stake could say he had entered that principle since the Manifesto was issued.

GFR **Dec 9** I received a telephone call from my brother Ezra F. Richards in Farmington informing me of the death of my father at his home in Ogden this morning at 12:14 a.m. Bro. Lyman handed me a letter of which the following is a copy.

---

12. Franklin's last journal entry is August 10. The circumstances of Franklin's death on December 9, 1899, are discussed in the biography written by his grandson Franklin L. West: "The last visit made by him in the discharge of his apostolic duties was to the Bear Lake Stake conference. [He had come home early from the St. George trip with President Snow because of an attack of 'nervous prostration'—hence no journal entries the latter part of May.] Failing to make any visible progress toward recovery, and thinking that the climate of the Pacific Ocean might be beneficial to him, he went to California, but receiving no benefit from the change, soon returned to Utah. Gradually he grew weaker, until the ninth day of December, 1899, when he peacefully passed away at his home in Ogden. Surrounding him when his spirit took its flight, were his faithful wife Jane and several other members of his immediate household" (*Life of Franklin D. Richards* (Salt Lake City: Deseret News Press, 1924), 248; paragraphing altered).

Tooele City, Dec 9th 1899

Elder Geo F. Richards.

My Dear Brother: Your revered father Prest. Franklin D. Richards died in Ogden, Utah at 12:14 a.m. today. He was born April 2, 1821, was 78 years, 8 months and 7 days old. He was ordained an Apostle on Feby 12th 1849, when he was 27 years, 10 months & 10 days old and thus he held the Apostleship in the flesh 50 years, 9 months & 27 days. Pres. Lorenzo Snow was ordained an Apostle the same day. Only one man, Pres. Wilford Woodruff, held the Apostleship longer in the flesh than he.

> Your affectionate brother,
> Francis M. Lyman

GFR **Tues. Dec 12th** I went to Ogden on the 10:13 A.M. train to attend my Father's funeral services, held in the Ogden Tabernacle at 1 P.M. I with my other brothers, acted as pall bearers.

Chapter 7

GEORGE F. RICHARDS

JANUARY 1900 TO AUGUST 1950

Tues. Jan 16, 1900 Telephoned to City for George to come home on account of the spread of Small Pox in the City 20 cases having developed to date.

Feb 20, 1900, Tooele City
F. W. Richards Esq.

Dear Brother Fred: Your letter of 17th inst. is at hand. You ask if I have any suggestion to make in relation to your letter of inquiry from Box B. All missionaries have to make a sacrifice, some more than others. After your return you would I think, view it as an investment and a profitable one too. If you were living near by I could do much for you, I think I would promise you your family would be cared for and your effects not be wasted. What else you do, Frederick, do not refuse to go. That course is dangerous. If you can not of your self decide to go, then represent to the mission committee by letter your circumstances, endorsed by your Bishop as to correctness with the statement that if they understanding the circumstances desire you to go, you will do so at any cost. Unless we are willing, when necessary, to sacrifice all for the gospels sake, we are not accepted of the Lord.

Friday, May 11, 1900 Went to Salt Lake to see brother Fred before he should start on his mission to the Northern States.

Tues. July 24th The pioneers of these now peaceful vales of plenty; the authors of our existence here and of our religious liberties. All hail to them. May the memory of their sacrifices, sorrows, hardships and noble deeds ever live in the hearts of the people and their graves be ever kept green.

Tuesday Sept 25th I dreamed a dream. I had a most pleasant night's sleep and rest and during the night dreamed that I was ordained an apostle under the hands of Prest. Lorenzo Snow and was told by him that there were other blessings for me which he had not the authority to give, greater than these.

Thurs. Dec. 20th By request of Mrs. Woodward at the Miners Hospital I visited her in relation to baptism, which she desires but had the idea that it could be performed in the hospital bathtub. She being too weak to be moved to fount I advised her since she had been baptized and not cut off to not worry but that her repentance would be accepted of the Lord.

Monday Dec 31, 1900 As it was the last day of the year & last day of the century, we stayed up until the new Century came in & noted that the moon and stars continued to shine and all nature seemed undisturbed by the ushering in of the 20th Century.

Thu Feb 21st [1901] It is just as easy to believe that God can command the elements even to the resurrection of the dead than to have believed 50 years ago that science by man should have been developed to its present standard: carriages without horses shall go, Steam, electricity, compressed air, &c. The resurrection is a reality.

Sat. Oct 19th Attended special High Council Meeting at Tooele at which the new Presidency of the Church were endorsed and the council pledged themselves to keep the Sabbath, Attend

Stake Priesthood meetings, pay their tithing & refrain from Blasphemy. Exceptions: ( ) must have weak tea and ( ) must open his store on Sunday to sell drugs, confectionary, ice cream, &c. I think the latter should refrain from the sale of ice cream &c on Sunday or resign his position as an alternate member of the High Council.

Mond. Mar 30th 1903 I made discovery of an error on the part of the Utah Lumber Co. people which would have meant a loss of $8–$10 to them had I not corrected it & notified them.

May 29th I went to Salt Lake City by Special [train] & saw President Roosevelt & the parade.

Sat. May 30th The Rocky Mtn Bell Telephone Co. agreeing to put an exchange in Tooele, I made application for a residence phone, $1.50 per mo.

Mond. July 13, 1904 It is reported that Apostle A. O. Woodruff died Sunday at El Passo Texas from Small pox. His wife preceeded him only a week or so from same disease in Mexico.

Sunday Sept 18th At this writing my business is in good condition, am able to meet all my bills and have a good business credit. My health is good and I am reasonably happy. My conscience is reasonably clear and my mind at ease. My spiritual duties are pleasant to perform and performing same gives me spiritual strength and much peace of mind & conscience. My sons and daughters are exemplary in their lives and respect and love their parents and one another. Legrand is a class teacher in Sunday School, a Ward teacher and is called to take the missionary course this winter at L.D.S. College or University which means a mission in a few months. Why should I not be happy?

Wed. Apr 5 [1905] Legrand & I went through the Temple, he for his Endowments, I for the Dead.

Thurs Apr 6 Legrand is making preparations to go on a

mission to Europe to the Netherlands. A party for his benefit & what other Tooele people gave him amounted to more than $40.00.

Thu Oct 5th I went to Salt Lake on evening train and in the evening attended a reunion of the Richards Family, was chosen temporary Sec'y and acted as such, paid my $1.00 initiation fee & by request made a talk.

Saturday Dec 16 I made ready to start on a trip East with Prest. Jos. F. Smith & party. I having been invited by Prest. Smith to go along. The purpose being to unveil and dedicate to the memory of the Prophet Joseph Smith the monument erected under the direction of Junius F. Wells for the church on the spot of his birth in Sharon, Windsor, Co. Vermont. Said dedication to take place on Dec 23rd the 100th anniversary of the Prophet's birth.

Dec 18 We left Salt Lake City at 7:20 a.m. on the Pullman car. There were 30 in all. The names of the party as listed are as follows: President Joseph F. Smith, President Anton H. Lund, President F. M. Lyman; Apostles: John Henry Smith, Hyrum M. Smith, Geo. Albert Smith, Chas W. Penrose; and others as listed: Seymour B. Young, Rulon S. Wells, Angus M. Cannon, John McDonald, Joseph F. Smith, Jr, etc. There were 12 upper and 12 lower berths in the car and an apartment in one end for ladies and another in the other end for men with toilets, wash stands, &c also a stateroom occupied by Prest. Jos. F. Smith and his brother John Smith the Patriarch. I had upper 9 and Alice & the boy Oliver had lower 10 berths while Pres. Lund had lower 9 and Susa Y. Gates upper 10, she having changed berths with my wife whose berth was upper 10 on account of the baby. On the way, we had singing and at night had prayers. Our car went with us from first to last and we slept in it every night except one. We arrived at South Royalton at 7:20 a.m. Fri Dec 22nd. Some of the party by sleigh went up to Tunbridge 5 or 6 miles where the Smiths once lived and where Hyrum Smith was born. Seymour B. Young, Susa Y. Gates, my wife, baby & I drove over to the monument by sleigh a distance of about 3 miles. Found Junius F. Wells and some ten or 12 others working at the cottage & monument making ready for the dedicatory services to take place the following day. The monument stands on a little knoll about 30 feet from the house. Its base is 12 ft square. It is 38½ feet high representing the age of the Prophet when he was martyred. The spire is said to weigh 45 tons and the whole monument 100 tons. I also got a walking stick cut from one of the apple trees cleared away to make room for the monument. Joseph was but 3 or 4 years old when he moved from here. The apple trees are said to have been planted by Joseph's father.

Dec 23, 1905 South Royalton. Arrived at the monument at 9:30 A.M. Others kept coming from all directions until they were counted at 437 present. Elder Junius F. Wells by request related how he had thought when near those parts some nine years ago that there should be a monument erected on the 100th anniversary of Joseph's birth. All of the monument except the spire was taken from the Mar and Gordon Park Quarry and the whole weighs 100 tons. The difficulty in obtaining a stone that would make the spire was depicted and it was told how a railroad had to be built down into the quarry to load the stone. A special dispensation had to be obtained from the Ry Co. A special train furnished and a Ry Supt sent along as the base was wider than the Ry rules would allow and it was wholly unsafe to stand it on edge. The difficulties in moving the stone from car to destination was depicted graphically. How that the bridge across the White River had to be strengthened and in driving piles found mud and quick sand so that it was necessary to put in mud sills first. The interposition of providence in reducing in 3½ hours and temperature 35 degrees and freezing up a mud hole in which an empty hay press was stuck just the day previous. How that the two base stones stuck 22 heavy work horses in a low wheeled wagon with tires 22 inches wide on level. The necessity for changing the Die from a higher to a lower tack to pass under the bridge top. How nearly it came to tipping off into the river which it likely would have done had it been on the higher trucks or wagon. It required two weeks to move one load over the ground 3 miles. The difficulty of putting the shaft in place was also depicted. It being polished surface had to be handled with care and new machinery had to be provided.

Tues. Dec 26 We arrived at Palmira N.Y. at 10 a.m. By teams we went up through the city of Palmira and beyond about two miles to the former home of the Smith family now owned by one Mr. Chapman. At the time the boy Joseph had his first vision he lived in a log house later torn down by Mr. Chapman's father and it was in that house the Angel Moroni appeared to him. The house now occupied by the Chapman family was built according to Joseph's mother's record by Alvin Joseph's brother in 1825 which agrees with Mr. Chapman's version. So Joseph must have had his visitation from the Angel in the old House. We saw a cannon ball found in the roof of this house while undergoing repairs a number of year ago. There were two of them and my father F. D. R. got one of them on one of his visits to this house. We saw the room which according to Mr. Chapman Joseph used to sleep in and were shown the corner in which the translating of the Book of Mormon was done, a curtain having been drawn across the corner for seclusion. On this farm which was once owned by the Prophet Joseph's father is a grove of hardwood timber and it is

supposed that it was here Joseph received his first vision in answer
to prayer when both the Father and Son appeared unto him. Mr.
Chapman avers that his Father never cut a tree that was alive out
of that grove and charged his son to never let an ax be used there
except on dead timber. He said he had obeyed his father's in-
junction but there have been trees cut. We surrounded the stump
of what was once a very large tree and sang Joseph Smith's First
Prayer. This grove is about a half mile from the house and between the house & the grove is a small stream of water running
through the meadow. Mr. Chapman says old residents tell that
Joseph used to baptize in this creek and even show where the dam
was put in to the creek. For the truth of this statement I could
not vouch. In the house are some pieces of furniture said to have
been made by Brigham Young. They show fine workmanship but
of obsolete patterns showing age in that respect.

Wed. Feb 7th, 1906 Prest. Joseph F. Smith phoned out from
City inviting Alice, Oliver and me to go into the City and attend
a social of the members of our Eastern party with their wives &
husbands to be held at the Bee Hive at 5 p.m. Friday Feb 9th, the
anniversary of the birth of Hyrum Smith the martyred Patriarch.

Thu Mar 22 [in the margin he writes:] "I dreamed I saw and
embraced the Savior." [In the manuscript he states:] "I dreamed a
dream in which I saw the Savior."

Sat. Apr 7 S. L. City, weather fine. Attended forenoon meeting and at close of the meeting when Prest. Smith concluded
making announcements, Pres. Lyman requested him to announce
that Pres. HS Gowans and counselors were wanted at the stand
after close of that meeting, which announcement was made. We
met Pres. Lyman who requested me to meet him in about 30
minutes at the Historians office. This I did and there met Elders
John Henry Smith, Geo. Albert Smith with Pres. Lyman also

Bishop Orson F. Whitney and David O. McKay. Then Prest. Lyman made known the intended action of the conference to release from the quorum of Apostles Jno W. Taylor, and M. F. Cowley, which with the vacancy caused by the death of Apostle Merrill would leave 3 vacancies which would have to be filled and we were asked as to the manner of our living and our faith in all the principles of the gospel, &c. Prest. Lyman said the spirit had indicated that we were the men. Each of us expressed our feelings & faith. I first, then Bro. Whitney & then Bro. McKay, after which we separated. Repaired to the afternoon meeting. In the evening I attended the Gen'l Priesthood.

Sunday Apr 8, 1906 I was in a good seat near the stand in the large tabernacle. At about 3:45 p.m. Pres. Lyman who had been talking for perhaps 20 minutes commenced to tell that John W. Taylor and M. F. Cowley had handed in their resignations as members of the Quorum because they were out of harmony with the President of the Church and their Quorum. These resignations were presented Oct 28, 1905 and accepted by the Presidency and Apostles. Prest. Lyman then presented the General Authorities. He presented the President & counselors, then the old members of the Quorum, after which Bro. Lyman deliberately read my name off and called the vote. There were no opposing votes. Then Orson F. Whitney's name followed with the same result. Then Bro. McKay's name with the same result and the curiosity of the people was satisfied. After meeting many friends shook my hand and offered congratulations and expressions of pleasure at my appointment. My dream of March 22nd wherein I saw the Savior seems to have prepared me in a measure for this call.

Monday Apr 9 The Presidency and Apostles and Council of the Seventies repaired to the Temple where we met in council and received valuable instructions from Pres. Joseph F. Smith, after which the new members were ordained and set apart members of the Quorum by President Smith in order as follows. Geo F. Richards, Orson F. Whitney & David O. McKay. All of the Presidency & Twelve were present except Geo Teasdale, Heber J. Grant and Reed Smoot. We had a regular Pentecost and brethren wept in one another's embrace.

Wed. Apr 18 This morning at 5:10 o'clock San Francisco was visited by an earthquake and followed with fire which destroyed nearly all the buildings in the city and did damage to other towns nearby. Details not yet received. I went downtown and secured my pass on Ry.

Sat. June 30 Malad Stake. The Lord designs to bless us. We should prepare ourselves by faith for what the Lord has for us. Too great wealth not accompanied by faith commensurate might prove a great disaster. The Lord knows best, perfect as he is. Offerings should be given liberally that the poor may be provided for regardless of their location.

Sunday July 1 Cleanse ourselves that we may go into the Temple to receive blessings, then live for their fulfillment. We may lose our wives or our husbands or our other blessings through unfaithfulness, as all our blessings are promised on faithfulness. We should keep the covenant to keep the commandments as fast as made known unto us.

Jul 24 Bear Lake Idaho. This <u>pioneer day</u> the 59th anniversary of the day the pioneers first entered the valley of the Great Salt Lake. It is fitting and proper that this day should be celebrated, not for the pleasures we may get out of it alone, but that we may keep green the memories of the people, whereby the Rising generation may know what our pioneer fathers and mothers have suffered and done for us; the fruits of whose labors we are here and now enjoying. Our establishment here in the valleys of the mountains is in fulfillment of the prediction of Isaiah, also the prediction of the prophet Joseph Smith who prophesied that the saints should go west and be established in the valleys of the Rocky Mountains and there become a great people. Persecution at Nauvoo may have been necessary to accomplish the Lord's purpose concerning us in that regard. It is well for us to account for the justice of God in permitting those mobbings and driving in this way. We came here willingly because we had to and the persecutions we received and the hardships attending the traversing of the desert between the Missouri and the Great Salt Lake has the effect of making us content with our lots though hard and bitter. There was nothing desirable to return to. When we have proven ourselves the Lord made bare his arm and we were blessed and prospered, not left alone to apostatize, but have been probed and goaded by our enemies sufficient to keep us awake to a sense of our true position and the allegience we owe to the Lord. The valleys have been rendered fertile, the streams have increased, the hills have prospected and are turning out their wealth, the climate has been tempered unto today this is a most favored spot and we owe a debt of gratitude to Him. We will not forget the integrity of the pioneers and the hardships they endured which cost many their lives. We will love them and cherish their memory forever.

Weds. July 25 Georgetown, Idaho. Learning that the No. 5 train was ten hours late I went up to William Dunn's where my wife & babies were. Wm Dunn & the folks accompanied me and we went down to the river to fish until train comes. I caught 3 fishes. I flagged the train at 6:30 which was 15 hours late.

Thu. July 26 Arriving home at 7:00 a.m., went home and had a bath and attended our regular Council meeting at 10 at Temple. Attended Prayer circle meeting at 6:15 p.m., Pres. Lyman presiding. I related a dream or Vision I had wherein I saw and embraced the Savior on the 22nd of March last. The seeing of Him was something beautiful but that in itself would have been of little significance as compared with the results of my embracing him. My whole being seemed to be thrilled with the power of His love and I was indeed in Heaven. The singing of the Hymn "I Need thee Every Hour" brings this vision afresh to my mind, hence this is my favorite hymn.

Sat. July 28, 1906 I went from Nephi to Mona. Spoke at each meeting. Save our children, they are dearer to us than worldly wealth. By a conscientious life prove to our children our consistency. <u>We know better now than we do</u>, then why clamor for more revelation? Let us keep our covenants by keeping the commandments as fast as made known unto us, attending to the little things and prove our spirits to be willing.

Tuesday Aug 28 I wrote my brother Fred the following being an extract from same. I am kept busy with the duties of my calling and enjoy same, except that I feel my inability keenly, especially when I have to stand before congregations to instruct them. [Beware lest] some little thing such as a non-observance of the word of wisdom, a neglect of your prayers, or anything of the kind should block your way. It is by the observance of these little things that men show whether theirs is an obedient and willful spirit. A man with a willing and obedient spirit can be used for positions of trust and honor though not otherwise very well qualified, but if qualified so much the better. . . . You, my dear brother, may be one of them and you should not hedge up the way of your coming to this honor. A straw thrown up indicates the direction of the wind, even so the small things of our lives indicate largely our future destiny. Do now put yourself in order, and by your actions say: As for me and my house we will serve the Lord, in these little things as well as in greater things.

Sund. Sept 2 We are only fully converted when we live and accept every law and principle through obedience and free agency.

Sat Sept 8th Testified to the truth of the gospel truth and of the divine mission of Joseph Smith and his successors and was nearly overcome with emotion thus testifying. Such an experience as I never before experienced.

Sund. Sept 9th Cowley. [In a meeting of priesthood leaders in Wyoming, he stated:] we would lay down our lives for the work, but we will not lay down our tobacco, &c. By indulging in tobacco, etc., we lower the dignity of the Holy Priesthood and rob ourselves of honor. We do not know how our bad habits block our way.

Thu. Sept 27 Attended a committee meeting on History, genealogy and Temple work for the Richards Family association from 3 p.m. until 6 p.m. .

Weds Oct 10 In the evening Prest. Francis M. Lyman notified me that I had been selected to take a mission to California and Northwestern States Missions; to attend the conferences, and to leave here tomorrow evening 9:30 for Los Angeles. Notwithstanding I am just in the middle of transferring my property and my wife is sick in bed with a baby but 3 days old, I answered promptly yes, I would be ready.

Oct 20 I stayed the night across the street from the mission house at a rooming house and had an awful night with the bugs.

Oct 21 At forenoon conference meeting 14 Elders and 122 members present. I occupied 30 minutes, encouraged the saints. Subject: the Holy Ghost and operations of the spirit. Wives should be true to their husbands regardless of their faith. Do not break up families. It is not necessary. Hold 2 street meetings each

Monday, Wednesday and Saturday night and bear testimony to about 1000 people each week in the street. It is not sufficient that we be good but that we work, work, work. The Gospel requires work all the time. It is the gospel which makes the man and not the man which makes the gospel, therefore put your faith on the gospel and not man. Study the Book of Mormon and obey its spirit and you shall know its truth. I occupied about 45 minutes and cried like a baby under the influence of the Holy Spirit as did some of my brethren. A veritable Pentecost. Not much out of the ordinary spoken, but much felt. How blessed to be in touch and to have our hearts attuned so as to feel the inspiration the Lord has for us.

Fri. Oct 26 Left for San Francisco and stopped of at San Jose for 2 hours on Saturday morning; thence off to Palo Alto where we stopped off for a short time and by cab visited the Stanford University grounds and saw how the earthquake had demolished or wrecked those structures, now in the course of re-construction. Arrived in San Francisco about 2 p.m. Saturday and went up on Knob Hill where we could better see the ruined city. About 16 square miles in the heart of the city was reported as representing the district burned. In the evening I attended a street meeting where there were in attendance about fifty or 75 people and the meeting was addressed by three of the Elders.

Thu. Nov 1 Advised President Robinson [mission president] to have local brethren do more work. Keep as many as possible active. Activity is the best means of maintaining the faith. While enthused the converted saints may resist evil and scoffs, etc, but if allowed to get lukewarm, they may conclude that it is not worthwhile. That some have thus concluded is apparent by the number who did not attend our meetings.

Sunday Nov 4 Portland. Attended Sunday School and occupied 20 minutes. The children being pure in heart are in perfect condition to receive the impressions of the Holy Spirit.

Sunday Nov 25 Home. I attended 27th ward S. School and Sunday service in the Tabernacle. After the meeting I assisted in setting apart of number of ward officers. I wrote to Bishop Orme in Tooele contributing to Tooele's poor 10 tons of coal to be distributed by the Bishopric where it would do most good. Later decided not to send letter but reserve contribution for Christmas, as at present I am short of money.

Sunday Dec 2 We should be willing to lay at the feet of the bishopric our substance and our time for the upbuilding of the kingdom. We have already covenanted that our all if necessary should be so used.

Sund. Dec 9 After meeting I had a couple of hours conversation with Bp Larsen and learned form him that he had been Bishop 3 years and last winter he and his Counselors with assistants visit the homes of all the LD Saints and nearly all the outsiders with good results. The Bp. Calls his people to go to the Temple and if they have no names of their own dead, names are supplied at the temple. It has a good effect. A splendid example.

Wed Jan 2, 1907 Attended a Quarterly Conference of the Twelve at the Temple from 10 a.m. until 5 p.m. Among other things, I told the President my health is good, & my shoulders broad and if he had any work more difficult than any other that he could trust me, to lay it upon me; that my greatest hope & most earnest prayr is that the Lord will sustain me in my calling & the discharge of my duties.

Weds. Feb 20 This day after a hard fight for four years, Senator Reed Smoot won out and retains his seat on a vote of 43 to 27. Cost to the Govt. of $50,000. The Church is vindicated at last. The Devil suffers defeat, Zion prospers. There are more people investigating the gospel, more tithing being paid, more temple work being done than ever before. We never were so numerous and so strong before. There is absolute unity with the Presidency and the Twelve and the other General Authorities so far as I have been able to discover.

Sunday Mar 3 Persecutions expected. They came but the work started and will endure forever. We may have to suffer, but whatever may be required we should be prepared for. By doing the small duties we plant our feet in the narrow way and fix our faith permanently.

Thu Apr 18 Called on the Presidency later, no special instructions given me except to preach the Gospel and instruct the Elders to get the Spirit of their mission and then work with zeal and earnestness and do not go to cheap shows and other attractions but be dignified.

Thu May 9 Alice & I attended the theater, which I failed to enjoy "The Cabbage Patch." I feel as if I would not want to go again soon.

Fri May 31 I attended a council meeting in the temple with the Presidency & Twelve & 1st Council of Seventy until about 2 P.M. At close of meeting I received appointment to the Box Elder Conference in Brigham City and left on 4:10 train for Brigham City.

Saturday June 1, 1907 At 2 p.m. meeting there were present 511 out of a total population of 7984, about 6%.

Sunday June 2 Present at this meeting 1628, 18 out of 20 bishops and 25 Bps Counselors 11 High Counselors & 3 alternates. Elder Grant spoke twice and sang twice.

Saturday June 29, 1907 Davis Stake Conference in Syracuse with Pres. Lyman and Elder HJ Grant. "Only the obedient can be used by the Lord."

Sat July 14th After 4 P.M. went to dinner and after dinner canvassed balloted expressions 80 in number on names for Stake Presidency. We did not take those having highest votes for the positions. But we were very clear on whom we did decide upon.

Thu Aug 29 There was a card at the office from Joel written at Salt Lake 8/26/07 11 p.m. saying Nina had been operated upon at the hospital at about 9 o'clock that night, Mama & George being present and that she stood the operation fine but had not come from under the influence of the anesthetic entirely at that time. The card did not say what was her trouble but I suspect it to be appendicitis.

Sat Sept 14 The general authorities have 55 or 56 stakes and a number of missions to look after and we love them all alike and want to bless and do them good.

Friday Oct 25 I resolved to read the Church Works through commencing with the Book of Mormon. I have read the Pearl of Great Price through over on way from Bighorn, and do not know how many times before. Do not remember if I have read either of the other two books of the Standard Works through, but have read much of them through many times. Read 20 pages of Book of Mormon this evening, 1st 20 pages.

Sund. Nov 3, 1907 Unexpectedly my nephew Stephen L. Richards Jr. came in to a.m. meeting and spoke. In afternoon meeting, Bro. Stephen L. Richards & I were the speakers.

Thurs Nov 28 Thanksgiving at Thatcher. Pres. Andrew Kimball drove Bro Smith & me about for two or three hours and had a nice dinner at his home.

Weds Dec 4 El Paso, Texas. We left El Paso about 7:30 a.m. on car for Ciudad Juarez across the Rio Grande River, which forms the line between US & Mexico. Then took the train for Dublan, the terminal of the road, a Mormon town.

Tues Dec 31 My son Legrand who has been absent more than thirty-two months laboring as a missionary in Holland is expected home in February. His has been a successful mission. The Lord has greatly blessed him in the acquirement of the Dutch language and in the preaching of the gospel. Joel and the younger children are in school and hard worked. All are devoted to their religious work. I will be 47 years of age Feb 23 and Alice will be 44 in May. We have had fourteen children all well born without blemish. Two have died. Amy at 4 years of "Purpuria Hemangia" and Alverda at 16 mo. of scarlet fever. George my son has had & buried three children. Nerva has had one girl now 3 years old. We are happy. Our finances are not most favorable but I hope to soon be on sure footing.

Friday Feb 7, 1908 While waiting in the Omaha Station reading the New Testament one Elder Redd approached me not knowing who I was, offering me a Book of Mormon and asking if I had ever seen that book. By this means we discovered one another and there were three other Elders present plying their trade to others.

Monday Feb 24 Elder Smith and I took stage from Mesa 60 miles to Roosevelt [Arizona] for $6.00 each. On board the stage were three ladies. A gentleman who rode with the driver and the driver of Mesa. We saw the Superstition Mts., Black Gulch, Boulder Creek, Fish Creek, Fish Creek Mts., & Fish Creek Canyon. We left Mesa at 6:15 a.m. and reached Roosevelt at 5:30 p.m. A pleasant ride and much thrilling scenery.

Thu Mar 5 The Gen'l Authorities are united but a cloud is even now hanging over the people which gives the authorities great concern. Whether the Lord will scourge us as he did

Ancient Israel who disobeyed council remains to be seen. If the glory of God were to rest down upon us I fear many because of the dross would be consumed. The dead branches would kindle a hot fire for the consuming. The vineyard must be trimmed. We are living in the eleventh hour of this dispensation. The work is to be cut short in righteousness. Now is the time to prepare.

Sunday May 3 Cache Stake Conference in Logan. The speakers were in order as follows. Pres. Jos. F. Smith and Pres. Anthon H. Lund. Pres. Smith's testimony was especially inspiring. A most powerful testimony referring to the crucifixion of the Savior and the martyrdom of the Prophet. Many tears were shed in the congregation and the President himself broke down in his feelings.

Saturday June 13 I attended a meeting of the YWMIA officers in the Barrett Hall. I spoke briefly. Subject: The chief mission of woman and the influence education has upon her mind as relates to that mission. Sending our girls abroad to become specialists detracts from home life and the spirit of that higher life in the home. A study of domestic science and art inspire in the girls a desire to be a queen of a home of her own. Mothers should give their girls all the education possible along those lines in the home. They owe it to their posterity, for what the daughters become, their daughters will become largely in a domestic way.

Sunday June 21 Richfield Utah. It should only be necessary for us to know what the Lord wants of us & we should do it. 75 years ago he told us he would like us to keep the word of wisdom.

Sat July 11, 1908 I spent the day home studying until 6 p.m. when Alice, baby and I went for an auto ride up to the mouth of Big Cottonwood Canyon with Bro. Heber J. Grant & his wife.

Monday July 27 In the past two days I have had more responsibility entrusted to me than ever before being the <u>senior</u>

member of our Council in attendance and consequently having to direct, preside at meetings, present the officers and the business that was necessary in the organization of the Ogden Stake of Zion, the 57th stake of the Church. I feel wonderful well over it. It was a strenuous two days time.

Thurs Aug 6 Logan. I arrived home at 6 P.M. Our children are all home tonight the first time in several years. Twelve in all living, two are gone before, Amy and Alverda.

Sat Aug 8 I obtained the endorsement of Sister E. B. Wells of the change of presidency of the Relief Society of the Weber Stake, releasing sister Jane S. Richards who has been President of the Weber Stake Relief Society since its first organization by Brigham Young.

Sunday Aug 9 Between 12 and 1 o'clock with my brother Charles and Bro. Middleton of the Weber Stake Presidency called on Aunt Jane S. Richards who is one of the Relief Society General Board and who has presided over the Weber Stake Relief Society since July 1877 having been called by Pres. Brigham Young just the month prior to his death. The first Stake Pres. of Relief Societies in the church. She is now 85 years of age. The brethren thought Aunt Jane S. Richards should be released and I went to see her upon this point. She received the suggestion with good grace. I administered a blessing to her before leaving.

At 2 P.M. meeting the Tabernacle was fairly well filled. I spoke of the responsibility as the greatest ever placed upon me in my calling the organizing of the two new stakes and the completing of the organization of the Weber Stake. Some delicate matters had to be handled but all had come out well and the Lord had abundantly blessed us. The gospel net catches all kinds of fish. There are some who seek office and when they do not get it become disgruntled. Another class who when asked to hold office refuse unless it be what they specially desire especially so in small wards where they think their services can not well be dispensed with. There is another class who when relieved of office for the betterment of the cause become disaffected. Notwithstanding the many offices filled in these three stakes no such spirit as has been mentioned above has been apparent. This shows good training and well established faith.

Fri. Aug 21 Pres. Jos. F. Smith & wife Edna and I left Montpelier for Afton, Star Valley at 9 A.M. We came on to Afton & were serenaded by the Brass band as we entered the town about 10 o'clock P.M. Our ride of fifty miles by team was not altogether unpleasant, we enjoyed one another's company, the luncheon, scenery &c.

Sept 9 I should have attended a meeting of the Religion Class General Board at 4 p.m. but was so illy disposed physically that I remained home and lay down an hour or more after which I felt some better. As I lay on my bed I had some thoughts such as I never before had. When one is sick he realized more than at any other time except perhaps at funerals of loved ones how narrow is the space between life and the hereafter and the necessity for our doing all in our power while here and in life and health to strengthen the bridge and make our passing pleasant and without dread. This, it is within my power to do with the Lord's help who is always willing to aid us when we take the initiative. I went with my sons Geo. F., Joel and Geo L. Tate to the fair grounds to see the Buffalo Bill show but we were unable to obtain tickets as there was not sufficient tent room so we lost an hour or more of time and car fares.

Weds Oct 14 Alice and I attended a social function and dinner by the First Presidency in honor of the general authorities at the Lion House. The Old Guard of underground days and others were invited. I made a speech of about 10 minutes. Reminiscences seemed to be the order of the day. I did speak of the conversation had with Dr. H. J. R. at time of Crusade at which time he told me plural marriage must cease. I answered never in this world. I expected we would be driven to the wall and at last God would make bare his arm in behalf of his people but when the manifesto came I received it as the word of the Lord. So I had received every revelation and every instruction from the Authorities and had never found myself in rebellion and am always on hand to do what I can for the Church and to go and come as my Presidents direct.

Tues Oct 27 I got out form for keeping record of stakes and who visit them for submission to Pres. Lyman believing that its use would obviate the difficulty or monotony of the same ones visiting a stake too often unknowingly and also the same ones going together too often.

Thu Nov 5 Home. My health good except what seems to be chronic ailment a result of cold taking about two months ago. My left lung seems to be affected at least I experience pain in that region. I also have a wheezing in my Bronchial tubes which causes me to cough hard at times, principally at night towards morning. I once had a horse fall with me while riding on the range. The horse fell on me and I had a long spy glass swing under my left arm and I lay across the same. I thought my ribs might be fractured. I wonder if that accident has to do with my present soreness and if my lung has been long congested or otherwise ailing and if it is likely to be serious. I once when a young man in 1880 while going to school in Salt Lake to the University of Deseret ran nearly a mile to catch a belated train and ruined my wind. Any exercise requiring rapid breathing since then has the effect of making me nauseated and sick, sometimes vomiting.

Monday, Nov 16 I attended Ensign Stake Priesthood in the evening. Immediately after roll call about half dozen boys evidently deacons with a dash left the room. I received the impression from this action that they had been prevailed upon to be there for roll call and taking this in connection with what I had observed and heard of methods as a means of making a showing in percentages. It was on a par with boarding a street car unobserved by conductor and riding without paying fare. We should studiously avoid everything that tends to depreciate in the minds of the young the value of the principle of honesty and honor. He who is dishonest is dishonorable. To think of one selling his honor for five cents or to create a showing in percentages by any but honorable means.

Sat Dec 5 Preston, Idaho. Care for the poor. Winter now approaching, see that none suffer. The people should pay liberally their offerings that the bishop may have something with which to bless the poor. Read D&C 56:14, Mos 4:11. Some neglect to pay their tithing until the close of the year and then they can not. We should pay it as it comes in and thus avoid the greater temptation, which comes when we let our tithing accumulate.

Mon Dec 7 I spent afternoon and evening working on my looseleaf scripture commentary.

Sat Dec 19 Rexburg, Idaho. The Father gave his Son. The Son gave himself. We should give ourselves with each gift. Love the motive.

Mon Dec 21 We should continue to court our wives after marriage. Should we love them less because they have born our children, washed our dirty clothes, ironed, cooked our meals, etc. for years? There is often much deception before marriage, but we show our true character after.

Mon Dec 28 Mailed letters to all the stake presidents asking how many of their wards had not been visited by one of the General Authorities to attend meeting during the year 1908.

Mon Jan 4, 1909 I retired to bed about 9:30 but did not get to sleep until about 12:30 a.m. my mind dwelling on Spiritual matters.

Weds Jan 13, 1909 Before and after meetings I worked on my Commentary. Sat up until 12 o'clock midnight and finished copying Commentary of the Scriptures. Subjects from indexed pocket record to loose leaf record. Many days have I spent on this record and I consider it of very great value now although it may never be a finished record. It is intended that I add to as I may study and enlarge upon subjects however I have now all the leaves in that case that can be used to any advantage.

Sat. Jan 14 I spoke upon the subject of quorums. If we as officers live the gospel and do well our official duties the people will know it and love us and sustain us. If we are careless of our lives an indifferent to our duties, the people will know it and will not feel to sustain and love us. Under circumstances as first mentioned our labors will be a source of joy and satisfaction to us on the other hand if the latter prevail our duties become irksome and hard. Duty fully done brings pleasure. Duty but half done [brings] dissatisfaction and becomes a drudge.

Weds Jan 20, 1909 A resolution favoring statewide prohibition and pledging ourselves to work for same was voted unanimously.

Saturday Feb 13 Dr. Gill came up about 11 a.m. He swabbed from Edna's throat a piece of membrane and put it in a solution had it analyzed by a chemist and about 6 p.m. phoned up that it showed a diphtheritic germ and that it would be necessary to place us under quarantine. LeGrand was off at work and Joel out to a party. Anticipating such a condition I had notified

Elder John Henry Smith and he arranged with Elder Rudger Clawson to fill my place at Plymouth, Boulder Co., to dedicate their new meetinghouse.

Sunday Feb 14 The health officer came about 11 a.m. and put up the yellow flag indicating diphtheria within. Later Dr. Gill Richards came and administered anti-toxin to Sarah and those younger, seven in all not counting Edna who had hers Friday night. Edna has been feeling bright and cheerful. The clothing of LeGrand, Joel, Sarah and Ruby were spread out in the boy's room and fumigated for six hours or more when these four each had a bath, washed their heads in bichloride water three tables to a quart of water and went out of quarantine. All went to Aunt Seney's for the night. The girls to remain there and the boys to find another place in the morning to stay.

Monday Feb 15 Spent the entire day studying and writing letters. I enjoy immensely remaining in doors. If only our family members keep well I will have great cause to rejoice.

Weds Feb 23 This is my 48th birthday. I do not know if I was ever in better health or in better faith and spirits although I am in quarantine with my family. My sons LeGrand and Joel are staying at a room between State and Main street on 4th South St.

Tuesday Mar 30 Attended quarterly conference of the Twelve in the temple. Elder Grant paid me an undeserved compliment when he said I had forgotten more scriptures than he ever knew.

Tues. May 4, 1909 I spent two or three hours with my mother visiting and talking over temple and genealogy work. I heard my mother tell her experiences in crossing the plains coming to Utah. She rode in the conveyance with her husband, Willard Richards and my father Franklin D. Richards and his wife Jane.

May 19, 1909 I received the appointment to Uintah Stake, which necessitated my leaving Salt Lake on the 7:25 P.M. train. I went down stairs at conclusion of our meeting 2 P.M. and solemnized the marriage of my Son LeGrand to & with sister Ina Jane Ashton in the presence of about fifteen of the relatives. I then bid them goodbye, as I would not be able to attend the reception.

Tuesday June 1 I called at the Hist. Office with uncle Henry P. Richards to see about getting a genealogical record of the Richards family.

Fri June 4, 1909 At 2 p.m. the general conference of the Primary Workers commenced at Whitney Hall, 18th ward. I having received the appointment with Elder Hyrum M. Smith by the First Presidency to supervise the Primary work and aid the General Board, consider it my duty to be in attendance at their conference.

Sat Sept 25 I by special invitation accompanied Prest. Wm. H. Taft & party to Salt Air from 9:30 to 11:15 a.m. and attended organ recital in Large Tabernacle with the party.

Sunday Sept 26 Alice and I went to the large tabernacle at 8:30 a.m. when Pres. Wm. H. Taft and party were present. Pres. Taft occupied about thirty minutes in a practical discourse. Prov. 15:1 "A soft answer turneth away wrath, but grievous words stir up anger." A beautiful service was had after which the President and party viewed the school children on Brigham Street from A to Q streets.

Sun Oct 10 I attended Liberty Stake conference in the Assembly Hall at 10 a.m. and in the Tabernacle at 2 p.m. Bishop Joseph Warburton who is 79 years old had served as bishop for 48 years. He was released.

Tues Nov 9 I attended a missionary meeting at the annex of temple where thirty-one missionaries were set apart. I also instructed the missionaries along the lines about as follows: Why so much stress placed by us upon the subject and necessity for cleanliness and virtue. The success or failure depends so much on it. It is the Lord's work you are going to engage in. You enter into partnership with Him. The means by which He aids you is the Holy Spirit. This Spirit will not dwell in unholy tabernacles. You can not receive His assistance if unclean or unvirtuous hence failure, shame and dishonor are the inevitable result. The office of the Holy Spirit is diversified as are the demands or your necessities. Its promptings mean conviction. When a question arises ask the Lord which way and study it out and conviction will come. This is inspiration and the spirit of prophecy. You are a partner with the Lord in that you help to make efficacious his Atonement by presenting to men the plan by which they may avail themselves of the benefits of His Atonement. Until they receive the Law or hear it they are not capable of condemnation by the Law or Salvation by the Law. But when the law is come to them they are judged and either justified or condemned. Hence your testimony faithfully born becomes a savor of life unto life or of death unto death according as they obey or reject the same.

Tuesday Dec 7 At the breakfast table where we were all gathered about, I talked to the children about the housework and of the necessity for constant effort to overcome the evils of their dispositions and of doing deeds of kindness to one another such as is taught in religion classes. It was taken in proper spirit and I have hopes it will be productive of good. I had a similar talk with them a few weeks previous.

Wednesday Feb 16, 1910 Alice and I went to the temple and were endowed each for one and I paid $9.00 to 12 men who also were endowed for one man each and Alice and I were sealed for these thirteen couples and also for my Uncle George Longstroth, my mother's brother. We were nine hours in the temple and the last to get out.

Thu Mar 24 Am happy in the love of the brethren and the knowledge of the truth.

Tues. Apr 12 Home. My sons Geo and Joel and I went to Farmington on 7:45 O. S. S. train where we were met at station by livery man and three saddle horses and we three went up the Farmington Canyon as far as the Rice Ridge Slide. We found the bridges all gone and had to ford a stream a number of times. We could go no further than we did on account of snow. We spent about 2 hours while up in the canyon target shooting.

Sunday June 19, 1910 At the 2:00 p.m. meeting I spoke of the flagrant disregard of the word of wisdom and instructed the Bps to visit every user of tobacco & warn them that such disobedience could not be rewarded by recommends to the temple. When warned then do not recede from the position taken.

Saturday June 24 Sacrifice and self denial the strait gate and narrow way. The small sacrifices required of us now if cheerfully met will prepare us to make greater ones later on if necessary.

Sat Sept 3 We arrived in Salt Lake 3:35 P.M. one hour, 20 min late. On this trip [an extended visit to Arizona] I traveled by rail 2426 miles and by team 248 miles a total of 2674 miles. On my return I found my wife in bed where she had been for about 2 weeks afflicted with sciatica, bowel complaints & kidney trouble.

Tues Sept 20 I went with Joel to Des. News Book Store where we selected and I bought for him the Standard Church Works. Joel expects to leave for a mission to Gt. Britain Oct 19th. Pres. Jos. F. Smith has been confined to bed since his return from Europe Sept 3rd. The other brethren are pretty well unless it be J. G. Kimball who says he has appendicitis on both sides and indigestion in the middle and for this reason he positively refuses

*Franklin Dewey Richards, ca. 1847, while
serving as a missionary in England.*

Franklin D. Richards.

BORN APRIL 2ND 1821.

*Franklin D. Richards, ca. 1855, as a young
Apostle serving as president of the British Mission.*

Franklin D. Richards, ca. 1866.

*Franklin D. Richards with his wife
Jane Snyder Richards, ca. early 1880s.*

Jane S. Richards, mid 1880s.

Franklin D. Richards, mid 1880s.

Franklin D. Richards's home, Lincoln Avenue, Ogden, Utah, ca. 1884–85.

Lorenzo Maeser Richards, son of Franklin D. Richards and Jane S. Richards, about age twenty-three.

Franklin D. Richards, early 1880s.

Franklin D. Richards, early 1880s.

The First Presidency and Quorum of the Twelve Apostles at the time of President Lorenzo Snow, ca. 1898. Franklin D. Richards (middle row, far right) was president of the Quorum of the Twelve. From left, back: Anthon H. Lund, John W. Taylor, John Henry Smith, Heber J. Grant, Francis M. Lyman, George Teasdale, Rudger Clawson, Marriner W. Merrill. Middle: Brigham Young Jr., George Q. Cannon, Lorenzo Snow, Joseph F. Smith, Franklin D. Richards. Front: Matthias Foss Cowley, Abraham O. Woodruff.

to smile. Alice is able to be about the house but is not well. I have bought some electripodes for her to wear as a remedy for Rheumatic Sciatica.

Saturday Oct 8 Went to the Special Priesthood Meeting held in the Assembly room. At this meeting a copy of a letter by the First Presidency to be sent to all the presidencies of stakes was read. This letter instructs all Stake Presidencies to notify all the people of the contents of the letter and to instruct the Bishops to deal with offenders of the rule of the Church. President Smith made clear his attitude on the question. He said, "There is not a man in all Israel who is authorized to perform plural marriages. If any man shall say there is tell him he lies. The Lord has revealed that there is but one man at a time who has that authority. Any man who assumes that authority is a falsifyer and trying to injure me and the church and should you knock such an one down I shall not feel badly about it. Now is this clear? Do you see any loopholes? If so, tell me. If there is any way to make it plainer I wish you would tell me how to do it."

Tuesday Oct 1, 1910 The all important event of this day about which all my thoughts are entered is that there was born to us at 11:35 a.m. today a fine baby boy. Dr. Stephen L. Richards and nurse Alice Grover in attendance. This makes our fifteenth child of whom five are boys and ten girls, thirteen living and two gone beyond, three married, six grandchildren of whom three are living and three are not. Mother's age 46 yrs. Father's age 49 years past. We have great joy in our posterity. May the Lord be praised for ever more.

Mon Oct 17 Attended Ensign Stake Priesthood meeting in the evening and occupied about 20 minutes. Subject. We are all children. These members of the lesser priesthood are little men. We grown ups are big boys. The difference being that we have largely formed our habits, molded our dispositions and our characters. These are in course of development. All learn more or less from example. We imitate others. These younger ones especially learn that way. It is good to form habits if only of the right kind.

Thu Oct 27 In a conversation with Pres. Lyman this evening, he told me that he appreciated very much the fact that whenever and wherever I am wanted, I am always on hand. I told him any time he had any hard trips or unpleasant work that he could trust to me, that he need not hesitate in calling upon me.

Wednesday Jan 25, 1911 My son George and I attended the wrestling match at the theater between Yokel and Gehring, two world champions. After 3 hr 38 minutes without a fall it was declared a draw and we went home. I slept with my son George at his house.

Sunday Feb 19 Garland. I had good liberty and occupied about 1 hr 20 minutes. Faith as the first principle of revealed religion and moving cause of all action, hence all our righteousness is result of faith and all our indifference and neglect of religious duty is due to want of faith. We know better than we do. We need to have our faith stimulated. This may be done by more regularity and fervency in prayer, in attending to the worship of the Lord, partaking of the sacrament and hearing the testimony of the Elders, in searching the scriptures and in considering the evidence of the gospel truth.

Friday Feb 24 I feel that I have a very great deal to be thankful for and am very happy with my family and my home and in my membership in the Church. The fellowship I have with my brethren and the Saints and the favor of the Lord. For the understanding I have of the plan of salvation, the gospel and the assurances I have of its divine truth and saving power. For my calling and authority as an Apostle of the last days, one of the chosen

Twelve; that I feel as much in place as a I do in Council of the Twelve & Presidency; for the help and blessing of the Lord in my past labors; the things I have learned; the things I know and feel; for the peace there is in my soul. May the name of the Lord be praised forever. May his grace sustain me to the end.

Mar 28, 1911 No man can find out the truth by arguing against it.

Weds May 17 I signed a petition this day to the City Council asking that 3rd Ave be paved.

Mon May 22 Sanford, Arizona. Elder Smith and I were driven 3 miles by a mail driver and took the Denver and Rio Grande train at La Jara for Santa Fe 6:50 a.m. About 11 a.m. we were halted on account of a burning bridge and detained an hour. This delay caused us to lose our right of way and consequently our train connection at Santa Fe. As we got down on the LaGrande river about noon it got quite warm. We were due at Santa Fe at 3:36 p.m. but didn't arrive until 5 p.m. thus failing to get the 4 p.m. train to Larry on the mainline of Santa Fe Ry. And had to take the 7:20 p.m. train. This delay caused us to miss the no. 1 train and we got the no. 9 at 10:00 p.m. for Bluewater.

Tues May 23 Arrived at Bluewater at 4 a.m. and were met at station. We retired to bed and got about 2½ hours sleep. Attended a meeting called for 9:30 a.m. I spoke of the necessity for a course of life such that we know that we are approved of God. We left Bluewater with two saddle horses and a light four spring buggy with single seat and top seat. We drove about 12 miles and camped on the bank of a stream in the timbers. Here one of the saddle horses became frightened and ran off with the rope about 20 feet long dragging. We camped outside but had a good night. Elder Smith and I had a cot to sleep on.

Wed May 24 We broke camp at 6:30 a.m. When we got

about 2 miles beyond Sawyer on the Continental Divide the hind wheel broke down. We decided to unload our things and put a skid under the axle and Elder Smith and I remain and care for the things while Bp Hakes would go back to Sawyer and either get another wheel or another rig of some kind. Ramah. 4 p.m. We arrived here in a lumber wagon at 2:20 p.m. In view of our misfortunes thus far present circumstances, Elder Smith and I have decided to not visit Pine ward.

Sunday June 25 I spoke upon prohibition. Referred to the attitude of Pres. Smith & general authorities and read Luke 16:19–33, Lazarus & rich man. If you heed not the prophets ye would not hear one raised from the dead. Who is going to lead you? Saloon men or the prophets?

Sat July 29 I received appointment to Mexico to be at Juarez Aug 25th and it will require until Sept 25th to complete the itinerary arranged by the Stake Presidency for my visit.

Friday Aug 18 I this day shaved clean the first time for perhaps twenty-five years that I have been without mustache.

Saturday Nov 11 I subscribe for two daily newspapers, the Evening News & Morning Herald Republican and when at home spend from 30 min to one hour on each to keep up with the news of the times. Just now, China is fighting for freedom, a sort of revolution. The Italians are trying to interfere with Turkish rule in Tripoli and Mexico has not settled all her differences growing out of the recent revolution.

Thu Dec 7 I attended regular weekly council meeting. At this meeting Pres. Jos. F. Smith suggested the name of Elder Chas. W. Penrose to fill the vacancy of 2nd Counselor in the First Presidency and Elder Jas E. Talmage to fill the vacancy in the Twelve. Each spoke endorsing the selections and voted to sustain them, after which we all laid on hands and Pres. Smith set brother Penrose apart 2nd Counselor in the First Presidency, Elder Talmage not present and to this time not conferred with on the subject of his call.

Fri Dec 15 Alice and I received invitation to attend the Salt Lake Theater but reading the comments of the news we decided it was not sufficiently dignified and did not go.

Sat. Dec 30 I went to Tooele on the 7:45 A.M. train. I met Elder James E. Talmage on the train, he and I having been appointed to attend the Tooele Stake Conference. At noon brother Talmage and I met with Pres. Gowans and told him what we decided upon in our Council meeting last Thursday, this on my suggestion, that we thought a change in presidency of the stake at this time would be proper and that Pres. Gowans should be ordained a Patriarch. Pres. Gowans assented with good grace & feeling.

Sunday Dec 31 Tooele. At the 10 A.M. meeting held in the meeting house, the sacrament was administered with individual glass service, the first time either of us three apostles had seen such service used.

Tues Jan 9, 1912 LeGrand is improving. The doctor pronounces his case small pox and he with his wife and babe are this day quarantined.

Thur Jan 18 My son George and I visited the Latter Day Saints Gym in the evening and witnessed what is known as the tournament of the State. Pres. Jos. F. Smith, Pres. Francis M. Lyman and other leading men were present. I here witnessed the first boxing I ever saw with gloves and it was woefully wanting in science and replete with abusive slugging. The wrestling was interesting.

Thu Apr 18 The sinking of the Titanic Steamship off

Newfoundland through striking an iceberg by which more than 1500 lives were lost is one of the catastrophies of this century.

Sunday Apr 21 In the afternoon referred to the sinking one week ago of the Titanic of the White Star line, the largest steamer afloat 883 feet in length. The loss of life is reported 1635, about 750 rescued mostly women and children. It was thought that the Titanic was a life boat of itself unsinkable which fact no doubt caused the officials to be careless for notwithstanding they had been warned by wireless of icebergs they were going at almost full speed. We learn our dependence still upon Providence. While the Titanic was capacitated to carry above 3000 passengers, they only had life boats for 1000 or less. Had they had a sufficient number all could have been rescued. Again only one operator was on the Carpathia who picked up the survivors and he was just leaving his instrument for the night and it was by mere chance that he heard the call for assistance, 60 miles away. Each ship should have 2 operators so there would be one at his post all the time. These lessons we should profit by. Also that life is uncertain.

Tues May 14 Independence. This is the 48th anniversary of my wife's birth. We called on Joseph Smith, the son of the prophet Joseph Smith and President of the Reorganized Church. We also called on Fred Smith the grandson of the Prophet and the designated successor to his father in the Presidency of the Reorganized Church. We were treated nicely by them.

Thu May 16 Independence. Saw the old home of David Whitmer and met one of his grandsons, Mr. Geo W. Schweich. He & his mother and daughter want to go to Utah. He is a firm believer in the Book of Mormon and declares that he has repeatedly heard his grandfather assert that his testimony to the B of M is true. It was here that the Prophet and a number of the brethren were detained in chains fifteen days while under going many indignities at the hands of their enemies under the pretense of a trial.

Thu May 23 Nauvoo. We saw the old cemetery, the temple site where stood the temple, the Nauvoo house, the Nauvoo mansion, Joseph's cottage, Emma's grave, the graves of Joseph and Hyrum being near by but not definitely designated. Father Willard Richards' home lot and the grave of Jenetta Richards. Her remains were removed in 1867 by the Reinbolds who have possessed the lot since it was deserted in 1846. The remains were moved from near the house to the Southwest corner of the lot and the stone slab about 16 inches wide and about 3 feet high laid on the grave.

Thu May 30 I gave to each of the boys 160 Acres which is situated about two miles and a half west of Tooele City. George the North quarter, LeGrand the South and Joel the middle. This by mutual understanding and endorsement of both of the boys & LeGrand who were present, Joel is in England.

Sund. Jun 9 Am well but feel that I need more sleep. My rest was greatly disturbed during the night by vermine.

Tues July 2 My sons & I were talking about trading for an auto so went down to 8th So and State to look at a machine.

Sat July 6 I went down town and attended to some business and went with my sons to see an auto with a view to trading some Tooele land for it. The car a $4500 Thomas Flyer, six cylinder, 60 horse power, five passenger of 1910 model offered at $1200. I spent the day and evening at home. Mama took the little ones for a trolley ride.

Tues July 30, 1912 Am feeling some better today. Between 1000 and 2000 of our people from Mexico have within the past few days moved out of the Mexican colonias and are cared for at or near El Paso. I called on Dr. Stephen who prescribed further for me. They are convinced that my severe headaches and nausea is due to exposure to the suns rays in making the trip from Malad to Snowville, 40 miles torture, two weeks ago in an open automobile. I wrote to my son Joel in Preston, England.

Thu Aug 22 Called at Dr. S. L. and Gill Richards' office and consulted them and comparing my symptoms with those given in the book became convinced conclusively that my trouble is what is termed "heat exhaustion" and the cause same as I had attributed it to.

Sunday Sept 15 I attended the funeral services of Pres. Hugh S. Gowans who died 80 years of age. He was 29 years the stake president of the Tooele Stake and for 16 years I was his counselor.

Tues Oct 29, 1912 I have been out of the house but once since I took my bed Sept 23rd. I think I have had typhoid along with the return attack of my former trouble, head exhaustion or sun stroke.

Mon Nov 4 Being forbidden by the doctors to read on account of my eyes, the time drags. I sit up all day but retire early.

Sunday Nov 17, 1912 Aunt Jane S. Richards died between 2 & 3 P.M. today in her 90th year.

Thu Dec 26 I attended weekly Council meeting and then with others of the brethren walked up to Capitol hill and saw the ground broken for the new Capitol building.

Sund. Jan 26, 1913 I attended Pioneer stake conference. I occupied 30 minutes principally upon the love of God for us which led him to give his son to a life of sorrow, suffering & finally to death upon the cross for us; the love of Christ for us ditto and why we should love the Lord & how manifest it, 1st by being good children, 2nd by being obedient to his laws & covenants, 3rd by helping & blessing others.

Thu Feb 6 Am feeling better. At our Council meeting today we decided that the temple to be built in Canada should be at Cardston.

Thu Feb 13 At the Council meeting it was decided to try putting two companies through the temple in one day commencing tomorrow and word was given to the temple workers to that effect. This on account of the crowded condition of the temple.

Thu Mar 6 I went to Stauffer's and had electric treatment for my eyes at 10 A.M. Went through the temple after 1:15 p.m. for Adam Langstrothe of Yorkshire, Eng. Born about 1490.

Fri Mar 7 I went down to the temple in the morning with a view to going through twice for endowment work but learned that that was contrary to the rule so returned home.

Tues June 3 Arrived home at 6:30 p.m. on the train I finished Oliver Twist by Dickens, 528 pages read during the trip.

Fri Jul 11 I this day received from the tailor my black coat and trousers which I had quit wearing but later decided to have repaired and cleaned using the vest to make repairs. It now answers the purpose of a best suit.

Thurs Aug 14 I attended regular Council meeting in the temple. All of the First Presidency and the Twelve and Patriarch were present except brother Smoot who is in Washington. Pres. Lund arose and said we are in need of presidents to replace those in New Zealand, Australia, South Africa, Netherlands, Samoa and more particularly the European Mission. It was moved and seconded and carried that Hyrum M. Smith be called to fill that vacancy. Pres. Smith asked me if LeGrand was fixed so that he could go and preside over the Netherlands Mission. I told him that I thought he could and would and perhaps better now than at a later period as he was contemplating going into business with other parties and it would probably be better to go now than after he had obligated himself with others in a business. It was then moved and seconded and carried that LeGrand Richards be called and appointed to preside over the Netherlands mission. Pres. Smith gave me the liberty to tell my son LeGrand what had taken place; accordingly after meeting I went over to where LeGrand is employed and told him about it. He had been expecting it so many had told him he was going to be called.

Oct 7 [At special meeting with Stake Presidents, he refers to some statistics. The average home teaching in the church was 30%, ranging from 1% to 89%. He makes a suggestion as to how to improve the visiting of members—reduce the number of assigned families to 8 per companionship, visit 2 families a night, one night each week.]

Tues Oct 21 We are having the hot water boiler attached to the furnace this day, a very necessary improvement which will give us hot water night and day during the winter when furnace is operating without expense after first cost of installing.

Fri Nov 7 I set apart LeGrand Richards to Netherlands to preside over that mission; Ina Jane Ashton Richards to accompany her husband.

Jan 21, 1914 [In the flyleaf of volume 17 of his journal he wrote the following:] "Pythagoras devoted his evenings to solemn reflections of the events of the day. The writing of a daily journal has the effect of reviewing the events of the day. This review rivets these things upon the [mind]. One should take time to sort his thoughts and label them."

Weds Feb 25 Went to the City and County Bldg and met with the Mayor and the commissioners on question of paving 3rd Avenue. It was agreed that they would pave from E to N streets this year and continue on to a finish next year.

Fri Apr 3 Word comes this a.m. that between 10 and 11 p.m.

last night Torreon, Mexico fell into the hands of the Mexican Constitutionalists under Villa as General. A bloody and decisive struggle.

Wed Apr 8 I recommended to the mission presidents that when they have opportunity they should interview the elders as to their discreetness and general conduct towards the opposite sex, and ask if they are obeying counsel. This should put a check on any practices, which might if not detected lead to serious consequences.

Mon Apr 20 The Atlantic and Pacific fleets of the US are on their way towards Mexican waters. The relations between the two republics are very much strained and Pres. Wilson has asked Congress to give him authority or endorsement to call out the Army and Navy to compel respect for our flag and to preserve the national honor.

Tues Apr 28 I have these thoughts upon the subject of public address or oratory. First the subject matter must be worthwhile. Second, the audience must be made to feel what you have to give. To make them feel it the speaker must feel it himself. If one speaks with feeling the accent will be in the right place and many other rules of delivery will be complied with unconsciously. Be easy and natural and sufficiently deliberate to emphasize where necessary.

Sat July 25 Morning session was a Relief Society meeting presided over by Pres. Emmeline B. Wells. In afternoon meeting I was the last of five speakers and occupied 25 minutes. Subject: church history and scenes in early church history I have visited. Testimony of Sister Wells agrees with my mother's testimony as to the mantle of the Prophet Joseph Smith falling on the prophet Brigham in temple grove on Temple hill, Nauvoo.

Tues Sept 8 The war news of Europe claims a part of my

time each day though I scarcely ever mention it in my diary. It is in its bloodiest form just now. Many nations involved.

Fri Sept 25 The war in France between the Allies French and English and the Germans is being waged with continued fierceness. Also the Russians and Austrians are doing bloody work. Surely there never was so far as I have heard such a battle of world powers. The casualties are reported by the thousands almost daily. My son LeGrand is still in Holland presiding over the Netherlands mission.

Mon Sept 28 Spent the remainder of the day at my desk reading, studying, and writing. I find that I can study religious subjects and get new ideas and can link them together better when I have pen or pencil and paper at hand. The war news indicated bloody fighting on enormous scale both in Austria and France with thousands laying down their lives every day and many thousands wounded daily. I think of the widows and fatherless; of parents, sisters and others mourning and the poverty and distress and pestilence to follow.

Thurs Oct 1, 1914 "All Continental missionaries released. All well." This we interpret to include Holland so suppose that LeGrand and family will soon be leaving Holland for home or some other mission.

Sun Oct 25 Attended High Council meeting and catechized them and found three of them using tea or coffee. They promised to quit their use.

Thur Nov 5 The election returns show that Sen. Reed Smoot was re-elected to the Senate. He has served twelve years in that capacity. An able senator, one who is in complete touch with Pres. Smith.

Tues Mar 30, 1915 The city in preparation for street paving 3rd Ave from N St East is putting in new water mains of 6" pipe on South side of street and have made excavation in front of our house. I have engaged Walsh plumbing Co. to deepen our service pipe from mains to the house to prevent future freezing.

Tues Apr 6 We are anxious about our son LeGrand and family in Holland not having heard anything from them for about three weeks and the last word was that the baby was very sick with whooping cough.

Tues May 4, 1915 I attended a meeting of the First Presidency and the Twelve in the Temple. Elder James E. Talmage read to us from the manuscript of his book on the life of the Savior.

Sun May 23 The boys and girls are entitled to the Spirit of the Lord to guide them in all their religious work if they live for it and that is all the Prophets have and it is by this means that the children of Israel were led out of bondage and the church is organized and the gospel restored. I urged the young people to use the strength of their young man and womanhood in the cause of the Lord.

Thurs Jun 17 At this meeting Pres. Jos. F. Smith who just returned from the Sandwich Islands proposed that we build a Temple in Laii, Hawaii, it was unanimously agreed upon.

Sun Jun 27 We are well taught but have need of being impressed with the necessity for doing as well as we know.

Weds Jul 14, 1915 My son LeGrand and family are still in Holland, LeGrand being on his second mission to the Netherlands and this time president of the mission. One baby, Jane born to them in Holland makes them four children, all girls and all learning to talk Dutch.

Fri Aug 20 I here awoke and later dreamed again that I saw my wife neatly dressed and not particularly occupied which seemed to invite me to embrace her which I most happily did. This dream impressed me with this thought that there are two things which mitigate against demonstrations of affection on my part; first, pre-occupation or being pre-occupied or over industrious and, second, lack of prime appearance on her part. Dress better and work and worry less would call forth demonstrations of affection.

Sat Oct 30 Subject: the sacrifice the Father made and that of the Son were for the salvation of man. All our sacrifices are for the same purpose, all our gifts of time or money privately or publicly, voluntarily or on call. No nobler calling or labor.

Sun Nov 14 At 2:20 p.m. attended a meeting of the stake presidency and bishoprics and spoke to them on the "Home Evening."

Tues Nov 30 I finished reading "Jesus the Christ" a book of 800 pages by Jas. E. Talmage. An excellent contribution to church literature.

Wed Dec 1, 1915 Later held a home evening meeting, inaugurating the same. We are to hold the first Wednesday of each month. Geo and Edith and Joel and Georgina and Wayne were with us. At this meeting I gave all the unmarried children 3 cents for each year of their age and this is to be repeated at each meeting.

Fri Dec 17 I had a dream last night which impressed me with the fact that I am not doing my Temple work as fast as I should. I saw in my dream a large orchard of fruit trees of heavy foliage. I was irrigating the orchard but had neglected to watch closely the water. Now I observe that the leaves are all brown and withered from the drought. I thought what a shame that these trees had been so neglected. I saw a woman who may have been my mother or grandmother who seemed to be living on the place. She called my attention to the effects of the drought and as near as I can remember she indicated to me that if watered well now these trees would come out in the Spring. I apply this to my responsibility to do or have done our Temple work. I fear if I were to go on the other side I would realize my neglect of Temple work as I felt my neglect of the orchard.

Mon Feb 7 [1916] I invited Pres. FM Lyman to go with me to the Temple and we inspected it with the view to increasing the capacity of the Temple, as many people are turned away for want of capacity. . . . I also suggested having three companies daily instead of two as at present.

Weds Mar 1, 1916 Later George, Joel, Clarence and wives and children came and we had a home evening meeting, singing, reciting, games, refreshments, etc.

Sat Jun 10, 1916 Beautiful weather. According to appointment I met Pres. Jos. F. Smith at his home, the Beehive house at 9 a.m. today. He asked me how I would feel about an appointment to succeed the present President of the European Mission leaving my family at home until it should become more safe at sea. I answered that what is his will in the matter I should conclude is the will of the Lord and I desired to do the will of the Lord. I told him I felt it would be a tremendous responsibility, but others with the Lord's help had accomplished such work and that I was hopeful; that I appreciated the expression of confidence. The President then asked me how soon I could get ready. I told him my son LeGrand and family are to sail from Holland the 17th inst. And would probably be home about July 10th or before and I would like until that latter part of July to make ready and assist LeGrand to get established in some business if possible. He said that would be all right and to make my arrangements accordingly. He said he had talked it over with the brethren, meaning, I suppose, his counselors. I came home and made known to my family the above information. It broke up my wife's feelings and the children cried with her. The Lord has said we should live together in love so that we should mourn for those who die. We should so love that we sorrow at separation. It is pleasing to the Lord that we love one another so it cannot be an offense that we sorrow at parting. My true feelings are that I would naturally shrink from such responsibility and having to leave home and loved ones for such a time as this mission will mean, but that having put my hand to the plow, there is for me no turning back. I appreciate the honor if I can succeed and I believe I shall have his help else he would not through his servant have called me. Perhaps I have said enough. God's will be done and all glory, praise and honor be his forever through Jesus Christ.

Sun Jun 25 The news of today is that war with Mexico is almost a certainty. Pres. Carranza (Karanza) having acknowledged responsibility for the Karanzal attack and treachery of the Mexican troops.

Weds Jun 28 [Having recently purchased a new Oxford Bible for four dollars,] I worked at my desk until the middle of the afternoon reading and marking my new Bible from my old one.

Sun Jul 2 I spent the remainder of the day at home comforting my wife. Yesterday July 1st the Allies (British, French, Russians, and Italians) commenced a concerted offensive movement against their enemies the Germans, Austrians and Turks, which seems to be telling and makes it appear that the Teutonic allies had reached the limit of their military power and that the tide of war is going against them.

Fri Jul 14 Invited the advice of the First Presidency whether it is safer to go by American line or just as safe to go by Canadian Pacific or Allen line. Elder Reed Smoot responded to a letter of inquiry and stated he felt they were equally safe, however the

"Department of the Interior advises to go by the American line." I left the letter with the First Presidency, Pres. Smith not being in. His advice will decide us on this point if he feels to advise.

Sat Aug 5 Alice and I and George and Edith went to the President's office at about 11:30 a.m. and received blessings at the hands of Pres. Smith and Pres. Penrose. Pres. Smith blessed and set me apart to preside over the European Mission. Pres. Penrose set apart my son George a missionary to Gt. Britain and Pres. Smith set apart Edith May Richards a missionary to Gt. Britain. Then Pres. Smith gave Alice a good blessing to remain home. These blessings were taken by the stenographer. Pres. Smith and Pres. Penrose gave instructions.

Mon Aug 7 I wired home at 11 a.m. from North Platte and again on reaching Omaha. We are all well and have enjoyed the trip thus far, the only unpleasantness being the separation with my loved ones on leaving. Elder Orson F. Whitney of the Council of the Twelve came to the Ry Station to see us off. Others out on their trips. Both Pres. Jos. F. Smith and Pres. FM Lyman kissed me good bye.

Mon Aug 14 By phone made appointment with _____ of the Canadian Steam Ship Co. to meet at 11 a.m. at hotel where I was staying and when we met we talked over matters pertaining to our travel with the Allen Line or Canadian Pacific line and objections made by certain women's organizations of England to our people traveling on same ships because as purported, our Elders undertake proselyting on the ship and thus become objectionable company. He admitted that he thought these were unfounded rumors but suggested that some instruction to Elders on that point may not be altogether in vain.

Thur Aug 17 One of the stewards told me that once we leave last sight of land, all windows will be sealed up and every thing appear dark, that we will from that time on be in the danger zone, liable to meet submarines. It begins to take on the appearance of war times.

Sun Aug 20 Last night I dreamed that I saw Kaiser Wilhelm of Germany and had a talk with him. I said referring to himself and King George of England, "You boys are having a quarrel which is causing much bloodshed and sorrow." The emperor acquiesced in the statement and seemed to be sorry. My sympathy went out for him and I was about to say if there is anything I can do for you, I will be glad to serve you and then I checked myself remembering that what he might want of me would be something adverse to the interest of the King of England and the English people. It is too cold to sit in my room to read and write with the window open and with it shut and light on it is too dark to see well making it unpleasant studying. The large guns on the rear which shoot a 100 lb shell and can be fired from 8–11 times per minute; seven men to the gun. Should an enemy submarine appear this ship would no doubt turn the heel and the boat (stern) and run and shoot. Then our chances for getting off the boat if struck by a torpedo is lessened. If on a neutral boat and held up no effort of escape would be made, the submarine would not sink the ship and after a search had been made if searched at all, she would be permitted to pass on. If I am not mistaken in my conclusions, it is too unsafe to recommend that our Elders go to and from by this route during war times. Had I known what I now know, I think I should have come by American liner. We are notified by printed notice to darken the port holes at night so that no light can be seen. Not allowing to even light a match on deck. After daybreak the whistle blew about every two minutes on account of fog for an hour or such until it cleared up a bit. I did not undress for the night as a precaution in case of submarine attack.

Mon Aug 28 This day the affairs of the European Mission were turned over to me. With Pres. Smith I went through the house and the accounts of the mission on inspection tour and signed the books of transfer.

Tues Sept 5 A brother Caron of McGrath, Canada in soldier's uniform called on us at 10:30 a.m. He reports Major Brown and his LDS men at Somerset barracks, Shorncliffe, England.

Wed–Thurs Sept 6–7 To Blackburn and Clitheroe, the birthplace of my Mother. Saw and visited the old castle many centuries old and from its walls viewed the country for miles around and it is one of the most beautiful scenes I have ever seen.

Mon Nov 6, 1916 It has been three months since I left home and I have been blessed to exceed all my former hopes or expectations. Surely the earnest prayers offered for me are not offered in vain. On each occasion I was richly blessed by the Lord and had good freedom of thought and delivery. This has been one of the best days of my life.

Wed Nov 29 During the three months there have been 33 branches organized or reorganized with local brethren and sisters exclusively. Most of these in the past have been presided over by Elders from Zion. For the months of July, August and September the Elders spent 3350 hours more visiting Saints than in visiting investigators and in tracting combined. We are trying to reverse this record having the Saints nurse the Saints and as far as possible liberate the Elders to do real missionary work. Have as far as possible all the Saints working. These are war times when women do men's work. We are trying to employ our women in officering our auxiliary organizations, doing branch teaching, praying and preaching in the meetings, etc. During the past 3 months we have called, set apart and issued missionary certificates to about 270 lady missionaries. These are doing good work tracting, etc. It is requested that these missionaries spend at least one hour each week tracting. These women are mostly employed in shops and munitions factories and have but little time to give to the work. I feel very much encouraged in my work thus far and believe the Lord has inspired these new movements of women's work in the Church.

Mon Dec 11 The Salt Lake newspapers came today announcing the appointment Thurs Nov 23rd of Elder Heber J. Grant as President of the Council of the Twelve succeeding Pres. F. M. Lyman. I wrote Pres. Grant as follows: "Dear Brother: Word has just reached us through the Salt Lake papers of your appointment as the President of the Council of the Twelve. This I recognize as being perfectly right and in proper order and I endorse the action with all my heart. I declare my loyalty to you, my President, and I thank the Lord that one so worthy and capable was in line to succeed to this important office. May the Lord bless you always with the spirit of your high calling as an Apostle and as President of His Chosen Twelve. Affectionately and Sincerely, your brother, George F. Richards."

Christmas Dec 25 After turkey dinner, my son Geo and I walked down where the poor live and distributed about 6 dozen small oranges and several dozen penny packages of sweets, one to a child as we felt they were deserving, judging from their appearance.

Thurs Feb 1, 1917 This day Germany's radical and desperate methods of submarine warfare go into effect, the announcement of which was made yesterday to the United States and published in the English papers today.

Fri Feb 2 The papers have comments on Germany's attitude in regard to the war and neutral countries are very wrought up. Germany gave only 8 hours notice to the United States of her intended vigorous submarine warfare on all kinds of ships, sinking them without notice. Great Britain notified Pres. Wilson that if Germany carries out her threats, Great Britain and her allies will resort to reprisals. The U.S. has given notice that no passports will be given to people desiring to go to Europe. A German ship was sunk in an American harbor by her crew to avoid being taken possession by the US Government.

Weds Feb 7 The Des. News of Jan 18, 1917 received today states that Stephen L. Richards, Jr. having been selected to fill the vacancy in the Council of the Twelve Apostles, was ordained by Pres. Jos. F. Smith. This appointment is a splendid recognition of Stephen's ability and devotion to the work of the Lord and will no doubt meet with the hearty approval of the Saints who know him, as it meets with mine.

Thurs Feb 8 I was under the painful necessity of asking Sister _____ to keep out of our kitchen and larder when not invited.

Sunday Mar 18 We should never get so old as to quit working physically and mentally. The powers become atrophied and dormant by non-use.

Mon Apr 9 Birmingham: I met with the 6 Elders of the conference and gave special instructions and asked each Elder as to his conduct. Inquiry a safeguard. They will expect me to enquire again and so be circumspect.

Mon May 15 Dreamed of my wife, fond embraces.

Sun Dec 9, 1917 I am well and happy but I would love to see my wife and children.

Mon Dec 10 This evening's paper announces the capture of Jerusalem by the British. This is glorious news as the British have already signified their purpose of opening the way for Jews to return to the land of Palestine by driving the Turks out of the country which it seems they are doing in good order.

Sat Jan 26, 1918 At 8:35 a.m. I received a cablegram from Pres. Lund as follows: "Appendicitis yesterday caused death of Hyrum Mack Smith." I walked down town and sent a cablegram to Pres. Jos. F. Smith as follows: "Condolences. God bless bereaved."

Fri Apr 5 From the Millennial Star I learn that when my father came to England in 1846 the mission headquarters were at No 135 Duke Street. Between that time and Jan 1847 they were moved to No. 6 Dorel Piazza. Before Jan 1848 they were moved to 39 Torbuck Street. Later they were moved to No. 15 Wilton Street and in 1855 to #42 Islington Street. From there a move was made by Elder Heber J. Grant about 1905 and a little later to Durham House, 295 Edge Lane, the present headquarters.

July 4 Geo and I went downtown and witnessed an Independence day celebration which comprised a parade and review of American troops. The US soldiers marched 4 abreast and it required 12½ minutes for them to pass a given point. The English people were out in good force. The most people I ever saw assembled on one occasion. American flags were generously displayed. It seems strange that after 142 years Great Britain should acknowledge the justice of the cause for which the American Colonies fought and freed themselves from the oppressions of their mother country. It almost appears now as if Gt. Britain is glad that it happened and joins with us in celebrating the anniversary of that event with as much enthusiasm as the Americans themselves. Both countries are now fighting side by side for a more extended application of those principles of freedom for which the colonies fought. The application of those principles are to be worldwide. That means for Russians, Germans, Austrians as well as for the allied countries. Mr. Winston Churchill at Central Hall London today said, "A great harmony exists between the Spirit of the Declaration of Independence and all we are fighting for now. . . . Deep down in the hearts of the people of these islands there lies the desire to be truly reconciled before all men and before all history with their kindred across the Atlantic Ocean separated by the blunders of a bygone age." Germany must be beaten. She must know she is beaten.

Fri July 19th I went with my son and others to Knotty Ash Soldier's rest camp and saw some of our Utah Mormon boys and met Lieut. Brigham H. Roberts, chaplain for the 145th.

Sat Oct 5 The influenza is reported as being general and quite malignant. It is reported that at Knotty Ash Camp, 50 American soldiers were buried today.

Mon Oct 7 The headlines of the "Post and Mercury" this morning are as follows: "Enemy appeal for armistice. Joint overtures to Mr. Wilson. Immediate conference wanted. President's 14 points accepted." This looks like the approach of the end. What tremendous responsibility rests upon Pres. Wilson and the Allies to determine steps! What far-reaching effects will result from their action!

Tues Nov 5 Had a visit from a Sargent Torgenson from Ogden. He told of their troop ship. 1700 men on board. "About a thousand of the men had the influenza. 40 of them were buried at sea including 2 from his bunk room. He was taken from the ship on a stretcher to a hospital. He said 70 American soldiers were buried yesterday in Liverpool and that a week ago there were about 80 buried in one day."

Sun Nov 10 The Kaiser and the Crown Prince have abdicated and renounced the throne and rights to same in Germany.

Mon Nov 11 Official announcement of the signing of the

terms of armistice by army made. Whistles were blowing, guns were fired, bells ringing, flags flying and work men and work girls were thronging the streets singing and hollering, etc. This certainly is a great day as it is the ending of the war at 11:00 a.m. today with a complete victory for the US and the Allies.

Fri Nov 22 I received a cablegram from Presidents Lund and Penrose dated Nov. 19th which gave the information that Pres. Jos. F. Smith died Nov 19th. I wired regrets and condolences; also cabled the other Presidents of the European Missions.

Tues Dec 3, 1918 This day I received from Pres. Jos. F. Smith a personal letter dictated on his 80th birthday anniversary as he lay in bed and signed by himself. He died on the 19th, six days later. I also received a personal letter from Pres. Heber J. Grant written Nov 12th. One paragraph reads as follows: "I hope that it may not be long now before your wife will have the pleasure of joining you. . . . I see no reason why she could not go at the earliest date convenient for her. I can well appreciate how much real joy and happiness it will be to you after the long separation from your wife, to have her with you in the missionary field."

Mon Jan 13, 1919 I had a touch of appendicitis trouble yesterday and today if what I think is appendicitis trouble is what I think it to be.

Fri Jan 24 I received a cablegram from my wife signed Alice Richards which reads as follows: "Sail Metagama, Feb 24th. Successor leaves April. All well." There is so much meaning in the above cablegram and of a pleasing character that I felt that my cup of joy is running over.

Jan 30 There now remains but three of us missionaries in Durham House and but 13 Elders from Zion in the conferences, each one of whom is a president. We have four local brethren, all young men and two lady missionaries giving all their time as missionaries and a corps of 368 Lady Missionaries who are giving such time as they can spare to missionary work.

Fri Feb 7 President Heber J. Grant. Along with the routine work of the presidency, each of the preceding presidents has had a special labor to accomplish which has particularly distinguished him and his administration. It will prove to be the case with Pres. Grant. I firmly believe that the Lord has raised him up to preside over the Church at this time and that there is a special work for him to accomplish which is of great import in preparing for the coming of our Lord whose glorious advent is near, even at our door. His love of God is known by his devotion to the Lord's work and the faithfulness with which he has kept the commandments. His love for the Saints is proven by his many and exceedingly generous gifts. He will have in his administration the gifts of God through the Holy Spirit and the sustaining love and prayers of the Saints with their loyal devotion to their religious duties all of which is sufficient guarantee of his future success.

Being the very embodiment of honor and honesty the funds of the Church entrusted to his care will be carefully and honestly administered. He possesses also that business acumen which coupled with his wide business experience admirably qualify him for the trusteeship. Pres. Grant is a plain spoken man. With him a spade is a spade. His expressions are rarely ambiguous. He is frank and outspoken. He not only speaks the truth, but he speaks the whole truth and nothing but the truth. He has never been regarded as being physically strong, but intellectually and spiritually he is a giant in strength.

He is as fearless and scathing in his denunciation of the wrong doer as he is gentle and loving in his commendation of the pure in heart and faithful. His integrity is beyond all question, and this is one of the chiefest qualifications necessary for one holding the exalted office of President and mouthpiece to God's chosen people. No president of the Church has ever departed from the ways of the Lord or lead the people astray, and none shall.

I recently dreamed of Pres. Grant in which I received his kiss of love and approval, which I greatly appreciated. I dearly love Pres. Grant and rejoice exceedingly in my association with him in the councils of the Priesthood.

Feb 23 This is the most direct and definite word I have received in regard to my release but it means that I will probably be leaving about the first of May. I suppose that I, like most of the missionaries, will welcome the change when the time comes. My loved ones at home are a great drawing card and loadstone, and when my mission here is ended, I shall hurry home to labor in other fields.

Weds Mar 12 The weather is cold. The snow covers the ground. We have been out of coke and have had no fire in the furnace for several days. I go about with my coat on in the house.

Sun Mar 30 Mother had a little sickness on the way but was well on landing. This has been one of the happiest days in my life or hers.

Apr 17 [He writes a letter to Pres. Grant regarding the number of missionaries serving. He is notified that eleven missionaries will be arriving in May and reports that with the departure of three elders in May, they will be down to four Elders from Zion and a few local missionaries.] "10 of the 13 conferences will be left entirely in the hands of the local priesthood leaders. Many valuable lessons are being taught through the shortage of Elders from Zion and the trying circumstances through which the mission has been passing the past few years. The saints are learning to sustain the local brethren in their various offices and to stand on their own foundation of faith without being constantly nursed by the Zion Elders. Local talent is being developed and appreciated, and the officers are learning to serve in humility and kindness. The bringing of so many more people into active service has been a great blessing to them as well as to the work. I think them fully equal to the average missionary from home."

Sat Jul 6 It is 35 months today since I left home for my mission. Attended fast meeting and made a few remarks on war and peace and as this is the day set apart by the King and the Mission President on which to give thanks for peace, I lead in prayer.

Friday July 25, 1919 Our sons Geo, LeGrand, Joel, Oliver and Ray met us in Ogden. At Salt Lake the other members of the family met us. We are all well. We had a grand reunion and most happy time. My daughters Sarah and Nina each had been married and each has a nice baby and in all eight grandchildren have been born to us during my absence. Our granddaughter Jane passed away during that time.

Tues Sep 2 I this day took possession of office room No. 213 in the Office building of the General Authorities. In the evening I attended a lecture in the large tabernacle by Reuben Clark on the League of Nations.

Tues Sept 23 I saw Pres. Woodrow Wilson and the pageant or parade. It was grand by reason of the numbers. I and members of my family attended the services in the Tabernacle at 8:15 p.m. I think the house was never before so packed, and I suppose [there were] many thousands on the grounds and streets adjacent who could not obtain entrance. The President's remarks which lasted for about an hour created a very favorable impression of the Covenant of the League of Nations. I was introduced to Pres. Woodrow Wilson by President Heber J. Grant who told that President that I had spent nearly three years in Europe while the war was progressing. Pres. Wilson while shaking hands with me leaned forward and remarked, "You know that I have not mis-stated the conditions over there." I answered in the affirmative.

Tues Nov 4 Cardston. In the evening I attended the MIA meeting and spoke to those present following Major Brown who spoke on the League of Nations covenant. A busy and interesting conference. Financial conditions in Canada very adverse. Loss of crops through drought, loss of potatoes through frost, and loss of cattle and horses for want of feed and on account of the cold and snow. A serious outlook.

Thurs Nov 19 The Senate this day rejected the League Covenant and Treaty and adjourned. The Republicans desired certain reservations which the Democrats would not have and the Republicans would not ratify without reservations.

Sat Dec 13 The thermometer reached 10 degrees below zero. Sleighing is good in and about Salt Lake but we see no sleighs, no horses—the automobiles have displaced horses.

Thurs Jan 8, 1920 Attended regular council meeting. I witnessed an exhibition of Church moving pictures in the basement of the Office Building

Sat Feb 1 I attended a special meeting yesterday afternoon with the Stake Presidency and the visiting brethren where the matter of cost and size of Temple to be built were considered, also site, the latter to be further considered later. It was decided that a Temple having rooms to seat 100 would be large enough. The attendance at this conference was, by percent of population the largest I have ever seen, I think. The Sunday meetings were attended by nearly 50% of the population of the stake.

Mon Feb 2 With Pres. Grant and others I drove about Mesa looking at properties with a view to deciding upon a Temple site.

We arrived at a conclusion and arranged to purchase 24 acres in the Eastern part of town for that purpose.

Thur Feb 12 In the evening, Geo, LeGrand and Joel and their wives came in on my invitation and I made representation to them of opportunities for investing in land with profit in the Gila Valley, Arizona. I had been offered a farm of 120 Acres for $5000, ½ cash with balance by note over 5 years. Water for 90 acres.

Fri Feb 13 Made application for a loan of $2750 at the bank with which to purchase land in Arizona.

Tues Feb 17 In the midst of the influenza's prevalence we have thus far escaped and we are very grateful to the Lord for this fact. Many are dying from the dreaded disease.

Thur Mar 18 I was appointed chairman of a committee on the revision and correction of the Book of Mormon, the other members being Elder Ivins, Talmage and Ballard.

Mar 19 On the auto stage from Lund to Cedar City were seven other men and much profanity. I protested and it had the effect of cutting most of it out. While driving from Cedar to Parowan, the steering rod broke when we were near a culvert and we narrowly escaped what might have been a very serious accident. Returning from Parowan to Cedar we ran short of gas and were stranded for about an hour in a cold wind and rain.

Mon Mar 29 I spent the forenoon reading the Book of Mormon with a view of detecting errors to be corrected in the next edition.

Tues Apr 13 Held consultation with _____ on subject of his making an index for the Book of Mormon.

May 7 Advised that the boys be informed what qualifications are necessary to be advanced in the priesthood and to go to the Temple and plead with them to make the necessary preparations.

I gave the attitude of the Church on profanity, using tobacco and tithe paying as qualifications.

Tues May 18 I have missed the marks, I am sure in the matter of keeping my diary in the past in that I have aimed principally to show how and where my time has been spent. Many important things I have omitted to record such as dreams, occurrences temporality with my life. One of the most important things of my life was the seeing of the Savior in a dream which was, I think, in the month of March, 1906, before I was called into the Council of the Twelve. I failed to record it at the time and later when I came to make a record of it, I could not tell the date I received it. I wonder if it was not so with the Prophet Joseph with respect to the bestowal of the keys of the Priesthood by Peter, James and John. We teach not the exact date. I think I will try and do better and be more careful in the future.

Fri May 21 I was with the Book of Mormon committee from 9 a.m. to after noon. After supper I made ready and took the train at 11:30 p.m. for Idaho Falls to attend the Bingham Stake Conference. I recommended that we make an effort to get 10% of population at the opening session of stake conference. Spoke of unsettled business conditions, scarcity of money and extravagance of the people and advised the practice of economy. Get out of debt and keep out and be free. Debt may mean bondage.

Tues May 25 Sat about 6 hours in committee meeting reading the Book of Mormon.

Weds May 26 I attended the Book of Mormon committee meetings reading the Book of Mormon 5½ hours.

Tues Jun 8 I attended two sessions of the Book of Mormon committee of which I am chairman. Six members of the Twelve are members of this committee.

Weds Aug 25 Worked in my office correcting footnote

references to Book of Mormon. In the evening I attended a meeting in the tabernacle where Democratic candidate for VP of US, Roosevelt was the principal speaker.

Mon Sep 6 We had a good conference. We may not remember what was said, but we will remember what was felt. It is well to be impressed often with the truth and beauty of the gospel. This is usually accomplished in our meetings. We are made more appreciative of the gospel and live better lives.

Tues Sept 14 Our company of two car loads left for Zion's Canyon about 9 a.m. We had dinner there and then with two carriages and two extra horses we went up above the weeping rock and cable to where we could see the narrows. This is surely a wonderland, nature's garden. While it differs from other National Parks it is of itself one of the greatest.

Weds Sept 15 Pres Grant and Elder Lyman called for me at 6:45 a.m. and we went up the canyon and attended the Dedicatory exercises for the opening of the park.

Tues Oct 12 I with J. F. S. worked on Book of Mormon Table of Contents for new edition. I having prepared a new and extended Table of Contents, Bro. Smith is checking it up with me.

Thurs Oct 14 I attended Weekly Council meeting in the Temple. At this meeting Elder David O. McKay was to visit the Islands of the Pacific.

Tues Nov 9 I attended Book of Mormon committee meeting and later we appeared before the Presidency and presented some important matters pertaining to that work. Bro Ballard and I spent some time working on B. of M. committee work.

Fri Nov 12 To accept a call is to covenant to magnify same.

Thurs Nov 25 Thanksgiving day. I took Estella to the football game on Cummings field. This is the first game of this kind that I have ever watched through. U.A. college won over U of U 9 to 3.

Tues Dec 28 This day I was presented as a member of the Book of Mormon committee, with a copy of the new edition of the Book of Mormon in each of four kinds of binding, this by the First Presidency.[1]

Fri Jan 21, 1921 I spent the forenoon in my office and the afternoon from 2:00 to 5:30 p.m. in Book of Mormon committee meeting, where we heard Joel Ricks on Book of Mormon lands. A number of other prominent Book of Mormon students were present.

Mon Jan 24 I attended B of M committee meeting from 9 to 1 p.m. Elder Ivins presented his views of Book of Mormon geography. Attended to business in my office with Elders Ivins and Talmage.

Tues Jan 25 I studied Book of Mormon geography most of the day, several hours with A. W. Ivins and Jos. F. Smith, Jr. Spent the evening studying the Book of Mormon.

Weds Jan 26 Continued my study of the Book of Mormon lands. My ideas in the past have been that the Nephites were located in the Northern part of South America, but am beginning to believe that they were from the first in Central America.

Mon Feb 21 Have had some lameness in my right arm for some days which disturbed my rest nights but last night I had no trouble. I am wondering if the same power that enlightened my mind while speaking in the conference did not heal the bodily affliction. I asked for that blessing and I received it.

Wed Mar 2, 1921 This day Pres. Anthon H. Lund passed

---

1. Later editions of the Book of Mormon, including the 1948 edition, state, "First issued in double-column pages with chapter headings, chronological data, revised foot-note references, pronouncing vocabulary, and index, in 1920."

away quietly. I made out my income tax report and mailed it to the Collector of Internal Revenue, SLC. This is a gloomy day for the Latter-day Saints.

Mon Mar 7 I phoned Pres. Heber J. Grant telling him that I was at my office and that I was not very busy and would be glad if I could do something to lighten his load. I told him that I had offered to assist Elder Talmage and had filled appointments for him to attend conference so that he would not be so long away from his office. Have offered to assist Joseph Fielding Smith at the Temple and have done some sealings at his invitation. Pres. Grant thanked me and said he was in a meeting at the time. I told him I did not desire to put my nose in others business but that I could usually be found in my office when not attending meetings.

Wed Mar 9, 1921 While in Logan I went with Pres. Cardon to the home of Elder Greender whose body was lying in state, ready for burial. Elder Greender died from gas fumes in an out house in Ohio where he was laboring as a missionary two months out. He left a bride of one week when he went away.

Thurs Mar 10 I attended a meeting in the Temple as usual from 10 a.m. to about 3 p.m. At this meeting Pres. Charles W. Penrose was chosen as First Counselor and Anthony W. Ivins was chosen as Second Counselor, or rather their names were suggested by Pres. Grant and sustained by unanimous vote of the Council. Each spoke expressing their feelings of endorsement. The Presidency retired for a few moments and on their return presented my name for President of the Salt Lake Temple and I was sustained unanimously. The time of setting apart was deferred until my assistants are selected. Pres. Grant stated that I could select my own Assistants stating that Joseph Fielding Smith and Brother Albert Davis were the Assistants to Pres. Lund. I know of no special labor that could be added to my present duties in the Church that I would appreciate and enjoy so much as that of presiding over the Temple and Temple work and workers, and engaging in the work itself. I regard therefore this appointment as very great added honor which, with the help of the Lord and the assistance of my counselors and the First Presidency over me, I hope to magnify satisfactorily to the Lord and all concerned. I spent the evening at home with my family.

Fri Mar 11, 1921 I attended a committee meeting of what has been known as the Book of Mormon committee to whom has been delegated the labor of revising the Doctrine and Covenants which I may now properly style the Doctrine and Covenants Committee. Later we went before the Presidency of the Church with recommendations. I received instruction from Pres. Grant and endorsed by Pres. Penrose that all Temple marriages should be solemnized by the Apostles where possible.

Mon Mar 14 Elder Jos. Fielding Smith and Brother Albert Davis went with me to the President's office and we were set apart to preside over the Salt Lake Temple. I met with the Presidency later and considered plans for the proposed Arizona Temple to be built at Mesa.

Tues Mar 15 I presided at the Temple for the first time. After meeting I had my assistants together and we talked to them in regard to being kind and helpful to others and seeing that others do likewise. People coming to the Temple for the first time regard it as heaven on earth, the holiest place, and the workers the best of men and women, angels symbolized. Do not disappoint them. . . . The Temple must be clean. Received letter of instruction from the Presidency concerning the affairs of the Temple.

Wed Mar 16 After consulting with my assistants, I instructed Bro. _____ to admit to the Temple the number the Temple seating capacity will allow and when there is room, to let those who desire it go through twice the same day.

Sat Mar 26 Phoned 2 city Bishops about members from their wards who are reported to have come to the Temple as tobacco users. I asked the Bishops to try and clean them up before they come here again.

Thurs Apr 28 I did some ordaining, marrying and setting apart of Temple workers. Attended weekly Council meeting of the Presidency and the Twelve while attending to the marrying.

Apr 30 Told my experiences on a mission and in my early farm life calculated to encourage the people who are coming up through much tribulation. We are sustained by that which we hope to attain in the future and for which we are striving. The lesson applies to our religious life as well.

Wed May 25 Instructed the cooks to not serve raw onions and cooked cabbage.

Mon Jun 13 I arose at 5:30 and went through with my morning's work as follows: blackened my shoes, took physical culture exercises, had a cold water bath, shaved and dressed before 7 a.m.

Tues Jun 21 We had above 60 couples sealed and married during the day. We are conducting four companies through the Temple daily, three days a week. I this day sealed all of the couples except about four.

Fri Jul 29, 1921 I attended D&C committee meeting from 9 to 12 with other members of the Twelve where we read the revelations which do not appear in the present edition of the Doctrine and Covenants, about twenty in number with the view of recommending to the First Presidency certain of them to be included in the edition we are just now preparing.

Tues Sept 13, 1921 The articles of incorporation of the

Taylor-Richards Motor Co. of which I am President are dated this date [Geo and LeGrand and the Taylor brothers are the principals].

Fri Sept 30 Attended to Temple duties during the day. I am to do all the sealing of the living wives to husbands and children to parents except where special request has been made for one of the other brethren to attend to it for them.

Jan 21, 1922 I spoke of the two powers. The war is still on. Are we doing God's will as Jesus did, or are we doing our own will as Satan did his own will? We should let the Church leaders interpret the will of God. The President and a majority of the Twelve never go wrong. Follow their lead.

Sun Apr 2 While addressing the parents class in the 27th ward, Pres. Grant's daughter called with auto for Bro. J. A. Widtsoe and me and took us to Pres. Grant's office where the Presidency and the Twelve were met.

Mon Apr 3 I attended a meeting in the Temple of the Twelve, the Seventy and Mission Presidents from 9 a.m. to 6 p.m. A very interesting meeting.

May 20 On the way home, we paid $5.00 to Brigham City Cop for exceeding the speed limit. This only marred the pleasure of our trip.

Mon May 29 The Presidency approved the recommendation to honorably release Sister Edna L. Smith at the closing June 30th from her position as Matron of the Temple. This action taken on her own suggestion.

Mon Jun 26, 1922 I went before the Presidency to consult them about the reception to be tendered Sister Edna L. Smith, the Matron of the Temple, the matter of a successor came up. I told the brethren that since I had such a good opportunity I thought I might express my thoughts as to a successor to Sister

Smith. So, I told the brethren that I thought it somewhat more proper and preferable to have my own wife as an assistant to me in this Temple work than somebody else's wife provided the brethren felt that she is worthy and capable of filling the bill. The brethren in chorus said she is just the woman for the place, none equal to her and said further that they had already considered the matter and decided upon her. Tears came in Pres. Grant's eyes as he spoke of it.

Thur Jun 29 The Richards Family Reunion was held at Salt Air and I rode out and back with my son LeGrand leaving here about 6 p.m. returning at 11:00 p.m.

Sun July 9 I spent the day at home resting and sleeping and visiting with members of my family who came to see us. This is one of the most restful, pleasant days I ever spent. I had no appointment for this day, no conferences being held.

Fri Aug 25 I attended and presided at a meeting in the World Room of the Temple at 5 p.m. for Temple workers at which Pres. Grant was present and he and I spoke. My wife Alice A. R. Richards was sustained to preside over the Sister Workers of the Salt Lake Temple and she was set apart by President Heber J. Grant, assisted by myself and Brother Davis. Mother made a short talk expressing her appreciation of the appointment and the hope that she may successfully and satisfactorily fill the same. At the close of the meeting the sisters congratulated Mother and expressed their satisfaction with the appointment.

Wed Sept 6 Spent the evening at home, Mother and I alone, an unusual circumstance.

Thurs Sept 21 I fully expect that we will soon be doing three evening sessions of endowment work as we are now administering endowments three days a week and that we will be doing evening baptismal work. I hope the Spirit of the work will continue to increase among the people so that there will be the demand for evening work five days of the week, three for endowment and two for baptisms. Surely there is no more important work than the redemption of the dead. Other work can be carried on over there but the ordinances must be attended to here. I wonder how far the work over there is being impeded by our neglect here? May not those who accept the gospel there need the Priesthood and other ordinances so they can engage in the work of preaching.

Sat Oct 14 I spent the forenoon at the temple and in the afternoon my sons Geo and Ray and I went to the football game, U of U and BYU teams.

Nov 27 Arrived in the city at 7:45 a.m. and went directly to the Temple. Held special meeting at 9 a.m. with about 170 young people from Provo who came up to do baptismal work in the temple.

Thurs Feb 15 At midnight I was seized with a severe pain in what I thought to be my stomach and opposite in my back but it was on the right side of the sternum.[2] I suffered excruciating pain for about 7 or 8 hours. I received some relief about 7:30 a.m. through prayer and hot pack applications. Mustard and lard poultices and plasters were used until my body was blistered.

Mon Jun 25 I attended the quarterly meeting of the Twelve and witnessed the parade of Pres. Warren G. Harding and party. In the evening I attended the lecture of Pres. Harding. I had tickets for admission but Mother and I could not get admission to the tabernacle so we went to the Assembly Hall where we heard distinctly the President's talk.

Aug 7 "Brothers George F. Richards and Joseph Fielding Smith, Brethren: The Presidency feel that it would be wisdom for

2. This is clearly an acute gall bladder attack but was not recognized as such, nor was it treated.

you brethren to go a week or ten days ahead of the dedication of the Canadian Temple, so as to be making all arrangements for the dedication and initiating the people into the work that they will have to do. Sincerely yours, Heber J. Grant, A. W. Ivins."

Weds Aug 29 Two sessions, morning and afternoon finished the dedication services, eleven sessions in all. We commenced taking records before 6 p.m. and I finished sealing the last couple at 2 a.m. 75 people received endowments and nearly all of them were sealed as husband and wife. I regard the services all the way through as a great success and the evening endowment service was a fitting climax and to me it seemed to more fully sanctify the Temple.

Oct 11 [On a train to Portland with Alice and Ray] At about 3 a.m. our car was visited by robbers. One man, gun in hand, was discovered. The trio consisted of two colored men and a woman. They were put under arrest by a sheriff who happened to be in the next car forward. A pair of pants were among their lute. We count ourselves fortunate in getting off with our lives, cash and other valuables.

Thurs Jan 17, 1924 We are having a rushing time at the temple today and evening. It is impossible to accommodate all who come for endowments.

Sat July 12 This is the season of the year when the brethren who desire a vacation or outing are at liberty. There are two Sundays together without conferences and no weekly meetings of the Council of the Twelve and Presidency are being held. My religious duties take me from home so much, it is a rare treat to spend so much time at home and I have no great desire to go away on a vacation. Thoughts about my journal. When I think that some one may undertake to look through my journals after I shall have gone hence with a view to accumulating information for a book on my biography, I feel ashamed that I have written so much into my journal that is of so little worth and so lacking of interest. I have thought that notwithstanding I have been closely associated with others in the making of Church history, I would leave the making or writing of such history to the Church, and that leaves me but little to say about such matters.

Sunday July 13, 1924 I think that from this time forth I shall write in my journal with the thought that it may sometime be read by someone other than myself.

Wed. July 16 I finished reading the biography of my Father. This is a well written book. The subject is a worthy one. The life of my father as there portrayed is most interesting and inspirational. When I think of the accomplishments of my father, it makes me feel very small and inadequate for the responsibility which has come to me from the Church. I do feel that the Lord has helped me in every direction of my life actively. I have been measurably successful in raising my family. Notwithstanding I have but one wife, I have 15 children, 5 boys and 10 girls.

Tues Aug 19 I suffered all day from pain in the stomach. Had a pot of hot water and a little cream in it during the day. On arriving home I cleaned up and went to bed. Had an enema of hot water, soap and turpentine and hot applications to my stomach and after a while I had a little relief.

Wed Aug 20 This morning I am clearly jaundiced.

Fri Sept 12 The doctor desired to ascertain if possible the cause of my recent illness. Three young ladies attended me. I had my stomach washed out. Then I took four small cakes, a glass of water and after about a half hour or so this was taken from my stomach to be tested. Then a tube with a metal ball about as big as the end of my little finger, was inserted in the stomach and finally through the pyloric orifice where the bile from the gall bladder was extracted to be tested.

Mon Sept 15 By appointment I went to the Doctor's office where I had taken an x-ray photograph of my diaphragm. I had to take a glass of white preparation and had a spy to see what became of it I suppose. Then I ate a bowl of mush and I suppose, magnesia which looked like plaster of paris. This is all I am to take until after another examination which takes place at 4:30 p.m. [Later in the afternoon the doctor gives him a summary of his findings.] Gall bladder inclined to become inflamed. He said that he thought it would be well to drain the bile or gall off occasionally, but the ordeal is so terrible having to insert a tube into and through the stomach into the intestine, that he did not order it done, but said that if I have more trouble such as I have had on several times of late, I am to come to the office and be treated.

Fri Oct 3, 1924 We have had the amplifiers in use at one or two of the former (general) conferences but at this conference the discourses were broadcasted so that the people by the thousands, if listening in would hear. Pres. Penrose being indisposed did not get to conference but in his own home heard distinctly the discourses. He sent a brief message to the conference.

Thurs Oct 30 In the evening I took my wife and three daughters to the Pantages Show. Mother and I figure that as we have no auto we are entitled to some pleasure and we are justified in spending as much as the interest on an auto investment would amount to in shows for ourselves and those whom we may invite to join us. Then there is the difference in the gas and upkeep to our credit.

Mon Nov 10 On my request, the agent for the Super-Neutrodyne Radio Sets placed one in our home last Friday, the 7th on trial. Last night I listened to broadcasted lectures, music, etc. from Salt Lake, Hastings, Nebraska, Oakland and San Francisco.

Sun Nov 23 About 20 of our family came in and between 9 and 10 we heard the LDS services broadcasted from the Des. News K.T.P.T. President Grant was the speaker.

Fri Feb 6, 1925 This day I received notice that I would be expected to speak over the radio Sunday evening, Feb 15th, 9 o'clock. It will be my initial radio speech.

Thurs Jun 4 At 4:30 held an investigation of the discourteousness of some of our temple employees and administered my disapproval of some things that have been said and done.

Sat Jun 13 Our interest in the people leads us to not only pray for them but to plead with them to walk in paths that are straight so as to have the Kingdom of God, the kingdom of peace within. . . . Find peace and make peace for others.

Jun 20–21 Assigned to Price stake conference. My stomach trouble became intense about this time and continued through the night. I suffered very greatly. This is like the spell I had while visiting Los Angeles and the other time when in Millard Stake. I turned yellow.

Weds July 29 I read William Jennings Bryan's speech prepared to deliver in court at Dayton, Tenn in defense of religion and Christianity and denouncing evolution. [He later presents the speech to Pres. Grant, who agrees to the printing of it in the *Improvement Era*.]

Mon Aug 10 My son George took dinner with me and after dinner I spent several hours inspecting autos with the thought of buying one. I rode out in the Lafayette, the Marmon and the Franklin. [After buying a Franklin used car for eight hundred and fifty dollars, he wrote, "It will cost me something to have the car put in first-class condition."]

Tues Sept 1 We went up on the boulevard and saw the K.K.K. cross fire on the mountains.

Thurs Sept 3 Pres. Grant announced that the Presidency had had under consideration for some time the matter of attempting to open up a mission in South America and had finally decided to call a member of the Council of Twelve and a member of the First Council of the Seventy and the President of the Mexican Mission to go and do the job. The personnel will be Melvin J. Ballard of the Twelve, Rulon S. Wells of the Seventy and Rey L. Pratt of the Mexican Mission.

Tues Oct 20 I met with my sons Geo, LeGrand and Joel and we decided to go in together and form a company for the sale of Chrysler cars. Decided to organize with a capital of $25,000, I to be the President, George, the Secretary, Joel at a salary of $230 per mo to be manager/treasurer and we four and Mother to be the directors. We have secured the building on 4th South between Main and West Temple.

Mon Oct 26 Called at the Richards Motor Co. place of business on 4th South between Main and West Temple, this being our opening day.

Thurs Dec 10 [He made the following entry while on a mission tour of the Southern States Mission in Greenville, South Carolina:] I spoke on Joseph Smith, a prophet. It was one of the best discourses of the trip. I spoke of some who expressed their feelings that our doctrine would be fine if we would leave Jos. Smith out of it. This work is founded upon revelation and these came through Joseph Smith. He cannot be eliminated. The work would be all upset. There would be no foundation.

Mon Dec 21 Our trip through the Southern States has been a wonderful trip for Mother and me. We have been in about 25 states, made 49 public addresses and have spoken at a number of missionary meetings. The Lord has been very good to me and made my efficiency about 200% above normal.

Mon Mar 8, 1926 I asked the chief of police for the privilege of parking my car without restrictions on Main St. North of the East gate of the Temple. He said he thought they were not marking the cars up that far. I told him I wanted to be within the law. He said for me to try it. I take it that should my car be tagged he will see me safely over the difficulty.

Mon Jun 14 I bought from Taylor-Richards Motor Co. a two door Ford Sedan. They gave it to me at cost which with accessories, viz. speedometer, foot feed, extra tire, cover, chain and lock, etc., cost me $574.35. I bought this for my sons Oliver and Ray which they both appreciate much. I think this will be a good investment in tying the boys to their father. I desire to help them to do the things they desire to do that are right. I desire that they should be happy.

Weds Oct 13 All well. Mother and I were in the Temple at 7:50 a.m. this is about our usual time. . . . 15 hours spent in the temple this day.

Fri Oct 22 We returned to the Temple (late in the evening) and saw that the work was going all right. We still have six sessions each of four days each week.

Sat Nov 13 I am very happy to have my wife with me for the remaining part of my mission (tour of Central States Mission). We have held 2 lengthy meetings this day with 50 missionaries from the East Kansas and Independence Conferences. These were spirited and profitable meetings. Mother and I are free from colds and are happy together.

Fri Nov 19 To Nauvoo. We saw the homes of the first four President's of the Church and the homes of a number of prominent men of the Church. The home of Willard Richards had been torn down and a new house built in its place. In removing some sand which had been washed in about the house, they found the stone slab which had been placed on . . . Jenneta Richards' grave. She is Heber John's and Rhoda Ann's mother. They removed her remains to a remote corner of the lot where the slab now lies. This removal was made in 1867. The inscription on the stone slab is as follows: "Jennetta Richards, born at Wakesfield, England, Married to Willard Richards Sept 24, 1838. Died July 9, 1843. buried in lot 1, block 103 where they lived in Nauvoo at time of her death." I could not read the inscription very well as I had to kick about the snow and dirt to find the slab, and Mr. Reinhold said he had the wording of the inscription at home and I obtained it from him there. I saw enough of the inscription on the stone slab to know that it was Jeannetta's tomb stone.

Weds Dec 8 Attended a committee meeting of the Richards Family consisting of Fred S., Charles C., Stephen L. Richards and myself, self constituted. SL and I were appointed to arrange with the genealogical Society to make a survey of the Richards Family Record and report to us. We made this arrangement.

Sat Jan 1, 1927 I spent most of the day at home. In the evening the grandchildren and most of the parents came and we had a program, played games and served ice cream and cakes.

Mon Feb 21 Made out and filed my income tax report and paid $15.10 tax for 1926.

Weds Feb 23, 1927 I am 66 years old today.

Sat Mar 26 Mother and I accompanied George and his family to Tooele to do some trading. I drove the car, George's Chrysler from near State St. To Erda and at Erda the car skidded in the loose gravel and tipped over. Mother had her back quite badly hurt and had a bruise on her cheek bone near her ear. We returned in the car but it was damaged to the extent of about $25.00

Tues Apr 19 I called on Pres. Grant and recommended to him the furnishing of the Salt Lake Temple endowment rooms with upholstered noiseless chairs. He asked me to ascertain the cost. I proceeded to learn through the Idaho-Utah school supply how much such seats would cost.

July 1 Mother and I went with Joel to see an installed Baker Automatic Oil Burner in a home in the SE part of town. We there met a service man, Mr. Foot. From there we came to our house and after looking things over he to install a plant and service it free for one year for $500. I told him that if he buys a car of Joel, i.e., Richards Motor Co. so as to apply the burner on the car, I would have one installed. Mrs. Gundy, at whose home we saw a plant in operation said they had used theirs two winters and that they were more than satisfied with it. She says they get no suit (soot) from it and the comfort and convenience of it is beyond description. 100 gal of oil is the same as 1 ton of coal, oil costs 8 cents/gal.

Fri July 8 I played my first game of golf. My sons George and LeGrand prevailed upon me.

Weds July 20 I took my car and George and LeGrand with us and their three boys and we played golf at Nibley Park. My son LeGrand made me a present of a set of golf clubs, bag and balls, 6 clubs. They are fine. I have played but four games. The first score was 77, the second was 74, the third was 71 and the fourth 68.

Thur Jul 28 The plumbers completed their work installing the sprinkling system at a cost of $120. I played two rounds of golf. I had several teeth pulled.

Sun July 31 This is my vacation period. No conference appointments.

Mon Aug 29 I attended services under the direction of the First Presidency of the Church at the grave of President Brigham Young where a name plate was placed on the iron fence surrounding the grave. This is the 50th anniversary of Pres. Young's death. The First Presidency spoke and we sang "Come, Come Ye Saints".

Mon Sept 19 I had the humiliating experience of receiving a puncture to my auto tire as we were opposite ZCMI on So. Temple street and of having to repair it.

Weds Oct 5th Attended meeting of the Mission Presidents and the Twelve from 9:30 a.m. to 4 p.m. Some of the thoughts had at the mission presidents meeting: 1. advantage of hearing what other Presidents are doing; 2. Exchange of ideas; 3. Use of local saints; short term missions, and acquire the habit of doing missionary work.

Thurs Oct 20 Mother and I with other General Authorities of the Church and their wives, occupying two Pullman cars, left for Mesa Arizona to attend the Temple dedication.

Sun Oct 23 I was one of the speakers in the first and 10th or last session.

Thurs Nov 24 Thanksgiving Day. I played "golph" with my sons Geo and LeGrand in the forenoon and in the afternoon took my son Ray to the football game (U of U and UAC) . . . neither obtained a score.

Sat Dec 31, 1927 This is the last day of the year 1927. It has been a very eventful year, a good year for me and my family. Today I am happy and in our home more comfortable than ever before. The installation of an oil burner in our furnace contributes much to our comfort.

Sun Jan 1, 1928 This is the inauguration of the new order of things as pertaining to the Sunday schools and Priesthood class study of the Church. The plan might be stated as follows: Sunday morning Sunday School and Priesthood class work; and Tuesday evenings MIA and Priesthood quorum work; Friday nights for recreational evening, dancing, etc.

Mon Aug 13 This day is opening day for the public at Richards Motor Co. office and a parade was had with four DeSoto cars, a band in band wagon, banners, etc. The principal streets of the city were traveled.

Mon Oct 22 after the theater as we turned the corner of 7th Sou and State going West, a man stepped in front of our car and was struck and lifted up into the air and thrown out to one side. He got up and swung his arms and seemed to be unhurt. I think it was purely carelessness on his part.

Thurs Nov 8 This day I put my Franklin Car in the Franklin Motor Sale Co. shop to be sold, and I bought a new Delux four door sedan of the DeSoto make of the Richards Motor Co.

Fri Mar 15, 1929 I prepared a 2 paged letter and sent to members of the family appealing for help with our temple work. We have had baptisms and endowments for: Longstroth names: 1387; Gill names: 3799; Shackleton names: 90; Total: 5276 names.

Weds Apr 17 I played a game of golf with Prests. Grant, and Nibley and FY Taylor. Pres. Grant made a score of 41, the best score he has ever made. I made a score of 42, the best score I have ever made. The score was as follows: 6, 5, 4, 5, 4, 5, 3, 3, 7.

Sat Aug 25 [At a stake conference in Driggs, Idaho, he spoke on safeguarding the young.] I spoke of the responsibility of parents and the home, the instinct and love of parents for children, the force of example and a large family. Chaperoning is a benefit in that it prevents temptation from being presented. The individual must have it in the soul so as to die in fighting if needs be to preserve these ideals, their morality. A man should defend and safeguard woman's virtue as he would her life if in danger.

Tues Oct 15 [At a meeting in Tijuana, Mexico] I spoke, Pres. Pratt interpreting for me. I had plenty to say but did not feel the freedom in speaking that I usually do. There were some young people, Americans, who were whispering and laughing most of the time. Perhaps that accounted for it.

Sunday Apr 6, 1930 Mother, Ruby, George, Joel and I were in attendance at this meeting where admittance was had by ticket. It was a remarkable occasion. The address by the Presidency to the Church and to the world was read by Pres. Grant in 39 min. It was well read and its contents were a remarkable and impressing presentation of the Gospels history and truth. The voting by the Conference by the quorums was well done and impressive as also was the Hosanna shout.

Weds July 2 We decided to drive across the desert by night to escape the intense heat leaving St. George at 10 p.m. we drove through to Las Vegas arriving there about 2:30 a.m. We halted for me to get an hours sleep thence on, arriving at Barstow at 9:00 a.m. The ride was pleasant with all car windows open and in my shirt sleeves without collar. I stood the drive well and did the trick with but little sleep.

Thurs Dec 4 In our meeting I mentioned that my appointment was to Star Valley this week. Pres. Grant said he thought I ought not to have to make the trip. Pres. Ivins said he made the trip once in winter and suffered much from the cold. It was decided to authorize the Presidency of the stake to ordain a bishopric which seemed to be the pressing need for a visitor.

Thur Jan 8, 1931 Had a busy day and in the evening went to the tabernacle and heard and saw the illustrated lecture of

Richard Byrd on the expedition he conducted to the South Pole. It was intensely interesting.

Mon Aug 1, 1932 Mother and I have bought a ticket each for golfing at Nibley Park Course for the month of August and we go and play golf nearly every day since the first.

Fri Aug 5 1:30 a.m. we received a telephone call from Mercedes, our granddaughter who was visiting with her parents in Glendale California, saying that her brother LeGrand had met with an accident while bathing in the ocean by which he had been hurt internally requiring an operation which was performed in a hospital in Los Angeles. At 8:40 p.m. I called LeGrand in Glendale and learned that LeGrand Jr. had passed away about 4 p.m. that afternoon. I told him that I would take the train in the morning.

Sat Oct 8th I was the first speaker at the morning session of conference. I occupied 25 minutes. Subject: cause of the financial depression and remedy.

Sat Oct 15 Attended football game at U of U stadium between U of U and BYU. I was then introduced to the Vice President of the United States, Mr. Curtis, along with Pres. Ivins. In the evening I attended the Republican rally in the tabernacle and heard Sen. Smoot and VP Curtis talk.

Fri Oct 21st I attended a Father's or Dad's program at KSL and made a brief speech myself. The following are the words I wrote while the program was on and which I spoke into the microphone: "As the father of 15 children, naturally, I am proud first of the mother who bore them, and of the children, 13 of whom are still living; and through them I am the happy grandfather of 46 grandchildren and several great grandchildren. It is needless to say that I believe in large families. Mrs. Richards and I, in the raising of our family, have come up through much financial tribulation, but those things are all forgotten in the joy we have with our children. Sometimes we hear the expression by married people, 'we cannot afford to have children these times, it is too expensive.' Money values cannot be compared to these values. These are riches which carry over into and through eternity. Those who have shunned family responsibilities of this character will never in this life know the joy they have missed. God bless the fathers, and not forget the mothers."

Mon Nov 7 Mother and I went to the tabernacle to hear Pres. Hoover, but were unable to get in so went to the Assembly Hall and heard his address.

Tues Nov 8 Election day. The Election is a veritable landslide for Democracy [Democrats] for which I am not responsible.

Mon Mar 20, 1933 I attended a homecoming reception tendered Reuben J. Clark and family in the 20th ward on their return from Mexico where they had been for about two years.

Thurs Apr 6, 1933 The General Conference of the Church convened and I attended the meetings of the conference. At the morning meeting Reuben J. Clark was sustained as the Second Counselor to Pres. Heber J. Grant in the First Presidency.

Thurs Nov 9, 1933 This day the Richards Motor Co. [defunct] through the receiver returned to us more than a thousand dollars which was distributed among the stock holders. This comes at a most opportune time for taxes.

Mon Mar 12, 1934 At about 8:07 a.m. an earthquake tremor was felt distinctly throughout the city. Later, about 11 a.m. another shake was felt and the schools of the city were closed. It was reported that there were fears that the Parley's Canyon Reservoir might break and flood the Southern end of town.

Sat Nov 17 I had a bad dream at night, which impressed me that to have a violated conscience is a taste of hell and torment.

Sat Apr 27, 1835 Two of the Elders came with a car belonging to one of the Saints and took us out to Florence or Winter Quarters where we have about 600 Saints buried. On our return trip we came to a golf course and Pres. Daynes and I played 18 hole game, two of the Elders acting as caddies for us.

Sat Nov 16 In the evening we went to see Will Rogers in his last performance at the Capital theater.

Tues Feb 9, 1937 [In Mexico City] Pres. Ivins and I went with Pres. Pratt in his auto about 25 miles to the pyramids of the Sun and the Moon and the ruins of a great city being excavated. We climbed to the top of the Pyramid of the Sun, the largest, which occupies about 10 acres and stands 2 or 300 feet high. All in all it kept me wondering.

Fri Apr 9 Thirty-one years ago today I was ordained an Apostle. Today I had occasion to go to the President's office and in the presence of President Clark and President McKay, President Grant informed me that the Presidency are still undecided upon a Patriarch to the Church and they have decided to release me and Sister Richards from presiding over the Salt Lake Temple and have me attend to the work of the Patriarch to the Church until such time as a Presiding Patriarch may be chosen, the change in my calling to take place at the end of the month. I was privileged to inform my wife of this action on behalf of the Presidency. President Grant said that the Presidency think that someone other than one of the Twelve should preside in the Temple and that he should not feel or think that it is a life job. Changes may take place from time to time.

Thurs Apr 15 At the council meeting today, Pres. Grant reported that the Presidency had decided to release me from being President of the Salt Lake Temple and make me superintendent of all the Temples of the Church and the Acting Patriarch to the Church.

Thur May 13 9:00 a.m. Arrived in Honolulu. Pres. Wooley of the Oahu stake met us and placed leis on us and accompanied us off the ship. A large concourse of people met the ship. Bands played. The Natives sang and the throng waved their hands. Leis were placed about our necks.

Tues June 8 I administered 13 Patriarchal blessings.

Mon June 14, 1937 Thoughts: A person cannot be exalted without companion in holy matrimony, as the exalted are to have eternal increase. The Savior so far as we know was not married and had no children, yet he is exalted. Provision will be made for the faithful that they lose no blessings such as others who are faithful receive for which they are not responsible. Some of the most faithful sisters in the Church have never been married, and some who have been married have never had children—but they will be cared for hereafter and will have husbands and children. If worthy, parents who have lost in death little children, shall be privileged to rear them to manhood or womanhood in the Millennium. . . . The Lord will care for his own.

Sun Aug 1 I attended the centennial celebration of the arrival of the first missionaries to England. This was held in the large Tabernacle and was filled to over seating capacity.

Sun Oct 3 In closing the conference, Pres. Grant said that if there any officers of the Church, general, stake or ward who do not keep the Word of Wisdom or pay their tithing, they should step aside and let others lead whose example is as it should be.

Fri Feb 18 [1938] I with others inspected five sets of plans, two for Idaho Falls and three for Los Angeles Temples and made report to the First Presidency.

Weds Apr 6 I was notified by phone of a meeting of the

Presidency and the Twelve at the Presidency's office at 9 a.m. At that meeting we were informed that on account of Bp. Sylvester Q. Cannon's failing health it is proposed to release him from his office as Presiding Bishop of the Church . . . the Presidency named my son LeGrand and his selection gave general satisfaction as shown by unanimous vote. Pres. Grant invited me and we went down to LeGrand's office and presented the matter to LeGrand. He accepted in a proper spirit and while we were there he selected his counselors, Marvin Ashton and Joseph L. Wirthlin.

Tues Jun 14 We went to Manti where we attended the 50th anniversary of the dedication of the Manti Temple. The services began at 10 a.m. in the open air East of the Temple. Pres. Grant and I were the only General Authorities present.

Fri July 8, 1938 This day 100 years ago, the law of tithing was given.

Tues Aug 30 My health is good and has been for a long time. Dr. Jackson recommends golf as a means of prolonging life and maintaining health. Activity is life. Idleness is death-dealing.

Tues Nov 8, 1938 I dreamed of the German Kaiser. Last night I had a remarkable dream which left upon my mind a good and wonderful impression. I dreamed that I and a number of other men of non-German extraction were gathered in a group for some unexplained purpose where were the German Keiser or Ruler, no name attached, and a number of uniformed German soldiers. They seemed to be engaged in sharpening their swords and otherwise preparing for war or executions or something of the sort. They fell in line and marched round in a large circle. Then we non-Germans were marched in a smaller circle before them, and as they marched one after another chopped out of the circle and I was one of them. If it was for execution or what not

I did not know, but I walked straight toward the Kaiser who was sitting apart from the other soldiers. He seemed to be well uniformed and a very dignified personage. I addressed him as if I had an appeal to make to him though I had no fear, and he gave me attentive audience. While I do not remember the exact words I used and I do not remember that he said a word, I addressed him about as follows: I am your brother. In the Spirit world you were a son of God. I also was His Son. We lived together in the same Heavenly family. We loved each other as brothers. As I spoke feelingly and deliberately, I seemed to feel that his feelings were touched so that he believed my words, and that he believed and felt as I did, a real brotherly love for one another. It became so intense that we embraced each other and kissed each other on the lips, a brotherly kiss or kiss of affection. Then, I saw these soldiers marching again, and the Kaiser stepped out of line as he passed, and again kissed me on the lips. This ended the dream, and I was left with the thoughts, "Why can we not feel thus toward all men for we are really and truly brothers?" I was made to realize as never before that the commandment to love our neighbor as ourselves and to even love our enemies is possible and the command is consistent. [He later referred to this dream in a conference talk and named the Kaiser as being Hitler. This dream preceded the known atrocities that subsequently occurred during the war.]

Jan 4, 1939 I attended services at 7th South and 251 West where the corner stone of the main building as storehouse for the Welfare Work of the Church was laid, my son LeGrand, as Presiding Bishop laid the stone and made a very appropriate speech, along with Pres. Grant and others.

Fri Sept 1, 1939 This early morning in Europe, war broke upon Poland by Germany air bombers dropping bombs on Warsaw and other cities in Poland. The war is now on.

Sat Sept 2 I was up at 5:30 a.m. listening to the radio news from Europe.

Weds Dec 13, 1939 I thank the Lord that he has blessed us with means with which to help others. I have paid out this year so far $179.50 to poor people in payments for endowment work. In this I figure that I am killing four birds with one stone—the Lord, myself, the person employed and the dead.

Tues Feb 6, 1940 In the evening I took Mother, Geo and Edith, LeGrand and Ina to see "Gone With the Wind."

Mon May 6 I received a letter from ___ of Missoula, Montana, in which he asks: "Will you please write me a sentence or two upon what factors you consider to be keys which will lead to a successful life?" In answer I wrote as follows: "High ideals, strong self-reliance, and sincere trust in God."

Weds May 8 Paid Elvin J. Homer $10 for 20 names end [endowed]. Since I commenced keeping a record, I have had endowments myself for 304 men and have paid out $737.00 for temple work and genealogical search.

Weds July 17 I listened to the Dem. Convention proceedings in Chicago, over radio, at which F. D. Roosevelt was nominated for a third time.

Thur Aug 1 Palmyra, New York. The first meeting of the conference was held in the Sacred Grove from 9 to 12 o'clock. Pres. Evans made introductory remarks, followed by a number of missionaries after which LeGrand and I each spoke. The Lord helped me wonderfully. Our group left after meeting and drove about 27 miles to the old home of Peter Whitmer where the Church was organized with six members, Apr 6, 1830.

Fri Aug 2 We traveled more than 400 miles to Nauvoo where we spent the night. We called at Carthage on our way and Bro McRay showed us through the jail in which Joseph and Hyrum

Smith were martyred and John Taylor was seriously wounded. Father Willard Richards was the only one not injured. He directed in caring for Bro. Taylor and for the bodies of the Prophet Joseph and the Patriarch Hyrum Smith. Hot day.

Sat Aug 17 We had shower installed in our bathroom. I listened to Wendell Wilkey's speech of acceptance of Presidential Republican Nomination.

Tues Aug 27 I took time off in the middle of the day to see the Premier picture "Brigham Young." It is marvelous, and while I would have had it different in some places, I think it will not hurt us, but will be the means of allaying much prejudice and creating much sympathy for the LDS people.

Mon Sept 16, 1940 I had an invitation from the Airways Company with other members of the Twelve and Presidency and our wives to fly in their 21 passenger car at 5 p.m. today and have accepted the invitation for myself and my wife. Later we had our air trip of 45 minutes and enjoyed it immensely.

Mon Oct 28 I heard Pres. F. D. Roosevelt and his opponent in politics Wendell Wilkey over the phone. Politics are rife in the U.S. as presidential election nears and in Europe as the war increases in intensity and in geographical expansion.

Thurs Apr 3, 1941 Attended regular Council meeting of the Presidency and the Twelve, fasting. We fast the first Thursday of each month and have the sacrament.

Tues Apr 8 We arranged our itinerary for Mexico City, leaving here May 9th by auto.

Tues May 20 [They visit San Marcos.] We saw the place where 2 of the brethren were shot to death by a squad of soldiers in the revolution about 20 years ago because they would not renounce their religion.

Sat July 12 The Dr. recommended that I cut down on my

preaching. Mental exertion, such as preaching, is just as hard on the heart as physical exertion. He said I might be able to play a game of golf by September.

Sun Dec 7, 1941 This morning war broke out between Japan and the US, the former having bombed Honolulu, Manila and various other English and American held ports, etc.

Mon Dec 8 A number of nations declared war against Japan.

Sat Dec 13 I finished reading the life of my father, Franklin D. Richards by his grandson, Frank West. I am proud of my father and his accomplishments.

Sat Apr 4 [1942] I attended three sessions of conference held in the Assembly Hall for General Authorities, Stake Presidencies and invited guests. I was the first speaker in the 2nd session on Genealogy and temple work. The Lord blessed me with good thoughts and power of expression.

Sun Apr 5 I attended the 10 a.m. meeting of the General Conference held in the Temple, 5th floor; general authorities and stake presidencies, and presidents of High Priests quorums present. The first meeting was a broadcast meeting until 12 noon. We then had a 30 minute recess and reconvened at 12:30 for the second session of the day. The Twelve administered the sacrament. I passed the sacrament to the general authorities on the stand. A glorious time.

Sat July 4 I spent the afternoon studying the scriptures and can find no scripture that says that the Patriarchal order of the Priesthood is to descend from father to <u>oldest</u> son. From Abraham to Ephraim in no instance was it given to the oldest son. In this dispensation there have been deviations made from the order of Father to the oldest son, the order has been as follows: Joseph Smith, Sen., Hyrum Smith, John Smith (Hyrum's uncle), William Smith (Hyrum's brother), John Smith (Hyrum's son), Hyrum G. Smith (John Smith's grandson). Hyrum Smith had two sons when he died, viz. John and Joseph. Both were too young to act. After William Smith was rejected, John Smith, Hyrum's Son was made the Patriarch to the Church.

Sun Sept 13 Pres. Grant called on me at my home and spent about 30 minutes. We talked freely over Patriarchal matters and he revealed to me whom he had in mind for the office of Patriarch of the Church.

Sat Nov 28 LeGrand and I arrived here in New York at 7:45 a.m. We took a taxi to Manhatten Towers hotel, the building in which we hold conference meetings. Here we took a small room with 2 beds, toilet and bath for $4.00 per day. Not very comfortable, but the best we could do under the circumstances. 520 soldiers stationed here.

Tues Apr 6, 1943 I met with the General Authorities at 8:30 a.m. to receive instructions pertaining to the holding of Regional Conferences.

Sun Apr 18 Burley, Idaho. I attended the three sessions of the Regional Conference. Six stakes were represented. This was a continuation of the 113th Annual conference of the Church.

Thur Jun 16 The meeting of the Twelve and the First Presidency was held at the home of Pres. Grant. Pres. Grant is looking well. His voice is weak and he is not able to walk about. Pres. Clawson is very weak and ill in bed at home.

Mon Aug 16 In the evening, Mother and I with Joel, Georgina and Helen drove to "Hill Field" and saw the famous bomber plain, Memphis Belle, which had been in a number of fights with the enemy. This was on public invitation and afforded us an opportunity to see Hill Field at close range.

Thurs Oct 7 At 10 a.m. the Twelve met with the Presidency in their office in the Church Office Building and President Grant ordained Spencer Kimball and Ezra T. Benson Apostles and set them apart [as] members of the Quorum of the Twelve.

Tues Jan 18, 1944 This morning I had surgery to remove the prostate gland, Dr. Richard Middleton, operating. The operation seemed to be a success.

Sun Jan 30 I am unable adequately to express the gratitude I feel to the Lord for His care of me, his protection and blessing. I feel that I would like to live forever under the influence of the Lord's Spirit and in His presence.

Tues June 6, 1944 The Allies early this morning invaded the European Countries. I spent the afternoon listening to the radio bulletins announcing the progress of the war of invasion. The invasion seems to be progressing according to plans, but better than was expected and with fewer casualties.

Weds June 28 [He received a letter of appreciation from the stake presidency in Twin Falls after a stake conference.] Such compliments when deserved are very encouraging to one whose limitations are so well known to himself but who is trying to live by and advocate the truth. May the Lord help me to be worthy of my calling and of the confidence of the Saints.

Fri Sep 1 I wrote to my son Ray who is on his way to Pearl Harbor (Lt JG in the US Navy), and to my grandson Lt. Joel Richards, Jr who is somewhere in the Pacific and included tracts by Hugh B. Brown and the Des. News Church Edition.

Fri Jan 12, 1945 I visited and administered to Elder Hugh B. Brown at his home.

Weds Feb 7 Pres. Grant by phone requested me to come to his home to see him, and sent his car for me. I spent about an hour and a half with him as he lay in his bed. I gave him a blessing before leaving him.

Fri Mar 9, 1945 It was 63 years ago today that I lead my wife to the altar in the Endowment House and she was sealed to me for time and eternity; my father Franklin D. Richards officiating. I received my endowments in 1876. My bride received hers that day.

Mon May 7, 1945 News came over the radio at 7:45 a.m. that Germany had unconditionally surrendered to the Allies. We had the radio in the car and listened to the report of the German Generals and the Allied Generals signing the unconditional surrender.

Tues May 8 Listened to VE day radio talks by Pres. Truman and Churchill and others.

Mon May 14 Pres. Grant is failing fast and may pass away at any time. Pres. George Albert Smith is in Chicago planning to go on to New York and Washington. I suggested to Pres. Clark that we send for Pres. Smith and he endorsed the suggestion and said it would be done. Pres. Clark said that Pres. Grant might pass on at any time. The Doctor said within the week. Pres. Clark said that when Pres. Grant dies, he, Pres. Clark would take his place in the Quorum and that if Pres. Smith should be away, I would have to take over, hence, my suggestion that Pres. Smith be called home from the East. Pres. Grant died at 6:30 p.m. Failing to get Pres. Clark on the phone, I consulted with Joseph Fielding Smith and suggested that we call the Twelve together for a meeting at 8 a.m. tomorrow. He volunteered to notify the brethren who were in town which I appreciated. Pres. Clark called to notify me and I told him what I had done.

Tues May 15 I attended and presided at a meeting of the Twelve and the counselors in the First Presidency, in arranging for the funeral services and burial of Pres. Grant. I asked Pres. Clark and Pres. McKay to conduct the meeting and the work of preparations to be made. Pres. George Albert Smith is on his way home from the East.

Thurs May 17 Pres. Smith came to my office and I reported to him what had been done up to now in preparation for the funeral and burial of Pres. Grant. He seemed to be satisfied and pleased.

Mon May 21 A special meeting of the Twelve in the Temple from 10 a.m. to 3:30 p.m. At this meeting Pres. George Albert Smith had charge. We had our prayers. I was sustained to be President of the Quorum of the Twelve Apostles. Pres. Smith then announced his counselors, J. Reuben Clark Jr, and David O. McKay. At my office I planned a release of myself from four committees and appointed others instead. Left office at 6 p.m. Evening at home.

Sun July 24 Attended the ground breaking of the new "This Is the Place" monument and participated in turning ground with the shovel.

Weds Aug 8 Word by radio says that Russia has declared war on Japan.

Thurs Aug 9 This morning's paper announces that Atom-bomb dropped on Nagasaki, Japan. The second city to be so bombed. It is called an aerial terror.

Tues Aug 14 At 5:01 p.m. the radio reports that Japan has accepted the terms of surrender.

Thurs Oct 11 Attended regular Council meeting at the Temple. Elder Matthew Cowley was ordained an Apostle by Pres. Smith. We now have a full quorum.

Tues Feb 5, 1946 At work at the office as usual. Am to be at my office before 8:30 a.m. and leave at 5:00 p.m.

Weds Feb 6 I am pleased to learn that Elder Benson and

his missionary companion, who went by airplane, had arrived in England.

Fri Apr 19 When we reported Mother's condition to Dr. Gill at 7:30 a.m. he said we should have her at the hospital and that he would send for her. The hospital ambulance came at 9 a.m. and we took her to LDS Hospital where she received attention. Mother suffered terribly from her short breathing and suffocating feeling. We administered to her at times and prayed fervently for her.

Sat Apr 20 Mother's condition grew worse and she suffered much all day and night.

Sun Apr 21 My dear wife endured her suffering until 1:45 p.m. when she passed away peacefully. I went to my apartment where I spent the night alone.

Weds Apr 24 This is a crucial day in my life, having to lay her away whom I have loved and with whom I have been associated as husband and wife for more than 64 years.

Sun May 12 [Mother's Day] I am feeling well physically, but had a lonely day and mourned for my dear wife.

Tues May 28 At my request my son Ray brought my journals from 1010 E. 3rd Ave. My son George is thinking of studying them with a view to prepare for writing my biography.

Weds Jun 5 This day I bought a record book to be used in making a record of my tabernacle discourses and possibly some other discourses and radio talks that I have made. Sister Wetzel is intending to type them for me on her spare time. I shall pay her a fair price.

Mon July 8 I worked over my diary, covering over several years period, selecting therefrom items to go into my history in the Church Historical Record. I have assembled the books of my diary from the beginning. I commenced writing a daily record in

1883 and from memory I wrote items of my life work up until that date. I have requested my son George, should he survive me, to have my journals filed with the Historian's Office.

Sat July 13 I spent much of the day working on my journal in my office, making notes for a biography. I have gone through my journal from 1910 to 1946 in that way.

Tues Dec 24 Pres. Levi Edgar Young called on me at my office and in tears of affection expressed love for me. I received a letter from Elder Widtsoe written in his own hand which I copy:

> Dear President Richards; at this holiday season, let me express my gratitude to you for your intelligent leadership, kindly consideration and steady wisdom. Your long and faithful experience in the cause of the Lord is now blessing the Church greatly. May the Lord continue to bless you abundantly and give you constant joy in your labors. Your fellow workers support you and cherish you.
> Affectionately yours,
> John A. Widstoe.

Pres. Richard L. Evans called and extended seasons congratulations and love, which I greatly appreciate. Elder Harold B. Lee called and extended greetings in words of love and appreciation beyond my power to express.

Tues Mar 4, 1947 Last night I had a pleasant dream of my deceased wife, a comfort of great magnitude. She was dressed in white and so beautiful and so sweet.

Tues Mar 11 Pres. Geo. A. Smith called at my office with a problem desiring my views.

Tues Apr 1 This day the Twelve meet in our quarterly conference. The meeting was different from previous meetings. The whole time was taken up in consideration of important matters instead of testimony bearing.

Mon Apr 7 I attended a special meeting of the General Authorities, Stake and Mission Presidents and Bishops held in the Assembly Room on the 5th floor of the Salt Lake Temple from 9:30 to 2:00 o'clock. The three members of the First Presidency were the speakers. I offered the opening prayer. The sacrament was administered by the Twelve and other General Authorities.

Apr 10 At the 10 a.m. meeting Elder Henry Dinwoody Moyle was ordained an Apostle. . . . Eldred G. Smith[3] was ordained Patriarch to the Church and Joseph L. Wirthlin and Thorpe B. Isaacson were set apart as counselors to LeGrand Richards in the Presiding Bishopric.

Thurs May 1, 1947 [George documents the beginning of the centennial celebration of the arrival of the pioneers, which ran from May 1 to October 15, 1949.[4]]

Thurs July 10 I talked with Joel on the phone this morning as he lay in bed in the hospital. He was feeling fine. Sister B___ H___ called on me at my apartment by appointment and gave me the green light after months of waiting.

Sat July 12 I revealed to my daughters my engagement and

---

3. Elder Smith served as patriarch to the Church from 1947 until he was given emeritus general authority status in 1979. He continued to attend regular meetings of the General Authorities in the Salt Lake Temple on the first Thursday of each month until shortly before his death on April 4, 2013, at age 106.

4. All living pioneers were invited to a reception in the Hotel Utah lobby and then to a "magnificent program" in the Tabernacle, where each of the two hundred pioneers present received a certificate. Then they went to the Brigham Young monument on Main Street, where Mayor Earl J. Glade and President David O. McKay spoke. Floodlights illuminated the Brigham Young monument and the Eagle Gate, and a large American flag was raised atop a forty-foot pole on Ensign Peak.

an invitation for them and their husbands to attend the wedding on July 20th.

Thurs July 17 I had blood serological test. OK.

Fri July 18 We secured our license and arranged for our recommends. Bessie came in about 7:30 p.m. and brought two of her suitcases. We had strawberries and ice cream refreshments and spent a pleasant hour together.

Sun July 20th At home until about 5 p.m. when I met Bessie at the Temple and we were married at 6:00 p.m. My son George performed the ceremony. LeGrand and Joel acted as witnesses. All my sons and daughters and their companions were invited. They were also invited to supper at 7 p.m. at the Temple Square hotel. I was already the richest man alive, and the Lord has given me another jewel for my crown. All of my sons and daughters and their wives and husbands were at the Temple to witness the marriage ceremony and at the supper.

Thurs July 24, 1947 The pioneer centennial is in full measure. I was at the 9 a.m. unveiling and dedication of the "This Is the Place" Monument. Each of the members of the First Presidency spoke and Pres. G. A. Smith was Master of Ceremonies. We witnessed the parade in which the Presidency were featured. I saw nothing during these exercises that would suggest that the Twelve had any place in the celebration.

Mon Sept 8 Last week the temperature in my office ranged about 87 degrees. Today it is about 77 degrees and the change is appreciated.

Weds Sept 10 I had a lady ask if I was a brother of LeGrand Richards. Pres. George Albert Smith asked how I keep looking so young. I answered, "I guess it is because of my association with the young."

Thur Oct 16 In the evening I attended Salt Lake Stake 100th organization anniversary.

Fri Oct 17 I attended the burial services of Captain Mervyn Bennion.

Dec 3 Bessie and I were invited to go by "plaine" to visit others of the islands to visit the Saints and hold meetings with them. We have accepted the invitation.

Fri Dec 5 The ride from Honolulu to Laie and about the Temple gave me one of the thrills of my life and I was lead in my enthusiasm to say that I thought it the most beautiful place in the world.

Mon Dec 8 Sister Richards [Bessie] and I went by air plaine from Honolulu to the Island of Maui to mission headquarters of the Hawaiian mission. In the afternoon of the day we were taken by auto up in the hills where a monument has been erected near a LD Saint meeting house in commemoration of a sacred event in the experience of President George Q. Cannon as the first LDS Missionary to the Sandwich Islands as they were known in earlier days, now known as the Hawaiian Islands. Pres. E. Wesley Smith there told us the story, which occurred in 1850. 100 people had gathered for a meeting and Pres. Cannon, then 20 years of age, was addressing the people and a peculiar phenomenon occurred. Pres. Cannon saw that all but three of that congregation had a white skin. Later 97 of them received the Gospel. When Pres. David O. McKay and Hugh J. Cannon visited that place and Pres. McKay offered prayer.

Weds Dec 10 Pres. Smith took us up the Canyon to the terminal of the auto road through which Pres. Geo. Q. Cannon came on foot from Lahaina, the first LD Saint to visit Wailuku, when the Lord or an angel spoke to him as he was about to return and told him to go on into the town, that he would be kindly received. We took plane at 2:45 for Hilo on the Island of Hawaii about 50 minutes of pleasant ride and beautiful view of the two Islands.

Dec 18 We took "Pan American" air plane at 9:20 for San Francisco.

Fri Feb 6, 1848 Of 149 births in the family there has not been a death of a mother in child bearing.

Mon Mar 15 Between the dam and Las Vegas, LeGrand dosed and the car left the road. No damage done.

Fri Mar 19 In the evening we went to the Tabernacle and heard the colored woman singer, Marian Anderson.

Weds Mar 24 I had a checking up at the Salt Lake Clinic which shows my weight 171 lbs; my urinary organs normal; blood pressure almost normal; my heart action as good as it was ten years ago; lungs OK, etc., etc. Limit of two meetings per day. Daily noon-time rest of one hour.

Sat Apr 3 I spent some time in preparing what I might want to use as a conference talk.

Sun Apr 4 I was the second speaker in the morning session.

Thurs May 13 In the evening Bessie and I went with LeGrand and Ina to the home of Elder Harold B. Lee to supper and for the evening. Brother and Sister Marion G. Romney were the only other visitors.

Weds May 26 President Clark visited me at my office. He favors having more assistants to the Twelve.

Tues June 8 I met Israel Smith, President of the Re-organized Church for the first time.

Sat June 12 I went to see Bro. Spencer W. Kimball who is ill at home with a heart ailment.

Fri Oct 1, 1948 Attended morning and afternoon sessions of General Conference and in the morning session, after Pres. Geo.

Albert Smith's opening remarks, I was announced as the next speaker. I occupied 18 or 20 minutes with good liberty and help from the Lord. I feel well satisfied.

Sun Oct 17 Attended the 1000th Tabernacle Choir broadcast at 9:30 a.m. by invitation. Attended and spoke at the evening meeting of the Salt Lake Stake Conference. Elder Bruce R. McConkie conference visitor.

Fri Nov 12 I spent the forenoon at my office and the afternoon and evening at home. I have high blood pressure and am advised by the Doctor and others to rest as the only cure for high blood pressure, except diet.

Thurs Nov 18 I attended regular weekly meetings in the Temple and attended to office work after. Evening at home reading the typed manuscript of a book for missionaries by my son LeGrand.

Sat Nov 27 I had a good night's rest and sleep with my dog collar on and my left hand in a pack.

Tues Jan 11, 1948 My lameness does not seem to get better. I'm sorry.

Weds Jan 12 Am still alive and wrestling with my lameness.

Thurs Jan 13 I had a number of visitors during the day. Elders Jos. Fielding Smith and E. T. Benson administered to me.

Sun Jan 16 Word comes from Los Angeles that Pres. George Albert Smith who was attending Los Angeles stake conference had been taken to a Los Angeles Hospital. He is to have a medical checking up. How serious his ailment is not known to me.

Tues Jan 25 I hope my condition is improving. The News reports the temperature 22 degrees below zero at the airport. We cannot get much detail in report of Pres. Smith's condition. May it please the Lord to spare President Smith's life and give him speedy recovery.

Salt Lake City, Utah, Tues Mar 15, 1949 [In Bessie's hand-writing:] At the request of my dear husband, President George F. Richards and by the assistance of some notes taken and from memory, I am undertaking to bring his journal history up to date. His last recording having been Feb 3. On that date he went to the LDS Hospital for inspection and treatment. He received that day a blood transfusion consisting of one pint of blood. . . . [He received a second unit the next day.] On the 12th of February he was released to come home and for a few days seemed to be progressing nicely, but the results were not all we expected. His prime trouble from the beginning seemed to be nervousness and neuritis and altho' receiving regular treatment from the Salt Lake Clinic his condition seemed to grow worse so that he was re-turned to the hospital on the 20th of Feb and on the 1st of Mar was operated upon for prostate gland trouble by Dr. Richard Middleton. He was released from the hospital to return home on Mar 9, 1949.

Tues Mar 22 I feel that I am making progress in recovering my health and am very thankful to the Lord, and to the Saints for their sympathy and their prayers. I hope to fully recover my health so as to be able to take up my religious duties as formerly.

Weds Mar 30 In the afternoon LeGrand took me to the Church Offices Building to see the brethren. I saw Prests. Clark and McKay and eight of the Apostles and two of the First Council of the Seventy and Patriarch and many other friends. We also in-spected the improvements made in the building interior. My trip did me good and no harm.

Mon Apr 4, 1949 I listened to all the conference proceedings in the tabernacle except 30 minutes when the broadcast changed to broadcast President Truman's talk on the announcements of the 12 nations representatives as they and their countries to the

United States signed the North Atlantic Pact, which I was glad to hear.

Thurs Apr 7 Elders Harold B. Lee and Spencer W. Kimball at the request of the First Presidency came from their temple meeting and brought the Sacrament to us, and gave me a blessing. This I appreciate greatly.

Mon Apr 11, 1949 I slept well last night and feel pretty well but my battery is nearly run down and I am quite weak.

Thurs Sept 22 I took taxi and went to the Temple for 9:00 a.m. meeting of the Twelve. We were photographed as a group by newspaper men. At 10 a.m. the First Presidency came, and by their invitation, the other General Authorities came and we had a meeting and the Sacrament. I offered the opening prayer and after Pres. Smith, was asked to speak which I did with good liberty. We were to come fasting. With this request, I complied. After several spoke at request of the President, we closed the meeting and had lunch after which the Presidency and the Twelve returned and finished our meeting.

Tues Oct 11 I went to the KDYL radio station in the Tribune Office and made a recording of a Christmas talk to be given over this station Christmas morning at 9:45 a.m.

Sun Oct 23, 1949 I am free from pain and aches but feel tired, and having no appointment, I remained home all day. I wrote at my desk composing a Christmas sentiment for the members of my family.

Christmas Greetings . . . 1949

My dearly beloved sons and daughters and family. Your Mother and I have dearly loved you, and have desired and prayed for your present and eternal welfare. We have tried to make our way of life such that, if followed, would bring to you peace, happiness and salvation. As a family, we are reported to be one of the largest and best families in the Church. It is to be hoped that this record may be maintained without blot or blemish. Let us not be tempted to violate conscience either for wealth or pleasure. May the Lord bless you to know the right and to do the right in every condition of life. We are making the cross we are to bear through life and eternity; we are making it heavy or we are making it light. May the Lord help us to make our cross light like even as the yoke of the Savior. Lovingly, Father.

Weds Jan 11, 1950 We left the hospital at 9 a.m. I phoned Pres. Smith and asked to be excused from my meetings tomorrow.

Sat Jan 14 Today's News publishes an article on Boy Scouts of America reorganization or election of officers. Quote: "New members of the Executive Board are President George F. Richards, Gov. J. Bracken Lee, and Robt H. Bradford of the Salt Lake Council." This on account of the large number of scouts in my family in general, and on account of Ray's personal record in scouting and because of my support of the scouting movement.

Tues Jan 31 I am reading "Jesus the Christ" by Apostle Talmage of 800 pages. I understand that Elder James E. Talmage wrote this book at the request of the First Presidency, and that he wrote it while he was in the Temple, occupying a small room on the fifth floor at the East room, East of the large Assembly Room.

Sun Feb 5 We went to the Temple grounds thinking to attend Emigration Stake conference, only to find no conference being held. We were a week ahead of time.

Tues Feb 28 I had a fairly good night. For an hour or so after I first got up I felt short of breath which is a very unpleasant feeling. I suppose it is caused from nervousness, but why nervousness? That I do not understand. I gave some thought to what I might say in General Conference.

Mon Mar 20 I spent several hours at my office where I attended to important business and inspected the offices of the General Authorities. Each and every one has a room well furnished.

Thurs Apr 6 Brother Claude Petersen, the secretary to the Twelve, took Bessie and me to the 10 a.m. conference meeting and returned us after meeting. I was the first speaker after the presentation of the business of the conference. My remarks were well received and by some of the brethren referred to as a masterpiece. I listened to the afternoon services over the radio. Several of the brethren called me over the phone congratulating me on my conference talk of this morning, among them were Pres. Clark and Harold B. Lee, who praised it very highly.

Fri Apr 7 I attended special meeting in the upper room of the Temple from 10 a.m. to 1:40 p.m. for special invited guests consisting of all the General Authorities of the Church, Stake Presidents, Bishops, Mission Presidents, etc. I offered the invocation. The sacrament was administered. I asked the blessing on the bread, and Jos. Fielding Smith on the water. The Twelve broke the bread and all the other General Authorities assisted in passing the sacrament. The speakers were the three members of the First Presidency.

Tues May 30 Decoration Day. We decorated graves in the Cemetery and then went to Farmington Cemetery and looked up the graves of many of our family relatives—Richards folk, Robinsons, Millers, etc. We visited my wife Alice's birthplace and mine.

Sat Aug 5 In the evening Geo and Edith came and George and I played checkers for a while and we listened to the war news on the television set which we had installed today on trial by my grandson, Dean Cannon.

Mon Aug 7 Received a letter from my son Joel in Portland reporting his recent trip to Alaska. After 8 p.m. I was taken seriously ill with pains in the stomach, through the body, shoulders, arms and hands. We phoned Dr. _____. It was about 11 p.m. He concluded that my trouble was nervousness, and prescribed placing a cloth wet in cold water on my chest, changing same for about 15 or 20 minutes to quiet the nerves.

Tues Aug 8 I remained indoors all day nursing myself and being nursed. I brought my journal up to date, answered a letter to Joel at Portland by pen.

Tues Aug 8, 1950 [Note written by Bessie:] 29 South State, Apt 716. Salt Lake City, Utah. At 10:53 p.m. this day, August 8th, 1950, at the above address, my beloved husband George Franklin Richards, age 89 years and 5½ months passed away from this earthly life. He suffered a heart attack, which although quite severe at the last was not of long duration for which I thank the Lord. He had a slight attack yesterday, but seemingly recovered. Today he has complained of pain in his chest, and altho' he was not in bed, he was not feeling well. He wrote several letters, one of them to his son Joel. He called his sons, LeGrand, Oliver and Ray on the phone and visited with them. His daughter Lucena called in at noon and visited with him and in the afternoon his son George came and played two games of checkers with him.

At 5:30 p.m. Apostles Spencer W. Kimball and Matthew Cowley administered to him. At 6:30 p.m. he retired to bed but could not rest. At 9:30 p.m. he complained of a sick stomach, and at 10:53 he passed peacefully away. Dr. _____ was with him. His two oldest sons George F. Jr. and LeGrand and myself, his second wife, Betsy. We called all his sons and daughters and their wives and husbands and they came and spent until 2 a.m. at the apartment during which time we had a <u>sad</u> but <u>spiritual</u> feast.

He was one of God's noblemen. Beloved by all who knew him. He was a kind, loving husband and father and we shall greatly miss him. "A man without guile."

My heart is full. I loved him dearly. May God bless his memory. This beloved Apostle of Christ.

INDEX

INDEX

Redfield, Harvey D., 43
Relief Society, 191, 204, 262, 300
Repentance, 283
Resources, in Salt Lake Valley,
    136–37, 139–41
Resurrection, 192, 283
Revolution, 203
Reynolds, Brother, 195–96
Reynolds, George, 212–13
Rich, Ben E., 230
Rich, Charles C., 65–66, 90–91, 188
Richards, Alice Almira Robinson:
    as Salt Lake Temple matron, 20,
    344, 345; marriage of, 207, 368–
    69; children of, 251–52, 298,
    309; Salt Lake Temple dedication
    and, 256; teeth of, 267; prayers
    of, 278; temple work of, 307–8;
    health of, 309; dream of, 321–22,
    372; Joseph F. Smith blesses, 325;
    cablegram from, 332; arrives in
    England, 334; death of, 371
Richards, Alice L., 73
Richards, Alverda, 298, 300
Richards, Amelia, 145
Richards, Amy May, 244–45,
    263–64, 298, 300
Richards, Ann Dalby, 185
Richards, Bessie, 374, 375–76
Richards, Charles C., 185, 353
Richards, Charles (son of
    Franklin D. Richards), 233
Richards, Charlotte, 203
Richards, Curtis, 153
Richards, Edith May, 325, 381–82
Richards, Edna, 304–5
Richards, Eliza Ann, 201
Richards, Elizabeth McFate: plural
    marriage and, 13; marriage of, 75;
    health of, 96–97; death of, 113,
    121, 124, 126
Richards, Emily S., 237–38

Richards, Ezra F., 186, 236, 280
Richards, Franklin D.: and family of
    Willard Richards, ix; on Willard
    Richards, 10; life of, 10–16;
    George F. Richards on, 18; death
    of, 280–81; biography of, 348
Richards, Franklin Snyder: birth
    of, 141, 272; illness of, 179;
    called to Europe, 188; Joseph
    Smith Translation and, 196; as
    Congressional delegate, 211;
    argues before Supreme Court,
    223–24, 230, 236; represents
    Church, 260, 262
Richards, Frederick W., 282–83,
    292–93
Richards, Fred S., 353
Richards, George F. Sr.: as son of
    Willard Richards, ix; life of,
    17–22; receives endowment, 186;
    education of, 204; marriage of,
    207, 368–69; Francis M. Lyman
    on, 238; Franklin D. Richards
    visits, 245; as patriarch, 257–58;
    letter from Franklin D. Richards
    to, 258–59; health of, 377; death
    of, 382–83
Richards, George F. Jr.: children of,
    298; recreation with, 308, 310,
    346, 381–82; land given to, 315;
    called to England, 325; invests
    in Chrysler dealership, 351;
    biography of George Sr. and, 371
Richards, George Spencer, 105, 182,
    218
Richards, Gill, 304–5
Richards, Harriet, 152
Richards, Heber John (1), 6, 28–29,
    61
Richards, Heber John (2), 6, 30, 61,
    114, 184, 195
Richards, Henry P., 306
396

mission, 323; blesses Richards family, 325; death of, 332

Smith, Joseph Fielding, 341, 342, 369

Smith, Joseph III, 225, 227, 228, 239, 269, 314

Smith, Joseph Jr.: calls Willard Richards as Apostle, 6–7; Wilford Woodruff's vision of, 15; blesses Willard Richards, 23; English mission and, 24; persecution of, 32–35, 41–42, 102; presidential campaign of, 37, 40; trial and incarceration of, 39, 42–45; biography of, 62; remains of, 68–69; apostleship of, 106; Willard Richards' vision of, 110–11; revelation of, 183–84; plural marriage and, 238; appears in vision, 254–55; Salt Lake Temple dedication and, 255; letter written by, 270; monument to, 285–87; home of, 287–88; George F. Richards on, 351. *See also* Martyrdom of Joseph and Hyrum Smith

Smith, Joseph Sr., 67, 68, 287–88

Smith, Josiah, 224

Smith, Livona, 74

Smith, Lucy Mack, 68, 70, 236

Smith, Lyman, 67

Smith, Moses, 75–76

Smith, Robert, 98

Smith, Robert F., 47

Smith, Samuel H., 54

Smith, Samuel H. B., 182

Smith, Warren, 182

Smith, Willard, 182

Smith, William: to return to Nauvoo, 48; on counseling police, 60; as Patriarch, 60; family of, 63; to remain in Nauvoo, 63;

sustaining of, 68; apostasy of, 82; fellowship of, 123; residence of, 225

Smith, W. R., 178

Smoot, Abraham O., 160

Smoot, Reed, 295, 320, 324–25

Snake bites, 89

Snow, Eliza R., 182–83, 195, 220

Snow, Erastus: "Word & Will of God" and, 106; consecrates Ensign Hill, 141–42; on remaining faithful, 158–59; organization of counties and, 182–83; speaks in Ogden Tabernacle, 185; St. George Temple and, 187; Church property and, 193; Mountain Meadow Massacre and, 206; in hiding, 210

Snow, Lorenzo: organizes Box Elder and Cache Counties, 182–83; St. George Temple and, 188; Church property and, 193; women's rights bill and, 198; Seventies and, 212; death of, 215; Logan Temple and, 218; goes into hiding, 222; released from penitentiary, 230; residence of, 236; Moses Thatcher and, 254; as Church President, 276; sets apart counselors, 276–77; hardships of, 277–78; on debt, 278–79; on tithing, 279–80

Snow, Minnie, 236

Snuff, 62

Snyder, Jane. *See* Richards, Jane Snyder

Sod houses, 110

South America, missionary work in, 350

Southern States Mission, 351–52

Southwick, Dr., 44–45

Spain, 274

INDEX

Time management, 238–39

Titanic, 313–14

Tithing: gathering, 62; European
Saints and, 172; of Brother
Roberts, 176–77; temples and,
198; Church leadership speaks
on, 235; Franklin D. Richards
on, 241, 264; Hugh S. Gowans
to teach, 273; Lorenzo Snow on,
279–80; George F. Richards on,
303; Church officers and, 361

Tobacco: quorum quits, 62;
Franklin D. Richards smokes,
124; B. H. Roberts on, 215;
Wilford Woodruff on, 262;
priesthood resignations over, 268,
293; temple attendance and, 308,
343

Toothache, 188

Torgenson, Sergeant, 331

Toune, W. B., 180

Train robbers, 347

Travel: of George F. Richards, 20–21,
285–88, 297–98, 301, 308,
311–12, 314–15, 337, 339, 347,
357; Willard Richards on, 30–31;
of Franklin D. Richards, 168,
170, 179, 200–202, 205, 242

Trials, 121

Turley, Theodore, 29

Twelve Apostles: Willard Richards
called to, 6–7, 30; Franklin D.
Richards called to, 11, 177;
migration and, 90; John E. Page
removed from, 91; as successor to
John Taylor, 231; Moses Thatcher
removed from, 271; George F.
Richards called to, 288–90;
Heber J. Grant as President of,
328; temple marriages performed
by, 342

Union Pacific Railroad, 178

United Order, 185

United States: disagreements in,
112–13; sanctions with Mexico,
129; rights in, 136–37

United States government, 93–94,
147–49, 172, 220–21

Utah: surveillance of, 220–21;
statehood of, 224, 260, 261,
267–68

Utah Lumber Co., 278, 284

Utes, 118–19

Van Cot, Brother, 85

Vancouver Island, 67

Vision(s): of Wilford Woodruff,
14–15, 254–55; of George F.
Richards, 19, 288, 292; of Joseph
Smith, 110–11; of Franklin D.
Richards, 273. *See also* Dream(s)

Voting, 237, 265, 266–67, 270, 273

Wallace, George B., 182, 274

Wallace, Thomas, 180

Wang, Charley, 196

Warburton, Joseph, 306

Wasson, Lorenzo, 44–45

Watson, Robert S., 215

Watt, George D., 73n3, 132

Wealth, 248, 290

Weber County, 177–78

Weber Stake, 191

Wells, Daniel H.: government of Salt
Lake Valley and, 139; sets apart
Franklin D. Richards, 168–69;
speaks on United Order, 182; St.
George Temple and, 188; Church
leadership and, 190; Seventies
and, 212; ordered to court, 220

Wells, Emmeline B., 300, 319

Wells, Junius F., 285, 286

Wells, Rulon S., 351

West, Caleb W., 261, 267

402